AF334114

The Role of Pedagogy in Shaping the Socio-Political Reality of Society

The Role of Pedagogy in Shaping the Socio-Political Reality of Society

Edited by

Leon Miller

Cambridge
Scholars
Publishing

The Role of Pedagogy in Shaping the Socio-Political Reality of Society

Edited by Leon Miller

This book first published 2024

Cambridge Scholars Publishing

Lady Stephenson Library, Newcastle upon Tyne, NE6 2PA, UK

British Library Cataloguing in Publication Data
A catalogue record for this book is available from the British Library

ISBN (10): 1-0364-0695-4
ISBN (13): 978-1-0364-0695-0

CONTENTS

Preface

The oppressed gain freedom, justice, and greater self-determination by relying on developing their capabilities and cultivating their humanity. Pedagogy is involved because gaining the desired outcome (i.e., the liberation of individuals and society) requires the cultivation of the humanity of both the oppressed and the oppressor (Freire, Pedagogy of the Oppressed 2005).

A major concern of social, ethical, political, and philosophical inquiry since the beginning of civilization has been structuring social systems that promote human and social development and improve the quality of social life. Social theorists and political philosophers have come to agree that integrating strategies for promoting human development with strategies prescribed by political philosophy for social development is essential for accomplishing the goal that social action aims to achieve. The goal of organized social activity, in short, is described by classical political philosophy as "the good life". But in more detail, a description of "the good life" includes social order, cohesion, solidarity, justice, social harmony, prosperity, and sustainable peace. Consequently, social theorists and political philosophers from the major centers of civilization assert that accomplishing the goal that social action aims to achieve requires the cultivation of individual members of society. This means that there is an inextricable link between the philosophy of education and political philosophy. In this respect, education is viewed as playing a role in shaping the socio-political reality of society because it is an institution established to improve the quality of life for both individuals and society. Therefore, the classical social theorists and political philosophers of the major centers of civilization did not subordinate education to politics. However, the significance of the connection between the two is often under-analyzed, at best, or completely overlooked, at worst. Yet, when you think about it, improving the quality of social life begins with improving the quality of the characters of the members of society; thus, cultivating qualities of good citizenship is an essential aspect of educational training. Which makes educational philosophy the foundation of the study of the social, economic, religious, and political disciplines that shape social life.

Social theorists and political philosophers assert that the cultivation of the individual is the basis of social development because it establishes the conditions for a well-integrated and well-functioning society. The philosophical significance of the relationship between education and public life is due to the fact that, on the one hand, individuals are trained by society's educational systems to make a valued contribution to society. However, on the other hand, establishing the best possible social system is fundamentally conditioned by the education of the individuals who participate in creating social reality. Education in a broader and more holistic sense is the process of enhancing the quality of individual participation in society, which results in increasing the quality of social life. Linking the philosophy of education with political philosophy takes learning out of the confines of the institution and makes it a part of the process of creating desired social ends (i.e., it contributes to establishing a learning society, to a humanistic approach to social marketing, and to strategies for linking good governance with human, social, and sustainable development). In addition, linking educational and political philosophy creates a holistic value-based approach to human development, increases individual and social well-being, and contributes to achieving sustainable peace. Therefore, this book explains the connection between pedagogy and endeavors at human, social, and sustainable development.

This book explains how the principles and values prescribed by social theorists, political philosophers, and ethicists can be expressed as factors for establishing the shared values and common goals of social stakeholders. The shared conviction is to improve the quality of life of each member of society as a means of increasing social capital and public value. This includes explaining why pedagogy is essential for maximizing the benefits the members of society enjoy in their relationships with each other and with the environment. Indeed, this involves educating the overall public, civil leaders, and public authorities in the factors that improve public-private relationships, improve the goods and services offered to the public, increase the effectiveness and efficiency of governance, increase social entrepreneurial activity, and increase the resources available to society.

This approach to social formation bridges the gap between public authorities and the general public by training both in processes and activities that establish value-creating networks that increase social goods. It is a state-of-the-art approach to social formation that endeavors to remedy the social problems resulting from pedagogy merely being treated as instrumental to political and economic purposes, i.e., as a means of training individuals how to find their place in a social reality increasingly dominated by powerful social and economic agents trying to maximize utility, which actually does not contribute to human, social, and sustainable development but, conversely, has put humanity on a path that is not sustainable. Therefore, the principles discussed in this book are relevant to many geographical, socio-cultural, economic, and political contexts.

Acknowledgements

The idea of compiling an edited book that explains the role of pedagogy in shaping the socio-political reality of society began with having the opportunity to represent Tallinn University of Technology for the European Union's Asian-Pacific Project. I was assigned to the South Asian aspect of the project. My first South Asian engagements were with several institutions of higher education in Northeast India that were interested in what was at the time a new state-of-the-art approach to improving the social and economic conditions of society as well as promoting sustainability—the co-creation of value concept. Northeast India happens to be one of the most conflict-prone zones in South Asia; thus, it was important that the project also included a strategy for achieving sustainable peace. Thanks to the support, guidance, and interests of Doctor Glen Christo of Lutheran Christian University (who was at that time the rector of the college), the late Doctor S. R. Lyndem (who was at that time the rector of Union Christian College), assistant professor Banshaikupar L. Mawlong of the Political Science Department of Union Christian College, and Doctor Charles Reuben of the Department of Political Science at Synod College, I was successful in establishing cooperation and collaboration, playing a role in several publications, and ultimately acquiring funding for research in the Shillong region (in the state of Meghalaya of Northeast India). However, what is equally significant was the opportunity to learn about the particular issues and concerns of Khasi culture, learn more about their worldview, and struggle for a greater sense of self-determination.

This was followed by an invitation from assistant professor Dr. Chakali Bramhayya (with the agreement of Professor Gaan Narottam, who was at the time the head of the Department of Political Science and Human Rights), to participate in a conference and to offer workshops at Indira Gandhi National Tribal University. Thanks to Doctor Bramhayya's invitation, I had the opportunity to learn about the tribal cultures of the Amarkantak region of Madhya Pradesh, India. However, more importantly, during this visit, the department hosted a cultural event that featured Bodo cultural arts. The Bodo people are the largest ethnolinguistic group in the Assam state of Northeast India. A small group of students from the cultural program at the university offered me the opportunity to gain firsthand experience of Bodo culture by visiting what is referred to as the Bodoland region of Assam. Therefore, special acknowledgement goes out to Mr. Sui Sui Boro, Mr. Swmaoshar Brahma (who is now an assistant professor of Political Science at Gossaigaon B.Ed. College in Assam), and Mr. Manek Narzary who arranged a visit to Bodoland. This included the opportunity to offer a peace research workshop at Bodoland University in Kokrajhar, Assam, and to spend time in the Raimona village in the Gossaigaon region of Bodoland, which provided me with a firsthand experience with Bodo culture. The Raimona village visit was amazing in many ways: e.g., there is a sense of pristine humanity, nature lovers would appreciate the beauty of the Brahmaputra valley, and it happens to be the last human habitat in that part of India. After the village, there is a frontier wilderness until the Bhutan border. So, one of the highlights of my days in the village was being able to enjoy the view of the mountains in Bhutan.

However, this book is also the outgrowth of a larger project affiliated with The Network of Religious and Traditional Peacemakers and the activities of its Asian Working Group. The project was organized by the Regional Peace Network. The Regional Peace Network is an affiliate of the Asian Working Group of the Network of Religious and Traditional Peacemakers that has a special focus on the role of peace education in promoting greater self-determination and improving the relationship between the government and the people in the regions where the project operates. The international board members of the Regional Peace Network played a special role in guiding the initial stages of the project and advising me on how to move forward.

Thus, the original idea for the book grew out of my firsthand experience with both Khasi and Bodo cultures, their struggle for human rights, and their interest in pursuing a peaceful approach to greater self-determination. Of course, a struggle for greater self-determination can often mean a conflicting relationship with governmental authorities. Therefore, in cooperation with Assistant Professor Manek Narzary (who is now working as a colleague and co-researcher), we attempted to establish a model of conflict reduction and peacebuilding that is based on an approach to pedagogy that empowers individuals and social groups to live in accordance with what they value and achieve what they aspire to do and/or be. We decided that a viable first step would be offering an international webinar in which international scholars could critique the idea and address the relevancy of the concept for their particular social context. Fortunately, there was interest from Taiwan, Vietnam, India, Russia, Cambodia, and the USA.

Therefore, special acknowledgements go out to Assistant Professor Manek Narzary, who was the organizer of the webinar. However, Assistant Professor Narzary organized the webinar under the leadership of Dr. (Fr.) Abhilash VJ, SDB, Ph.D. (the principal of Don Bosco college), and with the support of the webinar coordinating committee of the college. Assistant Professor Narzary is, as well, a contributor (co-author) to one of the articles in this edited book. Finally, I should acknowledge the excellent contribution of Assistant Professor Nobin Narzary as the moderator of the webinar and the role of members of the college webinar coordinating committee in chairing the parallel sessions of the webinar: Dr. Anuradha Goswami, Assistant Professor Jelly Basumatary, and Assistant Professor Nobin Narzary from the English Department, Assistant Professor Bhumiraj Mushahary from the Department of Political Science, as well as IT experts Jugami Bargoyary and Basil Koikara.

Notes on Contributors

Doctor Leon Miller (the editor) is an instructor of Ethics, Comparative Religion, Intercultural Communications, and Intercultural Relations. He has written many peer reviewed articles on the relationship between values, happiness, and success. He is an award winning author with a publication award from Emerald Publishing. He has also written a number of articles for wellness magazines on holistic well-being, self-cultivation, personal growth, and the integral experience. He is the founder and coordinator of "A Value-based Approach to Sustainability Planning" and "The Regional Peace Network". He is a research fellow affiliated with several European and International Peace Research and Peace Education Associations.

Doctor Saphimosha Blah is an assistant professor of philosophy at Saint Mary's College in Shillong, India. She has a special interest in environmental ethics, indigenous philosophy, the philosophy of religion, and culture.

Dr. Indrani Choudhury is Associate Professor and Head of the Department of Philosophy at Saint Mary's College in Shillong, India. She received her PhD from the Department of Philosophy at North-Eastern Hill University, Shillong, in 2001. Her research articles have been published in a number of academic journals and edited volumes on gender issues, environmental ethics, and social and political philosophy. Her areas of interest range from post-modern ethics to contemporary social and political issues, existential and ecological concerns for self-preservation, and conflict resolution.

Audrey Cohan, Ed.D., is Senior Dean for Research, Scholarship, and Graduate Studies and Professor of Education at Molloy University. She co-authored *John Dewey: America's Peace-Minded Educator* with Dr. Charles F. Howlett and focuses on John Dewey in her writing and teaching.

Professor Oleg A. Donskikh is the Head of the Department of Philosophy and Humanities at Novosibirsk State University of Economics and Management and Professor of the Department of Philosophy at

Novosibirsk State Technical University. His sphere of interests includes the history of philosophy, the origin of language, social philosophy, and the philosophy of education. He is the founder and editor-in-chief of the scientific journal "Ideas and Ideals." He has published a number of books on philosophy, e.g., Essays on the History and Philosophy of Science and Witnesses of Infinity (Metaphysics in Poetry); The Formation of Russian National Philosophy; Will for Dignity, Ancient Philosophy (Mythology in the Mirror of Reflection); To the Origin of Language; The Origin of Language as a Philosophical Problem; and Evolutionary Environments Homo Sapiens: an Endangered Species? In addition, his publications include contributing chapters to a number of edited books and publishing a number of peer-reviewed articles.

Dr. Amita Gupta is an esteemed assistant professor at the Center for Comparative Religion and Civilizations at the Central University of Jammu, specializing in Himalayan cultural heritage and comparative religion and civilizations. Her association with Lovely Professional University from 2020–2023 has seen her play significant roles in events like the Y20 Model Summit on Peacebuilding and Reconciliation: Ushering in an Era of No War and the Partition Horrors Remembrance Day seminar. As an academic who believes in being engaging, Dr. Gupta has introduced workshops on experimental archaeology and often lectures on diverse subjects, from archaeological investigation to civilization and peace studies. Beyond the classroom, she has made significant contributions to NGOs like the History Enthusiasts and the Asiatic Society for Social Sciences and Research. Her editorial roles and research at the University of Fribourg, Switzerland, underscore her international academic stature. Furthermore, collaborations with global entities like UCLA, the SAARC Cultural Center, Keil University, the University of Teheran, and the British Museum highlight her expansive network. Notably, Dr. Gupta has been recognized with the Namrata Joshi Gold Medal in 2015, the Swiss Government Excellence Scholarship in 2016–2017, and Foreign Travel Grants in 2016 and 2017. These accolades and grants have facilitated her academic ventures across Europe and Asia."

Dr. Dinh Hong Hai is an Associate Professor at the National University in Hanoi, Vietnam, where he serves as the Head of the Cultural Anthropology division within the Department of Anthropology. In 2019, he was appointed as an executive committee member of the International Association for Semiotic Studies and the Deputy General Secretary of the Asian Semiotics International Association. Additionally, he has been a scientific committee member of the division of culture, art, journalism, and media of the Vietnamese National Foundation for Science and Technology (NAFOSTED) since 2022. Dr. Hai has published over 30 books and 100 articles on related topics in both Vietnamese and English. He earned his MA at the Institute of Cultural Studies, Vietnamese Academy of Social Sciences (VASS) in 2001 and his M.Phil. from the University of Delhi, India, in 2006. From 2008 to 2010, he studied at Harvard University and defended his Ph.D. dissertation at the Graduate School of Social Sciences, VASS, in 2011.

Monalisa Hazarika holds an MA in Conflict Management and Development from Banaras Hindu University, India. She is one of the #Leaders4Tomorrow and #Leaders2Future under the United Nations Office for Disarmament Affairs (UNODA) #Youth4Disarmament Initiative and is currently working as a Project Assistant at SCRAP Weapons. Last year, Monalisa was invited to the UN headquarters in New York to present her project "ACROSS THE CHICKEN NECK", a product of her lived experiences in one of the politically volatile and highly militarized zones of South Asia, at the First Committee Side Event held on October 2022. She is interested in the nexus between the illicit trafficking of small arms and narco-insurgency in South and Southeast Asia, Additive Manufacturing, Dual-Use and Export Control. She is a 2023-24 Emerging Expert of the Forum on the Arms Trade, part of the Emerging Voices Network of the British American Security Information Council (BASIC), and a 2023 SIPRI Armament and Disarmament Summer School graduate.

Charles Howlett is Professor of Education Emeritus at Molloy University, the lead editor of the Oxford Handbook of Peace History (2023), and the author, co-author, and editor of numerous works in peace history and peace education spanning some 40 years. He is the recipient of the Peace History Society's Lifetime Achievement Award.

Professor Kwang-Kuo Hwang (1945–2023) obtained his PhD in social psychology from the University of Hawaii, Honolulu, Hawaii. Professor Hwang has retired from National Taiwan University. He was awarded the title of National Chair Professor by the Ministry of Education of the Republic of China. Professor Hwang has endeavored to promote the indigenization movement in psychology and the social sciences in Chinese society since the early 1980s. He had published more than 160 articles on related issues in both Chinese and English, in addition to eight books, including Foundations of Chinese Psychology: Confucian Social Relations

(English), Inner Sageliness and Outer Kingliness: The Accomplishment and Unfolding of Confucianism (Chinese), and A Scientific Interpretation of Song-Ming Neo-Confucianism (Chinese). He was past president of the Asian Association of Indigenous and Cultural Psychology (2010–2014) and the Asian Association of Social Psychology (2003–2005) and was the principal investigator of the research project "In Search of Excellence for Indigenous Psychology," sponsored by the Ministry of Education, Republic of China (2000–2008).

Prof. Manoj Kumar Mishra is the Coordinator of the Malaviya Centre for Peace Research, Faculty of Social Sciences, BHU. He holds a consistent first-class university record with an M.A., M.Phil., and Ph.D. from the School of International Studies at Jawaharlal Nehru University, New Delhi. His Ph.D. was on ethnic minorities in Central Asia. Currently, Prof. Mishra is concentrating on issues of human security, peace research, environmental security, and environmental conflict. He was awarded the International Fellowships for the Linnaeus Palme International Exchange Program, Sweden, and the Visiting Faculty at Karlstad University, Sweden, in 2022. He was awarded the UPSAM fellowship at the United Nations Mandated University for Peace, Costa Rica, in 2008–09, where he developed two exhaustive curriculums on peace, conflict, security, and development, one on environmental security and peacebuilding. He obtained an International Diploma in Peace Research from the University of Oslo, Norway, in 2012, which was granted by the Peace Research Institute, Oslo (PRIO). He has published books and over a dozen research papers in Scopus journals, peer-reviewed journals, and UGC CARE list journals.

Assistant Professor Manek Narzary was formerly an instructor of political science at Don Bosco College in the Chirang district of Assam, India. He played a significant role in organizing the activities that made the publication of this book possible. He was promoted to a new position with the Political Science Department at Zamduar College in Saraibil, Assam.

Doctor Ho Ngoc Son is currently an Associate Professor in Climate Change and Indigenous Knowledge at the Thai Nguyen University of Agriculture and Forestry, Vietnam. He obtained a master's degree (2004) and a PhD in global environmental change (2013) from the Australian National University. He has published many peer-reviewed articles on indigenous knowledge and climate change adaptation of ethnic minority people in Vietnam. In addition to research and teaching for university students, Dr. Son worked as a Deputy Director of the Institute of Forestry and Sustainable Development at the Thai Nguyen University of Agriculture and Forestry, where he led many research and development projects. All these projects aim at promoting equality, rights, voices, and empowerment for ethnic minority women in remote areas of Vietnam. His work is to ensure that vulnerable people are empowered to achieve their fullest potential and lead their lives in an equal, inclusive, and progressive society.

Dr. Ha Minh Tuan is the Director of the Hi-tech Agriculture and Forestry R&D Center (HACEN), Thai Nguyen University of Agriculture and Forestry, Vietnam. He holds a PhD degree in Agricultural Systems Management from the University of Adelaide, Australia. He has had extensive experience in research and on-the-ground management in a large number of areas, including in community development and resilience, gender studies, sustainable agriculture, agribusiness, agricultural systems research, livelihood development, transformative learning, participatory action research, disaster risk reduction and climate change adaptation. Dr. Ha has been working as a practicing scientist in both academic and development fields for a large number of international organizations and NGOs in Vietnam and overseas. He is a recipient of a number of competitive research grants, receiving two international and three national awards for his innovative research methodologies and impacts. Dr. Ha has so far published more than 80 refereed journal and conference papers and a large number of consultancy reports.

Hongyu Wang is Professor of Curriculum Studies at Oklahoma State University, USA. Her work focuses on curriculum theory, nonviolence education, and East/West inquiry. Her published books include The Call from the Stranger on a Journey Home: Curriculum in a Third Space (2004), Cross-cultural Studies in Curriculum (co-edited with Claudia Eppert, 2008), Nonviolence and Education (2014), Contemporary Daoism, Organic Relationality, Curriculum of Integrative Creativity (2021).

Introduction

Doctor Leon Miller

Knowledge of the highest good is our aim (i.e., knowledge of the master science). So, then, the course of study we are referring to has to do with the connection between the good for a single person and the good for society; thus, the course of study is nothing less than political knowledge (Aristotle 2004, 4).

The foundational principles of social and political philosophy stress that knowledge generation and dissemination play an important role in shaping the social, economic, and political conditions of society. Consequently, the principles establish a theoretical link between pedagogical and political philosophy. Applying these principles to human and social development is believed to be a means of elevating the human experience. Therefore, social theorists and political philosophers agree that the principles prescribe a strategy for achieving the highest good possible by means of organized social activity. The achievement of this good is the goal that human social action aims to achieve. In other words, "All political action has, in itself, a directedness towards knowledge of the good: of the good life, or of the good society. For the good society is the complete political good" (Strauss 1957, 343). Thus, the standard for political action is goodness, justice, well-being, and peace. This good is an ethical good, which implies that this moral or ethical good should motivate our actions, our relationships with others, market transactions, and the goal society aims to achieve. It is by applying this standard to social action that we achieve the happiness and well-being of the members of society (Odia Bhagavata, 1996, 21, 29, 35-37, & 69; Cicero 2004, 38-43 & 83-86; Aristotle 1998, 192-193; Confucius, 2005, 12).

An analysis of the fundamental principles of classical social theory, political philosophy, political economy, and ethics reveals that classical social theorists and philosophers envisioned human and social development in terms of the flourishing and prosperity of individuals and society, a just society, and sustainable peace. They envisioned that the refinement of humanity, in terms of the individual members of society developing virtuous character traits, would go hand in hand with civic virtue. In other words, they envisioned that the primary aim of the processes and activities for managing society would be the human development of the individual members of society, which in turn would contribute to social, economic, and sustainable development, a better public life, and consequently to a better socio-political order. The various theorists agreed that cultivating individuals so that they experience goodness and cooperate with each other to create a space in which they can enjoy personal and societal security is the whole aim of social life. Therefore, pedagogy is not only the means of providing knowledge and training individuals in particular skills, but it also plays a role in achieving a higher quality of social life. Thus, there is an inextricable link between education and politics, as was stressed by the social, ethical, and political philosopher Aristotle and is quoted in the epigram above.

The world's perennial philosophical and wisdom traditions also emphasize the connection between educational philosophy, political philosophy, individual freedom, and social justice. This was indeed evident in the political philosophy that shaped the development of the major centers of civilization. The ideas are based on principles that produce free citizens whose freedom includes not only social and political freedom but also the ability to experience happiness, good fortune, and higher levels of physical and mental development. This was especially evident in perspectives on self-knowledge, developing a virtuous character, and the prospect of enlightenment, all of which are drawn from a wealth of perennial wisdom. Such wisdom stands out as a unique and ideal example of the endeavor to cultivate individuals not only for the sake of citizenship but for improving the overall human experience. It was the vision of achieving this pedagogical, social, and political aim that drew people together into social solidarity, cohesion, harmony, and stability. The most respected and renown advocates of these principles asserted that, in the broadest sense, realizing the highest good possible requires more than political force. True freedom requires training individuals in how to develop their capabilities, how to exercise their right to life, liberty, and happiness, and how to pursue self-interest in ways that promote the common good (Tagore 1968: 99 & 186).

These principles prompted social development because they established a unified collective aim (i.e., shared values that motivated a willingness to cooperate to achieve a common goal). Although these principles, values, and ethics established fundamental ideals for organizing social activity, the full realization of these ideals was indeed thwarted by the persistence of social agents who attempted to exercise "power over" rather than as a means of empowerment. Their intention was to exercise authority over society and the control of its resources. Therefore, teaching the ideal of self-determination, the realization of shared goals, and common values becomes an enormous challenge. That is to say that it requires generating and disseminating a type of knowledge that is powerful enough to override the persistence of those who pursue power on their own behalf or on behalf of the powerful elite. Realizing the type of social dynamics prescribed by the principles underlying pedagogical and political philosophy requires integrating the interests of the powerful elite with those of the overall public (Dewey 1988, 225-226; Dewey 2021, 83-88). Therefore, realizing those principles as the basis of social activity requires generating and disseminating a type of knowledge that is powerful enough to override the persistence of relating to merely endeavor using others as a means to achieve instrumental ends.

This book explains various pedagogical and socio-political prescriptions for improving the conditions of society and, as well, the human condition. However, in line with the theme of improving the conditions of society, this book has two additional essential aspects. On the one hand, there is the aim of improving the well-being and life satisfaction of individuals, while, on the other hand, it also aims to increase social solidarity, cohesion, order, harmony, prosperity, and peace. In this respect, an overall concern of this book is explaining the factors that enhance the essential interdependence between the members of society and between the individual members and public authorities. The contributors to this book analyze the role that the generation and dissemination of knowledge play in personal growth and development, socialization and public life, personal and political power, and social justice.

In this respect, the book not only explains the connection between educational and political philosophy and the forces shaping the socio-political reality of society but, as well, the connection between developing the full capabilities of the individual members of society and social development. Although the book focuses on training students and social groups in a participatory and collaborative approach to social formation, it also explains the significance of training civil leaders, the general public, and public authorities. Therefore, there are aspects of the book that apply to both formal and informal learning. It is in this respect that the book explains the significance of integrating conceptualizations of personal and social well-being with those for realizing the goal that human social action aims to achieve. In other words, the book demonstrates a state-of-the-art approach (and an empirical basis) for linking personal well-being and happiness with social interdependence and a well-functioning society. Thus, this book describes a way to implement an approach to pedagogy that is both state-of-the-art and innovative while at the same time being very much in line with the fundamental principles of social theory and political philosophy.

This book emphasizes the significance of linking political philosophy with citizenship education in light of what has become known as the *Creating Public Value* concept in public administration and political theory (Mark Moore 1995). Citizenship education, in this respect, means training individuals and social groups in the connection between their own self-cultivation, the development of their capabilities, participatory governance, and improving the quality of social life. By developing their capabilities, individuals enjoy greater substantive freedoms and have greater opportunities to engage other members of their community in co-creating social life. Thus, developing capabilities promotes human rights, social justice, and self-determination while, at the same time, diminishes conflict and increases social harmony. By explaining the relationship between human development and political activity, we teach individuals and members of a community to become active agents for greater social justice. In this respect, the exercise of rights, achieving justice, and experiencing greater self-determination is a matter of training individuals and social groups in the connection between achieving what is in their best interest, promoting and protecting the collective interests, and increasing the enjoyment and benefits they experience in their relationships with other members of society. However, citizenship education also involves transforming formal and nonformal learning activities into models of ideal social interactions. Thus, what occurs in such interactions models the ideal ethos of pedagogy but, as well, an ideal of social relations and participation in political communities.

The co-creation of value concept, which is becoming increasingly popular, is the basis of the participatory aspect of the model. The co-creation of value concept is also often referred to as the co-creation of social reality concept, participatory governance, collaborative socio-political activities, deliberative civic engagement, and communitarian social order (Miller 2022, xi). This approach is based on teaching individuals and social groups state-of-the-art strategies for transforming the prior development paradigm into an approach that balances economic development with human, social, and sustainable development. These fundamental principles are relevant for addressing and resolving current human, social, economic, and political challenges because they are based on state-of-the-art strategies for transforming the precariousness of the human condition into a means of achieving social goals. That is to say, it increases the willingness of the multi-level stakeholders to engage in value creation networks in order to achieve their individual goals. Therefore, the development we aim for begins with training individuals and social groups by means of practical lessons on the connection between human, social, and sustainable development. This approach teaches individuals and social groups how to achieve the value goals they aim for, but in ways that are proactive and avoid reactionary responses to social challenges.

This book explains an approach to social and political philosophy that is integrated with pedagogical philosophy as the basis for teaching future leaders of society how to ameliorate the persistent problems faced by many communities, e.g., ethnic, racial, class, gender, religious discrimination, conflict over access to natural resources and their fair distribution, disputes over policies and rights, and environmental and climate challenges. It explains an inter-disciplinary approach to human, social, and sustainable development that increases the effectiveness and efficiency of governance activities, improves the relationship between the government and the overall public, and, equally important, reduces conflict and promotes peacebuilding. The focus is on empowering individuals by engaging them in processes of self-cultivation that will lead to achieving a better quality of life, enhancing their role as citizens, co-creating their social reality, and improving their relationship with their natural surroundings. It should be kept in mind that, although this approach is transformational, it is meant to be applied within a particular community context as a model for social development. That is to say, it establishes a model of how local citizens and public authorities can cooperate to realize the shared goals and common values that reflect their particular social, cultural, economic, political, and sustainability aspirations.

The book emphasizes the role that formal, informal, and alternative learning activities, plus the knowledge generated by means of public-private value-creating networks, play in what is experienced as social reality. Therefore, the book explains why the dynamics that occur as a result of the linkage between these three approaches to education reflect aspects of education that are inherently political in nature (Freire 2005).

Although most of the contributors to this book are scholars engaged in the educational profession, the scope of the contributions also includes practitioners who are deeply engaged in enhancing the relationship between civil society and the government. In this respect, the contributors demonstrate a concern for training individuals and social groups in the types of processes, activities, and interactions that not only reflect a Constructivist approach to pedagogy but, as well, a Constructivist approach to co-creating social reality. Thus, this book is concerned with elevating the life experience of those who participate in formal, informal, and alternative learning programs. However, the focus is on teaching participants the role that the development of their capabilities plays in their having happier, healthier, and more successful lives. Achieving this requires teaching the participants the role they play as citizens in achieving the highest good possible by means of organized social activity.

When teaching individuals and social groups about the relationship between their own self-cultivation, the nature of citizenship, and social justice we are taking part in the endeavors of a long tradition of scholars who attempted to maximize individual and social well-being. Such scholars shared the intention to cultivate the whole person—not only for the purpose of citizenship but to motivate individuals to live in accordance with their deepest convictions (i.e., the freedom to be their authentic selves, to live in accordance with what they have reason to value most, and to achieve their aspirations) and thus experience the most rewarding and fulfilling life possible. It also aims at training individuals and social groups on how to be well-integrated within the fabric of existence. This pedagogical tradition includes some of the greatest thinkers in the world throughout history and some who are most admired today.

The Structure of the Book

The book is divided into three main sections and a conclusion. Section one addresses the role of pedagogy in shaping the socio-political reality of society from a philosophical perspective (Aristotle, Taoism, Sri Aurobindo, and Confucius). Section two also addresses the relationship between pedagogy and social development, but from the perspective of either Critical Pedagogy, a Constructivist perspective on pedagogy (including the relationship between formal learning institutions and informal learning taking place in cooperation with civil bodies), or peace education. The third section addresses the relationship between pedagogy and social development from the perspective of indigenous knowledge.

The conclusion provides a comprehensive summary of the role of knowledge generation and dissemination (i.e., schools of philosophy, ideologies, and systems of knowledge generation and dissemination) in shaping civilization and progressing civilization to the present stage of global social existence.

Section One: Pedagogy and Social Development from the Perspective of Philosophy

Section one begins with Professor Donskikh's article entitled Pedagogy and Social Development from the perspective of Aristotle's philosophy. He describes Aristotle's approach to education and his system of personal growth and development that aims to cultivate individuals who are self-sufficient and responsible human beings. In other words, for Aristotle, education was a system of self-cultivation that resulted in individuals being aware of the interdependent and complementary relationship between themselves and the state. From the point of view of the development of society, Aristotle presupposed that society is organized with the aim of having well-educated citizens, which means that the state establishes a just social system. The system of education should provide the possibility of a step-by-step movement towards proper citizenship based on virtue and reason. The content of education should be designed in such a way that each period of human life from five to twenty-one years has its own end, becoming the foundation for the next one.

Doctor Hongyu Wang's article "Daoist Pedagogy: Attunement, Nonviolent Intervention, and A Virtuous Process" explains the impact of education on social development from a Daoist perspective. The article focuses on the relational aspects of Daoism, which emphasize attunement with nature and others, thus having implications regarding nonviolence and nonviolence education. The article begins with an explanation of a fundamental concept in Daoism (wu wei). Although the concept is usually associated with "going with the flow" or "being in the flow," it also has implications regarding attunement, which raises questions about non-interruption and allowing things to take their own natural course. The author then addresses what this means for classroom management and the teacher's intervention in the student's learning process (especially in the case of teaching nonviolence). However, the ultimate aim of the article is to reflect on what it means to educate and to be educated.

Doctor Indrani Choudhury's article, is entitled The Role of Pedagogy in Peace Initiatives for a Sustainable Future: with Reference to Sri Aurobindo's Philosophy. Her paper emphasizes the role of peace education in conflict reduction and peacebuilding, drawing mainly on insights from Sri Aurobindo's philosophy on how human beings face and negotiate with socio-political realities and how this process, in turn, shapes our ideas of the future of education for children and young adults in a conflict-ridden society. The article explains the idea of peace through education by thinking along three dimensions: (1) its internal dimension (i.e., peace as an outcome of Satya, meaning as an outcome of self-realization), (2) its external dimension (i.e., a common goal based on shared values, which sparks a collective moral consciousness), and (3) reconciliation, which involves tolerance.

Emeritus Professor Kwang-Kuo Hwang and co-author Doctor Leon Miller contribute an article that analyzes Confucian education principles to determine how they provide a means of sustainable social development at the multi-levels of social interaction. The article proposes that Confucius established the Mutual Trust Model (互信模式), based on his Five Constant Virtues (五 常), as a means of teaching principles of ethics, social relations, governance, and, as well, relations between different cultures and nations. Therefore, the article provides a viable approach to theorizing about social development at the multiple levels of social activity.

Section Two: Pedagogy and Social Development from the Perspective of Critical Pedagogy or a Constructivist Perspective on Pedagogy

Emeritus Professor Charles Howlett co-authors an article with Professor Audrey Cohan, which describes pedagogy and social development from the perspective of peace education. The title is John Dewey's Constructivist Approach to Peacebuilding. Dewey is one of the founders of American Pragmatism and, as well, a renown educational and social philosopher, a social and educational reformer, and an academic. His Constructivist ideals are the foundation of his democratic philosophy, which has been expanded to include his beliefs on peace and justice. The article explains the aspects of Dewey's call for social action that are especially relevant for peacemakers. Thus, the article explains new pathways for encouraging positive interaction between individuals and the members of a diverse society, as well as between society and its environment. This article raises the question of whether it is possible for policymakers to implement what Dewey advocated in terms of democracy, education, human development, and basic human rights? The authors point out that Dewey's ideas for peace education complement the views of many current policymakers who favor peacebuilding efforts for transformative change as opposed to attempts aimed at peacekeeping, which maintain the existing social order intact. The article points out the lessons that peace and justice advocates working in conflict zones—such as South Asia, for instance—can learn from Dewey's peace education theories, and how might they adapt them to their own contexts?

Doctor Hai's article describes the interface between Vietnam and France in education, the science of the humanities, and anthropology. He explains that after almost a thousand years of growth, the scholarly traditions of Vietnamese people, which were heavily influenced by Chinese civilization, began to crumble in the late 19th century. By the early decades of the 20th century, this bookish academia (known as 尋章摘句) had come to an end, with the last royal examination being held in 1919. So why did this thousand-year Confucius education come to an abrupt halt? His article explores the impact of French academia on Indochina for over a century, which fundamentally changed the scientific thinking of Vietnam's intellectual class. This shift led to significant changes in the country's human sciences, including the development of anthropology throughout the 20th century.

Ms. Monalisa Hazarika and her co-author, Prof. Manoj Kumar Mishra, write about the recruitment of child soldiers in struggles for greater self-determination and autonomy in Northeast India. They explain how the children are provided new rebel outfits and then oriented (educated, or perhaps better to say reeducated) to risk their lives for a cause. These impoverished children are lured into warfare by the promise of being able to escape their desperation by fighting for their freedom and dignity, as well as that of their people, and being provided with resources they would otherwise not be able to afford. This article critically analyzes such an approach to training youth on how to earn freedom, self-determination, and dignity. The article then proposes peace education theory as a tool to bring about positive social change in the context of Northeast Indian societies and explores the efficacy of such an intervention, framing recommendations from Freire's *Pedagogy of the Oppressed*.

Doctor Blah writes about the role of justice in avoiding social conflicts at all levels of social interaction. She uses the Northeast of India as an example of a context where the extent of diversity in ethnicity, culture, language, tribal status, religion, historical grievances, economic disparities, political marginalization, land disputes, and response to migrants make it one of the most conflict prone zones in South Asia. The author explains that because of the large tribal population in the region (e.g., Scheduled Tribes), conflicts are often centered on the role of government and government authorities in protecting the rights of the tribal people. One way of summarizing the nature of the conflicts is that they are a demand for justice. The author then goes into detail to explain the nature of justice and its role in establishing sustainable peace. The author then compares one of the most respected theories of justice (Justice as Fairness by John Rawls) to the sense of justice of one of Northeast India's cultural groups, the Khasi culturee. The author concludes by explaining a peace education approach to reducing the conflictual tension between tribal people and the various levels of government. This peace education model is based on a theory of justice that aligns the most cherished values of a tribal community with those of the Indian cultural and religious traditions and those of the theory of justice proposed by John Rawls.

Assistant Professor Manek Narzary, and his co-author Doctor Leon Miller, contribute and article entitled "Education: Society's Cornerstone Institution for Improving the Quality of Social Life". Their chapter describes education and learning as social goods thus involve not only the interests of the students, the teachers, and the school but of the community and entire society. The chapter points out that given the complexities of society (especially when there is a high level of ethic, cultural, and language differences) it is the nature of the relationship and communication between individuals and the overall society that determine the quality of social life. In this respect the chapter emphasizes why a Constructivist approach to teaching, interacting, and communicating promotes relational and interactive dynamics that result in complementary, mutually beneficial, and mutually enhancing agent-structure interactions. The chapter emphasizes that the effectiveness of this approach lies in the fact that it is simultaneously a method of teaching, an approach to personal growth and development, a strategy for social development, is based on a state-of-the-art perspective on social theory and, as well, is based on a communication theory effective for promoting and disseminating constitutive socio-political values and principles.

Section Three: Pedagogy and Social Development (with an emphasis on the role of indigenous knowledge in social development)

Doctor Gupta provides the opening article for section three with "Indigenous Knowledge and Social Development in Northeast India". The author defines indigenous knowledge as the collective memory of a cultural group that dates back to the earliest stages of its existence, which explains the best way to manage the challenges of existence. The focus of indigenous knowledge is on how to maintain harmonious coexistence between the members of the community, between the community and the forces it is confronted with in its environment, and, as well, maintaining a harmonious balance between tradition and modernizing. The author then explains that education in this sense is not only of a formal, nonformal, and alternative nature but a living experience occurring between individuals and elders, individuals and designated guides, and individuals and nature (i.e., including the forces shaping the nature of existence). Therefore, education for the tribal cultures of Northeast India is akin to a treasure house of knowledge, wisdom, and intricate cultural narratives, resilient social structures, and insightful systems for human growth and development that have stood the test of time.

Doctor Ho Ngoc Son and Doctor Ha Minh Tuan describe indigenous knowledge as the foundation of a cultural group's identity, cultural heritage, civilization, livelihood, and coping strategies, which the group has relied upon and adhered to for untold centuries. The authors argue that because it has proven to be effective for so many centuries, it is, no doubt, still relevant for dealing with such issues as food insecurity, reducing inequalities, climate change, and other challenges that humanity is trying to resolve through the Sustainable Development Goals. Indigenous knowledge in Vietnam, like in many other contexts where the indigenous population is equated with tribal villagers, is highly relevant to a sense of social development in that indigenous people are a great example of the challenge of blending time-tested traditions with new technologies, efforts to reduce poverty and inequality, improve access to education and healthcare, and promote civic engagement and community participation. Therefore, indigenous knowledge not only continues to be an essential source for insight into how to shape the culture's social, political, and economic future but also a learning source for the greater regional, national, and international society regarding how to live more peacefully, cooperatively, and harmoniously.

Conclusion: Knowledge, Power, and the Shaping of Civilization

The editor summarizes the role of pedagogy in shaping the socio-political reality of society by providing a comprehensive overview of the relationship between knowledge, power, and the shaping of civilization. The article provides an overview of the role of knowledge, schools of thought, and philosophy in shaping the civilizations in the Far East, Mesopotamia, and the West. The article uses India as an example to explain the role of knowledge, philosophy, cultural worldview, and schools of higher learning in shaping a civilizational state. The article concludes by explaining why insight into the role of knowledge in shaping civilization and the civilizational state is important to helping humanity deal with the challenges it faces as a result of civilization advancing to the global stage of social existence.

SECTION ONE

PHILOSOPHICAL VIEWS ON PEDAGOGY AND SOCIAL DEVELOPMENT

PEDAGOGY AND SOCIAL DEVELOPMENT FROM THE PERSPECTIVE OF ARISTOTLE'S PHILOSOPHY

PROFESSOR OLEG DONSKIKH

One ought not even consider that a particular citizen belongs to himself, but rather that all belong to the city; for each is a part of the city.
Aristotle Politics, Book 8.

Nowadays, when there is a serious restructuring of society under the influence of new means of communication, when it is necessary to teach in conditions of full accessibility to information, and when books move into virtual space, there is an urgent need to analyze and rethink the learning process and the education system as a whole.

Under these circumstances, it is not accidental to turn to classical authors who have made invaluable contributions to understanding key principles of education. Thus, in a modern monograph on this subject, we meet Plato, Aristotle, and the Stoics.[1] Rethinking ancient heritage in new contexts offers the opportunity to see new possibilities for thinking about the purposes and principles of learning. In this respect, Aristotle is one of the most interesting authors, known not only for his enormous intellectual contribution to different fields of knowledge but also for his Lyceum.

When we talk about the relationship between humanity and society, we come to the existence of two mutually contradictory positions: 1) people exist for society and, if necessary, are obliged to give their lives for this society; and 2) society exists to guarantee people their maximum dignified existence, in other words, to ensure their rights—"liberty, property,

---

[1] *Handbook of the Philosophy of Education. (*Ed. by R. Curren). Routledge, Taylor & Francis Group, 2023. Plato and especially Aristotle are mentioned many times, yet the title of the chapter, written by Nancy Sherman, on the Stoics is particularly revealing in this respect: "Stoic lessons for an uncertain future".

security, and resistance to oppression." It is possible to fix these positions with the terms *collectivism* and *individualism*. In the first case, society is primary in relation to humanity; in the second case, individuals are primary in relation to society. Hints of the possibility of the second position appear in the Renaissance period, and theoretical substantiation comes with the political philosophy of the 17th and 18th centuries and receives its pure expression in the *Declaration of the Rights of Man and the Citizen* of 1789. Since then, educational systems have been trying to strike a balance between the socialization of a human being and the creation of an independent individual. Depending on the implemented goals, this is not an easy task.

It is important to emphasize that for Aristotle, the main goal and the common end of education could be and was the education of a citizen, i.e., such a member of society who absolutely shares the values of this society and, belonging to this society, actively participates in their best realization. Aristotle has no special pedagogical texts, and his views on the upbringing and education of a citizen can be found in his political and ethical works, which he himself understood as practical disciplines. Accordingly, there is no consistently presented theory of education. When Robert Brumbaugh and Nathanial Lawrence try to present an outline of Aristotle's philosophy of education, they have to note that "such topics as the nature of the thing to be educated, the techniques of education, the process of education, the function of education, the effect of education, or the end of education are hardly discussed at all".[2] Therefore, we have to reconstruct Aristotle's views by taking into account his notes, which are scattered throughout various compositions. Notwithstanding, it is quite useful to outline the most significant tenets that define the frame of his approach to the matter:

1. The human being is a social creature, because by his nature he is striving to communicate, and this communication is arranged for the sake of some good.
2. By his nature a human being has a desire for knowledge.
3. The common end and common good of citizens and the state is the same, and this is happiness (good).
4. The amount of happiness is equal to the amount of virtue and reason.

---

[2] Robert Brumbaugh and Nathanial Lawrence. Aristotle's philosophy of education // *Educational Theory*, v. IX, No. 1, 1959, p. 1.

5. Happiness is not given casually or automatically; every citizen has to be trained in order to become virtuous and wise.
6. The way of life and training are multifaceted and at the same time they have to be moderate according to the principle of the golden mean.
7. Thus, human life is defined by the position in society. Therefore, in order to take the most appropriate standing it is necessary to comply with the established laws. Consequently, we have to go from politics to ethics and to other practical disciplines.

Aristotle himself states that the problem of upbringing and education is not well elaborated, and there is no agreement even with the goals: "Investigation on the basis of the education that is current yields confusion, and it is not at all clear whether one should have training in things useful for life, things contributing to virtue, or extraordinary things; for all of these have obtained some willing to decide in their favor. Concerning the things relating to virtue, nothing is agreed."[3] It should also be taken into account that, in certain details, the texts of Aristotle are different. Nevertheless, it seems possible to present some consistent and valuable picture of the link between pedagogy and social development based on Aristotle's views. This belief defines the aim of this article.

For Aristotle, practical philosophy starts with politics, then ethics, and then he lines up other disciplines in order of significance. Monique Canto-Sperber characterizes his approach by stating that for him: "Ethics is subordinated to politics; the common goal of these two disciplines is virtue, and life in the state creates the best conditions for cultivating the ability to enjoy life and endure suffering, without which it is impossible to acquire virtue. Living under good laws is the best means of ingraining in ourselves the habits that will lead to virtue. The realization of virtue and, more broadly, the public welfare thus depend on the legislator."[4] This approach completely conforms to a collectivist approach to social life, shared by Aristotle. W. Jaeger, in his famous research on Greek *paideia,* stresses the point that for Greeks, the highest goal is honor, and honor should correspond to virtue. W. Frankena formulates the principle goal of

---

[3]*Aristotle's Politics*, Sec. ed. (Trans. by Carnes Lord). The University of Chicago Press, 2013. p. 243.. by Carnes Lord). The University of Chicago Press, 2013. p. 243.

[4] M. Canto-Sperber, J. Barnes, L. Brisson, J. Brunschwig, and G. Vlastos *Greek philosophy.* V. I. Moscow: Graeco-Latin Cabinet of Y. A. Shichalin, 2006. p.442. (In Rus.)

Greek education as "the acquisition or transmission of excellences," insisting that *arete* (usually translated as "virtue") is closer to "excellence."[5] Anyway, the inner quality of a person in Greek Weltanschauung is immediately expressed by equivalent social merit. Aristotle states that "men seem to pursue honor in order that they may be assured of their merit; at least it is by men of practical wisdom that they seek to be honored, and among those who know them, and on the ground of their virtue; clearly, then, according to them, at any rate, virtue is better."[6] This necessitated conformity between virtue and honor (or recognized excellence) is, for Aristotle, the central point of his attitude towards education.

From the start, it should be asserted that Aristotle's practical philosophy is an extension of his theoretical philosophy, presented in particular in "Metaphysics". It is possible to find the application of the doctrine of actuality and potentiality in relation to education. "Teaching in accord with the philosophical principles of Aristotle is the causation of the actualization of the student's potentialities, especially in relation to the cultivation of the mind as a means of knowing the truth."[7] If we take into account Aristotle's understanding of knowledge, which includes sensation, memory, experience, art, science, and wisdom, the succession of steps towards a knowledgeable person is quite clear.[8]

In the first book of *Nicomachean ethics,* Aristotle stipulates that politics appears to be the master art, "for it is this that ordains which of the sciences should be studied in a state, and which each class of citizens should learn and up to what point they should learn them; and we see even the most highly esteemed of capacities to fall under this, e.g., strategy, economics, rhetoric; now, since politics uses the rest of the sciences, and since, again, it legislates as to what we are to do and what we are to abstain from, the end of this science must include those of the others, so

---

[5] W. Frankena. *Three historical philosophies of education. Aristotle, Kant, Dewey.* Scott, Foresman and Co. 1965. p. 15.

[6] Aristotle. *The Nicomachean Ethics.* (Trans. by David Ross). Oxford University Press, 2009. p. 7. See also Jaeger's comments: Jaeger W. *Paideia: the ideals of Greek culture.* (Trans. by G. Highet, v.1). Archaic Greece. The mind of Athens. Basil Blackwell, 1946. pp. 8-9.

[7] Collins P. Aristotle and the Philosophy of Intellectual Education // *The Irish Journal of Education.* v. 24, No. 2, 1990. P. 73.

[8] See: Ibid. p. 69.

that this end must be the human good."[9] However, though every human should strive towards this common good, it is not possible for those who do not have the required experience and possibility to control themselves. "Now each man judges well the things he knows, and of these he is a good judge. And so the man who has been educated in a subject is a good judge of that subject, and the man who has received an all-round education is a good judge in general. Hence a young man is not a proper hearer of lectures on political science; for he is inexperienced in the actions that occur in life, but its discussions start from these and are about these; and, further, since he tends to follow his passions, his study will be vain and unprofitable, because the end aimed at is not knowledge but action."[10] Therefore, we come to recognize the problem: politics should create citizens of defined quality, which means that they are virtuous and act in accordance with virtue—they do the right things. State life should be subordinate to this aim, completely including all practical occupations listed above: strategy, economics, and rhetoric.

Yet there lies the problem: in order for the state to function in accordance with the common end, everyone should freely participate in this end, but human nature does not enable it. In addition, virtue itself can be different for different people. In *The Eudemian Ethics,* Aristotle emphasizes that "the things productive of total virtue are all the things of law that have been legislated as to education for what is common. But as to the education of each individual, by which a man is simply good, it must be determined later whether it belongs to politics or some other study. Perhaps it is not the same thing for a man to be good as for each citizen to be so."[11] It is obvious that any citizen, in order to be good and virtuous, has to enjoy freedom; otherwise, his virtue is not a true virtue. If he is forced to behave in accordance with some rules without understanding why he should follow them, he cannot be named virtuous in any sense.

We come to a contradiction, which is well expressed by Stephen Everson: "Aristotle's ideal state is a community of free agents, but their free agency is substantially dependent on the existence of the state."[12] With this point,

---

[9] Aristotle. *The Nicomachean Ethics.* (Trans. by David Ross). Oxford University Press, 2009. p. 4.

[10] Ibid. pp. 4-5.

[11] *The Eudemian ethics of Aristotle.* (Trans. by Peter L.P. Simpson). Transaction Publishers. 2013, p. 70.

[12] Stephen Everson. Aristotle on the Foundations of the State // *Political Studies,* 1988. v. XXXVI, 89-101, p. 95.

we have to keep in mind that for Aristotle, 1) society is primary to the citizen, and so any citizen cannot separate himself from political life; 2) that citizen is defined not just by birth, territoriality, and kinship but also by the level of his morality and his virtue.[13] Therefore, the most important goal of the educational system is to prepare human beings for political life. This preparation cannot be done directly but through the upbringing of virtue. Also, it is obvious that not everyone will actively take part in political life because it depends both on their personal position and the state system.

In order to approach pedagogical matters, let us, following Aristotle's logic, start with the state system. In "The Art of Rhetoric," he states that "democracy is a regime in which they distribute offices among themselves by lot; oligarchy is that in which the distribution is done on the basis of property assessments; aristocracy is that in which they do so according to education (and I mean by "education" the one established by law), for those who have remained within the legal customs rule in an aristocracy, and these necessarily appear best—hence it has its name."[14] At the same time, Aristotle emphasizes the fact that any political regime can be deviated from and accordingly transformed. Therefore, the crucial task of a legislator is to establish such laws, which would provide the firmest foundation for the best regime (in which the common good is the same both for the state and the citizens). This means that one of the most important premises of this regime is the upbringing and education of the people, provided in the framework of recognized laws. Though it looks quite plausible that Aristotle would prefer aristocracy to other regimes, such a conclusion is not entirely correct.

Firstly, he realizes that the situation where only a part of society acquires proper education while others lack it does not produce the possibility to create the wholeness of society, which is necessary for normal and prolonged life. Secondly, Aristotle, following the principle of the golden mean, understands that there should exist a balance between different social groups, and this is impossible without a common ground for concordance. Taking into account these deliberations, the only way to build a decent society is to cultivate virtue amongst all citizens. In this

---

[13] The Aristotle's concept of citizen is analyzed by R. Boyd's article "Boundaries, Birthright, and Belonging: Aristotle on the Distribution of Citizenship" // *The Good Society*. Volume 22, No. 2, 2013. pp. 215-235.

[14] *Aristotle's Art of Rhetoric*. (Trans. by Robert C. Bartlett). The University of Chicago Press, 2019. p. 39.

case, even though the level of virtue will be different amongst the different members of society, there will be some common ground, allowing society to unite. W. Frankena comes to the same conclusion: "Educational opportunity cannot be distributed in proportion to excellence (a formula of justice that Aristotle also suggests), since the achievement of excellence presupposes education; it must be distributed according to capacity for excellence, but such capacity can be determined only by education—hence it must be distributed equally. If education is a rattle, everyone should be given a chance to shake it for all it is worth."[15]

Aristotle emphasizes that the only firm foundation for education is not family or the example of elders but exclusively the legal system of the state. In order to prove this statement he uses two arguments: 1) the relationship between people can be quite different, and, therefore, the success of the process of upbringing can be negatively affected by contradictory emotions; 2) laws are objectively present in human life, and the attitude towards them cannot become emotional. Aristotle: "…If … the man who is to be good must be well trained and habituated, and go on to spend his time in worthy occupations and neither willingly nor unwillingly do bad actions, and if this can be brought about if men live in accordance with a sort of reason and right order, provided this has force — if this be so, the paternal command indeed has not the required force or compulsive power (nor in general has the command of one man, unless he be a king or something similar), but the law has compulsive power, while it is at the same time a rule proceeding from a sort of practical wisdom and reason. And while people hate men who oppose their impulses, even if they oppose them rightly, the law in its ordaining of what is good is not burdensome."[16] Thus, in order to create virtuous people an educator has to influence the souls of the pupils in such a way that they would love good and hate what is mean.[17]

Keeping all these previous considerations in mind we will try to present Aristotle's system of education, referring to the points mentioned in the above quoted article of R. Brumbaugh and N. Lawrence - the nature of the thing to be educated, the techniques of education, the process of education, the function of education, the effect of education, or the end of education.

---

[15] W. Frankena. *Three historical philosophies of education. Aristotle, Kant, Dewey.* Scott, Foresman and Co. 1965. p. 78.

[16] Aristotle. *The Nicomachean Ethics* (Trans. by David Ross). Oxford University Press, 2009. p. 200.

[17] Ibid. p. 199.

Aristotle distinguishes three periods of human life, dedicated to education, up to 21 years. Education starts from five years and then "once they have passed through the first five years, during the two up to seven they should become onlookers of the sorts of learning that they themselves will be required to learn."[18] Thus, the first period (from 5 to 7 years) can be named the preparatory period. Proper education starts "from seven years up to puberty, and again that following the age from puberty up to twenty-one."[19] Aristotle agrees with Plato that the main goal of education is to cultivate virtue through controlling pleasure and suffering: "For moral virtue is concerned with pleasures and pains; it is on account of the pleasure that we do bad things, and on account of the pain that we abstain from noble ones. Hence we ought to have been brought up in a particular way from our very youth, as Plato says, so as both to delight in and to be pained by the things that we ought; this is the right education."[20] Also for Aristotle it is obvious that humans beings are neither good nor bad by nature; their qualities are acquired through training. At the same time, it is clear that the principle goal of education is the virtue based on the knowledge of laws.

One more principle condition should be considered: to be virtuous means to be in a specific mental state, which in turn means that it is necessary to acquire the brought up ability to keep this specific mental state. The corresponding way of acting, which enable such a state, Aristotle describes in the following words: "The agent also must be in a certain condition when he does them; in the first place he must have knowledge, secondly he must choose the acts, and choose them for their own sakes, and thirdly his action must proceed from a firm and unchangeable character."[21]

Thus, different periods of life meet different challenges and consequently require different approaches. It is quite obvious that during the preparatory period (before the age of seven), we cannot talk about reasonable control of pleasures and sufferings. The behavior of children is regulated from the outside so that they learn good examples. During the second period, from age seven up to puberty, reason should gradually be involved for the sake of developing virtue. The virtue in turn is "the state of character which

---

[18] *Aristotle's Politics.* Sec. ed. (Trans. by Carnes Lord). The University of Chicago Press. 2013. p. 240.
[19] Ibid.
[20] Aristotle. *The Nicomachean Ethics.* p. 26.
[21] Ibid. p. 27-28.

makes a man good and which makes him do his own work well."[22] In other words, it is the disposition to choose good rather than bad, and for Aristotle, it means to reasonably choose a position in the middle. During the third period, from puberty to age 21, the orientation towards laws is added to education.

Describing the general approach to education, Aristotle emphasizes that at any stage, "everything mean should be made foreign to the young, particularly things of this sort that involve either depravity or malice."[23] Also, he discusses the subjects that have to be taught.

Let us start with the outlined periods.

In ancient Greece, schooling started at the age of seven. Plato and Aristotle regarded this age as too late and proposed five or even four years. Therefore, the *preparatory period* lasts from three to two years. One of the most important activities of this period is the acquisition of good speaking abilities. It is difficult to overestimate the role of this ability in a society where communication is prodigiously oral. At this stage, the child observes the activities of older children and participates in some of these activities, thus becoming accustomed to what he will do later. It is extremely important that the child learn to repress passions and whims. Aristotle, in many cases, accentuates the significance of habit.

The second stage is, in many respects, crucial. It can also be divided into two periods, when the study of letters at the first stage is followed by the study of meaningful texts, predominantly of moral content, during the second stage.

Greek education consisted of two parts: gymnastics and music. In its turn, music (or "the art of muses") comprised letters (reading and writing), numbers, literature (predominantly poetry), and music itself. There were three different teachers: trainers (*paidotribes*) for gymnastics, *grammatistes* for literacy and numbers, and *kitharistes* for music. Also, a child usually had a *paidagogos* – a slave whose duty was to accompany the child on his daily journey from home to school and back. H. Marrou points out the fact that the role of paidogogos had a moral constituent: "If the child had to be accompanied, this was because he needed protection

---

[22] Ibid. p. 29.
[23] *Aristotle's Politics.* Sec. ed. (Trans. by Carnes Lord). The University of Chicago Press. 2013. p. 240.

against dangers to be met with in the streets—and we know what they were. The pedagogue kept a continual watch over his charge, and this often came to be resented in adolescence as an unbearable tyranny."[24] Thus, moral issues were becoming habitual from the very beginning of the school years. However, these issues were not directly related to school education directly, because the teacher was not regarded as an authority in this respect. "The schoolmaster was only responsible for one small section of children's education—the mental side. He did not really educate his pupils. Education means, essentially, moral training, character training, and a whole way of life. The "master" was only expected to teach them to read, which is a much less important matter."[25] It seems that Aristotle shared the common views in relation to teachers. In the *Politics* he is stressing the fact that parents and not teachers are responsible for education. The succession of subjects taught starts with gymnastics, because "it is evident that education through habits must come earlier than education through reason, and education connected with the body earlier than education connected with the mind, it is clear from these things that children must initially be given over to gymnastics and to sports training."[26] The time for letters should be gradually increased.

In relation to all subjects, the most important rule according to Aristotle is that learning should be 1) moderate and 2) delimited to such matters, which would not be vulgar and inappropriate for a free person. "One should consider a vulgar task, art, or sort of learning to be any that renders the body, the soul, or the mind of free persons useless with a view to the practices and actions of virtue. Hence, we call vulgar both the sorts of arts that bring the body into a worse state and the wage-earning sorts of work, for they make the mind a thing abject and lacking in leisure. But it is also the case that, while it is not unfree to share in some of the liberal sciences up to a certain point, to persevere overly much in them with a view to proficiency is liable to involve the sorts of injuries just mentioned."[27]

For the modern reader, it can be quite strange that, being himself an exclusively hardworking person, Aristotle prioritizes leisure over work. This point should be clarified. It can definitely and quite rightly be

---

[24] Marrou H.I. *A history of education in antiquity*. (Trans. by G. Lamb). A Mentor Books, 1956. p. 201.
[25] Ibid. pp. 205-206.
[26] *Aristotle's Politics.* p. 237.
[27] Ibid. p. 243.

regarded as the continuation of the aristocratic approach to life. However, Aristotle's approach is much deeper.

Firstly, it seems to be assumed that there is a distinction between leisure for such aristocratic occupations as political and military activities and just leisure for pastimes.

Secondly, and this is central, this attitude toward leisure reflects the general attitude towards learning as such. The key to solving the problem can be found in the first lines of Aristotle's "Parts of Animals": "Regarding every study and investigation, the more humble and valuable alike, there appear to be two sorts of states, one of which may properly be called understanding of the subject matter, and the other a certain sort of educatedness. It is characteristic of an educated person to be able to judge successfully what is well said and what is not. We think of someone who is generally educated as a person of that sort, and we think being educated is being able to make such judgements—only we consider the one person to be a single individual able to judge about practically all things, the other about something of a delimited nature; for there might be another person well disposed in the same way as the person we have been discussing, but regarding a particular subject."[28] We can easily infer from these considerations that Aristotle argues in favor of fundamental education: the educated person should know many different things in order to make good judgments on various matters. Yet the pupil should not be deeply involved in specific subjects because this involvement makes him dependent, as well as any knowledge or activity directed towards something that violates his self-sufficiency.

Thirdly, at the same time, this approach means that Aristotle defends human freedom. It can definitely be regarded as an exaggeration, since it is obvious that there cannot exist any social position that would allow absolute independence. However, Aristotle presents the ideal type (in Max Weber's terms) of the educated person, which unites high moral standards with a high level of knowledge. This statement can be supported by the following words: "Being at leisure, on the other hand, is held to involve pleasure, happiness, and living blessedly. This is not available to those who are occupied, but rather to those at leisure, for the person who is occupied is occupied for the sake of some end that is assumed not to be

---

[28] Aristotle. *On the Parts of Animals*. (Trans. by J. Lennox). Clarendon Press, 2001. p. 1.

present, while happiness is an end, and something all suppose to be accompanied not by pain but by pleasure."[29] This image of an absolutely happy person is certainly the end, rather than a real state of mind. We also have to keep in mind that, for Aristotle, happiness means satisfaction.

In his views on the system of education, Aristotle stands apart from the schooling practices of his time. He accepts the subjects that were usually taught at school: letters, gymnastics, music, and drawing. At the same time, Aristotle, along with the practical usefulness of these subjects, stresses the importance of the development of character. Thus, if gymnastics develops courage, drawing makes pupils "experts at studying the beauty connected with bodies". Learning letters is useful because "other sorts of learning become possible through them."[30]

The second part of this period started when *grammatistes* were followed by *grammatikos*. Predominantly poetry was taught by beginning certainly with Homer, followed by the list of classical poets such as Euripides, Menander and Demosthenes. Texts were especially selected for education. Learning started with expressive reading, which was quite a difficult task because at that stage written text was not divided into words and sentences, there were no capital letters, etc. Since reading was only aloud, it was gradually transforming into recitation, and this was preparation to public presentations. Most important was *exPredominantly,ation* of texts. The purpose of these explanations "was ultimately moral, and he was thus in the mainstream of the old tradition, with its search for heroic examples of "human perfection."[31] At this stage, pupils started learning literary compositions, and a new teacher appeared: a *rhetor* (or *sophistes*). The exercises successively followed well-established logic, starting with fables and narratives, followed by discussions of law. In parallel geometry, arithmetic and harmonics were learned, which was vital for the development of abstract thought. Their importance was stressed by Plato, and Aristotle seemed to share this view.

At *the third stage,* we are approaching higher education, directly oriented towards the main goal of education for the citizen as such. "Aristotle's arguments for the importance of education are intimately connected with his arguments for its public sponsorship, and nowhere are these connections more obvious than in the case of his arguments from

---

[29] *Aristotle's Politics.* p. 236.
[30] Ibid. p. 245.
[31] Marrou H.I. *A history of education in antiquity.* p. 234.

constitutional unity (CU) and a common end (CE)."[32] W. Jaeger emphasizes the significance of legal studies, saying that "the culmination of Plato's work as a philosophical educator comes in his last and greatest book, when he himself turns lawgiver, and Aristotle closes the *Ethics* by calling for a legislator to realize the ideal he has formulated. Law is the mother of philosophy."[33] By this time, boys would have acquired the necessary habits to learn; they could also compose and declaim texts, etc., and they were well prepared to start learning rhetoric and philosophy. They have also already overcome difficulties related to natural problems with suppressing passions and various wishes. Aristotle stated that "it is difficult to get from youth the right training for virtue if one has not been brought up under the right laws; for to live temperately and hardily is not pleasant to most people, especially when they are young. For this reason, their nurture and occupations should be fixed by law, for they will not be painful when they have become customary."[34] The interdependence between the law and the good character of a citizen is again the focus.

Actually, the art of rhetoric was recognized as the most significant of all other arts in the 5th century, when the political culture of policies with democratic ways of administration was flourishing. It is no coincidence that the old sophists were the originators of higher education, and the central theme of their teaching was unquestionably rhetoric. Aristotle defines the art of rhetoric as "a capacity to observe what admits being persuasive in each case, for this is the task of no other art." This art also meets the criterion of a non-utilitarian nature: "rhetoric seems to be the capacity to observe what is persuasive concerning any given matter, so to speak. Hence, we assert that its technical skill is not concerned with any particular, definite class."[35] In addition, rhetoric is virtuous by nature if we remember that Aristotle presents a collectivistic view: "the greatest virtues are necessarily the ones of most use for others, if in fact virtue is a capacity for benefaction."[36]

---

[32] Curren, R.R. Justice, instruction, and the good: The case for public education in Aristotle and Plato's Laws. // *Studies in Philosophy and Education*, v. 12, 1993. p. 104.

[33] Jaeger W. *Paideia: the ideals of Greek culture.* (Trans. by G. Highet, v.1). Archaic Greece. The mind of Athens. Basil Blackwell, 1946. pp. 109-110.

[34] Aristotle. *The Nicomachean Ethics.* pp. 199-200.

[35] *Aristotle's Art of Rhetoric.* p. 11.

[36] Ibid. p. 41.

The study of philosophy is also necessary because it means training intellectual abilities as well as providing some theoretical knowledge, named by Aristotle "first philosophy", or "metaphysics", including, in particular, logic and physics (general natural science). It is necessary to keep in mind that philosophy at that time was in no way reduced to knowledge as such. As it was stressed by Pierre Hadot in his works, the idea of philosophy was a way of life. Hence, the importance of ethics cannot be exaggerated.[37]

Thus, by the end of the third period of study, a human being was supposed to acquire all the necessary abilities in order to be a good law-abiding citizen, having virtue (orientation towards others'), and being happy due to participation in political life.

At this stage, it is useful to turn to Aristotle's teaching practice. Its characteristic features are summarized in the following points: 1) integrity of knowledge; 2) wonder as the beginning of knowledge; 3) oral communication as a way of organizing knowledge; and 4) knowledge as a necessary and special element of lifestyle.[38]

The fourth point was already discussed, so we will turn to the others.

It is obvious that Aristotle, in his approach to any discipline, uses the deductive approach (presented by his logic). Any subject is built and successively taught, starting from the first principles. In our days, when any information is too easily accessible, instead of a consistent picture of the world, flat mosaic pictures of the world pile up in our minds. On this basis, specialization in some exclusively narrow fields is added. Such a person can become easily manipulated as he or she lacks the possibility to analyze the situation from different angles. Fundamental education, in turn, makes a member of society much more independent in his or her views and, respectively, in his or her actions. The fundamental approach does not just provide counter-mosaic Weltanschauung but also offers methodological support to any discipline. It is enough to look at the beginnings of Aristotle's works. The perfect examples of his approach can be found in physics, rhetoric, politics, and others. In all cases, Aristotle starts to speak about general principles, defining the discipline, the most

---

[37] Hadot P. *Philosophy as a Way of Life. Spiritual Exercises from Socrates to Foucault.* (Trans. by M. Chase). Blackwell Publishers Ltd, 1995.
[38] Donskikh O. Significance of Aristotle Teaching Practice for Modern Education // *Teacher Education in the 21st Century*. London: IntechOpen, 2019. p. 5.

basic terms, etc. Here is the first paragraph of "Poetics": Let us discuss the art of poetry in general and its species—the effect that each species of poetry has and the correct way to construct plots if the composition is to be of high quality—as well as the number and nature of its component parts and any other questions that arise within the same field of inquiry. We should begin, as is natural, by taking the first principles first."[39] Aristotle defines the specific feature of poetry (taken as a generis term) as *mimesis* and divides poetry according to *"media* of imitation, or different *objects,* or a different *mode."*[40] The logic is very clear, which allows us to reflect on the subject as a whole. Discussing this approach allows us to clarify the previously mentioned point referring to fundamentalism. If we take any discipline from a bird's-eye view, we will understand the overall content without the need to scrutinize the small details. This is quite characteristic of the worldview of an educated person.

Wonder, as the beginning of knowledge, is also crucially important. In modern pedagogical techniques, the use of problem-based methods seems to provide some substitution for Aristotle's wonder. Yet there is a significant difference: wonder grows from the general approach of the human being to the surrounding world. It is characterized by a detached individual view striving towards wholeness of understanding. Instead, modern pedagogical techniques provide artificially refined situations scattered over different subjects. It is a matter of self-sufficiency rather than specific training. The person is not limited by the artificial situation presented from outside.

In Ancient Greece, rhetoric played an exclusive public role: "celebrating the golden mean encourages tolerance and makes common action conceivable. It makes the public sphere a rhetorical space where community is invented and shared in performances of virtue through stories of significant individuals and momentous events. These rhetorical enactments of civic virtues are worth imitating because they teach lessons for making society itself more noble."[41] Referring to education, it is worth stating that the necessity of oral communication as a way of organizing knowledge is quite significant for the following reasons: 1) in order to communicate orally the pupil has to keep in mind some knowledge without constantly referring to the written text, and this is useful for the

---

[39] Aristotle. *Poetics.* (Trans. by M. Heath). Penguin Books, 1996. p.3.
[40] Ibid.
[41] Hauser, Gerard A. Aristotle on epideictic: The formation of public morality // *Rhetoric Society Quarterly,* 29:1, 5-23. DOI: 10.1080/02773949909391135 . 19.

development not only of short-term memory but of long-term memory as well. 2) The pupil has to learn how to ask proper questions with the purpose of receiving proper answers. This is a demanding task because it is necessary to immediately formulate consistent problems in the most appropriate and consistent way. In this respect, training is aimed at forming corresponding habits.

The last question that should be discussed in relation to Aristotle's approach to education is whether his views are still significant for an individualistic society. It appears that there are definitely some points of significance. The general answer is quite clear: everything relating to the formation of a responsible member of society through character building retains its significance. However, there are some important additional nuances.

At first, it should be emphasizing the necessity of forming character, which starts to be molded at the age of seven and continues up to twenty-one.

Second, it is vital to have highly developed communicative skills.

Third, the development of long-term memory is important in order to acquire a self-contained individual position in one's social life.

Fourth, the very orientation towards state laws is crucial for an individual belonging to a legal society. Yet there is an important difference in attitude: in modern society, the goal of the individual and of the state differs because, in an individualistic society, a human being lives primarily in search of self-identity, while in a collectivistic society, he should freely subordinate his nature to social needs. Excellence (which is the goal of a human being in Ancient Greece) does not mean uniqueness but actually the opposite: the repetition of the best examples, familiar to society and accepted by the corresponding culture.

Conclusion: Aristotle presents the system of upbringing and education of self-sufficient and responsible human beings who are aware of themselves as being part of the state. From the point of view of the development of society, Aristotle presupposed that it is organized with the aim of having well-educated citizens, which means that the state acquires well-recognized laws.

The system of education should provide the possibility of a step-by-step movement towards proper citizenship based on virtue and reason. The content of education should be

designed in such a way that each period of human life from five to twenty-one years has its own end, becoming the foundation for the next one.

In the first period (ages five to seven), the child just imitates the activities of older people. In the second period, children start learning gymnastics and letters, and this is the crucial stage for forming character because the way of education is tough and repetitive and does not presuppose any facilitation according to the age. The second part of this period, in addition to learning different subjects, includes more and more moral issues based on classical texts. The third period is designed to form a good citizen who has acquired virtue and reason and the ability to act for the well-being of society on the basis of knowledge of laws.

Although in an individualistic society the goal of society is not the same as the goal of the individual, Aristotle's approach to education has not lost its actuality in many respects, the most important of which is the formation of the responsible member of society.

Daoist Pedagogy: Attunement, Nonviolent Intervention, and A Virtuous Process

Doctor Hongyu Wang

Introduction

Until recently, the Daoist[1] meaning of education has not been systematically elaborated in the U.S. context, where education is often approached as a practical activity and the role of philosophy is not valued. The philosophy of Daoism has profound implications for today's education and society in addressing many of the challenges we are facing (Culham & Lin, 2020; Wang, 2021; Miller, 2022). In this paper, I explore what a Daoist perspective can offer educators for re-thinking pedagogical theory and practice, particularly through the notion of *wuwei* and what it means for teaching that deconstructs the mechanism of domination and paves ways for integrative personhood and sustainable relationships (Wang, 2021). Relational attunement, nonviolent intervention, and virtue-orientation are three of its elements that are organically connected to vitalizing pedagogical relationships and engaging in students' knowing, being, and interbeing through interconnectedness and compassion.

This paper starts by explaining the notion of *wuwei,* its original and contemporary meanings, and then elaborates on what Daoist pedagogy means in adopting the approach of *wuwei. Wuwei* is often considered as spontaneous movement, but its spontaneity is enabled by relational attunement to all aspects of a classroom. *Wuwei* is often perceived as passive, without agency, but its non-dual action requires intervention and interruption—not by force—to enable students' non-dualistic learning.

---

[1] I am using the Mainland Chinese version of the *pinyin* translation, *Dao De Jing*, rather than *Tao Te Ching*. This paper refers to *Dao De Jing* and *Zhuangzi* as texts, and the translations are the author's own. There are debates about who Laozi or Zhuangzi were or whether they even existed.

Furthermore, the value orientation of *wuwei* deconstructs our usual ways of thinking about what it means to educate and to be educated. This paper considers these three intertwined aspects to illuminate Daoist pedagogy in a dark time for our humanity today.

What is *Wuwei*?

Wuwei is not unique to Daoism; it exists in other Chinese philosophies (Fung, 1976; Slingerland, 2003, 2014), but this paper addresses Daoist *wuwei*. Translated directly from Chinese into English, *wuwei* is "doing nothing" or "non-action," which leads to the misinterpretation of *wuwei* as not making an effort, being passive, or not doing anything against what is going wrong. However, *Wuwei* is a particular form of action, "non-dual" action (Loy, 1988), "noncoercive action" (Ames & Hall, 2003, p. 38), or "non-imposing action" (Bender, 2023) that acts upon the world but does not objectify and dominate others or the natural world. It is an action that does not impose itself nor possess others, but an action that moves with what the situation calls for to enable mutually flourishing paths for all participants (Wang, 2019). In this sense, *wuwei* already addresses what went wrong in wartime, when Daoism originated, and also addresses the current human and ecological crises that have been a result of divisions between cultural groups and separating humanity from nature.

In contemporary Daoism, *Dao* is perceived as both the path and path-making, both a noun and a verb (Ames & Hall, 2003; Wang, 2021), as *wuwei* moves through *yin-yang* dynamics. Chapter 43 of *Dao De Jing* makes the connection between the influence and the yielding of *wuwei*: "The most yielding [thing] in the world prevails against the hardest in the world. . . . But few understand the benefits of *wuwei*." The opposite yet complementary cosmic energies—*yin* and *yang*—in their dynamic interactions demonstrate how softness leads to strength and how *wuwei* leads to *wubuwei* (being free to do anything without crossing the boundary). The relational nature of *wuwei* is also embedded in the central role of *qi* (vital energy) in interfusing all existences with connectedness, including between the internal self and the external world. According to Liu's (2016) *qi* theory, the unified, prime *qi* self-differentiates into *yin qi* and *yang qi,* and everything and everybody in the universe is born through the interactions between *yin qi* and *yang qi*. For the rising *yang qi* to meet the falling *yin qi, yin qi* needs to be above *yang qi*. Otherwise, the death of a current existence can happen, and a new existence cannot emerge. *Wuwei* emphasizes the role of *yin qi* to achieve harmony and follows the waterway of *Dao* that falls down to accumulate strength (Allan, 1997; Wang, 2008).

There is an element of spontaneous response in *wuwei* as it empties out the instrumental accumulation for a predetermined goal. As Slingerland (2014) argues, "Spontaneity in the West is typically associated with individuality—people just doing whatever they want. *Wu-wei,* on the other hand, means becoming part of something larger; the cosmic order" of *Dao* (p. 42). The relational orientation of *wuwei* situates spontaneous action in attunement to the whole and the individual's interplay with the whole. As Jacob Bender (2023) points out, "To harmonize the relations of persons and nature, we need to be perceptive to how things are radically novel convergences of relationships (and thus, novel focal points of nature") (p. 192). In Daoism, things are unique not because they are separate from one another but because they are embedded in interrelationships in different forms. In other words, the uniqueness of a thing or a person depends upon the nature of the converging connections.

By following the way of nature to act without forcing, *wuwei* leads to the transformation of all participants. As *Dao De Jing* (Chapter 57) says, "I adopt *wuwei,* yet the people transform themselves; I love quietude, yet the people reach the integrity of themselves; I do not act without the need, yet the people enrich themselves; I do not have excessive desire, yet the people return to the simplicity of nature." Such a way of governing through *wuwei* is also a way of teaching and educating. Here, the notion of nature does not necessarily mean the natural world but means the naturalistic principle of the cosmos (*ziran*) that is spontaneous, self-generating, and self-transforming (Lai, 2017; Wang, 2021). Nature also embodies such a power of self-organization beyond human control. While *wuwei* follows the naturalistic principle, it is also a capacity acquired through engaged practices of intentional attunement to relationality, cultivating discernment, insights, and intuition rather than relying only on rational thought.

Wuwei is at odds with modern education, which privileges the effective transmission of subject knowledge, skills, and dispositions with clear-cut external expectations that students are required to reach. The role of the teacher as the authority in the classroom is seldom compatible with the position of practicing *wuwei.* Although it is difficult to imagine practicing *wuwei* in today's U.S. education, which is controlled by standardization, commercialization, and a competition-oriented mentality, there are still opportunities for teaching as non-forcing and enabling that can be carved out of difficulties. As Daoism makes clear, force cannot win in the end; nor can forcing students to learn in order to meet externally imposed uniform demands. However, as constraints cannot be overthrown once and for all, educators and teachers need to open cracks now and then to show alternative ways of thinking, feeling, and doing, so that students understand and experience that there is always another way. Doll (2012) advocates for allotting a limited amount of time in the teaching schedule to let students play and explore the structure of a school subject.

Importantly, teachers' ability to open new possibilities is dependent upon their own cultivation of a personhood that is not confined by taken-for-granted assumptions and established norms. Without getting in touch with the quietude inside themselves and without practicing *wuwei* in their own lives, a teacher will not be able to open a crack for students to see the light. For educators, enacting the relational and non-imposing orientation of *wuwei* in the classroom requires not only their attunement to all aspects of the teaching and learning process but also ongoing efforts to transcend societal and cultural norms that often become internalized within educators' own mindset. Intervening nonviolently in these internalized norms on the part of teachers, in an ongoing process, is essential to practicing Daoist pedagogy.

Relational Attunement in Pedagogical Interactions

Attunement to the self, the other, and the world is necessarily relational. As a concept, attunement is musical, aesthetic, emotional, spiritual, and intuitive, bringing inner and outer relationships into harmony. *Wuwei* is attuned to the self and the other in the "living wholeness" (Aoki, 2005, p. 185) of body, mind, and the situation to both reveal and transform the world.

Listening is essential to attunement. In Daoism, attunement is listening through *qi*:

> Do not listen with your ears but with your heart; do not listen with your heart but with your vital breath (*qi*). The ears hear only the sounds, and the heart welcomes only what is pleasing to it. *Qi*, however, in its emptiness and stillness, is inclusive of all. (*Zhuangzi*, Chapter 4, "The Human World")

Here, listening through the ears is not adequate, and listening through the heart, although one step further, is still not enough, as neither can get in touch with reality as it is. Listening through *qi,* however, directly connects a person with the world in its holistic existence and dynamics. In such attunement, emptiness and stillness nurture new ways of seeing and understanding in one's effort to become united with *Dao.* Attending to both verbal and nonverbal languages, listening attends to both conscious, explicit thought and unconscious, implicit needs. Pedagogically, often what is unsaid is more important than what is said, and listening to discern what students are struggling to express can make a transformative difference to a teacher's ability to be attuned to students.

Relational attunement also takes time and effort. The practice of *Taiji Quan* looks effortless in masterful performance, but its practitioners spend a long time to achieve such attunement to their own bodies as well as the environment to cultivate the harmonious circulation of *qi* in their movements. Similarly, masterful acupuncture doctors appear to insert needles effortlessly, and patients do not feel pain. While their attunement to others' bodies and minds cannot be scientifically formulated, they treat illnesses effectively. But it takes many years of practice to acquire the art of holistic medicine.

To explicate what relational attunement means, I use the example of the swimmer from a parable in *Zhuangzi.* The parable describes a tall waterfall and how fish and turtles do not venture into the area. A man jumps into it, scaring the people standing by. But soon he swims out of the water and reaches the shore, happily singing a song. When asked by others what his magic is, he replies:

> I don't have any magic. It is due to habit, and I have acquired this ability after a long time of practice. I can accomplish it because I go with the natural. Going in with the swirls and coming out with the eddies, I am following the *Dao* of water and do not impose my idea, and that is how I can tread water. (*Zhuangzi*, Chapter 19, "Understanding Life").

The swimmer had grown up in a mountain area and was thus familiar with the nature of mountains. Then he moved to another area along the water, and he experienced and acquired the nature of water. Following the naturalistic principle of *Dao,* the swimmer was attuned to the way of the waterfall, and even when it appeared to be dangerous, he could tread water safely and playfully. In other words, he became one with the movement of water. From this parable, we can see that the swimmer does not seem to do anything special, and his *wuwei* is both natural and acquired. It is natural because the swimmer goes with the flow of water, and it is acquired as he has practiced it for a long time until he can spontaneously respond to the movement of water and its environment.

As this parable shows, the swimmer's relational attunement to the waterfall is built upon his awareness of what he can and cannot do after many years of practice, and his internal ideas have merged with the movement of nature. It also shows the role of constraints and how constraints do not become barriers when the swimmer is attuned to the movement of the waterfall and acts spontaneously in accordance with the boundaries. Relying on his embodied, experiential, and intuitive knowledge, which supports his attuned action, his acceptance of constraints becomes the basis for his transcendence of the limits in his extraordinary performance. Thus, attunement simultaneously attends to both the internal and the external, both constraint and potentiality, and both the conscious and the unconscious (Miller, 2022; Pinar, 2019).

Pedagogical Attunement

A teacher's attunement in the classroom is a result of crafting the teaching process with a focus on the relational dynamics within this context. Pedagogical interactions not only include teacher-student relationships but also include students' interactions with what they learn, students' relationships among one another, and the climate of the classroom. Through the teacher's attunement to students' spoken and unspoken desires and needs, to students' peer relationships, and to the rhythm of the world introduced into the classroom, students' inner world is respected, and they become attuned to the interconnections (Wang, 2022). Studies, on the part of students, are no longer about conquering subject knowledge and the world or becoming superior to their classmates, but about immersing themselves in their explorations, understandings, and interactions.

As Miller (2022) points out, "Education and teaching tend to be dominated by rational, logical thinking" or calculative thinking (p. 47). However, the *wuwei* approach values aesthetic, embodied, and intuitive knowing, which goes beyond instrumentality, rationality, and logic. In today's education, in which instrumental approaches center on scientific rationality, it is important that teachers practice pedagogical attunement to help students get in touch with the creative energy of life. By working with the constraints and attending to the contextualized situations, teachers can open new possibilities without provoking more blockages. The doubled gesture of attunement also suggests that we can combine both analytic and integrative modes of thinking.

A teacher's use of the World Peace Game in a variety of teaching settings to help students explore peaceful solutions to conflict demonstrates how far a teacher and students can go when teaching is attuned to students' creative potential, the nature of conflict, and the possibilities of collaboration in our tensioned world (Hunter, 2013). John Hunter (2013) adopts a *wuwei* approach to creating an empty space to allow students' emergence and becoming in their journeys, and students have shown their brilliance in dealing with global problems, working through the complexity of issues, learning from their mistakes, and coming up with surprising ways of achieving peace when it seems impossible. Students reach "new depths within themselves—new reserves of creativity, leadership, and integrity" and "integrate their view of [different] layers into their vision of the planet as a whole" (p. 66). These students' a-ha moments have not been the result of merely rational and calculative thinking, but of using integrative, playful, intuitive, and out-of-the-box thinking.

Hunter and his students' astonishing achievements have happened over several decades during a time when U.S. school reform has gone through an era of emphasizing STEM and intensifying standardization, and when the U.S. as a nation has gone to war multiple times. The broader context of increasing scientism, militarism, and nationalism has not diminished Hunter's effort to open space for students to think and imagine differently. Pedagogical attunement can create new spaces despite constraints. Hunter (2013) also discusses his own growth, which has led him not only into this pedagogical space but also into his own learning from students, who have inspired him during the process. He argues, "Not knowing the answer can be a genuine advantage for a teacher, because it means that you are not able to impose your own limits on your students" (p. 20). The teacher's attunement to the self—beyond a rigid and fixed identity—to expand their horizons is an essential part of pedagogical attunement.

Attending to intellectual, aesthetic, ethical, and spiritual experience as lived, relational attunement in pedagogical interactions is supported by the intertwined threads between self-awareness and awareness of others and the world, teaching and learning without forcing, deep listening, and the release of creativity that follows the pathway of *Dao*.

Nonviolent Intervention

I start with a parable in *Zhuangzi* to explain the two layers of nonviolent intervention in *wuwei*. A woodworker, Qing, was getting ready to make a bell stand:

> First, I fast to still my mind. After fasting for three days, I no longer have any thoughts about reputation or rewards. After fasting for five days, I no longer have any thoughts about blame or praise, skillfulness or clumsiness. After fasting for seven days, I suddenly forget that I have four limbs and a body. (*Zhuangzi*, Chapter 19, "Understanding Life")

Here, the approaches to meditation through sitting, forgetting, and heart-fasting are evident. Enabling the interfusing of the self with the world for creative activities happens first through fasting to empty Qing's mind from pursuing external rewards and to reach the level of self-forgetting. This work comes from within; it is not externally imposed by force but is an intervention in the sense of transforming one's mind in such a way that one becomes in tune with *Dao*. I think that contemplation and meditation that center the mind and ground relational attunement (Nagler, 2004; Miller, 2022) are forms of nonviolent intervention into the busy mind to empty out excessive attachment and instrumental pursuits. This work takes time and effort, but cultivating *qi* cannot be forced. Nonviolent intervention as a part of Daoist personal cultivation can help teachers go beyond the confinement of fixed ideas and ideologies as well as attachment to external fame, gains, and the pursuit of power. That is the inner layer of *wuwei*.

The parable continues:

> Only then do I enter the mountain forest and observe the heavenly nature of the trees until I find one that is a perfect match. I can see a completed bell stand already in it. Only then do I begin to work; otherwise, I would not start. I allow the heavenly energy within me to match the heavenly energy in the natural shape of a tree—this is probably why the wooden stand is thought to be so magical. (*Zhuangzi*, Chapter 19, "Understanding Life")

Here, Qing's *wuwei* in his crafting process is demonstrated by the sudden appearance of the image in a tree by meditatively connecting the *qi* within him and the *qi* in the world in a spontaneous, magical way. The inner layer and outer layer of *wuwei* become connected. Although the image appears in a tree intuitively, Qing has already intervened by building bridges between the inner and outer world, albeit in a matching way rather than an imposing way. His creation, the outer layer of *wuwei,* is a result of nonviolent intervention.

As a nonviolent intervention, *wuwei* is opposed to all forms of violence. In Daoism, victory through military or other forces should be mourned rather than celebrated because it is not only damaging to others but also damaging to oneself. Nobody becomes safer or happier as a result of war or a warlike mentality (*Dao De Jing*, Chapters 29, 31). Warfare can easily lead to its own vulnerability, as the extreme hypermasculinity can be changed into hyperfemininity, as the yin-yang converting tendency indicates. In this sense, *wuwei* is an intervention to dissolve violence before it emerges. The lack of attention to the message of peace and nonviolence in school curriculum (Wang, 2024) can be interrupted by presenting peace literature, particularly children's and young adult literature, in order to disrupt the normalization of violence in its various forms. *Wuwei* disrupts and uproots the logic of domination and conquest.

Contemporary Daoists in China argue that intervention is also necessary for practicing *wuwei* because the contemporary context is already marked by the intensification of the separation between humans and nature, a situation that must be addressed urgently (Deng, 2008; Lin, 2017). Lin (2017) distinguishes two modes of *wuwei*: first, unconditional *wuwei* at the cosmic level, existing in the universe in a self-generating process; and second, conditional *wuwei* at the human level, as becoming attuned to *Dao* after *Dao* is lost in the human world requires human intervention. I am not sure that human intervention is needed only *after* Dao is lost, because I think intervening in violence in thoughts, words, and deeds is necessary in everyday educational practice so that aggression can be curbed and compassion can be promoted on a consistent basis.

Pedagogy of Nonviolent Intervention

A pedagogy of nonviolent intervention deconstructs instrumental learning, enables students' relational learning, dissolves the mechanism of domination, and encourages contemplative and intuitive thinking. Conditions must be created in curriculum, teaching, learning, and the class environment to intervene in a hierarchical system of education to enable students' emergent growth.

As Slingerland (2014) points out, "To attain Laozian *wu-wei*, you need to undo rather than do, gradually unwinding your mind and body, shedding book learning and artificial desires" (p. 98). The accumulation of instrumental knowledge and fixed ideas in book learning, which often happens at schools and colleges, creates barriers to getting in touch with *Dao*. Clearing up the crowded mind is important for enabling relational attunement so that students' knowing and being are fully engaged on their own terms, rather than controlled by categorical thinking and the pursuit of external rewards and societal conformity. Through allowing the role of silence, contemplation, and stillness in the classroom, teachers can intervene in the normalization of instrumental learning and open time and space for loosening up the rigidity of academic studies (Ma & Wang, in press).

Here, experiential learning that integrates students' body, mind, and spirit and connects them with life, rather than book learning that is abstract, categorical, and disembodied, is important for enacting a pedagogy of nonviolent intervention. Learning and teaching on the basis of insights, intuition, and analogy that are compatible with Daoist ways of relational thinking is an intervention into conventional teaching and the normalization of violence in intellectual, emotional, social, and educational aspects (Wang, 2021, 2024). Such intervention is nonviolent because it goes through students' embodied experiences and their own sense-making and meaning-making processes rather than through the one-sided transmission of intellectual knowledge.

Lessons in forming a harmonious relationship with nature are also good ways of teaching relational learning through awe, wonder, and reverence for life (Miller, 2022; Culham & Lin, 2020). Such lessons work not only for schoolchildren but also for graduate students in universities (Wang, 2019, 2024). While children have fewer barriers to forming communion with the natural world, adults can also find surprising discoveries in establishing a nonviolent and meditative companionship with non-human beings and in unlearning the mechanisms of human control and the conquest of nature (Brown, 2008). For example, Brown intended to help her students in a college class to have a "healthy, emotionally complex relationship with their trees" (p. 83) through a companionship project, which became an enlivening process of students' listening to the trees and letting the trees speak back in their own languages. It did take time to happen, as students' experiences with plants disrupted their usual assumptions and habits. To a great degree, mainstream formal education encourages the separation between humans and nature, so pre-service and in-service teachers often need to question the assumptions that they have internalized in order to restore and cultivate their own and their students' capacities to become attuned with to vital energy of nature.

Pedagogical companionship can also serve as a way of nonviolent intervention to deconstruct the controlling mechanism of teacher-student relationships (Ma & Wang, in press). Such companionship includes pedagogical watchfulness, generosity, and pedagogical letting go to provide guidance and enable freedom (Aoki, 2005). Accompanying students through their struggles without presenting the teacher's solution is not easy, as teachers need to let go of their desire to control the outcome of student learning. Adopting the *wuwei* stance, pedagogical relationships of companionship dwell in time, suspend judgment, and create space for students' explorations and becoming (Wang, 2024).

Virtue-Infused *Wuwei*, and Virtuous Teaching

The notion of *de* (i.e., virtue) in Daoism has both cosmic and human layers of meaning. It is cosmic in the sense of harmonious life energy in the universe; it is human in the sense of "aligning oneself with the underlying patterns of the *Dao*" (Culham & Lin, 2020, p. 180). There are different interpretations of what *de* means in *Dao De Jing*, and I adopt Ames and Hall's (2003) approach to *de* as the particular embodiment of *Dao* in specific things and specific persons. Such an alignment of *Dao* and *de* positions human attunement to *Dao* through *wuwei* as a virtuous process that emphasizes the importance of compassion, non-competition, simplicity, quietude, and humility in order to reach harmony within the self and in the world. Cultivating virtues and the practices of *qi*—in meditation, *qigong, tai-ji quan*, or in artistic activities such as calligraphy and painting—support each other (Chang, 1963; Culham & Lin, 2020; Miller, 2022). The circulation of *qi*, which sparks the cultivation of a virtuous character, is oriented by the creative dynamics of *yin* and *yang*.

Dao De Jing teaches us that, contrary to the conventional understanding, the feminine is more life-affirmative than the masculine (Chapters 36, 76, 78). It is a natural law that when humans and plants are born, they are supple and soft, but when they die, they are stiff and hard. Thus, Daoist virtues associated with *wuwei* are unconventional, dissolving rather than reinforcing our attachments to moral regulation and aggressive force. As *Dao De Jing* states, the greatest *de* "grows everything and nurtures everything. It grows but does not occupy, nurtures but does not lord over, and guides but does not control" (Chapter 10). If we can cultivate such nurturing yet non-possessive and non-controlling virtues in education, the whole world will be transformed and revitalized. These virtues are associated with the vitality of life and the cosmos and are essential for establishing humane social relationships and sustainable relationships with nature.

The value orientation of *wuwei* is in direct contradiction to the normalized educational practices of today. In modern and contemporary education, standardization rather than the emergence of individual personhood in relation; the authority position of the teacher rather than students' own exploration; and calculative, goal-oriented teaching procedures rather than students' existential understanding and well-being are the driving forces that are imposing on students' bodies, minds, and spirits. What *wuwei* values is precisely what mainstream modern education does not value.

Virtuous Daoist teaching is relational, nonviolent, intuitive, attuned, centering students' being and becoming in contextualized education. Rather than following the taken-for-granted rules and official ideologies, virtue-infused Daoist pedagogy moves all participants in the direction of self-awareness, gentleness, kindness, nonviolence, sympathy, humility, and compassion. Culham and Lin (2020) discusses how *Dao De Jing* considers water as embodying the highest virtue: "Water nurtures all lives but does not aim for glory; water being very powerful yet very humble"; water stays in lowly places; "hence it is closest to Dao" (p. 50). It is such a waterway that we need to introduce into the classroom.

Understanding and accepting constraints is also both a cosmic and a human virtue, as climate change demands our attention to the limits of human transcendence of the natural world. Re-learning the value of ecological and human interdependence, which modern society has pushed away, we must unlearn our own established values and systems that put humanity at the center. The swimmer in *Zhuangzi*'s parable decenters his own ideas, accepts the constraints of the waterfall, and follows the natural flow. That is why the dangerous waterfall does not pose a threat to him; he does not disrupt the natural patterns for his own desires, and so he can swim freely with the waterfall.

As Jeffrey (2021) points out, "*De* transcends the conventional notions of righteousness and arises spontaneously of its self-so-ness" (p. 242). Self-so-ness, or *ziran*, is the nature of the self-generating and self-transforming universe in its spontaneous unfolding. Self-so-ness and *wuwei* are intimately related, with the former referring to the cosmic state and the latter as the way of running human affairs. Daoist virtues are related to both *ziran* and *wuwei,* transcending moral and ethical regulations that confine humanity; they are necessarily ecological and cosmic, reminding us that humanity is a participant in the cosmos, not a controller. Students at all levels need to experience such a wondrous connection.

Educationally, *de* not only means that the process of teaching and learning should be virtuous, but also means that students can become attuned to such virtues through outdoor education to directly experience the natural world, and that such learning "allows nature to work its magic on how the students relate to one another" (Miller, 2022, p. 80) to improve students' mutual connectedness. The human effort to become in tune with nature and become virtuous, which is the cornerstone of Daoism, provides guidance for establishing compassionate human relationships. With the infusion of virtues that bridge separation and division, classrooms become vitalized with a heightened sense of "awareness, alertness, focus, and presence. . . in a flow of universal spontaneity free of disproportionate coercion and control" and of the demand for "predetermined outcomes" (Jeffrey, 2021, p. 243). In this sense, spontaneity is a virtue that Daoist pedagogy cultivates to unsettle educational orthodoxies and attune students to vibrant life energy.

To conclude about something as indeterminate as *wuwei* is impossible, so I want to leave it open. It is worthwhile, however, to notice how the three aspects of Daoist pedagogy are intertwined and mutually supportive of one another: Attunement to the self and the world is a form of nonviolent intervention to disrupt norms, impositions, and violence; nonviolence is a virtue orientation in pedagogical interactions and relationships; and virtue is attuned to *Dao*. Threaded together, they form the foundation for the relational dynamics of Daoist pedagogy as an organic whole.

References

Allan, S. (1997). *The way of water and sprouts of virtue.* State University of New York Press.

Ames, R. T. & Hall, D. L. (2003). *Daodejing: A philosophical translation.* Ballantine Books.

Aoki, T. T. (2005). *Curriculum in a New Key* (W. F. Pinar and R. L. Irwin, Eds.). Lawrence Erlbaum.

Bender, J. (2023). Alienation and attunement in the *Zhuangzi*. *Sophia, 62,* 179-193.

Brown, S. (2008). *A Buddhist in the classroom.* State University of New York Press.

Chang, C. (1963). *Creativity and Taoism.* Harper & Row.

Culham, T., & Lin, J. (2020). *Daoist cultivation of qi and virtue for life, wisdom, and learning.* Palgrave Macmillan.

Doll, Jr., W. E. (2012). *Pragmatism, post-modernism, and complexity Theory* (D. Trueit Ed.). Routledge.

Fung, Y. L. (1976). *A short history of Chinese philosophy.* The Free Press.

Hunter, J. (2013). *World peace and other 4th-grade achievements.* An Eamon Dolan Book.

Jeffrey, D. M. (2021). Ancient Daoist wisdom and its associated principle of yin-yang for contemporary classrooms for foundations for a harmonious world. *Philosophical Inquiry in Education, 28*(3), 237-250.

Lai, K. L. (2017). *Introduction to Chinese philosophy* (2nd ed.). Cambridge University Press.

Lin, G. (2017). 无待自然与有待自然[Unconditional nature and conditional nature]. *Journal of Humanities, 7,* 1-7.

Liu, G. (2016). 生成 [Generativeness]. Science Press.

Loy, D. (1998). *Nonduality: A study in comparative philosophy.* Humanity Books.

Ma, Y., & Wang, H. (in press). Pedagogy of emptiness: A Daoist perspective. *Asian Pacific Educational Review.*

Miller, J. P. (with X. Li & T. Ruan) (2022). *Taoism, teaching and learning: A nature-based approach to education.* University of Toronto Press.

Pinar, W. F. (2019). *Moving images of eternity: George Grant's critique of time, teaching, and technology.* University of Ottawa Press.

Slingerland, E. (2003). *Effortless action: Wu-wei as conceptual metaphor and spiritual ideal in early China.* Oxford University Press.

Slingerland, E. (2014). *Trying not to try: Ancient China, modern science, and the power of spontaneity.* Broadway Books.

Wang, H. (2008). The strength of the feminine, lyrics of Chinese women's subjectivity, and the power of education. In C. Eppert & H. Wang (Eds.), *Cross-cultural studies in education: Eastern thought, educational insights* (pp. 313-333). Lawrence Erlbaum.

Wang, H. (2019). From the instrumental to the existential: An experiential approach to teaching mindfulness. In J. Lin, T. Culham, & S. Edwards (Eds.), *Contemplative pedagogies for effective and profound*

transformation in teaching, learning and being (pp. 87-100). Information Age Publishing.
Wang, H. (2021). *Contemporary Daoism, organic relationality, and curriculum of integrative creativity.* Information Age Publishing.
Wang, H. (2022). Freedom, interconnectedness, and curriculum attunement: A cross-cultural perspective. *Journal of Curriculum Theorizing, 37*(3), 1-16.
Wang, H. (2024). *Awakenings to the calling of nonviolence in curriculum studies.* Peter Lang.

The Role of Pedagogy in Peace Initiatives for a Sustainable Future: With Reference to Sri Aurobindo's Philosophy

Doctor Indrani Choudhury

Introduction

Is it reasonable to think that people in societies where there are a large amount of ethnic and racial differences, differences in culture and religion, and vast differences in social status can live together in harmony and solidarity? Can strife, recurring conflicts, and war-like situations compel us to better understand the need to realize the much-desired ideal of peace? These questions remain an enigma but come up in a much stronger, more disturbing form each time we ask ourselves what the word 'peace' would mean given the current domestic, regional, and global challenges. Since time immemorial, this world has witnessed many grievous conflicts, be it the struggle for independence of the colonized from colonial rulers, the two World Wars, the Cold War, the Russian invasion of Ukraine, or, more recently, the long-standing Israeli-Palestine conflict that is raging again. Alternatively, in South Asia, the recent incidents of conflict along ethnic lines in the northeastern Indian state of Manipur in India between the Meiteis, Kukis, and Zo communities that erupted on May 3, 2023, in the wake of the Manipur High Court judgment regarding the inclusion of the Meitei community under the Scheduled Tribe category raise many questions regarding why the so-called objectives and aims of people holding the echelons of power in state machinery cannot always go well with the expectations and grievances of people who find themselves caught amidst a crisis that is mired with violence, death, mistrust and misgivings, and vested political ambitions.

How do we even talk of peace when the death toll rises and thousands of people are rendered homeless, unable to make sense of how they are going to gather themselves, live the rest of their lives, and come to terms with the trauma and loss they have suffered? Indeed, this defies all logic. Such tragedies render the word 'peace' empty and meaningless.

Time and again, we cannot help but be convinced that we live in a time and age when it is difficult to adequately represent the idea of peace. The meaning of peace eludes us when we are constantly faced with the forces of divisiveness, violence, and hatred, which spread their roots in every aspect of human existence. Hatred, strife, and conflict are manifestations of the dynamics of human existence that we cannot pretend to ignore and wish away as non-existent. However, we need to focus on and study how peace initiatives can be brought about amidst these disruptive forces at play.

This paper emphasizes the role of peace education in conflict reduction and peacebuilding, drawing mainly on insights from Sri Aurobindo's philosophy on how human beings face and negotiate with socio-political realities and how this process, in turn, shapes our ideas of the sustainable future of education for children and young adults in a conflict-ridden society. So, to understand what prompts human beings to behave the way they do, one has to refocus on the fact that human beings are yet to fully evolve and need to be viewed as a part of the larger continuum. Education, therefore, should begin with a quest for self-realization. However, it remains to be seen if knowing oneself entails knowing others, too.

While explaining boycotts from a moral perspective, Sri. Aurobindo writes, "It is interest warring against interest."[1](Sri Aurobindo, The Morality of Boycott, 1907, p.126)   He reiterates in the context of British colonial rule, "If the British exploitation were to cease tomorrow, the hatred against the British race would disappear in a moment. A partial *adhyaropa* makes the ignorant see in the exploiters and not in the exploitation the receptacle of hostile feeling."[2] (Sri Aurobindo, The Morality of Boycott, 1907, p. 126) If we find the reasons engendering hatred, strife, and conflict, then mitigating it will also be possible.

Following Sri Aurobindo's views, we need to channel hatred towards the evil deed and not the evildoer per se. He says, "...like all Maya, it is an

---

[1] Sri. Aurobindo, The Morality of Boycott, Bande Mataram: Political Writings and Speeches 1890-1908, Pondicherry: Sri Aurobindo Ashram, 2002 p. 126. https://sri-aurobindo.co.in
[2] Ibid., p.126.

unreal and fleeting sentiment and is not shared by those who think. Not hatred against foreigners, but antipathy to the evils of foreign exploitation, is the true root of the boycott."[3] (Sri Aurobindo, The Morality of Boycott, 1907, p. 126) However, this tendency to perceive the Other in every being and to alienate oneself as someone unique and significant, hence supposedly deserving special attention, gives rise to a fissure within oneself. It is this desire to stand out of the ordinary that creates a distinct but separate consciousness: a consciousness that creates a false sense of individuated existence and also, along with it, a perceived self-identity markedly distinct from everyone else.

It is common knowledge that conflict almost always rests on how individuals perceive their control over resources, rights, and recognition. The perception that what is mine should remain with me or can be shared with whom I consider my own[4] (Butler, 2020, p. 11) leads to an overly competitive attitude and, after that, aggressive strife against others. So long as the process of othering continues to promote self-aggrandizement and self-preservation, one wonders if it would ever be possible to speak in a language of peace, let alone think of some form of peace education that can be imparted. Hence, the most coveted ideal of peace can only be achieved if individuals learn to reorient their expectations in life. One needs to dissect and deconstruct the politics of the ideology and identity formation process in order to be able to see through the purpose and intent lurking behind hatred and enmity. One needs to decide what is relevant and meaningful in the name of self-preservation. Is it a life that gives excessive resources to a few or enough resources to sustain many?

Similarly, one must reconsider whether something can be called a right if everyone cannot claim it. Furthermore, given the almost insatiable need for recognition, we must ask: can reducing one section of people to anonymity and recognizing a few be sustained for long? Depending on whether we answer these questions in the affirmative or negative, we will either be left with nothing but a dehumanized lot out to destroy everyone eventually, or we will explore the possibility of an alternative form of life where one can look beyond the mere satisfaction of serving one's interests. The ground reality shows us how, in an attempt to proclaim the primacy of

---

[3] Sri. Aurobindo, "The Morality of Boycott, Bande Mataram: Political Writings and Speeches 1890-1908", Pondicherry: Sri Aurobindo Ashram, 2002 p. 126. https://sri-aurobindo.co.in
[4] See Butler Judith, "The Force of Non-Violence An Ethico-Political Bond," Verso, London, New York 2020, p.11.

all-powerful individual selves, there is a mad rush to uphold the 'powerful' as the 'fittest.' It is this tendency to create a power cluster of a chosen 'few' against the 'nameless many' that gives rise to strife and conflict and a deep-rooted feeling of divisiveness. Against this backdrop, can we talk of peace? This alternative possibility, from a moral point of view, is worth pondering.

In an attempt to retrace the idea of Peace through Education

One perhaps needs to think along these three possible dimensions to reestablish Peace as an ideal that is possible to realize:

1. In its internal dimension, can we talk of Peace in connection with Satya (i.e., in connection with an inward quest for Self-realization), which ought to be a personal goal of whosoever pursues peace?
2. In its external dimension, should it be understood as a larger goal of collective awakening resulting from a common goal based on shared values, which sparks a collective moral consciousness of how peace eventually must find expression in a shared, amicable, and harmonious co-existence of human beings in a public space?
3. Or could there be a third possibility that peace can never be attained in its pristine form in the aftermath of a conflict? Furthermore, eventually, conflict resolution becomes a mere compromise or an attempt to come to terms with the trauma experienced and learn the lessons of healing through acceptance and acknowledgment of the inherent differences that people have.

It must be acknowledged that the sole purpose of education should be to explore the possibilities mentioned above for understanding how pedagogy can bring about peace initiatives and conflict resolution by working towards understanding how to strike a balance between what one has, what one wants, and whether one ought to acquire it by any means. It may be noted that a sense of lack seems to regulate what we want for ourselves and what we perceive in others. This, in turn, creates rifts and reasons for conflicting expectations, aims, interests, and claims.

We have brought ourselves to a crossroads wherein we are forced to raise the question as to how far education has succeeded in bringing about peace and restorative justice to smooth out the differences and chasms created to placate the insatiable desire of people to stand against others whom they do not consider to be one of their own. We need to explore how education can become an 'ideal' process meant to transform the lives of all. Furthermore, if education is meant to be a basic right for all, has it reached everyone in the same way as it should? Can we still talk of education as the only ideal through which a society may evaluate itself in all the contexts in which social transactions occur between its members? Much to our dismay, we are yet to see education take center stage in deciding why human lives should be valued regardless of who they are and where they belong.

Despite being a right, being truly educated remains a privilege that does not reach many who need it. No matter how justified and legally binding a claim may be, merely being human may not often be enough to avail of its immediate and life-long benefits. Undoubtedly, every human being who ought to enjoy the right to education in a way that transforms him or her both at a personal and a social level may be left deprived. Even a casual assessment of the not-so-privileged third-world underdeveloped nations would reveal a massive gap in access to education as per global standards. This lack of opportunities in education often places young individuals on the wrong side of social development, both materially and psychologically, pushing them towards either the disenfranchised, nameless, and voiceless or the unruly and violent segment of the population.

When it is a choice between survival and education, education often seems secondary for people who are trying to grapple with abject poverty, and more so when they find themselves caught in the middle of a crossfire of conflicts. The sheer vulnerability of such people often inclines them to be trapped in a disturbing reality that cannot be undermined. One is forced to explore possibilities regarding how we can gear up for the challenges of sustainable holistic education in such strife-torn contexts where young students might lack basic opportunities whereby they can hope to work towards honing their full potential and bringing out the best version of themselves. At this juncture, one may note that often it may not even be possible to decide if at all an individual would know how it is even possible to bring out 'the best version' of oneself, and what would that 'best version' eventually be? Should developing oneself entail understanding the relevance of living in a shared space and working for the betterment of all? Or does developing oneself mean self-aggrandizement in the strongest possible sense? Amidst cutthroat competition and the demand to negotiate the challenges of survival, often the former seems more plausible and the only escape route from an incessant struggle for self-preservation.

Education for Sustainable Development: A Holistic Approach

A mere cursory glance at the United Nations' proposed goals for sustainable development will tell us why we need to emphasize ensuring inclusive and equitable quality education and promoting lifelong learning opportunities for all. [5] The major question here is whether mere access to classroom doors ensures education for all or whether the need of the hour is to review how we impart education and how it needs to change.

Let us remind ourselves what education means and ought to achieve. Education ought to bring out the very best in us. However, the conditions under which that 'best self' finds expression are a far more multi-layered, complex process involving many factors.

The five main factors that invariably determine what we learn are

   (1) our capacity to learn,
   (2) the learning environment,
   (3) the ideals aspired for in learning
   (4) values imbibed while learning
   (5) and the outcome of learning.

These five factors largely determine how education can be more effective, provided one realizes that education involves a highly complicated and delicate relationship between the educator who teaches and the learner who is to be taught or educated.

Role of an Educator: Rebuilding Trust

The battered, anxiety-ridden existence of young minds in their formative years often gets trapped in their silences and restricts all possibilities of learning. This has been the fate of innumerable students who never got an opportunity to speak for themselves regarding how they want to be taught and what they expect from the learning experience they receive in the name of formal education.

---

[5] https://www.un.org/sustainabledevelopment/news/communications

Now, the question that one might ask is, 'Have we been able to draw ourselves away from the typically dark picture of educators engaged in any form of overzealous attempt to impose instructions that represent a rigid and repressive system of education? Or are we in a deeper crisis now, given the fact that with a deluge of information at our fingertips at the click of a button, we are truly at a loss as to how we can sift out and discriminate between the relevant facts from the irrelevant ones and eventually turn the facts received into interpretative knowledge? The question that follows here is whether educators have been able to play the role of a guide or a facilitator in the learning process or if they need help as to how they could engage in building up a meaningful relationship with their students. Nowadays, that significant 'connect' between an educator and his pupil seems absent, resulting in students who learn facts but need help grasping the knowledge skills involved therein. Consequently, pupils must apply what is learned in an aggressively competitive world. They lose their faith in education *per se* and suffer from a complete disillusionment as to what their capabilities and capacities are. The eventual outcome is a lack of self-esteem, violent, disruptive behavior, and a disturbingly negative attitude towards oneself, others, and life at large. The sordid picture drawn is quite a familiar fact cutting across the globe, thus turning education into a contesting site that increasingly needs to be reviewed and rapidly opening to new challenges with time. Youth, especially those with a difficult and troubled life, seem caught up in vicious circles of frustration with no sense of direction. 'Hard times' are even harder now. We are in what may be called a "moral aporia."[6] (Bauman, 1993, p. 8)

We do not seem to be able to come to an agreement as to what should be the correct and ideal pedagogy. The more a teacher tries to impress upon the pupils the need for discipline and obedience, the more the students tend to attempt breaking free and begin to defy any form of instruction, resulting in an uncomfortable tussle, often leading to dismal learning outcomes and driving both toward a situation no less than a moral conundrum.

Now, the question is, how can this situation ever change? Such a predicament calls for a review of how we perceive the teaching-learning process. Suppose the educator's role is to reach out to the learners, ignite a sense of curiosity, and rekindle interest in getting involved in the learning

---

[6] See Zygmunt Bauman Postmodern Ethics Blackwell Publishers: Oxford, 1993, p. 8.

process. In that case, the educator needs to work with each of them. The teacher cannot afford to be withdrawn and is a dispassionate provider with a top-down approach. There has to be mutual participation and interaction. The learner cannot be pushed out of bounds by a lack of amenities or a failure to demonstrate capabilities on predictable lines.

The pandemic in the recent past has already proved that technological advancements will continue to have a tremendous impact on how learning management systems will work in the future and pave the way for technology-based teaching aids across the globe, but what we cannot afford to forget is that one crucial aspect of education will always remain the bond that a teacher establishes with the learner. Technology is meant to aid learning by providing techniques, but it cannot regulate learning or act as a barrier. Technology will always be a much-needed tool to enhance learning experiences, but it poses severe hindrances for economically disadvantaged learners in underdeveloped and developing nations. As technology-based education emerges as a power to reckon with, it also decides and dictates who can afford to avail of its benefits and who is marginalized and thereby pushed to the periphery. This digital divide is as real as the fault lines it is creating among privileged and less-privileged learners, which, in turn, will have a damaging effect for generations to come.

One can also no longer ignore the possibilities and perils of machine learning replacing teachers in many ways unless the teachers redefine teaching as building an emotional bond needed to nourish the souls of the learners.

Towards Lifelong Learning Opportunities

Merely opening the doors of the classrooms to disadvantaged learners who cannot avail of the technology-driven online mode of instruction is not enough. The more significant challenge lies in retaining them in the classrooms. It calls for a change in the manner in which education is perceived. If education needs to be effective, it must be seen as something other than a product-delivery system tied to a time-bound curriculum. On the contrary, an open-ended, flexible system might work better for students who often need help to keep pace and find themselves caught between the demands of the formal education system and the drudgery of survival. The introduction of future-facing national visions like India's

2020 National Education Policy.,[7] is definitively a way forward to address this crucial problem.

The need of the hour is to renew the emotional bond between a teacher and a student. An educator should be more of a forerunner who leads by example and not an instructor who demands observance of rules but, all along, remains alienated and distanced from the actual situation in which the young students find themselves. Instead of expecting the students to always take the step forward to reach out to the teachers, the reverse situation would work better, where teachers go out of their way to reach out where their help as facilitators may be needed. If the young pupils are assured that they need not fear their teachers, they will immediately be more receptive to the ideas and values of their educators. Love replaces fear with trust and removes the barriers that often unconsciously inhibit learning. However, one needs to exercise caution against the tendency to make the pupils pliable enough to accept what the educator has to convey unquestioningly. Instead, the educator's ethical responsibility lies in realizing that each pupil is unique in his or her differences. As Levinas would have seen, "the responsibility for the other"[8]

(Levinas, 1981 p. 25) is of utmost importance. The Other's Being cannot be reduced to a timid, obedient, and vulnerable object that can be easily silenced or molded at will or, if the need be, conditioned either with force and punishments or a blind and uncritical acceptance of whatever is being taught through powerful rhetoric and the formidable presence of the educator.[9] The educator's foremost responsibility lies in recognizing that the learning experience is not a linear process where only the pupil learns from the educator. However, the educator needs to learn, in turn, from the pupil about what he or she wants and expects from the teacher. Hence, every pupil must be allowed to express himself or herself whenever he or she needs to do so. The merit of a successful educator lies in training oneself to listen and interpret both the language of words and the silences of "the significant other', that is, the pupils, without any imposition.

---

[7] https://www.education.gov.in/sites/upload_files/mhrd/files/NEP_Final_English_0.pdf p.51.

[8] Emmanuel Levinas Otherwise than Being or Beyond Essence trans. By A.Lingis, The Hague /Boston /London Nijhoff (Kluwer), 1981, pp. 25-26.

[9] See Burggraeve, Fr. Roger SDB, The Vulnerable Mastership of Children and Adolescents in Dignity Safeguarding of Children and Young People, published by Don Bosco Youth-Net ivzw, Edited by: Rein Meus pp. 9-32.

Such a rapport between the teacher and learner can improve the student's learning capacity and make the learning environment a happy and safe place that one would not want to abandon.

Finally, if what is aspired to in learning is sustainable development, then it is about time we focus on learning that will eventually remain relevant in the days to come. Education must be viewed as a process of lifelong learning opportunities rather than a product that reaches its expiration date and is rendered redundant, ready to be discarded, and replaced by the market's latest products. So long as learning outcomes are judged in terms of arbitrary grades and selective emphasis on disciplines determined by market-driven forces as job creators, authentic learning can never occur. If we follow the motto that 'what sells, survives,' education becomes a commodity with economic worth, and educators assume the role of mere service providers with a target to attract consumers. Both eventually stand defeated against the ever-burgeoning and aggressively competitive market-driven forces. We need to realize that proper education cannot be solely judged by what it contributes to material and monetary gain but by learning skills and values and rekindling interest in creating meaningful experiences in life. The world undoubtedly needs better doctors, scientists, engineers, managers, lawyers, and entrepreneurs. However, the role of artists, artisans, caregivers, nature healers, farmers, gardeners, counselors, teachers, and peacemakers are no less crucial, given the pressing need to shape a generation of better thinkers who can become conscientious citizens aware of their moral responsibilities towards the world at large. Perhaps this is what Mahatma Gandhi envisioned for a self-reliant India when he discussed basic education[10] so many years ago. An emphasis on interdisciplinarity is the order of the day. The mandatory instruction-based approach should give way to a care-based 'do-it-yourself' approach if education is expected to transform the lives of already battered young learners.

Learning that makes us better human beings and teaches us how to make this world a better place is what we need if we intend to achieve inclusive and equitable education as a sustainable development goal by 2030.[11] Education can prove to be a meaningful process when it enables the learner to realize that to live in a fast-changing social space that is

---

[10] See Gandhi M.K. Towards New Education, Edited by Bharatan Kumarappa, Navjivan Publishing House Towards New Education.doc (mkgandhi.org) web accessed on19/10/2023.

[11] https://www.un.org/sustainabledevelopment/news/communications

pluralistic to the core, one cannot avert making choices from the innumerable possibilities open to all. However, the actual task lies in learning to be responsible for the choices made with a firm belief that the presence of mutuality and reciprocity of love, trust, and respect depends on the choices made. Educators can create an environment whereby the learners are encouraged to ponder the choices made, like self-reflective beings, and live up to the newer possibilities they might be led to explore. One is reminded of what Sri. Aurobindo would have us think along the lines that no one can be taught but can only be made to think. He says, "The true basis of education is the study of the human mind, infant, adolescent, and adult. Any system of education founded on theories of academic perfection that ignores the instrument of study is more likely to impair intellectual growth than to produce a perfect and perfectly equipped mind".[12] (Sri. Aurobindo, The Human Mind, SABCL Vol 17, 1972, p. 204)

Peace Initiatives: Through an Ethics of Care

Ideally, education should be a process focused on teaching how to 'care' for all, bringing about a sense of 'we-feeling' among people, resulting in the holistic well-being of the human experience. It is needless to reiterate that human society should be viewed as a family where satisfaction lies in the realization that it is in one's interest to promote and protect the well-being of others.

Perhaps the future of inclusive education lies in tentatively working towards a better society. Hence, peace education that helps unlearn the lessons of aggressive self-aggrandizement and relearn the ability to widen one's vision of where the individual stands in the larger picture of cosmic reality is indeed the need of the hour. Furthermore, here we again turn to the spiritual teachings of Sri Aurobindo to understand a being's place on earth and how one can see oneself and others. Sri Aurobindo believed in an ever-evolving being when he talked about human beings. He stated, "Man is a transitional being; he is not final. He is the middle term of the evolution, not its end, crown, or consummating masterpiece"[13] (Sri.Aurobindo, The Human Cycle Volume 25, CSWA, p. 56) Because of

---

[12] Sri. Aurobindo, "The Human Mind, The Hour of God and other writings VI Education and Art A System of National Education Some Preliminary Ideas p. 204, 2003. edited.auromaa.org/Sri-aurobindo-ru/workings/sa/17/00641-e.htm
[13] Sri. Aurobindo, The Human Cycle Volume 25 The Complete Works of Sri Aurobindo, Published by Aurobindo Ashram Publication Department copyright Sri Aurobindo Ashram Trust 1997 Pondicherry, India, p. 56.

this tendency to perceive and create dualities where there are none, conflict arises. He said, "War is a dangerous teacher, and physical victory leads to moral defeat."[14] (Sri. Aurobindo, Vol 12, CSWA, p. 221) Hence, the primary aim of education should be to acknowledge this moral failure and work towards mitigating these superficial dualities that regulate human thinking.

He begins by drawing our attention to how the growth of scientific thinking has fashioned itself and, in a way, has also sown the seeds of this kind of perceived duality. He identifies two dominant but opposing strains of thought processes that emerge when we look at how science has progressed in the modern age.

According to Sri Aurobindo

"The growth of modern science has meanwhile created new ideas and tendencies, on one side, and exaggerated individualism, or rather vitalistic egoism, on the other—the quite opposite ideal of collectivism. Science investigating life discovered that the root nature of all living is a struggle to take the best advantage of the environment for self-preservation, self-fulfillment, and self-aggrandizement. Human thought, seizing in its usual arbitrary and trenchant fashion upon this aspect of modern knowledge, has founded on its theories of a novel kind, which erect into a gospel the right for each to live his own life not merely by utilizing others but even at the expense of others."[15] (Sri. Aurobindo, The Human Cycle, Vol. 25 CSWA, p. 56)

He goes on further to say, "The first object of life in this view is for the individual to survive as long as he may, to become strong, efficient, and powerful, to dominate his environment and his fellows, and to raise himself on this strenuous and egoistic line to his full stature of capacity and reap his full measure of enjoyment."[16] (Sri. Aurobindo, The Human Cycle, Vol. 25 CSWA, p. 56)

---

[14] Sri. Aurobindo, The Complete Works of Sri Aurobindo, Volume 12, Sri Aurobindo Ashram Trust (1997), p. 221.

[15] Sri. Aurobindo, "The Human Cycle Volume 25 The Complete Works of Sri Aurobindo, Published by Aurobindo Ashram Publication Department copyright Sri Aurobindo Ashram Trust 1997 Pondicherry, India p.56.

[16] Sri. Aurobindo, "The Human Cycle Volume 25 The Complete Works of Sri Aurobindo, Published by Aurobindo Ashram Publication Department copyright Sri Aurobindo Ashram Trust 1997 Pondicherry, India, p. 56.

But this tendency to forge ahead with excessive reliance on self-development dominated by the powers of reason may have limitations. He writes in The Human Cycle, "……rationalistic and physical science has overpassed itself and must before long be overtaken by a mounting flood of psychological and psychic knowledge, which cannot fail to compel quite a new view of the human being and open a new vista before mankind."[17] (Sri. Aurobindo, The Human Cycle, Vol. 25 CSWA, p. 22)

Excessive celebration of reason also points out the limits of rationalistic pursuits in comforting people and the need for looking towards what Sri Aurobindo calls "subjectivism and practical spirituality."[18] (Sri. Aurobindo, The Human Cycle, Vol. 25 CSWA, p. 24) We cannot forget that the Age of Reason has given us two world wars and colossal damage and loss to cope with, notwithstanding the challenges of surviving in the aftermath of such mindless devastation.

Sri. Aurobindo quite emphatically writes, "It is no longer possible that we should accept as an ideal any arrangement by which certain classes of society should arrogate development and full social fruition to themselves while assigning a bare and barren service alone to others. It is now fixed that social development and well-being mean the development and well-being of all individuals in society and not merely a community flourishing in the mass that resolves itself into the splendor and power of one or two classes."[19] (Sri. Aurobindo, The Human Cycle, Vol 25, CWSA p. 24)

However, at the same time, Sri Aurobindo reiterates that we cannot also afford to crush the unique spirit of an individual human being to a mere "member of a human pack, hive, or ant-hill; he is something in himself, a soul, a being who has to fulfill his truth and law as well as his natural or his assigned part in the truth and law of the collective existence."[20] (Sri. Aurobindo, The Human Cycle, Vol 25, CWSA, p. 24) Sri. Aurobindo believed that "individual thought, will, and conscience"[21] (Sri. Aurobindo,

---

[17] Ibid., p. 22.

[18] Ibid., p. 24

[19] Sri. Aurobindo, "The Human Cycle Volume 25 The Complete Works of Sri Aurobindo, Published by Aurobindo Ashram Publication Department copyright Sri Aurobindo Ashram Trust 1997 Pondicherry, India p.24

[20] Ibid., p. 24

[21] Ibid., p. 25

The Human Cycle, Vol 25, p. 25) should find room alongside others in a collective public space instead of becoming a dominant hegemonic force. The role of pedagogy should be such that it can impart an education that focuses on lessons of care and concern for all. The focus should be on the ability to listen to little narratives on realities and truths without emphasizing a singular dominant perspective, no matter how pervasive and resolute it may have seemed to date. Only a blend of intellectualism and spiritualism that teaches detachment from narrow, divisive self-interest can help us shape a sustainable future for all.

Perhaps any meaningful attempt towards sustainable development must focus on education that enables learners to explore the hitherto untapped powers of their minds and encourages them to understand that the value of one's own growth lies in building a shared space for all life forms.

As Thomas Gunn so aptly said,

> "Life should be a human undertaking.
> I know. I undertook it.
> Yet have found
> That in my every move
> I prevent someone
> From stepping where I step."[22] (Miller, Greenberg, 1981, p.155)

Acknowledgments

My acknowledgments go to Sri Vishnu Mohan Foundation, where a rough working version of some of the ideas discussed here was first read in the unpublished paper entitled "Right Education for Sustainable Development: Learning to Unlearn "in the Conference on Peace and Sustainable Development organized by Sri Vishnu Mohan Foundation Chennai on 3rd October 2021 https://youtu.be/KN-jUD36KmY?si=FL_f2ijqgu1QNSRH

Notes and References

1. Ghosh, Sri.Aurobindo, The Morality of Boycott, Bande Mataram: Political Writings and Speeches 1890-1908, Pondicherry: Sri Aurobindo Ashram,2002 p. 126

---

[22] Miller, Ruth, Greenberg, Robert A. Poetry An Introduction @1981 St.Martin's Press.Inc p. 155 web accessed on 1/10/2021

https://sri-aurobindo.co.in/workings/sa/01/0028_e.htm
web accessed on 18/10/2023

2. Ibid., p. 126
3. Ibid., p. 126
4. See Butler Judith, The Force of Non-Violence An Ethico-Political Bond, Verso, London, New York 2020, p. 11.
5. https://www.un.org/sustainabledevelopment/news/communications
6. Ghosh, Sri. Aurobindo, "The Human Mind, The Hour of God and other writings VI   Education and Art A System of National Education Some Preliminary Ideas Sri. Aurobindo Birth Century Library, Volume 17, Sri. Aurobindo Ashram, 1972, (2003) edited.auromaa.org/Sri-aurobindo-ru/workings/sa/17/00641-e.htm p.201
web accessed on18/10/2023
7. See Dickens, Charles. (1854) Hard Times Wordsworth Printing Press, London, p. 9.
8. Ghosh, Sri. Aurobindo, "The Human Mind, The Hour of God and other writings VI   Education and Art A System of National Education Some Preliminary Ideas Sri. Aurobindo Birth Century Library, Volume 17, Sri. Aurobindo Ashram, 1972, (2003). edited.auromaa.org/Sri-aurobindo-ru/workings/sa/17/00641-e.htm p.204
web accessed on18/10/2023
9. See Zygmunt Bauman Postmodern Ethics Blackwell Publishers Oxford 1993, p.8.
10. https://www.education.gov.in/sites/upload_files/mhrd/files/NEP_Final_English_0.pdf p. 52 web accessed on 30/10/2023
11. Emmanuel Levinas Otherwise than Being or Beyond Essence trans. By A.Lingis, The Hague /Boston /London Nijhoff (Kluwer),1981, pp. 25-26. web accessed on 1/10/2023
12. See Burggraeve, Fr. Roger, SDB, The Vulnerable Mastership of Children and Adolescents in Dignity Safeguarding of Children and Young People, published by Don Bosco Youth-Net ivzw, Edited by: Rein Meus. pp 9-32. web accessed on 1/10/2023
13. Gandhi, M. K. Towards New Education, Edited by Bharatan Kumarappa, Navjivan Publishing House. Towards New Education.doc (mkgandhi.org) web accessed on19/10/2023
14. https://www.un.org/sustainabledevelopment/news/communications
web accessed on 30/10/23
15. Ghosh, Sri. Aurobindo, "The Human Mind, The Hour of God and other writings VI Education and Art A System of National Education Some Preliminary Ideas Sri. Aurobindo Birth Century Library, Volume 17, Sri.

Aurobindo Ashram, 1972, (2003). edited.auromaa.org/Sri-aurobindo-ru/workings/sa/17/00641-e.htm p.204 web accessed on18/10/2023

16. Ghosh, Sri. Aurobindo, "The Human Cycle Volume 25 The Complete Works of Sri Aurobindo, Published by Aurobindo Ashram Publication Department copyright Sri Aurobindo Ashram Trust 1997. Pondicherry, India p. 56. web accessed on18/10/2023

17. Ghosh, Sri. Aurobindo, The Complete Works of Sri Aurobindo, Volume 12, Sri Aurobindo Ashram Trust (1997), p. 221. web accessed on18/10/2023

18. Ghosh, Sri. Aurobindo, "The Human Cycle Volume 25 The Complete Works of Sri Aurobindo, Published by Aurobindo Ashram Publication Department copyright Sri Aurobindo Ashram Trust 1997 Pondicherry, India p.56 web accessed on18/10/2023

19. Ibid., p., 56

20. Ibid., p. 22

21. Ibid., p. 24

22. Ibid., p. 24

23. Ibid., p. 24

24. Ibid., p. 25

25. Miller, Ruth. Greenberg, Robert. Poetry An Introduction @1981 St. Martin's Press.Inc p. 155. web accessed on 1/10/2021

Bibliography

1. Bauman, Zygmunt, Postmodern Ethics Blackwell Publishers Oxford 1993, p. 8.

2. Butler, Judith. "The Force of Non-Violence An Ethico-Political Bond," Verso, London, New York. 2020, p. 11.

3. Burggraeve, Fr. Roger SDB, The Vulnerable Mastership of Children and Adolescents in Dignity Safeguarding of Children and Young People, published by Don Bosco Youth-Net ivzw, Edited by: Rein Meus pp 9-32 web accessed on 1/10/2023

4. Dickens Charles, Hard Times Wordsworth Printing Press, London, 1854, p. 9.

5. Gandhi, M. K. Towards New Education, Edited by Bharatan Kumarappa, Navjivan Publishing House Towards New Education.doc (mkgandhi.org) web accessed on19/10/2023

6. Ghosh, Sri. Aurobindo, The Morality of Boycott, Bande Mataram: Political Writings and Speeches 1890-1908, Pondicherry: Sri Aurobindo Ashram, 2002, p. 126
https://sri-aurobindo.co.in web accessed on 18/10/2023

7. Ghosh, Sri. Aurobindo, "The Human Mind, The Hour of God and other writings VI Education and Art A System of National Education Some Preliminary Ideas Sri. Aurobindo Birth Century Library, Volume 17, Sri. Aurobindo Ashram, 1972, (2003) edited.auromaa.org/Sri-aurobindo-ru/workings/sa/17/00641-e.htm p.204

8. Ghosh, Sri. Aurobindo, "The Human Cycle Volume 25 The Complete Works of Sri Aurobindo, Published by Aurobindo Ashram Publication Department copyright Sri Aurobindo Ashram Trust 1997, Pondicherry, India, p. 56. web accessed on18/10/2023

9. Ghosh, Sri. Aurobindo. The Complete Works of Sri Aurobindo, Volume 12, Sri Aurobindo Ashram Trust (1997), p. 221. web accessed on 18/10/2023

10. Levinas, Emmanuel. Otherwise than Being or Beyond Essence. trans. by A. Lingis, The Hague /Boston /London Nijhoff (Kluwer),1981, pp. 25-26. web accessed on 1/10/2023

11. Miller, Ruth. Greenberg, Robert. Poetry An Introduction. St. Martin's Press, Inc. 1981, London, p. 155. web accessed on 1/10/2021

12. Mahapatra, Debidatta A. Sri. Aurobindo at 150 An Integral Vision of Evolution, Human Unity, and Peace, Sophia Studies in Cross-Cultural Philosophy of Traditions and Cultures A Springer Nature Publication, Switzerland, 2023. ISSN 2211-1107 ISSN 2211-1115 (electronic) ISBN 978-3-031-21807-1 ISBN 978-3-031-21808-8 (eBook)

13. Paranjape, Makarand R. (Ed.) The Penguin Sri. Aurobindo Reader, Viking Penguin Random House India, 2023.

Web Sources:

1. https://www.un.org/sustainabledevelopment/news/communications web accessed on 30/10/2023

2. https://www.education.gov.in/sites/upload_files/mhrd/files/NEP_Final _English_0.pdf p.52 web accessed on 30/10/2023

The Confucian Influence on the Relational Turn in the Social Sciences: Dialogue in Multi-level Social Theorizing

Doctor Kwang-Kuo Hwang and Doctor Leon Miller

Introduction

Confucius is regarded as ancient China's most respected social theorist, ethicist, political advisor, philosopher, social reformer, political theorist, and visionary. Consequently, he is considered the paragon of Chinese sage-like wisdom. It was his sage-like wisdom that qualified him to be thought of as the most venerable ancestral teacher of scholar-officials, heads of state, other teachers, and the general public. Because of the broad range of subjects that Confucius expounded on, his ideas influenced perspectives on social interactions taking place at multiple levels. Therefore, Confucianism developed into a viable system of human and social development that focused on maintaining harmonious relationships in every aspect of social activity. That is to say that he envisioned a means of "How to structure society so that the necessary normative constraints imposed by culture would bring out the best in human nature" and ultimately elevate the human experience (Miller 2016, 69). Therefore, his ideas are regarded as an excellent framework for explaining the role of pedagogy in shaping the socio-political reality of society. This article explains why and how Confucius' mutual trust model of social relations and his five constant virtues (which underpin self-cultivation and social development) continue to be relevant for enacting relational Cosmopolitan principles and ethics (i.e., reciprocity, mutuality, and equal respect), which Confucius referred to as 恕 – "shu" (Confucius 1869, 226).

Confucius established his school of thought in response to a socially and morally chaotic and violent era in Chinese history (i.e., the Spring and

Autumn period that was followed by the Warring States period). Paradoxically, it was also a period in which great freedom of thought was allowed to the intellectual elite, who are relied on to provide socio-political guidance, ethics, and morals as a guide for a better future. This meant that he responded to the need to address and provide a solution to challenges in social relations at multiple levels of social interactions. It was a time dominated by hard power and political Realism. He responded to this period by providing some of the world's most respected teachings on virtue ethics, moral behavior, leadership, etiquette, social relationships, social structures, governance, and world order. That is to say that he sought to increase the likelihood that individual social agents would interact on the basis of sincerity, integrity, and benevolence, which would be the determinate factor shaping the nature of the social world (Confucius 1869, 308-309). Confucius introduced a relational approach to social interaction in order to avoid relationships at multiple levels being reduced to self-seeking individuals pursuing their comparative advantage. Consequently, the recent relational trend in psychology has sparked renewed interest in Confucius's approach to human and social development. There is an increased interest in his mutual trust model as a means of offsetting the prior assumptions about "the self" as an autonomous and sovereign social agent who is willing to employ utilitarian ethics to maximize gains.

A cornerstone concept for Confucius was the principle "ping", which could establish cohesion, solidarity, social order, and sustainable peace (Confucius 1869, 266 & 319). He envisioned social justice as the fair distribution of social goods. He thought of an increase in social goods, social capital, and public value as resulting from improving the quality of character of the individual members of society, which would result in improving the quality of social life. He implied that social life reflects what is described by a System's Theory perspective on social dynamics, i.e., what benefits one part of the system benefits the entire system; thus, what benefits the entire system is beneficial for its components. This is a variation on the mechanistic view of existence in which social agents operate within closed systems in which their outputs are directly proportional to their ability to maximize and convert their inputs. In fact, Confucius envisioned social relations, at all levels of social interaction, as being shaped by the principle of "ping tianxia" (i.e., the peaceful coexistence of all under heaven). Thus, Confucius envisioned a world reconstituted along the lines of peaceful and harmonious relations in which every individual would engage in transactions that would contribute to elevating the human experience.

Confucius notion of learning, self-cultivation, and social development is based on his convictions regarding ontology (especially social ontology). In other words, Confucius' expertise lay in his insight into the nature and properties of the social world. Consequently, he developed a very comprehensive understanding of how the dynamics of social relationships affect human and social development. Confucius' social ontology was based on his understanding of the psychological states of individuals, what motivates interactions, the nature of the relationship between the general public and public authorities, and how to be well-integrated within the fabric of existence (i.e., he often spoke of the relationship between humanity, the social world, and harmony with Tao) (Confucius 1869, 299). He thought of "the value of life "in terms of a harmonious integration of the self, the other, and society.

Confucius proposed that there is a direct correspondence between personal virtue and civic virtue. Personal virtue is the outcome of engaging in the practice of self-cultivation, which results in developing the characteristics of sincerity, integrity, and faithfulness or reliability. When sincerity and integrity, for example, are the basis of how individuals relate in society, then personal virtue shapes social virtue, which is described as the basis of Confucius's mutual trust model of social relations that is underpinned by his five constant virtues. Confucius claimed that the self could be cultivated in a way that increases the likelihood that the members of society will experience happiness, well-being, good fortune, and flourishing. He proposed that self-cultivation results in an enhanced ability to discern how to fulfill basic drives in a way that is admired by the other members of society (Miller 2016, 71–72).

This article explains why the relational approach to sociology is a means of avoiding the problem of autonomous social agents focusing on self-interest and viewing the other as a threat that either has to be controlled or eliminated. The article also explains why the rise of the relational turn in the social sciences posed a challenge to substantialism and essentialism. The challenge had to do with whether it is more accurate to view the social world in terms of processes of dynamic unfolding relations or as substances (i.e., substances are the fundamental building blocks of reality, and in the social sense, individual social agents are self-subsistent or self-acting entities). Therefore, in addressing the relational turn in the social sciences and subsequently the social science response to substantialism and essentialism, it is necessary to provide a comprehensive explanation of social ontology. This includes an explanation of Confucian views on integrality and Chinese dialectics.

Section one explains the issues that sparked a growing interest in the relational turn in the social sciences with a special emphasis on the epistemological and ethical issues involved in the shift. This section analyzes the controversy over substantialism, essentialism, and relationality through the lens of social ontology. Section one ends by stressing how Confucian views helped to address and resolve these issues. Section two points out that Dewey is credited with initiating the relational turn in the social sciences. However, the section explains that it is very likely that Dewey was influenced by Confucian views on relationality and his views on ideal social existence. This includes emphasizing Confucian views on the constitutive nature of social relational patterns. In addition, section two explains the connection between Confucius' views on an integrative framework for interpersonal interactions and an integral model of the self. An understanding of his views on integrality helps to clarify the issue of the role of substances, essences, and processes in human and social development.

Section three explains Confucius' five virtues and harmonious relations and why these principles apply to multiple levels of social interaction. Section four explains social ontology from the perspective of Confucius' mandala model of relationality. The concluding section provides a summary of Confucius' perspective on the relationship between pedagogy, human, and social development and explains how his mutual trust model of social relations and his five constant virtues establish a viable framework for harmonious multi-level social interactions. The conclusion also explains how the Confucian approach to pedagogy and social development can be utilized to address contemporary conditions humanity faces at the second decade of the 21st century.

1. Relationality, Ethics, Epistemology, and Social Ontology

> *"Ontology—the realm of being, or of what is or exists—should be understood in relation to epistemology, which concerns the realm of knowledge, or of what is known"* (Meikle 1985, 178).

The world's most respected wisdom traditions and most renown philosophers address a broad range of issues and concerns that confront the human experience. The aim is to provide humanity with reliable knowledge (i.e., knowledge that will be beneficial to the human experience and will enable humanity to effectively manage its existence in the natural and social world). Reliable knowledge can be defined as "The kind of knowledge that gives unity and system to the body of the sciences and the kind that results from a critical examination of the grounds of our convictions, prejudices, and beliefs" (Russell 2005, 25). The attempt to address the dilemma of knowing and what can be known dates back to the very beginning of civilization. However, the issue of how to gain reliable knowledge is also associated with reconciling the difference between an understanding of the ontological nature of existence based on sensory awareness and the epistemological alterations in that understanding subsequent to interpretation. Without reconciling the difference, our understanding of reliable knowledge will not be based on the most accurate evaluative judgment. This difference can be thought of as the challenge to developing reliable knowledge, given the fact that there is a difference between the intransitive ontological nature of the phenomenal aspects of existence and the transitive epistemological nature of cognition (Bhaskar 2008, 11–14).

For philosophers, natural and social scientists, and the world's most respected wisdom traditions, there are three means for gaining knowledge that is reliable for enhancing human existence: (1) being sure that knowledge claims are reliable (epistemology); (2) gaining insight into the nature of existence and human nature (ontology); and (3) deciding how to apply knowledge to action, which involves ethics (e.g., applying knowledge to personal and social activities as well as to how to relate to the forces shaping the natural order). Because our understanding and explanation of being are based on the transitive epistemological aspect of cognition, discussions about ontology and epistemology necessarily involve the domain of ethics. Therefore, to completely grasp the significance of the relational turn in the natural and social sciences, it is important to understand how it contributes to our understanding of the role of epistemology, ontology, and ethics in enabling humanity to effectively manage the challenges it faces in the natural and social world. In short, reliable knowledge enables individuals to avoid the types of mistakes that are made because of faulty reasoning and understanding, which has ethical implications because faulty reasoning and understanding can result in poor judgment regarding the best choice of action.

Humanity's search for knowledge that cannot be doubted has gone through several paradigm shifts. The preclassical epistemologists proposed that the material world has an unseen, underlying nonmaterial essence, which plays a role in shaping the nature of existence and the human experience. Classical social theorists and philosophers stressed that human reasoning is an emergent quality sparked by fundamental principles that shape the natural order. The natural order was considered to have an underlying structure whose properties could be discovered by human consciousness, self-reflection, and collective reflection. However, since the scientific revolution, logical empiricism has been regarded as the most reliable means of gaining knowledge about epistemology, existence, axiology, reason, mind, language, etc. Consequently, essentialism, metaphysics, reductionism, empiricism, mechanism, substantialism, dualism, and causality all continue to influence the way some individuals think about the nature of existence.

Reliable knowledge requires rectifying what heretofore have been *epistemic* fallacies. The fallacies involve, on the one hand, responding to questions about the nature of being with answers that reduce the issue to how to formulate accurate statements about knowledge. However, on the other hand, "The philosophical vogues, which have influenced methods in the sciences, have had a very restricted ontology that has been fused with their atomist epistemology. The result is that entities (e.g., social classes) seem problematical unless they can be reduced to the permitted atoms (individual agents) or in some way construed of them alone" (Meikle 1985, 178). Acquiring knowledge by means of an epistemological approach based on methodological individualism will only admit for ontological consideration those aspects of things that can be atomically reduced in the way that describes them as discrete individual components. The relational turn in the social sciences introduced a challenge to the established paradigm: methodological individualism. That is to say, the relational turn challenges the view that "All social phenomena (their structure and their change) are in principle explicable in ways that involve only individuals—their properties, their goals, their beliefs, and their actions" (Elster 1982, 453).

Therefore, this raises the question of whether there is a reliable basis for knowledge that puts together fragments of information that had seemed irreconcilable. In other words, can the prior paradigms be reconciled, thus regarded as an *ex-post factum* of our pursuit for reliable knowledge, if they are superseded by a relational view of the nature of existence (Apel 1998, 43–44)? Thus, the question is, does the relational view better enable scientists to bridge what heretofore had been a gap between the noumenal structures or generative mechanisms that manifest as reality and human cognition? If so, this would mean that the relational turn in the sciences creates "A progressive deepening of our understanding of being and a progressive deepening of our understanding of the categories that are manifest in the natural and social world" (Bhaskar 2007, 197). This would mean that the relational approach has greater explanatory value when analyzing the connection between the overlapping domains of the real, perception and experience, and what is regarded as empirical facts by a particular domain of science.

The relational mode of thinking recognizes that what is taken to be reliable knowledge is, in fact, a symbolic representation of complex constitutive processes and relations. Relationality alters or expands the established paradigms by explaining constitutive processes and relations using such terms as integrality, systems, and the interconnected web. This provides humanity with better conceptual tools for delving deeper into the nature of existence, and with such tools, humanity is able to transcend subject-object and nature-human dichotomies. Thus, an expansion of the established paradigm allows for more accurately discerning how relations, processes, and transformations play a fundamental and essential role in existence. Consequently, relationality requires "A crucial rethinking of much of epistemology and ontology" (Barad 2007, 83), which has implications for both ethics and social ontology. It becomes evident that the benefit of establishing complementarity between epistemology, ontology, and ethics is that it provides a more effective means of integrating the various aspects of social activity (economic, political, and social-psychological) in order to balance a focus on the material aspects of existence with the inclusion of what humanity (or a society) regards as having intrinsic value.

Social ontology is the study of social properties, practices, entities, structures, and relations. A relational approach to social ontology focuses on the role that social transactions play in shaping social reality. Social ontology studies the nature and properties of the social world from an interdisciplinary perspective, which includes analyzing the relationship between subjective values and collective intentionality. The relational approach to social ontology is based on the assertion that "The real is relational," or, in other words, social reality is co-created by the collective rather than by the autonomous intentions of individual social agents. (Bourdieu 2013, 8). The social group forms a collective consciousness (in Durkheim terms), which, once internalized, forms the basis of an interior knowledge or embodied disposition—a "sociological habitus". In practice, the habitus accomplishes the integration of systems of relations in and through the production of [social] practice. In effect, these systems of relations establish the current practices that members of society engage in. However, they also reflect knowledge, wisdom, practices, and perceptions from a cultural heritage that are handed down from generation to generation, which produce the conditions for the durability of constitutive social principles, their reproduction, or their innovation. However, this can all be traced to a collective understanding of how to manage the conditions society is faced with in its effort to deal with the nature of existence (Bourdieu 1995, 78–79). Thus, the relational view of social ontology establishes a unique perspective on the connection between epistemology, ontology, and ethics.

Certainly, epistemology involves the endeavor to gain reliable knowledge regarding the nature of existence, and on the basis of that understanding, "Create ethical value systems in the intelligible world according to the demands of the human spirit and to guide human activities in the sensible world toward 'The Kingdom of Ends'" (i.e., the Kingdom of Ends is a Kantian concept that depicts an ideal realm where all individuals act in ways that enable them to realize intrinsic value ends) (Hwang 2012, 44). Therefore, the relational turn in the social sciences establishes a complementary connection between the moral grounding of civilization (ethics) and perspectives on epistemology and ontology. This is especially evident in how it addresses and resolves the difference in perspectives on substantialism, essentialism, and relationality. The debates over substantialism, essentialism, and relationality involve the scientific issue of "The nominal essence or substance of a thing that is necessary for the thing to be correctly identified as one of a certain type or in virtue of which the thing or substance tends to behave the way it does, including manifesting the properties that constitute its nominal essence" (Bhaskar 2008, 200). Consequently, contemporary natural and social scientists increasingly regard matters of knowledge about the nature of things and about doing the right thing in relation to these things as matters related to epistemology, ontology, fact, ethics, and value.

As recently as the turn of the century, 21st-century sociologists were "Faced with a fundamental dilemma: whether to conceive of the social world as consisting primarily of substances or processes, in static 'things' or in dynamic, unfolding relations" (Emirbayer 1997, 281). "The substantialist mode of thought is inclined to treat the activities and preferences specific to certain individuals or groups in a social context as if they were substantial properties, inscribed once and for all in a kind of essence" (Bourdieu 1995, 9). Substantialism takes discrete individual entities as the foundational units of analysis. That is to say that a substantialist approach to social ontology privileges individual things over relations and material productions over the relationships that produced them. Substantialism makes the reasonable claim that nothing outside of an entity can change its nature. The paradigmatic illustration of the substantialist view of the nature of existence is that entities are like billiard balls; they can bump into each other but maintain their fundamental identity. However, substantialism is also the basis of the established methodological individualism paradigm in the social sciences (in other words, the claim that the fundamental unit of social life is the individual). The implication is that there is an emphasis on an atomistic understanding of social life that prioritizes individuality.

Rather than analyzing existence in terms of essences or substances, the relational approach views individuals as existing in an interconnected and entangled web with others and with their environment. The proponents of relationality argue that entities and their relations cannot be viewed as autonomous, thus separate from one another or completely independent of each other. Certainly, any study of social activity, at any level of analysis, must take into consideration how the goals, beliefs, and value commitments of individual agents are impacted by those of other social agents. Thus, the relational view represents the area where sociology and social psychology overlap. It establishes a resolution to some of the moral, epistemological, and ontological issues addressed by some of the world's most respected social, political, and moral philosophers (e.g., Aristotle, Hume, Kant, and Confucius) (Bhaskar 2008, 11–20; also see Hwang 2014, 9 & 12-21). The relational perspective on epistemology, ontology, and ethics allows for a clearer understanding of the phenomena revealed to us by sensory experience and, therefore, for better judgement as to how to act in relation to such phenomena.

Over the last couple of decades, there has been a resurgence of interest in the classical approach to relationality, which is now impacting every level of social interaction. This means that there is widespread acceptance of the claim that regardless of the level of social interaction, the behavior of each social agent must take into account that of the other and is oriented in these terms (Weber 1978, 26). Consequently, relationality is now influencing quite a few scientific and academic disciplines, e.g., social psychology, pedagogy and social pedagogy, organizational behavior, leadership, governance, public administration, philosophy, and intercultural and international relations. Therefore, relationality is increasingly chosen as the preferred approach to analyzing social activity at its multiple levels of transaction. However, the term resurgence is used because classical social theorists and political philosophers stressed that in order to be harmoniously well-integrated (within oneself, with others, and with the forces shaping the natural order), it is necessary for individuals to realize they exist in an intricate, interdependent relationship with the whole (Aristotle 1959, 11–13).

Confucius's social theory is a good example of a relational approach to socio-political philosophy that integrates epistemology, ontology, and ethics to establish the fundamental principles of social life. Consequently, his view of the human experience, social relations, and nature-human relations reflects integrality. Confucius provides insightful resolution to the controversy regarding materialism, substantialism, essentialism, and relationality. That is to say that pre-Qin Confucians provided insight into the relationship between substances, essences, and relations with their explanation of the hexagrams of the I-Ching in its Ten Wings. The Ten Wings (十翼 *shí yì*) is a collection of commentaries (傳 *zhuan*) to the classical Chinese *Book of Changes* (易經 *Yì jīng*). Parts of the Ten Wings are traditionally ascribed to Confucius (or as commentaries written by his students).

The relational view ascribed to Confucius is expressed in his claim that "Heaven and Earth—all things material—exist. After the existence of all material things, animate beings came into existence, which is the outcome of attraction, transactions, and relations (e.g., for example, between male and female). With the existence of relationships, propriety and righteousness came into existence" (Hwang 2018a, 81, where he translates from *The I-Ching* 1977, 973–974). Therefore, what we conceive of and experience in regards to the nature of existence is shaped by the interactions and relationships between the material and animate things we witness in the space between heaven and earth, as well as the ideas we form about them. Hence, in earlier Chinese culture, there was a tendency to think of life as an open field that had to be cultivated, which determined one's life experience. The harvest is then a manifestation of the existential meaning one ascribes to the relationship between the animate and inanimate things experienced in life.

Self-cultivation and the role it plays in civic virtue are the keys to Confucius' relational approach to social activity. Self-cultivation is also the means of developing the sage-like wisdom that derives from developing a virtuous character and moral mind. In this respect, Confucianism integrates epistemology (i.e., the sage-like knowledge or wisdom derived from the moral mind), both ontology and social ontology (i.e., harmony, social cohesion, and solidarity, and ethics (humanness and developing a virtuous character—as the basis of civic virtue), which are manifestations of adhering to the underlying principles shaping the nature of existence—adherence to the Tao) (Hwang 2012, 100 & 107–109). The idea is that reliable knowledge (epistemological validity) is gained by discerning the principles underlying the organic and inorganic aspects of existence (ontology), which are the principles that also explain how individuals can have the most beneficial relationships with others and the environment (ethics) (Hwang 2012, 127–118).

The Confucian perspective on epistemology, ontology, and ethics is referred to as holistic, which places the substances of nature in an essential relationship to people and social life (i.e., with the forces of existence/Tao, individuals, and the social order all existing in harmonious interdependence). In this respect, a Confucian perspective on the complementarity between epistemology, ontology, and ethics is based on his claim that all systems operate in accordance with principles that regulate their existence and, in terms of social activity, manifest as relations based on the principle *li*. In other words, from his perspective, li is a principle that implies congruity (i.e., an ethical concept that explains the manifestation, growth, and development of things). The concept of (li) has three aspects according to Confucius' view of social relations and activity: (1) traditional cultural values, customs, beliefs, and norms; (2) etiquette (politeness, courtesy, and being considerate); and (3) propriety.

Confucius' explanation of an underlying existing interconnectedness is similar to the first, second, and third triad, which is an essential aspect of the philosophy of Pragmatism. The first, second, and third triads are complementary to how the principle of Tao is conceptualized. Tao is the first, which manifests as the ying-yang dialectic. The second are phenomena that manifest as a result of their generative yin-yang interaction. Humanity interprets the many manifestations is the third. Therefore, Confucius's Taoist yin-yang ontology, his principle of human-heartedness, and his benevolence establish the basis of both his approach to social ethics and reliable knowledge. From a Confucian perspective, it is the nature of the interactions that take place between individuals and individuals and nature-human relations that constitute being. Therefore, the Confucian view of social ontology is based on integrating knowledge about the forces shaping the natural order and knowledge about human nature into an explanation of the moral mind, the significance of society's relationship, the forces shaping the nature of existence, and how individuals can relate harmoniously at every level of social interaction.

2. Confucian Influence on the Relational Turn in Social Theorizing

"To be is to relate" (Foucault 2002, 105)!

"What exists in the social world are relations, not interactions between agents or intersubjective ties between individuals" (Bourdieu and Wacquant 1992, 97).

The American philosopher John Dewey is credited with playing a key role in initiating the "relational turn" in the social sciences with his advocacy of Transactionalism as a part of his contribution to pragmatic philosophy (1949). What Dewey had in mind by using the term *trans-action* is that human behaviors are not activities of the self alone, nor even primarily one's own, but are processes of the full situation of organism-environment transactions (Dewey 1946, 506). Dewey's analysis of the transaction between an individual and the environment can be read as a transactional Constructivist-type account of the processes that underlie the learning, growth, and development of both individuals and society (i.e., the construction of social reality is itself a process that is transactional). Thus, Dewey's work contributes to our understanding of Constructivist-type transactional and relational views on epistemology, pedagogy, and social relations. Dewey viewed transactional Constructivism as the framework for "Establishing cooperation in an activity in which there are partners and in which the activity of each is modified and regulated by the partnership. Possession of the capacity to engage in such activity is intelligence. Intelligence and meaning are the natural consequences of human interaction" (Dewey 1998, 55). In this way, knowledge, meaning, and social reality are co-constructed, co-created, and co-produced. In short, Dewey implies that human growth and social development involve transactional Constructivist-type dynamics.

The aim of Dewey's introduction of Transactionalism was to move beyond subject-object dualism. Dewey argued that there is no detached social subject interacting with a passive, unresponsive social reality. That is to say that he eliminates the breach between the subject and the object, which makes experience a result of the transaction between the impact that an experience has on the experiencer and, consequently, the impact the experiencer has on what is experienced. In this sense, Dewey's influence played a role in redefining our understanding and conceptualization of social relations, social life, and the ontology of social existence. His ideas contributed to moving beyond the Newtonian notion of the mechanical-like 'self-action' of autonomous individuals. The key to understanding Dewey's contribution to relationality is in his critique of the prior emphasis on describing social action by using the terms self-action and interaction and his preference for describing social action by using the term transactions. Self-action, of course, means that there is no external agency or force causing the action. The benefit of this perspective is that it affords the agent a great deal of autonomy. Interaction implies that the acts of individuals are the result of the attention they give to other things or other people in their environment. However, the term transaction implies that individuals exist in an interdependent relationship with others and with the natural environment, thus having an influence on each other.

However, the question is to what extent Dewey's views on a relational approach to social interactions were shaped by his experience in China (1919–1921), thus undoubtedly influenced by Confucianism. Of course, this would mean that if the connection is established, it would indicate that Confucian views on relationality influenced the shift in social science theorizing toward focusing on social relations and, as well, new ways of analyzing relational categories. What we do know for a fact is that Dewey regarded Confucianism as the moral foundation of Chinese culture. We also know that he held a high regard for the role of ethics, morals, and values in social life. He is noted for saying that the foundational grounding of Western civilization is not its political and economic systems but its moral foundation. In Dewey's own words, the Confucian ideals of filial piety and socio-political organization "Transmit Chinese civilization intact. Confucius contributed something without which China cannot endure" (Dewey 2008, 53 & 54). This has prompted David Hall and Roger Ames to point out that Dewey gradually began to find greater value in the Confusion view of social democracy over the Western view of the individually oriented notion of social life. They argue that Dewey's vision of relational (i.e., ideal type) community life was influenced by Chinese social practices and the continued influence of Confucian social theory on Chinese culture. They argue that indeed, Dewey began to view the Confucian communitarian approach to social life as a viable means for realizing an ideal type of community life (Hall & Ames 1999, 11).

"Dewey's activities and experiences in China contributed to the development of his views, especially in the areas of social and political philosophy. By becoming part of Dewey's life, the Chinese world became a medium for his ideas. However, Dewey in China is complex. Therefore, we must start with the topic that unites Dewey and Confucius more than any other – education" (Behuniak 2019, 40 & 41). Education was a central aspect of both Dewey's and Confucius' socio-political philosophy and practice. They both regarded education as a cornerstone institution of society and the primary social mechanism for human and social development. For both Dewey and Confucius, education is a process by which individuals develop their full capabilities, realize their full potential, and, thus, on the basis of their personal growth and development, contribute to the quality of life of society. Their relational philosophy of education included the principle of mutuality, in which there is self-reflection, learning, and growth for both the teacher and the learner.

For both Confucius and Dewey, the unique, raw, untutored, and originally unadorned qualities of the student are polished by the process of structured social relations. Structured social activity is not meant to restrict the freedom and creativity of the individual; both Dewey and Confucius prescribed a means by which an appropriate approach to relationality can transform raw potential into the individual's ability to make a unique and creatively beneficial contribution to society. "The assumption is that there is something native, spontaneous, and raw (zhi 質) in the human experience (one) that enters into relations (two) and thus comes to express patterns (wen 文) that integrate productively into broader wholes (three). This dynamic also indicates that harmony (he 和) is the normative measure that guides Confucius' philosophy", which corresponds to the 1-2-3 of Chinese cosmology and ontology (Behuniak 2019, 45). But conceptualizing cosmology and ontology in terms of 1-2-3 also corresponds with American Pragmatism conceptualizing cosmology and ontology in terms of the first (a noumenal quality), the second (a relational or transactional aspect of existence), and the third (experience—the interpretation of or meaning assigned to the transaction).

The philosophies of both Dewey and Confucius prescribe a means by which the members of society can live in solidarity (he 和) with each other and in harmony with the natural order. Therefore, both Confucius and Dewey emphasized the fundamentals of how to establish personal and social harmony. Of course, both Dewey and Confucius proclaim that such harmony (cohesion and social order) is the basis for realizing the goal social action aims to achieve. Instituting this harmony is established by means of the types of social practices associated with the relational approach to social activity. The basis of the relational approach is self-cultivation, which emphasizes zhongxin 忠信 (i.e., or what Confucius referred to as the consummation of one's authentic self). Cultivating zhongzin results in expressing oneself on the basis of cheng 成 (sincerity, authenticity, and genuineness). In other words, they both stressed that achieving harmony—within oneself, in social relations, and in relation to the natural order—is the most important lesson of pedagogy. Contributing to the harmony of society creates a feeling of great satisfaction and increases the benefits individuals enjoy as a result of the social harmony. Whenever harmony is achieved, the uniqueness of each individual part contributes to the wholeness and the experience of consummation. That is to say that social harmony, from both the Confucian and Deweyan perspectives, occurs when each participating part (he 和) finds its unique contribution to the whole. If this unique contribution is lost, then the result is a loss in value. In this way, their contribution to social reality provides insight into how to establish harmonious transactions at every level of social life.

The relational view of existence holds that things "Are not assumed to be independent existences present anterior to any relation, but they gain their whole being . . . first in and with the relations that are predicated on them. Such 'things' are terms of relations, and as such, they can never be 'given' in isolation but only in community with each other" (Cassirer 1953, 36). In other words, it is assumed that things indeed exist and that we experience them. Social knowledge is insight into the connection between these things, their causal factors, and the interdependent connection individuals have with these things. If our epistemological approach fails to take into consideration relationality because its reductionist methodology focuses on parts, then "It is clear that what is merely a part has taken the place of the original sensuous whole. We may borrow a drastic example from Lotze: If we group cherries and meat together under the attributes red, juicy, and edible, we do not thereby attain a valid logical concept but a meaningless combination of words, quite useless for the comprehension of the particular cases" (Cassirer 1953, 6 & 7). The solution is to understand the difference between substances, essences, and relations, which will enable us to explain the real connection between all things.

A particularly significant feature of relational sociology resides in its capacity to broaden the theory of the human subject not only as a self, agent, and actor but also through the development of the concept of the person; more precisely, through deeper research on the relational constitution of the human person as a social subject emerging from relational reflexivity (Emirbayer & Mische 1998, 962–992). Relational ethics require that we do not treat others as means to accomplishing an end or an outcome we desire. We must treat others as an end, never as a means to an end. Fundamental to the relational approach are the principles of mutuality and equal respect (regardless of social status) and that it is in one's best interest to promote and respect the human rights of others. Relational theorists propose that, because of the interdependent nature of social relations, these three principles are fundamental to the relational ethics of social action. Therefore, the relational turn in the social sciences increases "The possibility of creating a consummatory experience where transactions result in an outcome that one desires (within society and in intercultural relations). Thus, it enables individuals to be better integrated within their social and natural order" (Miller 2016, 31).

Consequently, the relational approach to social transactions at various levels is relevant to such fields as anthropology, education, social psychology, organizational behavior, business, social economics, philosophy, and international relations. This includes the growing interest in networks (e.g., social networks, value creation networks, governance networks, and social media networks) in social relations and in improving social and economic performance. In other words, social actions are a matter of interactions carried out either relationally, within, or between networks. This means that social life is actually a matter of interdependent relationships, or that individuals exist in a world of interdependent relations. Therefore, there is an interdisciplinary aspect to relational sociology. Applying this approach to social action, socio-political activity, political economy, international relations, and sustainable development is proving to create a generative force that produces both quantitative and qualitative improvements in performance. Thus, there is increased interest in applying the relational approach at various levels of social interaction and various aspects of social activity.

3. Confucius' Five Virtues and Harmonious Relations at the Multiple Levels of Social Interaction

Confucius' relational view of social life provides an alternative to the notion that individuals are autonomous, self-seeking social agents who engage in competitive, utility-maximizing relationships. The Confucian view emphasizes the concept of co-creation, where social life is thought of as comprised of social beings whose social make-up is shaped by nurturing moral cultivation and personal and collective reflection. This establishes Confucius as one of the earliest proponents of a relational theory for constructing social reality. Therefore, the relational approach to social ontology may provide a bridge between Anglophone and Sinophone views on transactional Constructivism (Paes & Linares 2019, 569). The principles underlying Confucius' relational ethics provide a reliable source of knowledge for co-creating a positive or progressive social transformation. That is to say that they describe the first principles of social existence from the perspective of what nourishes the body, mind, and spirit (Lui 2021, 16 & 17). In terms of the realms of epistemology, ontology, and ethics, the relational approach to social activity establishes the necessary conditions for social justice, knowledge proven reliable for experiencing good fortune and social flourishing, and harmonious relations with nature.

Confucius explains the cornerstone principles of his philosophy in chapter 20 of *The Doctrine of the Mean*. Confucius explains that the Dao (i.e., a constitutive force, universal principle, or, in more contemporary terms, cosmopolitan principles), which are manifest as appropriate relationships, can be described in terms of five virtues. The Five Virtues are benevolence (仁 – ren), righteousness (義 – yi), propriety (禮 – li), wisdom (智 – zhi) and trustworthiness (信 – xin), which signifies the accomplishment of Confucian theorization on relationality (Hwang 2018a, 79).

Benevolence (ren) is the characteristic attribute of personhood. The first priority of its expression is showing affection to those individuals a person is most closely related to. The character ren refers to the relationship between two people. Ren portrays the unity of two individuals and structurally implies the ethical dynamics that connect any two people. Yi (righteousness) means appropriateness and respecting the superior, which is one of its most important aspects. Loving others according to who they are and respecting superiors according to their ranks gives rise to the forms and distinctions of propriety (li) in social life (Confucius 1869, 299). The concept of Li and the principles associated with it involve social norms, traditions, and those aspects of social activity that are revered. However, it can also mean social etiquette. Confucius uses the term to mean conscientious observation of appropriate rules of conduct and social relations.

Confucius' references to the virtue of wisdom provide some clues into his thoughts regarding epistemology, ontology, and ethics. Above all, Confucius thought of reliable knowledge as an ability to discern and be attuned to the fundamental patterns of life in the natural and social worlds. Wisdom inclines an individual to act in accordance with the principle of Wu Wei (i.e., effortless action, going with the flow, and/or free and easy wondering). In other words, aligning one's inner inclinations with the forces shaping the nature of existence means flowing with the nature of things with sensitivity and grace (Confucius 1869, 244). Xin is translated as faithfulness, reliability, and trustworthiness (which were associated with having cultivated the inner virtue of sincerity). In terms of a person's moral character, Xin refers to self-management, intrinsic motivation, and perfect virtue. From an ethical perspective, Xin involves acts of the highest integrity. From an epistemological perspective, it involves discernment, insight, and wisdom. In terms of social relations, it has to do with what generates social order, legitimacy, and respect for authority (Confucius 1869, 118 & 240). From a psychological point of view, individuals who have cultivated Xin do not hide behind a persona. Therefore, in their social relations, they are neither deceptive nor manipulative; thus, they are authentic and can be taken at their word.

In the Chinese language system, the term morality (道德, Daode) is composed of two characters, Dao (道) and De (德), each of which holds its own meaning. Daode, of course, can simply refer to one's ethical principles. However, it can also imply integrity—of one heart and mind— and a level of awareness, discernment, and/or the type of demeanor that has been gained through self-cultivation. However, Confucius redefined the meaning of each syllable by referring to Dao as an unfathomable, dynamic, *potentia* out of which all things are manifested and transformed. De refers to principles that enable potential to manifest in a particular way. In short, the De (or principle) for displaying virtue in one's life, character, and demeanor, it is Shu (恕). Shu is typically translated as what you don't want done to yourself; do not do it to others. On an occasion when teaching his students, he attempted to summarize his whole doctrine in one brief phrase. he stated, "My doctrine is 忠 (zhong) and 恕 (shu) and nothing more". Zhong can be translated as sincerity, authenticity, keeping in mind the interests of others in your conduct, and loyalty. However, shu can also be translated as reciprocity.

4. Social Ontology from the Perspective of Confucius' Mandala Model of Relationality

The mandala depicts the connection between ontology and social ontology by illustrating the interdependent dynamics and relationships that exist within and between both the natural and social worlds. The first thing that stands out is that the model portrays a symmetry between the two sides in which one side interpenetrates the other. Therefore, the mandala illustrates a constant process of integration and reintegration. Life demands a constant exchange with other aspects of existence. Maintaining the integrity of any organic system (the human organism as well as a social system) requires making other aspects of existence a part of itself. The very basis of survival for the human organism is engaging in life-sustaining interactions, and for society, it is the ability to form structures of cooperative interchange. A prime example is food and drink. However, a more essential interchange is the process of breathing (i.e., a constant receiving, yin, and giving back in return, yang). Individuals cannot survive without participating in this interchange that the life process requires. This means that the continuous commingling between the human organism and various aspects of one's social and natural environments can be thought of as "the tie that binds" all of existence into integral relatedness (Miller 2017, 102-124).

Chinese thought contributes to relationality with its explanation of binaries. Chinese philosophy emphasizes that the two parts actually exist in interdependent co-existence. Any thought of one side of the binary dominating the other actually threatens the existence of both. Social harmony and justice, as well as individual liberty, lie in being liberated from a sense of opposition and duality by embracing interconnectedness. In other words, the mandala depicts mutuality, equality, and complementarity. In terms of individuals engaged in social transactions, complementarity means a relationship in which the interacting parties enhance each other's existence. Thus, the symbol illustrates that we live in a relationship-oriented or relationship-centered world in which relationality shapes the nature of our existence. From this perspective, the quality of life for the individual is dependent upon the quality of the relationships and the nature of the interactions the individual engages in. Confucius used the term Jen to describe a person who relates to others in a proper, fully human manner. Jen, in this respect, involves interacting with others in ways that ensure reciprocal benefit and promote solidarity.

According to Confucianism, the virtue of Jen is the essence of human transaction.

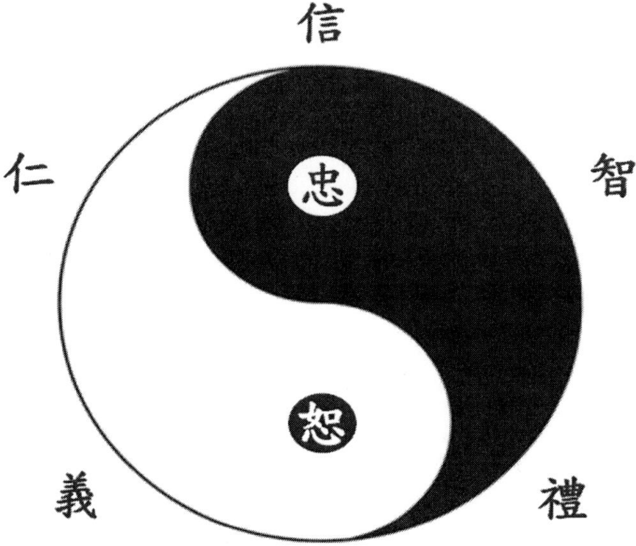

Figure 1: Depicts the Taoist origin of Confucius' mandala model of the connection between ontology and social ontology. Confucius viewed wisdom as the mediating factor in social relations. Self-cultivation results in having the wisdom to interact in the outer world with sincerity and benevolence, which are sparked by being true to one's inner nature (Hwang 2018a, 80–82). The arrangement of these five virtues (in relation to yin-yang dynamics and those of Tao) indicates the relationship between the self, others, and the forces shaping the nature of existence (Hwang 2018b, 179–193).

In the ancient Chinese conception of ontology and social ontology, phenomenal existence is the outcome of the attraction between yin and yang. In that respect, the distinct entity (e.g., either yin or yang or any other distinct entity in existence) is actually a component of a greater whole upon which it is dependent. From a Confucian perspective, how to act effectively and appropriately in social relationships and in relation to the forces shaping the nature of existence (li) cannot be separated from understanding our place in the natural, social, and cosmic order. Therefore, behaving in accordance with relational ethics (ren) is the manifestation of an inner quality that is expressed outwardly. Wisdom (zhi) enables individuals to discern how social action manifests as the "highest good" (yi or righteousness) for society.

5. Conclusion

The relational approach to social ethics and transactions can actually be traced back to antiquity. However, there has been a resurgence of interest in relationality in both the social and natural sciences. Therefore, there is an increase in viewing ontology from the perspective of relations rather than essences or substances, which has an impact on ethics and epistemology. In addition, the social sciences are increasingly convinced that it is more advantageous to the human experience to conceive, analyze, and theorize social transactions at every level in which they occur from a relational perspective. The refocus on relationality and its constitutive power results in a resurgence of the way social relations were viewed by classical socio-political theorists and philosophers. Social scientists, in particular, are adopting the relational view because it is increasingly evident that the quality of social relations plays a key role in the quality of overall health and well-being as well as in the overall quality of social life. In fact, there is an increasing body of literature that proposes that the quest for ontological security is best satisfied by the relational approach to social transactions at every level in which interactions occur.

In social terms, ontological security is the feeling of reliable continuity that individuals have regarding their state of being. The problem of ontological security (perhaps better stated as the problem of ontological insecurity) occurs when individuals feel themselves living in a world in which they increasingly experience the fear of unforeseen threats. Therefore, they experience themselves as increasingly disconnected from what will enable them to feel secure. "Ontological insecurity is aggravated by insisting on perpetuating a reality based on unrealistic imaging, which could be overcome by means of a more reliable approach to knowledge generation" (Miller 2014, 52). In other words, by analyzing personal security from the *subjectivism epistemological* perspective (i.e., with an emphasis on analyzing social activity from the perspective of what concerns the individual), there is a greater tendency for individuals to focus on safeguarding themselves. By analyzing ontological security from the perspective of methodological individualism, autonomous social agents feel that they increase their security when they effectively manage the threat that other social agents presumably impose. With such a view, social agents seek to maintain a competitive, comparative, and power advantage over the proverbial other. Confucius proposed an alternative approach to achieving ontological security. In his relational approach to social interactions, the other is viewed as a reflection of the self, thus personal and social security are increased by engaging in mutually beneficial interactions, and Confucius himself proposed that power is employed as a means of empowerment (Confucius 1869, 152).

Confucius described his relational view from an ontological perspective by stating that it involves the significance of humanity's relationship with the forces shaping the natural order. He spoke of ethics in terms of acting appropriately, thus effectively, in relationships with others and with the natural order. He spoke of epistemology as reliable knowledge that will provide insight into what will improve the relationships individuals have with others and with the forces shaping the natural order. In fact, he called the generation, dissemination, and regulation of such knowledge education (Confucius 1869, 283). Although Confucius taught social theory, ethics (i.e., self-cultivation), and socio-political philosophy, he constantly emphasized that his ultimate concern was conforming to the Tao. When asked why, he replied, "Because following *The Way* enables you to accomplish everything in accordance with the Taoist principle Wu Wei [i.e., by following the Tao, your life provides you with the feeling that the nature of things unfold in a way that enables you to experience your highest good]. Therefore, what individuals accomplish is harmonious with Tao" (Confucius 2016, 1378).

Therefore, contemporary social and political theorists increasingly agree that Confucius's ethics, value theory, and social theory continue to be relevant today (Kavalski 2018, 92). His relevancy lies in the fact that his social value theory provides a viable approach to human and social development, to society operating properly, to improving the quality of life, and to accomplishing the goal that social action aims to achieve. That goal is social stability, cohesion, harmony, solidarity, flourishing, prosperity, social justice, and sustainable peace. Confucius's ethics, value theory, and social theory continue to be relevant because, as was put by one of last century's most influential political philosophers, a social value theory continues to be relevant when "It includes conceptions of what is of value in human life and ideals of personal characters, as well as ideals of friendship and of familial and associational relationships, and much else that is to inform our conduct and in the limit to our life as a whole" (Rawls 1996, p. 13).

Confucius was not considered successful as a stateman, or perhaps it is better to say he was not successful in influencing the statesmen and/or heads of state of his time. However, he continues to be regarded as highly successful as an exemplary teacher, a pedagogical philosopher, and a socio-political philosopher. In addition, he is credited with contributing to foundational views on a relational approach to pedagogy and a relational approach to social activity. As a teacher, Confucius did not merely establish a school where students could come to learn on a daily basis for a prescribed period of time. He established a community where the participants dedicated a significant period of their lives to both learning and self-cultivation. In that respect, there was a great deal of comradery and collegiality in his community. The community itself was an example of the role that quality relations play in self-cultivation and social ethics. In other words, the relationships enrich the lives of the participants in ways that are transformational (rather than merely transactional, as is the case in so many educational contexts). This makes Confucius's philosophy of education a prime example of the role that pedagogy plays in shaping the socio-political reality of society. Indeed, Confucian pedagogy has and continues to make a significant impact on social behavior in several countries.

The relational basis of social interactions has both instrumental and consummatory benefits. His social theory continues to be relevant today because it prescribes a means by which individuals who engage in cooperative social activity can realize their needs and wants more effectively and efficiently, with a greater sense of social harmony and less social conflict than they can by viewing success as the peak of a social ladder, which can only be occupied by a single individual. From the exclusive view, social relations involve dominance and are regarded as involving a zero-sum game. The proponents of a relational orientation propose "That facts about individuals alone are inadequate in accounting for social phenomena. Facts and principles concerning social phenomena are not reducible to the knowledge of individuals" (Hwang 2012, 193).

Although Confucius's approach to relationality is based on his "Five Cardinal Relationships" model (i.e., ruler-minister, father-son, elder and younger brothers, husband and wife, friend-friend), social theorists agree that it applies to all social transactions and at every level in which they occur, e.g., interpersonal relations, relations with those a person is most closely related to, relationships between the members of a community or society, those between individuals and their public authorities, and regarding organization behavior and the relationships associated with institutions. There is even now a growing body of literature proposing that global affairs would be more constructive, peaceful, and stable if his theory were applied to international relations. Confucianism implied that there are three types of political systems that are legitimate: (1) ones that comply with the Mandate of Heaven (where Tao is the origin of the natural order, the Mandate of Heaven is the origin of the natural and moral order), (2) ones that comply with the Tao (i.e., the principles of nature and the laws of nature), and (3) ones that comply with the principles of relationality.

"Confucius combined propriety, benevolence, and righteousness and transformed the external ritual of propriety into a cultural psychological structure. He expected that humans, based on the mind of benevolence, could make moral judgments in line with righteousness after assessing the various role relationships in social interactions and then act according to propriety" (Hwang 2001, 193). He emphasized that it is as a result of self-cultivation, social relational processes, and reflexivity that we come to develop a sense of an authentic self, a sense of what it means to be a human being in good relations with others, and what it means to be well-integrated within the fabric of existence (Confucius 1869, 241-246). In other words, it is as a result of individuals cultivating their natural endowments that they come to forge relationships that are mutually beneficial, improve their skills of communication, engage in behaviors at the multi-level of social interaction that are deemed appropriate and in accordance with protocol and etiquette, and engage in behaviors that contribute to enhancing the eco-aesthetic dimensions of social life.

Because of the rapid transformation of China from a developing country at the end of the last century or millennium to becoming a world superpower, interest in "Chinese social theory has increasingly attracted attention from the international social science community" (Hwang 2000, 156). Therefore, international social theorists are discovering that an important aspect of Chinese social practice is "doing social relations" or "practicing social relations" (gao guanxi). This is a distinctive social phenomenon that originated in the Confucian socio-cultural tradition. The Chinese approach to social action can be described as prioritizing what is appropriate over what is effective and what will promote reciprocity over what contributes to utility maximization. It is believed that individual behavior is motivated by basic natural needs and socially acquired desires. From the perspective of the Confucian influence on social activity, the best way to satisfy those needs and desires is in a way that sustains beneficial relationships with others and with the environment, which the person relies on to satisfy those needs and desires. In short, a Confucian relational view of social interactions requires individuals to avoid acting in any way that would cause the other person to lose face. Losing face can range anywhere from feeling uncomfortable, feeling slighted, feeling embarrassed, or being made to look inadequate.

Confucianism eliminates the problem of relationships based on the notion of binary dichotomies, e.g., nature-human, male-female, ingroup-outgroup, and East-West. Therefore, the proponents of the Confucian view of social relations (at all levels in which they occur) believe that it reduces social conflicts by maximizing harmony, mutuality, trust, and reciprocity. In this school of thought, individuality is not diminished. What is diminished are the selfish and egoistic aspects of narcissism. The self is viewed as being encompassed within an inner circle with outer rings composed of a person's closest relationships, community, the larger society, etc. Self-cultivation enables a person to enjoy peak experiences and peak performance because it results in eliminating the sense of being limited by any of the circles. Therefore, with the circles having a liberating effect, the person feels a sense of harmony with existence and flows through it, enjoying the feeling of Wu Wie. In this sense, Wu Wei means moving freely and easily through one's natural and social worlds, disturbing others and other things less, and being disturbed less by others and other things. This is what the ancient sage Chuang Tzu, in his book on Taoism, referred to as "free and easy wondering" (Chuang Tzu 1998, 1–7).

References

Apel, Karl-Otto. (1998) *From a Transcendental Semiotic Point of View*. (Papastephanou. M. Ed.). Manchester, UK: Manchester University Press.

Aristotle. (1959) *Politics*. (Rackham, H. Trans.). Cambridge, Massachusetts: Harvard University Press.

Barad, Karen. (2007) *Meeting the Universe Halfway: Quantum Physics and the Entanglement of Matter and Meaning*. Durham, NC: Duke University Press.

Behuniak, Jim. (2019) *John Dewey and Confucian Thought*. Albany, New York: The State University of New York.

Bhaskar, Roy. (2008) *A Realist Theory of Science*. Oxon, UK: Routledge.

Bhaskar, Roy. (2007) Theorizing Ontology. *Contributions to Social Ontology*. (Latsis, Clive. & Martins, Nuno. Edits.). Oxon, UK: Routledge.

Bourdieu, Pierre. (2013) *Outline of Theory and Practice*. Cambridge, UK: Cambridge University Press.

Bourdieu, Pierre. (1995) *Physical Space, Social Space and Habitus*. Oslo: Institutt for sosiologi og samfunnsgeografi.

Bourdieu, Pierre. & Wacquant, Loïc. (1992) *An Invitation to Reflexive Sociology*. Cambridge, UK: Polity Press.

Cassirer, Ernst. (1953) *Substance and Function*. (Swabey, William. & Swabey, Marie. Trans.). New York: Dover.

Chuang Tzu (1998) *The Essential Chuang Tzu*. (Hamil, Sam. & Seaton, J. Trans.). Boston: Shambhala.

Confucius. (2016) *Delphi Complete Works of Confucius*. East Sussex, UK: Delphi Publishing LTD.

Confucius. (1869) *The Life and Teachings of Confucius*. (Legge, James. Edits.). London: N. *Trübner & Co.*

Dewey, John. & Bentley, Arthur. (1946) Interaction and Transaction. *The Journal of Philosophy*. Volime 43, Number 19, 505-517

Dewey, J., & Arthur F. B. (1949). Knowing and the known. Boston: Beacon Press.

Dewey, John. (1998) *The Essential Dewey* (Volume 2). Bloomington, Indiana: Indiana University Press.

Dewey, John. (2008) *The Middle Works of John Dewey* (Volume 12) Carbondale, Illinois. Southern Illinois University Press.

Elster, Jon. (1982) The Case for Methodological Individualism. *Theory and Society*. Volume. 11, Number 4, 453-482.

Emirbayer, Mustafa. (1997) Manifesto for a Relational Sociology. *American Journal of Sociology*. Volume 103, Number 2, 281-317.

Emirbayer, Mustafa & Mische, Ann. (1998) What is Agency? The American Journal of Sociology, Vol. 103, No. 4. (Jan., 1998), pp. 962-1023.

Foucault, Michel. (2002) The Order of Things. London: Routledge.

Hall, David. & Ames, Roger. (1999) *The Democracy of the Dead: Dewey, Confucius, and the Hope for Democracy in China*. Chicago: Open Court Publishers.

Hwang, Kwang-Kuo. (2000) Chinese Relationalism: Theoretical Construction and Methodological Considerations. *Journal of the Theory of The Theory of Social Behavior*. Volume 30, Issue 2, 155-178.

Hwang, Kwang-Kuo. (2014) Cultural System vs. Pan-cultural Dimensions. Journal for the Theory of Social Behavior. Volume 45, Issue 1, 2-25.

Hwang, Kuo-Kuo. (2018a) Enriching Social Network Theory with Theoretical Model of Confucian Five Virtues. *Archaeology and Culture*. Volume 1, Number 1, 68-86.

Hwang, Kuo-Kuo. (2018b) Five Virtues: Scientific Approach for Studying Confucian Ethics and Morality. *International Journal of Science Research and Methodology*. Volume10, Issue 3, 176-198.

Hwang, Kuo-Kuo. (2012) *Foundations of Chinese Psychology: Confucian Social Relations*. New York: Springer.

Hwang, Kwang-Kuo. (2001) The Deep Structure of Confucianism: a social psychological approach. *Asian Philosophy*. Volume 11, Number 3, 179-204.

Kavalski, Emilian. (2018) Chinese concepts and relational international politics. *All Azimuth*. Volume 7, Number 1, 87-102.

Lui, James. (2021) Introduction to Confucian Psychology. *Psychology and Developing Societies*. 33(1) 7–26.

Meikle, Scott. (1985) *Essentialism in the Thought of Karl Marx*. London: Gerald Duckworth & Co. Ltd.

Miller, Leon. (2017) Faith, Integrity, and Integral Being. *Indian Philosophical Quarterly*. Volume 44, Issue 1, 102-124.

Miller, Leon. (2016) Intercultural Communications and Global Social Existence: A cross cultural analysis of communication theory. *Review of Social Sciences*. Volume 1, Number 1, 26-37.

Miller, Leon. (2016) The Ontological Basis of Self-Formation and Social Existence. *Transcience*. Volume 7, Issue 1, 69-82.

Miller, Leon. (2014) Why European Liberalism Continues to Falter. *The International Journal on World Peace*. Volume 31, Number 2, 35-55.

Nordin, Astrid H. M., & Smith, G. (2019). Relating self and other in Chinese and western thought. *Cambridge Review of International Affairs*. 32(5), 636-53.

Paes, Lucas de Oliveira, & Linares. L. J. (2019). Letter from the editors. *Cambridge Review of International Affairs*. 32(5), 569.

Qin, Y. & Nordin, A. H. M. (2019). Relationality and rationality in Confucian and western traditions of thought. *Cambridge Review of International Affairs*. 32(5), 601-14.

Rawls, John. (1996) *Political Liberalism*. New York: Columbia University Press.

Russell, Bertrand. (2005) The Value of Philosophy. *Philosophy: Basic Readings*. (Warburton, N. Ed.) Oxon, UK: Published by Routledge.

The I-Ching or Book of Changes. (1977) (written by Richard Wilhelm and translated by Cary Baynes). Princeton, New Jersey: Princeton University Press.

Weber, Max. (1978) *Economy and Society*. Berkeley, California: The University of California Press.

Section Two

Pedagogy and Social Development from the Perspective of Critical Pedagogy, Constructivist Pedagogy, and Social Pedagogy

John Dewey's Constructivist Pedagogical Approach to Peacebuilding

Charles F. Howlett
and Audrey Cohan

John Dewey's Constructivist Approach
to Peacebuilding through Education

In the field of international relations, the dominant school of thought has been largely influenced by the late University of Chicago political scientist, Hans J. Morgenthau. In the aftermath of World War II, Morgenthau argued that war is endemic to our society and represents shifts in the struggles for power among nation-states (Guzzini, 2018; Morgenthau & Thompson, 1985). Better known as the "realist" school of diplomacy, the basic premise posits that once established powers feel threatened by new and rising states, the risk of war increases. Retaining a measure of power and stature requires that established states keep the balance of power intact, and they often resort to the use of military force and government suppression to reduce perceived threats to their national interests. To that end, the mantra "be prepared for conflict" has been the dominant framework for policy and action in much of international politics (Westoff & Howlett, 2019). This begs the question of how to reduce conflict and promote peace in key areas of strife? For example, given the existing realities of instability not only in South Asia but in other regions of the world today, is there an instructive lesson to be learned from John Dewey's views on peace education using a constructivist lens?

South Asia, in particular, has witnessed its share of conflict and disruption over the past fifty years. Countries in that region, such as India, Pakistan, Afghanistan, and Bangladesh, for instance, have been home to considerable internal and external disputes. Inhabitants in some of these countries have even been victims of harsh repression. These involve both tribal and religious conflicts as well as state actors determined to quell opposition to their rule, such as the now-ruling Taliban in Afghanistan. Some state actors have instigated unrest to gain a foothold in neighboring regions and unseat the ruling power. In most cases, peacebuilding efforts in this region have been top-down pacification attempts, many of which have been undertaken by power elites who privilege order over justice.

Even so-called peacebuilding missions, especially in the Middle East and North Africa, which have been undertaken by Western nations, have now become a rarity. Often, these were primarily military interventions, which were designed to promote a more open democratic way of life for citizens in conflict-ridden countries; however, in efforts to establish peace and a sense of domestic harmony, the results were hardly satisfactory due to the complexities of tribal customs, ethnic disparities, and religious beliefs. In some instances, religious-minded groups resented Western intervention even while continuing to exercise their authority over the populace at the expense of justice and social cooperation. There are other cases where government-led peacebuilding endeavors were carried out as examples of top-down pacification. Many of these have been initiatives with the expressed purpose of keeping a certain group in power and preventing opposition groups from exercising their rights. As a result, several ethnic groups may no longer seek recognition but complete autonomy.

Regardless of contemporary peacemaking or peacebuilding attempts and how these conflicts have been cast in the name of social order and political stability, it remains that such efforts can be characterized by their ethnonational underpinnings. Brenner (2022) posited, "Since the end of the Cold War, Western interventions have become increasingly rare in Asia, especially in the region's eastern parts," and he added, "the role of international actors is extremely limited in most peacebuilding" (p. 354). The end of the Cold War saw the competing ideologies of democracy versus communism no longer in play as they once were when the world's two superpowers—the United States and the former Soviet Union—sought hegemony over the region. Ethnonationalism versus ethnocentrism has now become the new Cold War rhetoric. The push for political autonomy rather than political recognition is what confronts South Asia today.

Is it then a useful dialogue to suggest that John Dewey's (1938) constructivist ideas will have any impact on peacebuilding philosophies, or is it more like threading global solutions through the eye of a needle? Are there realistic possibilities that can be formulated for paradigm shifts that would encourage peacebuilding efforts and a focus on human development rather than repeated conflict and despair? Autesserre (2017) stated,

"Admittedly, although foreign actors [i.e., the International Fellowship of Reconciliation, the Women's International League for Peace and Freedom, and the American Friends Service Committee] routinely contribute to conflict resolution, peacebuilding efficacy relies primarily on the actions, interests, and strategies of domestic entities" (p. 115). What lessons can peace and justice advocates working in conflict zones in various parts of the world, not only in South Asia, the Middle East, and Southeast Asia, but also in Africa today, learn from Dewey's peace education theories, and how might they adapt them to their own context?

The Possibilities of Other Pathways: Dewey as an Early Constructivist

The constructivist ideological foundation of Dewey's democratic philosophy for peace and justice has been largely ignored in favor of ethnocratic state building; it is a policy that seeks to bridge the gap between the postcolonial state establishment and a national rule insisting upon assimilation and centralization. What has occurred is not the implementation of Dewey's outlook for peaceful stability, but emergent resistance and continuous conflict. What peacemakers may want to consider is Dewey's call for social action—one that creates new pathways for encouraging positive interaction between those societies' inhabitants and the surrounding people and environment. In keeping with Dewey's educational ideas for promoting peace, is it possible for policymakers to implement what he advocated in terms of human development and quality of life improvement? Dewey's ideas for peace education complement the views of many current policymakers, who favor peacebuilding efforts for transformative change as opposed to previous attempts aimed at peacekeeping and maintaining the existing social order.

Dewey's Constructivist Theories for Understanding and Cooperation

To appreciate Dewey's role in peace education for social and political change, it is instructive to explain his constructivist approach to knowledge and understanding. According to Dewey, knowledge of how to act and conduct oneself responsibly is largely influenced by environmental factors. How one acquires knowledge is predicated on an intervention in which an individual responds to external, independent factors. This view was postulated in his famous 1896 essay, *The Reflex Arc Concept in Psychology*. In every case, Dewey perceives that reflection is a secondary reaction to the level of action required to address environmental stimuli. Which is important when dealing with issues such as violence, conflict, and social injustice. Dewey maintained that utilizing knowledge based on experienced objectivity is less effective than basing future actions on knowledge derived from the current situation (Dewey, as cited in Bowers & Boydston, 1972).

One of Dewey's principle arguments for addressing the social contradictions impacting knowledge and education is that parents and teachers can be examples of the main impediment to creative intelligence because they continuously try to influence and change their children—or students— thereby discouraging independent thinking. He maintained that there did not exist a set of guidelines or curriculums that would permit educators to encourage the desired changes in their students. Dewey's constructivist theory was necessary for allowing students to engage in elaborate and controversial topics needed to move society forward and away from entrenched habits and customs. Mason (2017) posits that "Dewey's perspective offers clues for how the strong opinions of a polarized culture can be used by incisive educators to better cultivate open-mindedness" (p. 49). Providing thoughtful comments and encouraging open discussions are suggested pedagogies. When it came to the problem of war and peace, Dewey's constructivist theories as well as strategies remained relevant to the problems facing the world today.

As pointed out in *John Dewey: America's Peace-Minded Educator* (2016), World War I proved instrumental in the development of his peace education theories. "A fair way... to estimate the post-war psychology," Dewey (1918) wrote, "is to take the spontaneous emotional predictions called out by the pressure of war and reverse them" (Dewey, as cited in Boydston, 1981, p. 112). "To state some of the human reactions from war," Dewey assessed, "...will teach us that reliance upon such undisciplined desires is one of the chief reasons why the course of events has in the past frustrated the ardent hope of men in the great crises of human history" (p. 116). What troubled Dewey was the detrimental impact of war on the democratic way of life, which he insisted was a crucial instrument for establishing more peaceful societies.

Democracy as a Way of Living and Its Relationship to Schooling

The ideal of democracy was the foundation supporting Dewey's constructivist approach to peacemaking. He considered it a social ideal and ethic that was considerably more than a form of government or even a political process. It was a way of life and how our actions should be governed. "To say that democracy is *only* a form of government," he wrote, "is like saying home is a more or less geometrical arrangement of bricks and mortar; that the church is a building with pews, pulpit, and spire" (Dewey, 1888, p. 240). The analogy between a form of government and structural arrangements belies the true meaning of democracy. These observable, concrete buildings represent more than living spaces or houses of worship, just like democracy is "infinitely more" than how society is governed. Thus, democracy, as he defined it, is a method of social self-realization for the individual in the community, which inevitably involves the equal self-realization of every other person.

According to Dewey (1888), a democratic community should be the "sole way of living" for all citizens. It was the basis for the "creation of a freer and more human experience in which all share and to which all contribute" (as cited in Bernstein, 1967, pp. 183–184). Dewey looked upon democracy in terms of his own Hegelian sympathies. He believed that democracy was an internally active social organism in which the individual citizen defined his objectives in terms of the social welfare of all its members. In many respects, democracy was a moral ideal for Dewey. It stood as a symbol for shared experience, human understanding, and cooperation.

Fostering this shared experience and developing human understanding and cooperation, Dewey maintained, could only be achieved through the educational process. Dewey's views about education highlight his constructivist theories on peacemaking. His philosophy of pragmatism was tied to experimentalism. He understood that the effects of schooling had to be judged against some standard of progress in life's experiences. As a pragmatist, he comprehended that his function in academia is to affect the here and now, to examine life in the present, and not as some transcendental experience.

Being a philosopher and teacher, Dewey considered it necessary to focus on the behavioral aspects of the here and now and to foster the kind of intelligent conduct that generates social progress. In that vein, he insisted that the whole child must be educated, not just his or her intellect (mind). Thus, he began to encourage a comprehensive, interdisciplinary curriculum that was activity-based with respect to experience. Simply put, he considered the school the engine of democracy, emphasizing the value of shared experience and integrating values, outcomes, and solving problems that solidify the people as a democratic nation.

Socialized Intelligence

The achievement of a social democracy was also based on justice and human cooperation, according to Dewey. Perhaps the first inkling of Dewey's attempt to formulate some type of social policy promoting the achievement of a democratic way of life through nonviolent principles—cooperation and mutual service—can be found in his writings about the child and curriculum as well as the relationship of schools to society. Perhaps it was not completely formulated at the time, but the intent and message became clear, especially when making the classic distinction between learning and doing. He proclaimed that "The divorce between the intellectual and the moral must inevitably continue in our schools (in spite of the efforts of individual teachers) as long as there is a divorce between learning and doing" (Dewey, 1897, p. 58). To unite learning and doing was essential, for it would then "go along with the more organic ethical relationships involved in methods of activity that would afford opportunities for reciprocity, cooperation, and mutual service" (Dewey, 1897, p. 60).

Dewey (1902) argued that "socialized intelligence" implies the "sharing of the intellectual and spiritual resources of the community." This is "the very meaning of the community," he insisted, and he suggested the dimensions for children to become members of a democratic society and delineated what they should study, including science, art, history, methods of inquiry, and communication, along with "habits of industry, perseverance, and, above all, serviceableness" (Dewey, as cited in Boydston, 1976, pp. 92–94). According to Dewey (1897), schools should empower students and consider the best interests of the community.

The focus on education highlights two key interpretations. First, schools should play a vital role when it comes to greater appreciation for tolerance and cultural respect. As Dewey (1916) wrote in *his magnum opus, Democracy and Education,* "The intermingling in the school of youth of different races, differing religions, and unlike customs creates for all a new and broader environment" (p. 21). Secondly, schools are an integral part of a society, and as "society becomes more enlightened, it realizes that it is *not* responsible for transmitting and conserving the whole of its existing achievements". Rather, it should transmit only those attributes that make for a better society, and "the school is its chief agency for the accomplishment of this end" (p. 20).

Another important component of Dewey's constructivist approach to peacemaking can be found in his vision of education, as it connects to fostering a cooperative society. The use of "serviceableness" represented a key component of how a just and moral society should be constructed. What has been noticeably missing in many studies examining Dewey's contributions to progressive education is the failure to explore his definition of the moral responsibility of the school and those placed in charge of its daily operations: "The school is fundamentally," he argued, "an institution erected by society to do a certain specific work—to exercise a certain specific function in the maintaining of life and advancing the welfare of society" (Dewey, 1897, p. 58). Schools are social communities. According to Dewey, and in one instance of his rare, elucidated language, he shared,

> Interest in community welfare, an interest that is intellectual and practical as well as emotional—an interest...in perceiving whatever makes for social order and progress and for carrying these principles into execution— is the ultimate ethical habit to which all the special school habits must be related if they are to be animated by the breath of moral life. (Dewey, 1897, p. 63)

Critics might argue that social progress, as related to schools and their mission, would not have an impact on communities, states, and nations, but Dewey, throughout his life—and through his multiple trips abroad— tried persistently to make the case for the schools as microcosms of society and, therefore, the training ground for the future (Wang, 2007).

Moral Ends of Education

In almost all of Dewey's earlier writings, one can find constructivist evidence indicating his deep concern for developing the proper mental and moral attitudes necessary for establishing useful social relationships. In *Psychology*, for example, which was written in 1886, Dewey pointed out that "moral feeling is the only explicit social feeling. In moral feelings, man feels his true self to be one that comprehends possible relations to all men . . ." (Dewey, 1886, p. 336).

A few years later, in *Outlines of a Critical Theory of Ethics*, he elaborated further by arguing,

The moral end must include the ends of the various agents who make up society. It must be capable of constituting a social system out of the acts of various agents as well as an individual system out of the various acts of one agent; or, more simply, the moral end must be not only the good for all the particular acts of an individual but must be a *common good*—a good that is satisfying to one and satisfies others. (Dewey, 1891, p. 32)

The analogy between a surgeon performing an operation and Dewey's philosophy as applied to social aims, that Mr. Joseph Ratner points out in this regard, is particularly helpful: "The surgeon [Ratner said] must remove the tumor, that is certainly clear; but the *method* he uses, *how* he removes it, is equally important, for the removal and the method of removal cannot be separated; they continually interact, and it is the consequences of their interaction that determine the life and health of the patient." (Ratner, 1939, p. 40). When applied to Dewey's constructivist theory of education, what stands out is that the method used to achieve a particular goal depended upon one important factor: the creation of a civilized integration of intelligent life.

Dewey's aim in education was to fulfill the notion of a democratic society in which all shared the fruits of productivity while at the same time contributing to the welfare of all. For Dewey, education was supposed to be both a moralistic renaissance enabling all individuals to learn to live together peacefully as well as a practical application of life's everyday experiences to the body of common knowledge already acquired. Promoting the civilized integration of intelligent life should be one of the primary goals of schooling. In *The School and Society*, Dewey (1899) pointed out that "a society is a number of people held together because they are working along common lines, in a common spirit, and with reference to common aims" (p. 12).

Equally important, in *Moral Principles in Education*, Dewey (1909) assailed the educational system in America for its promotion of philistine ethical habits: His prior work in *The School and Society* (1899) similarly described, "The social work of the school is often limited to training citizenship, and citizenship is then interpreted in a narrow sense as meaning capacity to vote intelligently, disposition to obey laws, etc." He forcefully continued, "But it is futile to contract and cramp the ethical responsibility of the school in this way" (p. 12). This position becomes even clearer in *Schools of Tomorrow* (1915), which he co-authored with his daughter Evelyn. With unmistakable conviction, they argued: "The conventional type of education that trains children to docility and obedience and to the careful performance of imposed tasks because they are imposed, regardless of where they lead, is suited to an autocratic society" (p. 218). Instead of creating an atmosphere of social harmony, they wrote, education had degenerated into a meaningless exercise in chauvinism. Education as a mode of social life that offered the best and deepest moral training was, according to Dewey, the only kind of learning conducive to a cooperative way of life.

Specifically, Dewey's peace education philosophy was derived from his own willingness to challenge the current state of teaching and the existing rigid formulas demanding discipline, obedience, and allegiance to the nation-state. Teaching solely for citizenship in lieu of fostering critical thinking was the dominant pedagogy. Even though Dewey believed that such social institutions as the home, local government, and church—rather than the school—were the basic force in shaping young minds, he did not agree with the opinion of more conservative-minded educators that the school must passively accommodate itself to external exigencies. He envisioned the school as a basis for energetic change. He argued that the school could indeed become a dynamic rather than a reflexive agency— one that would search out and reinforce positive ideological frameworks for reconstructing society.

This constructivist view acknowledges that society is capable of transforming itself while at the same time enabling each individual to realize his or her full potential in the process of change. Schools should be the key instrument for challenging the widely held perception that learning is nothing more than preparation for a useful occupation in order to put food on the table at the expense of one's mental capabilities. That current philistine outlook had to be discarded and dramatically revamped. The aim of education had to be conceived in a less exclusive way. "If we were to introduce into educational processes the activities that appeal to those whose dominant interest is to do and make," he said, "we should find the hold of the school upon its members to be more vital, more prolonged, and containing more of culture" (Dewey, 1899, p. 28). Education was more than a process of adjustment. It was a creative encounter between man and his environment that called for innovation and reform. Combining intellectual development—teaching independent thinking—with real-world experiences would be the best way to encourage social progress. To Dewey, education represented the most intelligent means for achieving his goal of a peaceful democratic world order (Dewey, 1899, p. 28).

Underlying Goal of Dewey's Lectures for Peace and Social Cooperation

It is quite possible to apply Dewey's views on peace education and peacemaking when addressing present-day conflicts. To do so requires a careful examination of Dewey's lectures and course teachings, which have largely gone unnoticed by most scholars. Rather, he is best known for his theories of pragmatism and as a leader in progressive education. In his 1902–1903 "Sociology of Ethics Course"—which many scholars consider the foundational cornerstone of his philosophy of instrumentalism—Dewey (1902–1903) wrote the following:

> The experimental verification of the ethical postulate is achieved through the reconstruction of the postulate itself. It is no longer the postulate that the individual as such will both contribute to and benefit from interest in the social good. It is the postulate that when individuals come into conflict, resolution is provided by reconstruction of the initially conflicting institutional of cultural processes in which they participate. (p. 15)

What Dewey's writings were interpreted to mean was that the issue of political, social, and economic conflict has the potential to be reconstructed for the benefit of all through the medium of learning. Such learning can be either in the classroom or through experience, as it is based on the development of moral awareness. Thus, social ethics "begins with the adjustment of the individual infant to his or her family and the subsequent continuation of this adjustment to larger social processes in the classroom and their subsequent experience." It is a lifelong process of learning since Dewey (1902–1903) concludes,

> Every particular individual is different from every other individual and every individual, is also 'the medium and bearer of social progress; and…he may come into conflict with social organization on the institutional side, which represents the formulation of the social process that has already been reached.' If education is anything, it is a conscious determination of social progress. (pp. 15-16)

More specifically, if education, which is designed to encourage cooperation over friction, is to serve the needs of society, it must be effective enough to reach the masses, not just the intelligentsia. "[T]there is a certain positive truth in the fact," Dewey wrote in his lecture course on ethics, "that civilized culture has to be renewed from below by persons who have not become too overweighted with the intellectual and ethical machinery." (p. 94) A valuable lesson, he noted, can be culled from examining the Russian anarchist Tolstoy's view of peace as a counterbalance to those who proclaim that military means are an ethical right predestined by an individual government's own desire to impose its views on the minds of its peoples. What a nation's government determines as positive and right may not necessarily square with what its citizens consider to be their moral and ethical beliefs, including their right to oppose war. Education is a pathway to individual growth and self-empowerment. The public, not the political establishment, should decide on such issues as waging military conflict or the suppression of civil liberties. In this interpretation, education leads the social direction.

In addition, as Dewey saw it, education is an extension of democratic ethics. It is the primary instrument for establishing the end: a democratic way of life guided by an ethical foundation that formulates a code of conduct aimed at resolving conflict. In "The ethical significance of democracy," Dewey posed the question in his December 10, 1902, lecture: what would that ethical conduct be? According to Dewey (1902–1903),

> It simply means that social conditions have gotten to the point where the dependencies, cooperations, and co-operations and the conflicts which have always been there and operative in determining the actual net value of experience have come out so clearly that people are forced to recognize them and deal with them, and that therefore they become more and more conscious standards, norms, and ideas in our actions. (p. 144)

Dewey's postwar lectures at Columbia during the 1920s also provide useful insights into his concern for the philosophical and educational perplexities of social cooperation and human understanding. They were conceived as effective and efficient techniques for social engineering. "Social philosophy," Dewey wrote in the syllabus for one of his courses, "is a technique for clarifying the judgments that are constantly passed of necessity upon social customs, institutions, laws, and arrangements, actual and projected" (Dewey, 1902-1903 – Philosophy 131–132, Social and Political Philosophy [Syllabus]). Insight into how Dewey sought to carry out his concept of peacemaking becomes explicit in one of his lectures for his course on social and political philosophy; in that lecture, he informed his students that the process of thought is, in actuality, a method for conscious social planning:

> No man knows what the morrow may bring forth. Yet what is wise today depends largely on what is going to happen tomorrow. Consider how much of our thinking is really an act of prevision in forming some kind of idea of what the sequence of events is going to be. In other words, how much of our thinking takes the form of planning and arranging what is now under our control with regard to future conditions and eventualities? Forecasting, anticipating, expecting, and planning for the future is one form of introducing continuity into experience. Dewey, J. (1902-1903) Philosophy 131-132, Social and Political Philosophy [Syllabus]

First and foremost, Dewey was a social philosopher. In his view, the primary function of philosophy was "to find an intelligent substitute for blind custom and blind impulse to habit and conduct" (Dewey, 1921, p. 125-126). It was his unique ability to make his philosophy "socially conscious", and as a teacher and professor, he believed that it was his duty to clarify students' thinking on society's problems. His lectures are a monument to that belief; they are an ample demonstration of his sincere conviction that philosophy and education serve no useful purpose in life unless they attempt to reconstruct one's thinking processes while at the same time aiding in the improvement of one's social conditions.

These lectures are important because they became the instrument for encouraging him to address the role of human nature and conduct. In 1922, Dewey published a rather astonishing work, *Human Nature and Conduct*, which was applauded by scholars and the general public at large. In this important study he observed that,

> There must be a change in the objective arrangements and institutions. We must work on the environment, not merely on the hearts of men...The world war is a bitter commentary on the nineteenth-century misconception of moral achievement—a misconception, however, which is only inherited from the traditional theory of fixed ends, attempting to bolster up that doctrine with aid from the 'scientific' theory of evolution. (Dewey, 1922, p. 111)

The critical insight Dewey provides is that environmental factors weigh heavily when positing constructive measures for changing habits of thought. How human nature guides one's conduct and how we think has largely been influenced by the environment. Dewey argued that it was possible to address how we can change the environment through intelligence rather than fall victim to the belief that human nature is some infallible construct responsible for inaction and moral paralysis. If all ends are fixed, then what difference would the means make? His work offers a compelling argument in favor of grassroots empowerment, an awareness of injustice and inequality as they currently exist in society, which can only be challenged when citizens themselves assume the responsibility for changing their own environments. It should not, however, be a top-down, mandated approach by elites or those in positions of power.

Grappling with Human Nature and Conduct to Propose a Peace Program

Turning attention to present troubles, the problem of war and social maladjustment, and seeking peaceful means to avoid future conflicts requires that educators and policymakers seek out and realize that "the chief means of continuous, graded economic improvement and social rectification lies in utilizing the opportunities of educating the young to modify the prevailing types of thought and desire" (Dewey, 1922, p. 89). What Dewey is arguing here is that education's responsibility is to provide learners with the appropriate habits of "flexible response", so when they enter adulthood, they will possess a disposition or mindset enabling them to develop a creative response to environmental changes necessary for mitigating violent impulses. At the same time, Dewey argued against theories treating human behavior as nothing more than an expression of instincts. Intelligence was a critical element in Dewey's social psychology, and he maintained that it was a collection of habits: "concrete habits do all the perceiving, recognizing, imagining, recalling, judging, conceiving, and reasoning that is done" (Dewey, 1922, p. 124).

Dewey's inspiration for writing his 1922 work, *Human Nature and Conduct,* came primarily from the views of the famous Harvard psychologist and philosopher, William James. One of the principle aims of this book was to address how education can be applied to the role of human nature and conduct. Whereas James' philosophical prescription for peace, as he explained it in his famous essay "A Moral Equivalent of War," was through national service in the form of physical labor for civic virtue, Dewey adapted it to the schools in the form of learning by doing in conjunction with the surrounding community (James, as cited in Ralph Barton Perry, 1967).

Like James, Dewey believed it was critical for schools to give students the ability to interact with their environment to improve it. As noted by historian Steven Rockefeller (1991) in his assessment of James' influence upon Dewey's thought, "The original and primary function of thought is the direction of practical action, solving problems, selecting means for the achievement of desired ends...." Rockefeller adds, "[I]deas and beliefs are understood to have an essentially instrumental function in guiding human activity through problematic situations to the realization of chosen purposes." (p. 198) By furthering James' "moral equivalent of war" in schools, Dewey believed it could generate a pragmatic assessment contingent upon "a new humanistic naturalism" in which an enlightened and educated army of students would be charged with fostering cooperation for communal building as the heroic good. In Dewey's own words:

> The very aim of the good man is itself a unification in thought, as the deed is in act, of the realities of the situation...In doing the deed, then, the universe of reality moves through him as its conscious organ, Hence the sense of the dignity and validity of the act—the essence of the religious consciousness. Hence the joy, the feeling of full life, and the peace, the feeling of harmonized force, which accompany the good act. (Dewey, as cited in Rockefeller, 1991, p. 202)

In *Human Nature and Conduct* (1922), Dewey encouraged students as citizens to develop the capacity for deliberation to combat routine and unintelligent habits and to stimulate original thought to address emergent situations. His work embodies a constructivist approach to peacemaking, one calling for imaginative intelligence to counter entrenched habits of mind such as acceptance of the custom of war when settling disputes. Turning "the mind of man to a tenable theory of progress" (p. 144) when dealing with the problems of war and social conflict.

Dewey pointed out that teaching science, art, and commerce could be compelling factors that make it possible for people living in different countries to cooperate with each other, thus making the world more interdependent. In terms of peace education, the lesson that still applies to this day remains Dewey's call for "a new movement in education to reserve what was socially most useful in the national heritage and to meet the issues of the emerging international society." (Curti, 1967, p. 1109)

Dewey's 1920s lectures, books, and articles related to world peace contained valuable ideas for seeking ways to minimize conflict in the world today (Howlett & Cohan, 2016). The constructivist nature of peace education should be based upon six fundamental principles Dewey established: (1) building a democratic community not defined by political prejudices; (2) teaching cooperation among local groups as part of the national mandate; (3) creating an environment based upon moral sensitivity aimed at eliminating ethnic and racial differences; (4) promoting critical thinking as an instrument to resolve future differences by examining current problems preventing communal cooperation; (5) empowering self-esteem and independent thought to challenge established modes of national behavior; and (6) appreciation and respect for local customs and cultural values. These principles were the basis for building a trusting community, one that was completely compatible with Dewey's (1923) environmental approach to social consciousness.

Supporting an International Organization for World Peace

It is these fundamental principles that led to his strong support for the establishment of the United Nations (UN) at the start of the new atomic age and only a few years prior to his death. He was outspoken regarding the proposed economic, social, and cultural agency—part of the UN—and he wrote two lengthy essays in support, which were both published: "Democracy in a World of Tensions: A Symposium Prepared by UNESCO" (Dewey as cited in McKeon & Rokkan, 1951) and "The Cleavage in Our Culture: Studies in Scientific Humanism in Honor of Max Otto", a fellow philosopher and friend of Dewey's. (Dewey as cited in Burkhardt, 1952). Both essays were largely expositions of his previous thoughts and reiterations of former writings. In each instance, a strong defense of the democratic culture premised on individual freedoms was the centerpiece of his message.

In particular, the United Nations Economic, Scientific, and Cultural Organization (UNESCO) publication emphasized support for cultural peace and political cooperation. While Dewey related the reasons for his optimistic stance in regard to the establishment of the UN and its underlying principles, he noted with a cautionary tone that the "Breakdown of traditional ways of dealing with conflict between nations is without doubt a large factor in bringing UNESCO into being". (Dewey, as cited in Boydston, 1989, p. 400) Nevertheless, "For long historic periods, recourse to armed conflict was successful in at least keeping the peace for a time, though it did not do away with the division of interests that generates war." (p. 400). Still, there remained an element of hope in UNESCO's work in "an effort to substitute the method of intelligence for that of force in arriving at agreement among national states" and "that it offers the peoples of the world a symbol of what is now desirable and of what may become an actuality in the future" (p. 400).

Dewey believed that the establishment of UNESCO represented a practical implementation that would put in place many of his peace education ideals. He did understand that peace has to be much more than simply the absence of war. The UN agency was an extension of his views on "conjoint communicative experience." In his view,

> As far as the work of UNESCO stands as a symbol of approach by the method of intelligence to the problems of international relationships, Dewey argued, "it also holds and sets forth the method that each several people needs to deal with problems and issues that are not exclusively their own but which it bears the primary responsibility for meeting. Responsibility for dealing with the sources of internal troubles that are due to rapid industrialization now rests most directly upon democracies of the older political type; they are the people with the longest experience of industrialization. (Dewey, as cited in Boydston, 1989, p. 406)

The key to peace may rest upon the principles of democracy, and many believed then that it was up to the United States to lead the way. As a political democracy where all citizens participate, examples of freedom are reflected for all, as expounded by Dewey. As a way of life, democracy encourages the free marketplace of ideas for fostering mutual cooperation and commitment to the community at large. Peace as a process starts from the bottom up, and that is what the political foundations of democracy should imply. It should be the dynamic principle applicable to every region now marked by turmoil, instability, and persistent violence.

How Current Peace Educators Have Promoted Dewey's Lessons

Are there lessons from current practitioners of peace education who draw upon Dewey's constructivist theories that are applicable to the current world situation? Certainly, such contemporary appreciation for Dewey's ideas about peace engenders a complete understanding of the "full social ends of education," which Dewey (1916) proclaimed in his magnum opus, *Democracy and Education.* What do they maintain about the importance of Dewey's environmentalist approach when it comes to sustaining societies' approach to the self-development of individuals necessary for the achievement of civic virtue?

One scholar, Regina Cortina (2011), maintains that Dewey's ideas were a powerful social force, calling into question the agency of the nation-state in fulfilling its role as an instrument of democratic openness. According to Cortina, the "full social ends of education" (p. 1196) embraced the notion of peaceful cooperation and equality among nations. This philosophy was not designed to strengthen the potential influence of any nation-state so that it could dominate or invoke power over other nations. She correctly notes that Dewey envisioned schools as social institutions designed to encourage young children to learn how to live and interact in their communities and, in a larger sense, "support the participation of people in local and national communities." In terms of our own contemporary outlook, Cortina applauds Dewey's insights for the current "ways in which social movements are shaping education in their quest for more fully realized forms of citizenship" (p. 1211). Where Dewey's educational theories still apply is the view that "Collective action leads to expanded definitions of citizenship and thus to a flexible education model that permits multiple national identities, encompassing a citizenship that is multilingual and multiethnic, even transnational in scope" (p. 1211). In Cortina's estimation, Dewey's emphasis on the full social ends of education in a democracy empowers social movements such as peace, which are collective action mechanisms for defining and constructing a global community without violence.

Canadian peace educator H. B. Danesh (2011) similarly argues that "Dewey's focus on moral and ethical issues is related to his interest in peace-based education. Peace is essentially a moral or spiritual state with social and political expressions. Therefore, peace education requires attention to moral and spiritual issues" (personal communication to Charles F. Howlett, January 22, 2013). In his estimation, Dewey's contribution to the study of peace was in advocating "a transnational perspective in which the best attributes of all societies came together to form a broader ideological base for the world" (personal communication to Charles F. Howlett, January 22, 2013). Peace studies scholar James Page (2008) also points out that the essential question in terms of Dewey's peace education contributions is, "Can peace, what we might describe as the action of interacting harmoniously and cooperatively with others, be regarded as a habit and one that may be encouraged through education?" He adds that "Such interaction does comply with the conditions of morality as suggested by Dewey" (p. 44).

African educator Moses Chikwe (2012) continues Page's line of argument by observing that Dewey's educational ideology,

> ....was central to the formation and shaping of a democratic nation by forming in the citizen-subject the moral responsibility of living with others and contributing to the upkeep of the nation. He already signaled the role of education in forming in everyone the idea of global citizenship by inviting us to look beyond the frontier of the nation. Hence, in educating the young, we are not just concerned with the national spirit but with the entire human community (global village). (p. 17)

And to that end, scholar Edward Brantmeier (2010) reinforces Chikwe's position, noting that:

> congruent with some aspects of peace education, this problem-based learning of Dewey requires exploration of real-world issues to forge real-world solutions. Peace education, aimed at alleviating various forms of violence (direct, cultural, and structural), has inherently been responsive to different forms of violence expressed in situated historic contexts and has morphed and changed with pressing issues facing humanity and the planet. (personal communication to Charles F. Howlett, April 4, 2013.)

Collectively, all these contemporary scholars agree that Dewey's constructivist philosophy remains relevant and applicable for addressing present-day conflicts. One of Dewey's more important contributions to the peace education debate is that we continue to overlook the distinction between nationalism and nationality. What these contemporary educators have drawn upon is Dewey's constructivist view that teaching for citizenship should not be based on the artificial ideal of nationalism—a political construct that largely evolved in the aftermath of World War I—but that of nationality—appreciation for cultural and ethnic diversity not tied to specific geographic boundaries. Dewey was correct when he argued that nationalism is a politically-made ideology created to solidify geographical demarcations, while nationality reinforces the concept of humankind as one. It strikes at the very heart of his environmental argument. Simply put, place the global village above the national spirit.

It is also important to keep in mind that these educators are reinforcing Dewey's constructivist approach to peace education by insisting that peace is a social movement requiring citizens to develop habits of mind necessary for creating social, economic, and racial equity. There is an emerging consensus among peace educators that the resolution of local conflicts is crucial to building peace (Autesserre, 2017; 2022). This is the pathway needed to prevent future wars and violence. These educators are following Dewey's lead, insisting that the end to violence and warfare in zones of conflict cannot rest solely with national leaders, vested elites, or even outside peace groups that try to impose their own ideas and policies. Many believe peace must germinate at the grassroots level, where the local inhabitants decide for themselves what is best for the society at hand. This is what local schooling and educators must seek to accomplish—teaching that rejects top-down, state, and outside interference. An education that finally places nationality over nationalism.

Conclusion

Given these observations in support of Dewey's peace education construct, can it be argued that the United Nations views on sustainability are appropriately suitable to the eminent philosopher's position as found in *Democracy and Education*? According to Dewey, "It is not enough to teach the horrors of war and to avoid everything that would stimulate international jealousy and animosity." Can this notion be a foundational guardrail and instructive in the resolution of global conflict, especially in the face of persistent violence? Dewey adds, "The emphasis must be put upon whatever binds people together in cooperative human pursuits and results, apart from geographical limitations" (p. 98). The compatibility between using education and furthering democratic ideals could not be clearer when developing an approach to social life based on harmony.

What may now be considered is how to apply Dewey's constructivist theories of peace education in ways that transform the current developmental models as well as recognize existing environmental problems. For those interested in building peace, can there be a focus on similar values as bridges to different ideologies? Dewey modeled a quest for a peaceful world, and can this lens be used to counteract conflict in South Asia and other regions throughout the world? Dewey's views do encourage a pathway for establishing a new model that enables a more harmonious relationship between nature and humanity. In other words, creating common goals aimed at minimizing conflict with many tribal villagers as well as state-imposed ethnocratic policies. Perhaps the real value of reexamining Dewey's ideological views on peace and social action is the need for developing feasible programs between states and societies—and the groups within those societies—that are dynamic, resilient, inclusive, and cooperative to become models for conflict resolution.

References

Autesserre, S. (2017). International peacebuilding and local success: Assumptions and effectiveness. *International Studies Review, 19*(1), 114-132.

Autesserre, S. (2022). *The frontlines of peace: An insider's guide to changing the world.* Oxford University Press.

Bernstein, R. (1967). *John Dewey.* Washington Square Press.

Brantmeier, E. J., Lin, J., & Miller, J. P. (Eds.). (2010). *Spirituality, religion, and peace education.* Information Age Publishing.

Brenner, D. (2022). *Pacification in Asia from the end of the Cold War to the present: Illiberal peacebuilding.* In C. F. Howlett, C. P. Peterson, D. Buffton, & D. Hostetter (Eds.), *The Oxford handbook of peace history.* Oxford University Press. doi.org/10.1093/oxfordhb/9780197549087.001.0001

Burkhardt, F. (Ed.). (1952). *The cleavage in our culture: Studies in scientific humanism in honor of Max Otto.* Beacon Press.

Chikwe, M. (2012). Civic education and global citizenship: A Deweyan perspective. *In Factis Pax,* 6(1), 1-25.

Cortina, R. (2011). Globalization, social movements, and education. *Teachers College Record, 113*(6), 1196-1213.

Curti, M. (1967). John Dewey and nationalism, *Orbis,* 10, 1103-1119.

Danesh, H. B. (Ed.). (2011). *Education for peace reader*. EFP Press.

Dewey, J. (n. d.) *Syllabus for Philosophy 131-132* (Social and Political Philosophy,) Seth Low Library, Columbia University.

Dewey, J. (1886). *Psychology*. Harper & Bros.

Dewey, J. (1891). *Outlines of a critical theory of ethics.* Greenwood Press.

Dewey, J. (1897). *My pedagogic creed.* E. L. Kellogg & Co.

Dewey, J. (1888). *The ethics of democracy.* Andrews & Company Publishers.

Dewey, J. (1899). *The school and society.* University of Chicago Press.

Dewey, J. (1902-1903). *Sociology of ethics: The class lectures of John Dewey, 1,* 15-16; lecture 33, p. 12. Intelex Electronic edition.

Dewey, J. (1909). *Moral principles in education.* Houghton Mifflin Co.

Dewey, J. (1916). *Democracy and education.* Macmillan & Co.

Dewey, J. (1921). *Reconstruction in philosophy.* Henry Holt & Co.

Dewey, J. (1922). *Human nature and conduct.* Henry Holt & Co.

Dewey, J. (1923). The school as a means of developing a social consciousness and social ideals in children. *The Journal of Social Forces, 1*(5), 513-517. doi.org/10.2307/3005121

Dewey, J. (1938). *Experience and education.* The Macmillan Company.

Dewey, J. (1972). The reflex arc concept in psychology. In F. Bowers, & J. A. Boydston (Eds.), *The early works of John Dewey, 5, 1882-1898* (pp. 96-109). Southern Illinois University Press. (Original work published 1896)

Dewey, J. (1972). Ethical principles underlying education. In F. Bowers, & J. A. Boydston (Eds.), *The early works of John Dewey, 5,* (pp. 58-60). Southern Illinois University Press. (Original work published 1897)

Dewey, J. (1976). The school as a social center. In J. A. Boydston (Ed.), *The middle works of John Dewey, 2,* (pp. 92-94). Southern Illinois University Press. (Original work published 1902)

Dewey, J. (1981). The post-war mind. In J. A. Boydston (Ed.), *The middle works of John Dewey, 11, 1899-1924:1918-1919, Essays on China, Japan, and the war* (pp. 112-116). Southern Illinois University Press. (Original work published 1918)

Dewey, J. (1972). Discrediting idealism. In J. A. Boydston (Ed.), *The middle works of John Dewey, 11, 1899-1924: 1918-1919* (pp. 180-185). Southern Illinois University Press. (Original work published 1919)

Dewey, J. (1989). Democracy in a world of tensions. In J. A. Boydston, (Ed.), *Later works of John Dewey, 16,* (pp. 399-419). Southern Illinois University Press. (Original work published 1951)

Dewey, J., & Dewey, E. (1915). *Schools of tomorrow.* E.P. Dutton & Co.

Guzzini, S. (2018). *Hans J. Morgenthau and the three purposes of power.* Danish Institute for International Studies.

Howlett, C. F., & Cohan, A. (2016). *John Dewey: America's peace-minded educator.* Southern Illinois University Press.

James, W. (1967). The moral equivalent of war. In Ralph Barton Perry (Ed.), *Essays on faith and morals* (pp. 311-328). World Publishing Co.

Mason, L. (2017). The significance of Dewey's "Democracy and Education" for 21st-century education. *Education and Culture, 33*(1), 41-57.

McKeon, R., & Rokkan, S., (Eds.), (1951). Democracy in a world of tensions: A symposium prepared by UNESCO. University of Chicago Press. https://unesdoc.unesco.org/ark:/48223/pf0000133513

Morgenthau, H. J., & Thompson, K. W. (1985). *Politics among nations: The struggle for power and peace* (4th ed.). Knopf.

Page, J. (2008). *Peace education: Exploring ethical and philosophical foundations.* Information Age Publishing.

Ratner, J., (Ed.), (1939). *Intelligence in the modern world.* Modern Library.

Rockefeller, S. C. (1991). *John Dewey: Religious faith and democratic humanism*. Columbia University Press.

Wang, J. C-S. (2007). *John Dewey in China: To teach and to learn*. State University of New York.

Westoff, L. M., & Howlett, C. F. (2019). Peace history: Curricular challenges and innovative opportunities. *Journal of American History, 105*(4), 939-970.

A Century of the Interface between Vietnam and France on Education, Science of Humanities, and Anthropology

Doctor Dinh Hong Hai

Abstract*: After almost a thousand years of growth and development, the scholarly traditions of Vietnamese people, which were heavily influenced by Chinese civilization, began to crumble in the late 19th century. By the early decades of the 20th century, this bookish academia (known as 尋章摘句) had come to an end, with the last royal examination being held in 1919. So why did this thousand-year Confucius education come to an abrupt halt? This article aims to explore the impact of French academia on Indochina for over a century, which fundamentally changed the scientific thinking of Vietnam's intellectual class. This shift led to significant changes in the country's humanities sciences, including the development of anthropology throughout the 20th century.*

Keywords: *French academia, humanity, social formation, anthropology*

Introduction

Education serves not only as a bridge that connects civilizations throughout human history but also as the foundation for creating cultures. It acts as a seed that helps in the development of scientific knowledge across the globe. After the Enlightenment, Western education gained dominance over all the education systems that had ever existed in the world. This education quickly gained a leading position and was spread to all continents following the colonial conquest of great powers.

Today, scientific knowledge from Western civilization has influenced every aspect of social life across the world. Education systems, too, have followed the Western model, becoming a common approach in countries across the globe. General education has become a mandatory condition for all countries' educational systems, regardless of their size or economic status. Though there may be variations between undergraduate and graduate education in different countries, they all align with the direction of the universal scientific achievements of humanity, led by the West.

For centuries, Vietnam was heavily influenced by Chinese Confucian education, but by the end of the 19th century, the country had not yet developed its true science. Despite centuries of scholarship spanning the dynasties from Lý-Trần to Lê-Nguyễn, Vietnamese academics had only managed to produce notes, chronicles, and preliminary research, with no theoretical or methodological advancements. However, after just a few decades of absorbing Western learning through French education, Vietnam became one of the academic centers of the world with advanced education in the first half of the 20th century at that time, such as the École française d'Extrême-Orient (EFEO), Indochina University, Institut Indochinois pour l'étude de l'homme (IIEH), etc. These "Westernized" academic centers created illustrious names in the world of science such as Alexandre Yersin (infectious diseases), Leopod Cadiere (religious studies), Paul Pelliot, Henri Maspero (Sinology), Gustave Emile Dumoutier (art), and Madeleine Colani (archaeology).

Many of the academic centers and famous scholars mentioned above were associated with the humanities. The French colonial exploitation had a significant focus on the human factor, making Indochina and Vietnam the ideal places to test new research methods and conduct research related to humans and human society. This academic background quickly influenced the high-level intellectual class in Vietnamese society, completely changing their perception of scholarship, science, and education. They realized that the traditional way of learning through rote Confucian memorization, "bookish academia" (尋章摘句), was no longer suitable for the general development of the world, and thus, there was a need for educational reform in the country.

During the early 20th century, several reformers attempted to lead the Vietnamese people towards a new path by incorporating Western learning and education. Nguyễn Trường Tộ, Phan Chu Trinh, and Phan Bội Châu were among the prominent advocates of this idea. Their progressive ideas influenced the intellectual class of society and gave rise to a new group of intellectuals who had a nationalistic spirit but held Westernized thought. This group promoted educational reform according to the Western model and paved the way for a revolutionary transformation in Indochina society, particularly in Vietnam. This transformation marked a significant shift from the Confucian education model to the modern Western education model, with emphasis on the science of the humanities as the key. One of the most notable outcomes of this transformation was the birth of anthropology in Vietnam, which is clear evidence of the influence of French education on the formation of the science of the humanities in accordance with the Western model.

1. The Interface between Vietnam and France on Education and Academia

Similar to trains and automobiles on road and rail transport, French academia functioned as a "vehicle" of science introduced to Indochina to serve the French's colonial exploitation and as "the introduction of the Enlightenment spirit in Vietnam at the beginning of the 20th century" (Nguyễn Phương Ngọc, 2014: 49). Though this completely new type of "vehicle" was unfamiliar to the majority of local people, its efficiency was quickly popularized. Since then, "Vietnamese intellectual elites and businessmen became really close to contemporary Western education" (Nguyễn Thụy Phương, 2018: 84), creating "the turn of the Millennium" of Vietnamese scholarship (Nguyễn Thuyết Phong, 2018: 96).

For several decades only, French academia became an indispensable part of modern academia in Vietnam, especially the science of humanity, advancing the latter into the region's leading, cutting-edge academia. This is due to the changing mindset of the local radical intellectual class from a Confucius education to a Western one. Ignoring all political factors, this article will focus on the role of scientific theory and methodology that changed scientific thinking in both France and its colonies after the French Third Republic. Thereby, comparing human development and social formation in Vietnam based on French anthropology to that in the world in present-day Vietnam.

If we were able to conduct large-scale comparative research on academia, we could see enormous differences between Vietnam and the Western world over the past thousands of years. One of the largest differences, up to the late 19th century, is the synthetical thinking of the Oriental ideas and the analytical thinking of the Occidental ideas. Vietnamese education synthesized and recorded predecessors' experiences into textbooks and canons for by-heart learning, under the control of a king in accordance with the Chinese Confucian model. Meanwhile, in Western education, learners make academic notes and analyze the nature of things and phenomena. This method has been applied since the time of ancient Greco-Roman civilization. When this education influenced such cultures in the Sinosphere like Korea, China, Japan, or Vietnam, it made a breakthrough that completely transformed the Confucian societies formed by "a mixture of religions that is acutally some political apparatus, because the government and theocracy are tied together" (Nguyễn Xuân Thọ, 2018: 39)[1].

Following Western missionaries and traders to Vietnam, the process of academic infiltration, exchange, and transformation began in the 17th century. By the mid-20th century, Vietnamese education was completely dominated by the theoretical and methodological systems of Western academia. Since then, it has created a great transformation in which Vietnamese academia has been forced to change towards "Westernization." Thanks to its strategic geo-political location in Asia, Vietnam has become a hub of East-West academic interaction over the past century. Since the 17th century, when the first-stage scholars (for example, Francisco de Pina, Alexandre de Rhodes, Charles B. Maybon, Jean-Baptiste Tavernier, William Dampier, John Barrow, etc.) set foot on this land, culture and education in Vietnam have so far undergone a wave of "Westernization" for centuries, with deep French imprints.

Receiving a scientific background from the West, Vietnamese people quickly realized the great values, theories, and methodologies coming from that world. This was also the key for Vietnamese intellectuals in the early 20th century to open the door so that Vietnamese academia could get out of the restrictions of Confucianism and the giant shadow of Chinese civilization to revive the country. Since then, the Confucian education in Vietnam (which was based on *ký, chí, biên, lục* (記, 誌, 編, 錄/ notes and descriptions, or at higher levels *bình, chú* (評, 注/ comment, explanation), had new instruments (methodologies) and means (theories). It is possible to assert that, if train and automobile are extremely effective means of

---

[1] The way of selecting talents through literature, poetry and learning by heart the so-called "sages' canons" is clearly no longer appropriate… This Confucius regime of education and examination was popular in four countries, but Japan renovated the country in 1868, China abandoned it in 1900, Korea in 1894, and Viet Nam in 1919 (according to the book *Khoa cử Việt Nam* [System of former competition-examinations] by Nguyễn Thị Chân Quỳnh, Literature Publishing House, 2007).

transport, the methodology and theory of Western academia are particularly effective means for the modern academia of Vietnamese people.

This was the precondition for radical intellectuals (for example, Phan Chu Trinh, Phan Bội Châu, Nguyễn Trường Tộ, Nguyễn Tư Giản, Nguyễn Lộ Trạch, Phạm Phú Thứ, Phan Thanh Giản, and others) to advocate the policy of national renewal based on advanced Western education. In this period, among ideas of renewal, "learning" became a national-level importance, represented by the tendency of *modernization* (duy tân - 維新) advocated by Phan Chu Trinh with the motto

"Khai dân trí, chấn dân khí, hậu dân sinh."[2] Successive generations of Westernized intellectuals absorbed and applied new knowledge from the West to Vietnamese academia quickly and effectively.

Only after the first few decades of the 20th century did the cause of academicization in line with the Western model dramatically progress. As a result, in Indochina, with Vietnam as a hub, major academic centers were formed, with well-known scientists, both French and Vietnamese, working at École Française d'Extrême-Orient (EFEO), Université Indochinoise, and Institut Indochinois pour l'étude de l'homme (IIEH), such as George Cœdès, Pierre Huard, Paul Levy, Paul Guilleminet, Leopod Cadiere, Henri Maspero, Gustave Emile Dumoutier, Madeleine Colani, Paul Pelliot, Đỗ Xuân Hợp, Nguyễn Thiện Lâu, Nguyễn Văn Khoan, Nguyễn Văn Huyên, Vũ Đinh Tụng, and others. These scholars made significant contributions to converting Indochina into an academic center of the "France Far East" (as described by Doumer, 2018: 620).

After Vietnam regained its independence in 1945, the country's science and education moved to a new stage with two separate branches: the first branch followed the Soviet Union in the north, and the second branch followed the West in the south. Though labeled as "colonial" academia, the French imprints are still deeply rooted in almost all modern scientific and educational institutions of an independent Vietnam, even to this day,

---

[2] *Khai dân trí*: Abandoning the bookish way of studying, opening schools for popularizing the modern writing system of Latin script for Vietnamese language (*chữ quốc ngữ*) and practical scientific knowledge, and eliminating lavish customs; *Chấn dân khí*: Awakening the spirit of patriotism and self-reliance, making the masses aware of their own rights and obligations, so as to escape from the venom of autocracy; *Hậu dân sinh*: Developing economy, setting up associations and unions for business, maintenance, production and consumption of domestic goods.

of which the most prominent is France's science of humanity. Thanks to that foundation, in the post-Đổi-mới period—after 1986—contemporary science of humanity in general and anthropology in Vietnam, in particular, have experienced a boom of development in the context of international scientific integration. This research will evaluate the role and position of the French academia as well as of humanities scientists during this stage of the development of Vietnamese science. Thereby, it will provide specific proofs of the development of contemporary Vietnamese academia based on the foundations laid by the French a century ago.

2. The Formation of the French Sciences of Humanities in Vietnam

Before the French social sciences and humanities flourished in Indochina, right within France, this academia had undergone a big transformation right after the French Third Republic. Theoretically, the French science of humanity had gone from evolutionism, determinism, ethnocentrism, and many other ideological movements to functionalism, structuralism, relativism, positivism, and so on. Methodologically, that science had also changed from an "armchair" study to "field" research.

In the 20th century, the study of humanity in colonial Indochina underwent significant changes. Previously influenced by views of evolutionism, determinism, and ethnocentrism, the policy of "civilizing" colonial peoples, which had been imposed through various governance and scientific measures, shifted to a perspective of relativism. This new perspective emphasized respect for the subject and recognition of indigenous cultural identities. Additionally, French Indochina became a major research and fieldwork site for French scientists in the Far East, allowing for the implementation of new methods and modern scientific and educational institutions. As a result, Hanoi became France's academic capital in Indochina. The transfer of theory and methodology from EPHE to EFEO marked an important starting point for this process.

From EPHE to EFEO

The establishment of EPHE (École Pratique des Hautes Études), administered by Sorbonne Université in 1886, was a great leap in French academia. This project was conducted by a number of famous scientists, as noted by Bauberot: "In the four Oriental Studies Departments, there are two divisions about the Near East and two divisions about Asia. The

Indian religions were carried out by Sylvain Levi beginning in 1887, and the Far Eastern religions were practiced by Leon de Rosny" (1992: 234). "From EPHE to EFEO" marked a major move of the French science of humanity from "armchair" to "fieldwork" because, only 14 years after the birth of EPHE, a similar scientific institution, the École Française d'Extrême-Orient (EFEO), was founded in 1900 in Viet Nam.[3] This was the foundation for the science of humanity in Indochina to develop into a modern and radical science.

Following the establishment of EFEO, the French built the Université Indochinoise in 1906, the Musée Albert Sarraut in Phnom Penh in 1905 (present-day National Museum of Cambodia), the Musée Henri Parmentier in 1919 (present-day the Museum of Cham Sculpture, Đà Nẵng), the Musée Khải Định in 1923 (nowadays the Huế Museum of Royal Fine Arts), the Musée Finot in 1926 (now the Viet Nam National Museum of History), the Musée Blanchard de la Brosse in 1929 (now the Museum of History in Hồ Chí Minh City), the Museum of Archaeology in Thanh Hóa in 1936, and the Indochinese Institute of Human Studies in 1937. It is possible to say that these important institutions of science and education laid a "cornerstone" for modern Vietnamese academia. Since then, the French system of academic theory and methodology has been deployed both in France and Vietnam. That foundation helped French and Vietnamese scientists gain development breakthroughs and make Vietnam a key academic center with many great contributions to the academic world.

Under the direction of archaeologist Louis Finot, former Vice Director of EPHE and the first Director of EFEO, the agency conducted much archaeological research and obtained significant results. Large-scale explorative excavations in Indochina found archaeological vestiges of pre-historic people in Hòa Bình that shocked the archaeology circle and brought the name *Hoabinhian culture* to the world map of science. Then, the discovery of Đông Sơn culture was not only a long step forward for the science in colonial Indochina but also a great achievement of French scientists. In the south, the finding of the Mỹ Sơn Sanctuary of the Cham,

---

[3] On 15 December 1898, Indochinese Governor General Paul Doumer (1857-1932) signed the Decree on establishing the Mission archéologique permanente en Indochine. On 20 January 1900, Paul Doumer signed the Decree on renaming it École Française d'Extrême-Orient (EFEO) and officially recognized by French President Émile Loubet (1838-1929) in an ordinance on 26 February 1901. Louis Finot (1864-1935), former Vice Director of EPHE, became the first Director of EFEO.

together with excavations of Óc Eo and Funan cultures, made the French science of humanity in Indochina, led by the EFEO, a big center of science in Asia. It is research results of academic works during this period that helped the world recognize such names as *Dongson culture, Hoabinhian culture, Champa culture*, etc. This was a gap which the thousand-year Confucian academia in Vietnam was unable to fill due to the lack of theory and methodology.

In the transformation of science in Indochina, theoretical and methodological changes were the cause of great academic alterations during this period, including the use of theoretical foundations for new approaches to research subjects in the field. Here, the system of theories, methods, and research techniques, as well as modern scientific disciplines and views, mostly followed the models being implemented in France, such as laboratory science, data collection, practice, etc. A number of humanitarian works done in this period inherited outstanding scientific achievements after the French Third Republic; all took a purely scientific perspective, with the school's functions separated from the church.

Thanks to that radical system of theory and methodology, Vietnamese intellectuals could shift from their old approach of compilation or note-taking to new methods introduced from French science (separated from the previous Court-dominated work of noting classic references), becoming independent professional scholars. Some prominent intellectuals of this period (Huỳnh Tịnh Của, Thiều Chửu, Trương Vĩnh Ký, Phạm Văn Ký, Nguyễn Văn Huyên, Trần Văn Giáp, Nguyễn Khắc Khoan, and others) left classic scholarly works, such as *Đại Nam quốc âm tự vị* [Dictionnaire Anamite] by Huỳnh Tịnh Petrus Của, *Hán Việt Từ điển* [Sino-Vietnamese Dictionary] by Thiều Chửu, *Tìm hiểu kho sách Hán Nôm, Phật giáo Việt Nam từ khởi nguyên đến thế kỷ 13* [Understanding Sino-Nom Vietnamese Buddhist Textbooks from beginning to 13th century] by Trần Văn Giáp, etc. Their influence is still very great on the current generations of Vietnamese scientists.

The Change from "Colonial Civilization" to "Colonial Research"

In fact, the colonial civilizing[4] and exploitation by the French was a long-term planned strategy, as described by Animonier, to "develop the latent

---

[4] It can be considered as a cause of industrialization and modernization in the Indochinese colony rather than the political view of *civilizing* that "France became

resources – material and spiritual – of this land. At the same time, it is necessary to create stronger cultural ties than to use violence, so that in the long run, attachment to France and distant lands will one day flourish" (1889, 2018: 22). This process took place throughout Indochina, in which Vietnam was always a center due to its strategic position. The use of indigenous labor forces was a priority, so the study of Vietnamese people, both physically and culturally, was always on the agenda of the colonial government. It was these policies that formed a generation of Westernized Vietnamese intellectuals and French scientists who had a passion for Vietnamese culture and people. They were also the leading scholars who made great contributions to Vietnamese academia after the country regained its independence.

To boost their colonial civilization and the academicization of native intellectuals, French officials first had to rely on their humanity scientists to learn about the cultures of indigenous ethnic groups. Indochina was France's strategic area where, during the war, the updated French scientific theories and methods were experimented with. This was the root of the great advance of the humanities in Vietnam in comparison to other countries in the region. Many well-known French researchers arrived in Indochina, and a number of important studies of the then French academia were claimed in Indochina. Following missionaries from previous centuries, colonial scientists, both French and Vietnamese, continued to conduct long-term research on Vietnamese culture and society. Among scientists of this period, it is noteworthy to mention significant contributions in terms of theory and methodology made by such scholars as Marcel Mauss, Paul-Levy, Levy-Bruhn (in France), Marcel Granet, Léopold Michel Cadière, George Condominas (Vietnamese ethnology), Édouard Mestre (Vietnamese religions), Nguyễn Thế Anh, and Daniel Hémery (Vietnamese history). Until now, their imprints are still profound in 21st-century Vietnamese academia. For those achievements, the influence of the French humanities foundations from big academic centers and the outstanding role of EPHE are undeniable.

---

an important messianic power that patronized the intellect and spirit beyond its borders and within other empires and powers" (Salon 1983: 32, cited by Nguyễn Thụy Phương 2019).

After a period of the costly military and political use to rule the colony,[5] along with the strong resistance from native people, the French government finally realized that their policy of violence-based "civilizing" in the early stages had gone wrong, turning French colonists into "invaders" and that their "civilizing" cause was misunderstood in a negative sense, both politically and scientifically. It was the time when studies on humanities played an extremely important role in colonial exploitation and the operations of French political institutions in Indochina were changed from protectionism (bảo hộ) to direct governance (trực trị) under the direction of General Governor Paul Doumer. From this point, the study on indigenous culture and people became one of the focuses of the *direct-rule* administration, creating a premise for the development of the French science of humanity in Indochina. Doumer himself was a famous scholar with numerous academic works.[6]

The Formation of the French Science of Humanities in Indochina

To create a "Far East capital of France", Doumer built a series of leading modern infrastructure in the region, with a transportation network of thousands of kilometers of road, railway, river and seaports, and other facilities to serve the administration. Among numerous achievements of this stage, the most prominent is that the Domer administration built Hanoi the first Asian city with electricity (Doumer 2018: 21).[7] To operate such a modern apparatus, the colonial government needed "modern people." This was the reason why many new decrees were issued to create a true science of the French Indochina, for "training indigenous employees and servants

---

[5] "From 1860 to 1895, the total expense reached to 750 million gold francs. Only in 1888, 35 million gold francs were spent on the army and 10 million on navy" (Nguyễn Xuân Thọ, 2018: 528).

[6] For two thirds of the century after regaining independence, the majority of Vietnamese people (including intellectuals) only know "chief colonist" Paul Doumer in a negative ideological perspective without knowing that he was an outstanding French scholar and politician who was elected President of France in 1931 and assassinated in 1932. His huge academic work (*L'Indo-Chine française: Souvenirs*), published by Thế Giới Publisher in 2018 in Vietnam, shows a different perspective of Doumer.

[7] The striking projects built in the early 20th century include Doumer Bridge (Long Biên) in Hà Nội, Tràng Tiền Bridge in Huế, Indochinese University, the Opera House and the Cathedral in Hà Nội, Notre Dame Cathedral in Sài Gòn. The north-south railway was even extended to Yunnan, China, with a total length of 2,400 km (Doumer 2018: 575).

for local admistrative apparatus or professional agencies under the General Government of Indochina" (Paul Beau, 1906, Decree No. 1514a. Article 9).

Apart from their administrative mechanisms, the French also placed importance on the science of humanity by building educational and scientific institutions and introducing eminent students from Vietnam to high schools, colleges, and universities in France. This was the first generation of Westernized intellectuals who were methodically trained at French schools and returned to Vietnam to serve the French apparatus of direct governance. Many of them were also the pioneers who helped create Vietnam's independent science after 1945. With the advancement of Western science of humanity in terms of theory and methodology, the French science of humanity in Indochina also changed quickly. Studying and training Indochinese people not only served the ruling mechanism but also aimed at a more important and "humane" mission: to have an insight into the people in the colony (Paul Beau, 1906, Decree No. 1514a).

In fact, the diversity of ethnic cultures and languages created numerous obstacles to the implementation of colonial policies. This was the reason why the French government had to send many leading scientists to Indochina in order to study this important area. And their research results went far beyond what the colonial government wanted. They were not only submitted research reports but also successfully conducted important academic projects.[8]

Since then, the French Indochina actually had an academic science of human beings (human studies), not only with research institutions but also with teaching facilities. The focus of teaching humanity science was the École supérieure des Lettres of the Université Indochinoise. Here, Oriental language and classical literature, history and geology of Far East countries, history of French and foreign literature, history of philosophy, and history of the arts were taught to residents of three Indochinese countries and even

---

[8] For example, Gourou with *Esquisse d'une étude de l'habitation annamite dans l'Annam septentrional et central*, Paris, EFEO 1936. *Les paysans du delta tonkinois*, Paris, EFEO, 1936. Colani with *L'âge de la pierre dans la province de Hoa Binh. Mémoires du Service Géologique de l'Indochine* 13, 1927. Cuisinie with *Les Mường: géographie humaine et sociologie*. Paris: Institut d'ethnologie, 1946. Condominas with *Nous avons mangé la forêt de la Pierre-Génie Gôo* (Hii saa Brii Mau-Yaang Gôo); *Chronique de Sar Luk, village mnong gar (tribu proto-indochinoise des Hauts-Plateaux du Viet-nam central)*, Paris, Mercure de France 1954, etc.

other Asian ones. It was from those institutions that an academic science on Indochinese people was born in Vietnam.

3. The Influences of the French Science of Humanities and Anthropology in Vietnam

Vietnam has a larger population and is more developed than Laos and Cambodia among the three Indochina countries. As a result, the French established important academic institutions in Vietnam's two largest cities, Hanoi and Saigon. In 1937, the Indochina Human Research Institute was founded in Hanoi, which played a significant role in developing the French science of humanities and anthropology in Vietnam. It contributed to the improvement of human studies in Vietnam based on contemporary French science and helped establish a separate branch of human science worldwide. Many leading ethnologists of the French science of humanities in the early 20th century were among the outstanding scholars in Indochina.

The French Science of Humanities in Vietnam

Apart from archaeology and sociology, ethnology was also a radical science in France, brought and applied in Indochina. Through Pierre Gourou's researches on people and geography, the French recognized a Southeast Asian "plant civilization" with numerous differences from the European civilization. From here, he learned about "peasants in the Tonkin delta" with irrationalism (duy tình) and small-holder characteristics, but their tropical farming knowledge was very valuable to the colonial government and academia (Gourou 1955, 1936). Meanwhile, French sociology, with the leading role of Durkheim, not only affected researchers in Europe and America but was also approached quite early by many Vietnamese scientists (for example, Trần Văn Giáp was one of Durkheim's students who graduated from EPHE).

Being used quite later than archaeology and sociology, French ethnology made a bold mark with research by Nguyễn Văn Huyên (a student of Marcel Mauss, Lucien Lévy-Bruhl, Marcel Granet, and Jean Przyluski) and Condominas (a student of André Leroi-Gourhan, Denise Paulme, or Marcel Griaule, Maurice Leenhardt). French ethnology was effectively exploited in statistics on demography, ethnoculture, and village culture in Vietnam. The deep imprints of French master ethnologists on these scholars not only created an important milestone for the Vietnamese academia but also widely spread within the Francophone community. In fact, if Bronislaw Malinowski, Franz Boas, and Margaret Mead were well-known field anthropologists in the English-language anthropological community, Nguyễn Văn Huyên and Condominas were also as famous in the Francophonie, especially in Indochina. Though their long fieldwork research could not be continued after the war broke out in Vietnam, their previous classical works are still greatly influential on Vietnam's anthropology to this day.

Nguyễn Văn Huyên's studies (recently collected in the two volumes, nearly 1,000-page Góp phần nghiên cứu văn hóa Việt Nam [Contribution to Vietnamese Studies]) showed a completely new approach to research on Vietnamese history and culture in the previous periods. That approach was also used by contemporary scientists in Europe, like Durkheim, Levi-Bruhn, Mauss in France, Malinowski, Evan-Pritchard in the UK, or Boas, Mead, and Benedict in the US; it was the methodological system for ethnology. Together with Nguyễn Văn Huyên, Condominas conducted field research in successive years on the M'nông Gar people in Vietnam's Central Highlands (similar to those of Malinowski in the Trobriand Islands). His important scientific works have been published in France and Vietnam (such as *Không gian xã hội vùng Đông Nam Á* [L'Espace social. À propos de l'Asie du Sud-Est, 1980], *Chúng tôi ăn rừng đá – thần Gôh* [Nous avons mangé la forêt de la Pierre-Génie Gôo 1954], etc. and translated into many other languages. His ethnological collections of thousands of artifacts have also been exhibited in France and Vietnam, with printed detailed indexes.

The deep imprints of ethnology, as mentioned above, provided the background for the French to take an important step towards establishing a comprehensive study of peoples in Indochina. This was the firm foundation for human studies or anthropology that covers *l'étude de l'homme* and *la science de l'humanité* in this colony. From French ethnology to French anthropology in Indochina, this was the clearest manifestation of the formation and development of human science and anthropology in Vietnam over the past century. Unfortunately, the fierce Indochinese wars from 1945 to 1954 and then from 1954 to 1975 prevented this foundation from further development, as expected by many scientists.

Science of "Studying Indochinese People"

Originally, the science of studying peoples in Indochina aimed at learning about the indigenous society and explaining why France's early military and political colonial policies encountered many obstacles. When this work was handed to scientists with profound academic and scientific foundations, it helped form an important scientific subject – human studies. Their research included not only reports to the protectionist government in favor of policy implementation but also world-known scientific works. This was the premise for boosting a scientific institution studying people in Indochina – Indochina Institute for Human Studies (Institut Indochinois pour l'étude de l'homme - IIEH).

On November 4, 1937, at the headquarters of the Institut Anatomique de Hanoi, a meeting of George Coedès, Vitor Goloubew, Jean-Yves Clayes, Louis Bezacier, Paul Lévy, Nguyễn Văn Tố, Trần Văn Giáp, Nguyễn Văn Khoan and Nguyễn Văn Huyên (EFEO); Pière Huard, Đỗ Xuân Hợp, Tôn Thất Tùng, Đào Huy Hách and Nguyễn Xuân Nguyên (Department of Anthropology, École de Médécine de Hanoi) decided to establish the Institut Indochinois pour l'étude de l'homme (IIEH) and draft the IIEH Statute, with operational principles adapted from the Statute of the French Institution of Anthropology (established in 1911). Then Indochinese General Governor J. Brévié signed *Decree 619 on February 3, 1938,* on the establishment of the institution and approving the statute.

With its principles and purposes, IIEH was France's first scientific center for human studies in Indochina and the world's first "research institute for studying Indochinese peoples". This was affirmed in Article 1 of the Statute: The goal of the IIEH in Indochina is to increase understanding of the people both physically and socially in the Far East. Then, the Museum of Humans (Musée de l'Homme) was opened at the Maurice Long Exhibition Center (present-day Palace of Friendship), displaying collections of daily utensils, ornaments of ethnic groups in the Central Highlands, jewelry and wedding costumes of the Việt, the Kh'mer, the Laos, the mountain dwellers in North Vietnam, and photo collections of M. Manikus and Đinh Văn Nội" (Ngô Thế Long, 2009: 38). Unfortunately, IIEH only operated for six years (1937–1944) and was dissolved right before the August 1945 Revolution in Vietnam. However, it was lucky that the French anthropology in Vietnam was formed.

The Formation of French Anthropology in Vietnam

Though the IIEH only existed for a short time, hundreds of its valuable researches helped to form a French anthropology in Vietnam in accordance with the model of the French Institution of Anthropology (Institut français d'anthropologie), established in 1911 in Paris. To confirm this, we could rely on research conducted by the IIEH in four aspects of anthropology: 1) physical anthropology; 2) cultural, social, and religious anthropology; 3) archaeology; and 4) linguistic anthropology. Thus, at the latest, French anthropology appeared in Vietnam in 1937, or 1938, if referring to the Indochina Governor General's decision.

In addition to their scientific publications, IIEH scholars devoted their efforts and even whole lives to studying Vietnam. Researching and exploring Vietnam, the Oriental land attractive to French scholars with its distinctive beauty, also equally charmed Vietnamese scholars through an academic perspective derived from theories and methodologies of Western civilization. Until the present, "in any historical phases and periods, exposure to Western schools has strongly encouraged literary composition and criticism in Vietnam" (Ngo Viet Hoan, 2018: 163). Unfortunately, wars interrupted the very fast development of Vietnamese anthropology at this stage, and finally, it had to take different turns. It was not until the early 21st century when Vietnamese scientists could return to the orbit carried by French and Vietnamese predecessors in the early 20th century.

The Role of French Anthropology to Vietnamese Anthropology at Present

Through the above-mentioned research, we can generalize the development of humanity science in general and anthropology in particular in Vietnam in three stages, as follows:

- Stage of formation (early 20th century to 1945);
- Stage of division (1954–1975)
- Stage of integration (since 1986).

The stage of formation was the time when Vietnam's humanity science got out of previous *bookish* activities to absorb western humanities, especially French ethnology. The stage of division took place with two distinct schools: the North followed the ethnological viewpoints of Russia and the Soviet Union, while the South went after Western perspectives. The stage of integration (as we see it now) is the influence of academic globalization and internationalization. Anthropology in Viet Nam, accordingly, has also acquired new academic schools that are more diverse and abundant, with scientific views similar to those around the world.

	Stage of formation	**Stage of division**	**Stage of integration**
Duration	Early 20th century to 1945	From 1954 to 1975	Since 1986
Scope of influence	Nationwide	North / South	Nationwide
Academia of influence	France	*North*: Russia and East Europe; *South*: France, US, UK	Worldwide
Subjects of influence	French sociology and ethnology	*North*: Russian history, culture studies, and ethnology; *South*: French sociology, Western anthropology	Russian culture studies and ethnology, Western anthropology and sociology
Research fields	People and society in Indochina	Ethnic groups and culture	Various fields
Training and research facilities	Indochina University, EFEO, IIEH, other training and research facilities	*North*: Universities, research institutes, training and research facilities; *South*: Universities, research institutes, training and research facilities	Universities, research institutes, other training and research facilities both in the North and the South

Different stages of development of anthropology in Viet Nam

In the development of contemporary anthropology in Vietnam, in 2000, the Ministry of Education and Training officially issued the training code for anthropology (code: 523146) in the list of training disciplines. In 2008, the Department of Anthropology was founded at the University of Social Sciences and Humanities, Hồ Chí Minh City National University (on the basis of the Subject of Anthropology founded in 2002 under Decision 111/QĐ-ĐHQG-TCCB by HCMC National University President on February 27, 2008). In 2010, the Department of Ethnology and Anthropology was founded under the Institution of Social Sciences (Decision 35/QĐ-TTg dated January 10, 2010). On September 29, 2015, the Department of Anthropology, University of Social Sciences and Humanities, Vietnam National University, was established, opening a new stage for training anthropology in Vietnam. The establishment of anthropology faculties at the two biggest training centers for social sciences and humanities confirms the role and position of this discipline in the 21st century.

Currently, the progress of "The Revolution 4.0" has been creating a new academic face of science and technology in Vietnam. The science of humanity is also in the process of transformation and increasingly deep integration into the academic world. Anthropology in Vietnam is now trying its best to affirm its pioneering role among the social sciences and humanities, with a foundation set by the French a century ago. To summarize contemporary Vietnamese anthropology, we can consider it the outcome of a "melting pot" made of theories and methodologies from three main schools in which French anthropology is a fundamental foundation.

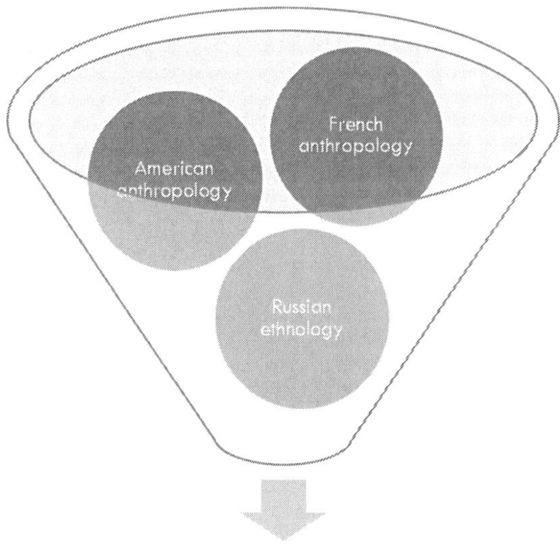

Vietnamese anthropology

Conclusion

It is possible to affirm that, in the first decade of the 20th century, French academia played a crucial role in the development of modern science in Vietnam, particularly through the humanities. Their influence led to the creation of a strong foundation for scientific exploration that incorporated modern theories and methodologies. This radical scientific approach has contributed significantly to humankind's understanding of science in general and Vietnamese science in particular. During the first half of the 20th century, the French systematically developed anthropology in Vietnam, producing scientific works of high academic value. This is an undeniable fact and has resulted in a great scientific legacy for both Vietnam and the world's scientific community.

Although Vietnam has inherited a significant scientific legacy, its usefulness has been limited due to various factors. After the French's withdrawal, North Vietnam, where a large part of the scientific legacy was kept, was embroiled in a war that lasted until 1975. The Marxist ideology of the Soviet Union prevented scientists from continuing their work. It wasn't until Vietnam implemented its "open-door" policy (1986) and integrated it into world science that French humanity science and anthropology were able to return. The reopening of the EFEO in 1993 was a significant achievement led by French and Vietnamese scientists after nearly half a century of closure.

Another important reason is that, after Vietnam gained its independence, the importance placed on learning the Russian language in the North and English in the South left valuable French-language documents in Vietnam nearly untouched (except for the personal efforts of some French and Vietnamese scholars and some scientific projects conducted by the EFEO Hanoi and the Embassy of France). It can be said that translating this documentary treasure of thousands of French works into Vietnamese and English is extremely necessary for the world's scientists to expand this scientific legacy. That is also a task that should be fulfilled by contemporary scientists in order to reconfirm the role of French science in the world in general and that of French anthropology in the Vietnamese one in particular.

Acknowledgments

Firstly, I would like to express my gratitude to Ngô Thế Long for providing me with important data that allowed me to contribute to this article as a guidance of Dr. Leon Miller. Finally, I would like to extend a special thank you to Hoàng Thị Bích Ngọc for her advice on French terminologies. It is truly an honor.

References

Alexandre de Rhodes 1991. *Annam-Lusitan-Latin Dictionary* (Từ điển Việt-Bồ-La), Thanh Lãng, Hoàng Xuân Việt and Đỗ Quang Chính trans. Social Sciences Publishing House, Hanoi.

Animonier, F. Etience and Roucoules, Emile 1889, 2018. *Educational policies in Cocochine at the end of 19th centuries*. Lai Nhu Bang translation. The Gioi Publishers, Hanoi.

Barrow, John 1793. *The Voyage to Cocochine*. Nguyen Thua Hy translation. The Goi Publishers, Hanoi.

Bauberot, Jean 1992. "Tư tưởng "lương hoa" (vô thần) và khoa học tôn giáo tại trường Đại học thực hành (EPHE)," [Atheism and Religious studies at EPHE]. Hội thảo *90 năm nghiên cứu về văn hóa và lịch sử Việt Nam* [International conference: 90 years of Vietnamese historical and cultural studies] organized by VASS and EFEO in Hanoi 1992.

Condominas, G. 1997. *Không gian xã hội vùng Đông Nam Á* [L'Espace social. À propos de l'Asie du Sud-Est, Paris: Flammarion 1980], reprint in Vietnamese, Ho Hai Thuy, Ngoc Ha, Thanh Hang translation. Cultural Publising House, Hanoi.

Condominas, G. 2013. *Chúng tôi ăn rừng đá – thần Gôh* [Nous avons mangé la forêt de la Pierre-Génie Gôo, Paris: Mercure de France 1954], reprint in Vietnamese, Nguyen Ngoc, Tran Thi Lan Anh, Phan Ngoc Ha, Trinh Thu Hong, Nguyen Thu Phuong translation. The Gioi Publisher, Hanoi.

Dampier, William 1688, 2011. *The Voyage to Tonquin*. Hoang Anh Tuan trans. The Gioi Publishers, Hanoi

Doumer, Paul 2018, 1905. *Xứ Đông Dương* [L' Indochine Francaise], Lưu Đình Tuân, Nguyễn Thừa Hỷ translation. The Gioi Publisher, Hanoi.

Flower, John E. 2020. "French Republic". *Britannica Encyclopedia.* https://www.britannica.com/place/France/Cultural-and-scientific-attainments. Acess Dec. 6th, 2020

Gourou, Pierre 1955. (Les éditions d'Art et d'Histoire, Paris 1936). *The peasants of the Tonkin delta: a study in human geography* (Behavior science translations). New Haven, Connecticut: Human Relations Area Files.

Huỳnh Tịnh Paulus Của 1895. *Đại Nam quốc âm tự vị* [Dictionnaire Anamite]. Imprimerie REY, CURIOL, Saigon 1895.

Maybon, Charles B. 1916, 2011. *Les européens en pays d'Annam* [The Europeans in Annam]. Nguyen Thua Hy translation, The Gioi Publishers, Hanoi.

Ngô Thế Long (2009). "Vài nét về Viện Nghiên cứu Con người Đông Dương (1937-1944)" [Several information of Institut Indochinois pour l'étude de l'homme – IIEH (1937-1944)], *The Social Sciences Information Review* No. 2/2009, pp. 32-40.

Ngo Viet Hoan 2018. "Studies on 20th Century Western and Vietnamese Theories of Literary Criticism," *Comparative Literature: East & West*, 2:2, 151-165, DOI: 10.1080/25723618.2018.1556841

Nguyễn Phương Ngọc 2012. *L'origine de l'anthropologie au Vietnam: Recherche sur les auteurs de la première moitié du xxe siècle*. Aix-en-Provence: Presses universitaires de Provence

Nguyễn Phương Ngọc 2015. "Vents d'Est, vents d'Ouest: L'introduction de l'esprit des Lumières au Vietnam au début du XXe siècle." In *Le Vietnam: Une histoire de transferts culturels*, Hoai Huong Aubert-Nguyen and Michel Espagne (ed.). Demopilis, Paris, 2015, p.49-67.

Nguyễn Thị Chân Quỳnh. *Khoa cử Việt Nam* [System of former Vietnamese competition-examinations], Vol. 1, An Tiêm Publisher, Paris 2002. Vol. 2, Literature Publishing House, Hanoi 2007.

Nguyễn Thụy Phương 2019. "Nguồn gốc luận thuyết của "sứ mệnh khai hóa" *Tia sáng* magazine. https://tiasang.com.vn/khoa-hoc-cong-nghe/Nguon-goc-luan-thuyet-cua-su-menh-khai-hoa-18534.   Access Dec.12nd, 2020.

Nguyễn Thụy Phương 2018. *New education in Vietnam 1940s*. Culture and literature Publisher. HCMC.

Nguyễn Thuyết Phong, 2018. "The Vietnamese Scholarship at the Turn of the Millennium: A Study of the Pioneering Works of Gustave Emile Dumoutier (1850–1904)". *ASIA Network Exchange*, 25(1), pp. 96–114.

Nguyễn Văn Chính 2007. "Một thế kỷ dân tộc học Việt Nam, và những thách thức trên con đường đổi mới và hội nhập" [A century of Vietnamese ethnology and challenge in innovation and integration], Jourrnal of Folklore Studies, No. 5(113), 2007.

Nguyễn Văn Huyên 1995, 1996. *Góp phần nghiên cứu văn hóa Việt Nam* [Contribution to the Studies of Vietnamese Culture – Complete works of Nguyen Van Huyen] Vol. 1-2, Trần Đỉnh, Đỗ Trọng Quang, Phạm Thủy Ba trasnlation. Social Sciences Publishing House, Hanoi.

Nguyễn Xuân Thọ, 2018. *Bước Mở Đầu Của Sự Thiết Lập Hệ Thống Thuộc Địa Pháp Ở Việt Nam (1858 - 1897)* [Les Debuts de l'installation du Systeme Colonial Francais au Vietnam (1858 - 1897)]. Hong Duc Publisher, Hanoi.

Paul Beau, Jean-Baptiste 1906. "Decree No. 1514a on May 16th, 1906". *Journal officiel de l'Indochine française* (JOIF), 11.6.1906, pp. 807-810.

De Rhodes, le P.A. 1651. *Histoire du Royaume de Tunkin* (Lịch sử của Vương quốc Đông Kinh). Lyon, J.B. Denenet en rue Mercière, à la croix d'Or.

Tavernier, Jean-Baptiste (1681, 2011). *Relation nouvelle et singulière du Royaume de Tunquin* [New and unique voyage of the Kingdom of Tunquin]. Lê Tư Lành trans. Nguyễn Thừa Hỷ Ed. The Gioi Publisher, Hanoi.

Trần Văn Giáp 1967. *Phật giáo Việt Nam từ khởi nguyên đến thế kỷ XIII* [Le Bouddhisme en Annam des origines au XIIIè siècle], Tueej Syx transslation, Vạn Hạnh Univerrsity Publisher.

Trịnh Văn Thảo 2019. *L'Ecole francaise en Indochine* [The French schools in Indochine]. Nguyen Tri Chi and Trinh Van Tung trans. Tri thuc Publisher, Hanoi.

Unlearning Northeast: Countering Militarized Realities with Peace Education

Ms. Monalisa Hazarika
and Prof. Manoj Kumar Mishra

Introduction

Soot-covered faces carrying equipment of almost half their weight is a sight we rarely hope to see but a chance reality in India's Northeast. The fallout of the incessant low-intensity conflict following the country's independence, the recruitment of child soldiers for the cause of greater autonomy, and an imagined homeland is a fairly recent phenomenon. While it could have been the mainstay of insurgent groups for decades and a successful endeavor in hiding from the purview of national and international attention, the issue has been brought to the limelight in the past decade with renewed energy on the part of researchers, journalists, and other intellectuals who have taken a greater interest in uncovering the truth. Children as young as nine have been brainwashed to fight for a cause that predates their generation and to which they can no longer relate through the use of a flimsy utopian future [Bhattacharya 2011]. Their youthful faces are exposed to extreme weather conditions and the harsh realities of life and death, rather than being tarnished by the UV lights of smartphones and electronic devices, akin to children their age. With rehearsed group dogmas at the tip of their tongues, they are the parroted personas of a number of rebel outfits that covertly or overtly involve youth in their operations under said education, or alternatively, "re-education" wing. [Sen 2015]. Their enlistment, whether forced or voluntary, is the result of their recruiters' efforts, who use a variety of socioeconomic and psychological tactics for their indoctrination.

Whether it be through the execution of drastic measures like kidnapping or more subtly through the fetishization of "uniform" and a chance to 'serve their motherland', the promise of a "way out" of their current pigpen is the greatest selling point. While we try to unravel the peripheral-mainlander deadlock, we need to consider a plan of action to counter the culture of violence and masculinity that has been ingrained into the societal fabric by romanticizing the gory details of destruction and glorifying the virtues of men who, defying morality, 'fought for the cause'. Targeting the hidden intricacies that fuel and sustain perpetual wartime societies requires studying the enthusiastic behaviors towards war and the normalization of violence resulting from experiences of nationalistic bias and expulsion from the mainstream narrative. In this regard, peace education has the potential to foster a climate conducive to positively addressing years of neglect and actual and perceived injustices for a pragmatic shift towards rekindled hope and understanding. Beyond a pacifistic phenomenon, it entails a continuous process of intervention to imbibe human-centric values and re-center the moral tug of war between the psychological and social modalities of the post-conflict generation. This paper aims to critically analyze the peace education theory in the context of Northeast Indian societies as a tool to bring about positive social change and explores the efficacy of such an intervention, framing recommendations from Freire's Pedagogy of the Oppressed.

Keywords: Peace Education, Northeast India, Militarization, Patriotism, Violence, Child Soldiers

Children of the Fractured Frontier

Northeast India, a region of inherent complexity with pulsating multiverses, is a scholar's laboratory of vastly understudied and erroneous microcosms. Depending on who is doing the 'seeing', the region often features a dissociated understanding as an exotic other and has been assigned a directional name for administrative convenience [Baruah 2020]. With an erratic gender designation, the frontier province was appropriated as an official place-name post-independence, giving rise to the controversial derivative label "Northeasterner" – a postcolonial coinage corresponding to an identity that equates to a person's geographical location, hierarchy and power relations, and racial inflection [Ibid]. Like any other peripheral territory, Northeast India is underscored as a geostrategic preeminence with extreme security vulnerability and a major contributor to India's national security anxieties. Unique to the mix, however, is colonial misadventure, political alienation, economic deprivation, state-sponsored persecution, and environmental dislocation [Nepram 2002]. This mainlander's "Shangri-La of escape" is an archival product of neglect, discounted grievances, and racialized treatment, where the feeling of otherness and alienation is sustained by the psychological one-upmanship of the 'mainlanders', evident from their classic center-periphery style of deliberate policy measures. As an anomalous zone with a vacuum of legal exceptions, the contrasts in the perceived and imagined borders, both "inside" and "outside" the region, point to the lived legacy of poorly thought-out decisions and ineffective conciliatory strategies [Baruah 2020].

Sharing porous borders with Myanmar, the regional epicenter of insurgent activities stationing over 40 recognized rebel outfits, the 'ungoverned' terrain has been successful in maintaining tandem with the peculiar socioeconomic and political milieu of the region, sustaining the durable disorder of closeted activities. Poverty and unemployment aggravate the impact of alienation, which is the case in Northeast India [Bhattacharya 2011]. Disparate economic backgrounds and a sense of helplessness magnify the vulnerability of young children and adults alike to being lured by the potential financial stability and comfort provided by the gun and the uniform. The fervent feeling of neglect due to incompetency on the part of the government has been responsible for drawing citizens to take the plunge. Whatever the ideology, from secessionism to banditry, the promise of getting paid and being able to afford a better lifestyle for their families has always been the prime motivating factor. This is particularly profound in Manipur, which has the dubious reputation of having the maximum number of militant outfits among all states in the country [Ibid.]. The Zomi Revolutionary Army (ZRA), operating in Manipur's Churachandpur district, is a classic example of how children from impoverished families are groomed to become guerrillas [Ibid.].

The Promise of Eternal Glory

Desperation is a powerful stimulus. It can be banked to maneuver one's psychological compass to embark upon suicide missions or orchestrate atrocities against their own kind. The recruitment of child soldiers in Northeast India is a case in point. Exploiting their physical and emotional immaturity, children are abducted, forcefully recruited, or coaxed into joining for an array of reasons. Driven by power, poverty, limited employment opportunities, domestic abuse, discrimination, revenge-seeking, and/or hope for a better lifestyle, children in this region can be forced into voluntary and forced recruitment. They also tend to partake in warfare in response to financial, cultural, social, and political pressures when "volunteering" seems to be the only viable option [Siddiqui & Siddiqui 2015].

As expendable pawns in armed conflict between the national armed forces and ragtag rebel outfits, they are easier to train, docile, and more susceptible to being under the influence of substance abuse, making them the preferred tool in warfare. They not only fight on the front lines as soldiers, spies, and, in some cases, decoys and human shields but also perform other tasks as aids, messengers, porters, cooks, or forced sexual services [Siddiqui & Siddiqui 2015]. Some argue that children from impoverished and marginalized backgrounds are more likely to be recruited than those from well-off and educated families, as the families of the latter are usually eager to pay hefty amounts for their release [Ibid]. Recent technological advances in weaponry and the widespread proliferation and availability of small arms, including lightweight automatic weapons, have contributed to their increased usage among children [Bhattacharya 2011].

The rapid proliferation and trafficking of small arms and light weapons, the ready availability of young recruits as a disposable and cheap resource with population explosion, and the rising civil wars and conflicts have made children susceptible to coercive methods and cheaper to retain [Beber & Blattman 2013]. Further, the ease of brainwashing them to fight for moral compensation of honor and revenge and shaping their expectations through misinformation blurs the line between forced and voluntary enlistment [Ibid.]. Other reasons for their marketability are their indigent backgrounds of low employment and educational freedom, making remuneration affordable and compliance in the face of punishments more likely [Ibid]. The decreasing popularity of militant outfits puts them in an unfavorable position to be cautious about recruits and have no option but to enroll children in the absence of viable alternatives [Bhattacharya 2011]. As pliable and governable subjects, they are preferred over their adult counterparts given their receptiveness to socioeconomic and psychological tactics of indoctrination and loyalty when caught by law enforcement. Beber & Blattman applied theories of industrial organization to rebel groups to understand the logic behind child soldiering, apart from them being easier to "intimidate, indoctrinate, and misinform than adults" [Beber & Blattman 2013]. This has to do with the low-risk cost of conducting such war crimes in the absence of regulating bodies to punish offenders and provide protection to children [Ibid]. This is especially true in the Northeast, where most scholarship has focused on the cessation of hostilities and preventing future outbreaks with peace accords, but little attention has been paid to the reintegration and fallout of former combatants, children, and adults alike.

The children are socialized to values of sacrifice for group honor and justice, which are expanded multifold in situations of perpetual conflict where they start to integrate themselves by opposing their 'common enemy'. This feeling of struggle against the 'external' forces can be motivated by revenge-seeking behavior or a moral obligation to fight for a cause [Bhattacharya 2011]. Seeking membership in such an organization not only fulfills their mundane needs but also confers a sense of power and purpose. As children from the obscure frontier tracks, the buzz associated with operating tools of slaughter against those that once wronged them becomes the foremost temptation that they couldn't have gotten otherwise. With technological advancement and the growing ease of evading national and international gun laws and export controls, children are given access to lighter and more efficient weapons, which require less brute strength and years of training to master [Ibid]. There have also been instances where they were employed as decoy cadres in designated camps when a rebel outfit was planning to surrender [Ibid]. Popular outfits such as ULFA have been known to "outsource terror", which was brought to light when two 8-year-olds—Ganesh Das and Babu Chetri—were arrested on charges of extortion on August 13, 2009, in Guwahati while collecting money from local shopkeepers [Ibid].

Whether it be through the execution of drastic measures like kidnapping or more subtly through the fetishization of 'uniform' and a chance to 'serve their motherland', the promise of a 'way out' of their current pigpen is the greatest selling point. The military uniform has been used as a recruitment device, through the "erotic potential of the uniform", in the words of Sharon Peoples, to seduce men or children, for that matter, into service [People 2013]. It seeks to create an interest in detachment and 'disinterestedness' in civilian life, which is painted to be the epitome of 'coolness' and also goes towards constructing an identity for those who aspire to heroic masculinity [Ibid]. These uniforms screamed 'manliness' to those who were ready to accept or reformulate their own individual identity by filling the potential for a more stimulating life and hidden apprehensions [Ibid]. This is also integrated into the wider umbrella of the military-industrial complex, which is the rather 'comfortable' relationship that can develop between government entities and defense-minded manufacturers, where 'war and weapons' are seen in tandem with 'peace and prosperity'.

Lack of access to quality education, healthcare, and other essential facilities of life hindered by widespread poverty increases their risk of recruitment. While poverty in itself is not the prime cause of child soldiering, it does influence the interplay of other contributing factors. Being outside the purview of the administration is a major vantage point for the militant outfits to pitch their policy to 'educate' and look after the children whose parents can't afford to educate them in missionary schools [Bhattacharya 2011]. This is a strategy adopted by multiple overground and underground factions, including the ZRA, the Kuki Liberation Army, the Kuki Revolutionary Army, and the United Kuki Liberation Front, where the new recruits are fed and clothed while living with adult cadres and given training in handling weapons only upon attaining 14 years of age [Ibid]. Militant outfits engage in such investments given the minimal capital, high returns, and lower risk factors. There are virtually no restrictions or heed and are almost never faced with sanctions despite having strict national and international laws. Owing to the lack of bargaining power to demand better pay, children are the quintessential commodity in times of financial hardship and low budgets, which has been the case for most outfits in the region [Ibid]. These groups also maintain cordial relationships with the locals by organizing cultural shows to bolster support for their operations.

Child Soldiers of Northeast India

How do we define a 'child soldier'? Fraught with cultural construction and familial responsibilities, the notion of childhood is contested across societies. The Paris Principle on the Involvement of Children in Armed Conflict (2007) defines "a child associated with an armed force or group" as any human below the age of 18 who is or has been recruited by an armed force to carry out both combat and non-combat activities, with little heed to their forced or voluntary enlistment [Vinet 2023]. While historically considered non-participants in an armed conflict, the reality of employing children shifted with their usage as "powder monkeys" to deliver essential cannon ammunition and the deployment of 'Hitler Youth' in the Second World War [Ghosh 2018]. The Khmer Rouge in Cambodia is believed to have been the first regime to train young children, which evolved with the advent of the Cold War [Ibid].

It would be erroneous to believe that the recruitment of child soldiers by insurgent groups in Northeast India is an isolated event given the lack of any systematic monitoring of the issue and the failure to devise comprehensive strategies to protect and prevent the same [Bhattacharya 2011]. Given the asymmetric conflicts and unique state of affairs, the case of child soldiers in the Northeast has few parallels with the rest of the world. The argument has failed to register on the agendas of government agencies despite receiving major attention from academics, policymakers, and human rights advocacy groups due to the paucity of documented cases. Amidst popular discourses on child soldiers around armed conflict and extremism in Africa, guerilla warfare and drug peddling in Latin America, or the curated portrayal of forced conscription as "volunteering" in neighboring Sri Lanka and Nepal, India's northeast remains vastly overlooked or ignored [Roul 2014]. When probed on the status of children involved in armed conflict during the combined third and fourth periodic reviews of the Convention on the Rights of the Child, the Indian delegation responded that it was aware of such recruitments from non-governmental organizations and media reports but was unable to establish a figure due to the clandestine nature of the armed groups [Ghosh 2018]. India had categorically stated that the country "does not face either international or non-international armed conflict situations", dismissing such criticisms by claiming that the issue hardly ever existed in the country [Roul 2014]. They further added that they have institutionalized schemes for their rehabilitation if any such child is found, which is far from the truth.

Living at the crossroads of armed violence and democracy deficits, the plight of child soldiers, who occasionally go missing only to return as uniformed cadres, doesn't receive attention beyond their families. Further, there is a significant gap in the perception of the said 'soldiers'. A 14-year-old wielding an assault rifle could be seen as both a child and a young adult, depending on the observers. According to notable journalist Rajeev Bhattacharya, the highest enrollment of children in varying degrees has been observed among the Kuki-Chin-Mizo outfits active at Chandel, Churachandpur, and Senapati in Manipur, North Mizoram, and sections of Assam's hill districts [Bhattacharya 2011]. In an article in the Indian Defence Review, Bhattacharya pointed to the prevalence of children with arms in the ranks of various militant outfits in Manipur and Nagaland, including the National Socialist Council of Nagalim (Isak-Muivah) (NSCN-IM), the National Socialist Council of Nagaland (Khaplang) (NSCN-K), and the Naga National Council (NNC) [Ibid]. He further added that they were also found across ceasefire-designated camps of four militant groups—Dima Halam Daogah (DHD), Black Widow, United People's Democratic Solidarity (UPDS), and Karbi Longri North Cachar Hills Liberation Front—in the Dima Hasao and Karbi Anglong districts of Assam [Ibid]. In 2013 alone, there were two comprehensive reports that featured this uncharted issue in India. The Asian Centre for Human Rights, in their "India's Child Soldiers" report, conservatively estimates the existence of at least 3,000 children in militant outfits across India, with 500 of them stationed in the Northeast and Jammu and Kashmir [Asian Centre for Human Rights 2013]. Another report by Child Soldiers International pointed to the absence of monitoring mechanisms, both domestic and international, making it difficult to investigate the precise numbers or current patterns of recruitment and use of children by armed groups in India or their physical and moral exploitation in the hands of armed groups [Siddiqui & Siddiqui 2015].

The involvement of children in armed conflict has been prevalent in Manipur since the 1990s and gained traction with the abduction of Angom Langamba in 2008 [Tombing 2018]. It led to a public outcry after the mother of the child held a press conference lamenting the involvement of a local underground militant outfit, and 20 other cases of child abduction between the ages of 10 and 16 were brought to light [Ibid]. In 2012, the "People's Revolutionary Party" lured three teenage Manipur boys into the jungles of Myanmar with the promise of unspecified employment and the assurance of their parents' comfort as bait to wage war against India [Siddiqui & Siddiqui 2015]. Over the years, multiple cases of forceful conscription were reported, including the kidnapping of 14-year-old aspiring archer Alice Kamei and 15-year-old Sanahanbi Khaidem from Manipur by the banned Revolutionary People's Front in 2013 [Tombing 2018]. The Manipuri militant groups of the PREPAK and Cobra Task Force, however, claimed that children voluntarily enlisted in their groups, joining the ranks of combatants and support personnel [Roul 2014]. Similar incidents involving the GNLA using children as fighters in Meghalaya occurred in 2012, with the state police estimating over a hundred children stationed at GNLA hideouts in the Garo Hills [Ibid]. The infamous and violent Khaplang faction of the NSCN made headlines in Nagaland in February 2008 when they kidnapped 39 boys from Arunachal Pradesh to become fighters for their faction [Ibid].
Cases of employing children to carry out dreaded activities, while not new, shocked the state of Assam when its infamous banned outfit ULFA used two children from 9th and 10th grades to plant bombs in the Tinisukia

district amidst the Independence Day celebrations in 2016 [The Northeast Today 2016]. While initially confessing to doing so for money, they later changed their stance to have done the same to "Save Assam" [Ibid]. A study conducted by Northeast Research and Social Work Networking (NERSWN) in 2014 titled "Impact of Conflict on Children in Assam and Manipur" on four children from the conflict-hit districts of the two states revealed the contrasting scenarios of how children end up being involved in the murky business of armed groups [Karmakar 2014]. While one was kidnapped and coerced into joining a militant group, the other decided to take up arms at the urging of the village elders [Ibid]. The third managed to escape the rioters and spent eight months living in a relief camp, while a fourth became an orphan after losing his parents in a crossfire [ibid.]. According to a report by the Manipur Alliance for Child Rights, 100 of the 147 kids housed in an observation home in the Churachandpur district were found to be involved in insurgency-related activities [Ibid]. According to an official statement by the Assam Rifles, the Khaplang faction of the NSCN conducted an aggressive recruitment drive along the border villages on the Indo-Myanmar border in Manipur, Nagaland, and Arunachal Pradesh, where at least 15 school-going students were reportedly kidnapped and taken to the Ngiakching Camp in Myanmar for military training [Choudhury 2015]. Additional Superintendent of Police Priyadarshini Laishram, in her 2012 paper "Conflict and Child Soldiers—Manipur Case", estimated the number of child soldiers in the region based on the data available on surrendered cadres [Shah 2022]. Between 2004 and 2014, 270 out of the 1252 returnees were children, some as young as 8 years old during the time of recruitment [Ibid]. There are also recorded cases of 12-year-olds who 'willingly' took up arms under the premise of serving their motherland and joined the Khaplang faction of the NSCN [Mukhim 2016]. At 15 years old, he was among the few people who escaped the camps and lived to tell the tale [Banerjee 2015].

Unlearning Northeast:
Recommendations for a Way Forward

Demobilization and Reintegration

Robbed of a healthy childhood, releasing children from the ranks of the armed forces, while a preeminent move, is only a necessary first step towards their recovery. Providing the opportunity for a fresh start is not only a moral and legal obligation of the state but also an important pillar of creating sustainable peace. Whether serving as active combatants or serving staff, the cessation of war or the signing of peace agreements does not necessarily give them the closure they require, as they have been living in a perpetual survival mode where violence is the norm. This is especially true in communities dealing with the aftermath of a conflict where basic services are scarce or have not been resumed at operational levels. Thus, reintegration efforts must be backed by long-term commitments and adequate services that cater to not only their immediate needs of physical and mental health support but also a viable alternative to bearing a weapon and becoming valued members of their communities.

A 2018 report from the Office of the Special Representative of the Secretary-General for Children and Armed Conflict put forth a comprehensive set of principles to guide reintegration efforts regardless of race, sex, age, religion, ethnicity, opinions, disability, or any other status of the child [Office of the Special Representative of the Secretary-General for Children in Armed Conflict 2018]. As enshrined in the historic 1989 Convention on the Rights of the Child, the first and foremost priority of any reintegration program should be the "best interest of the child" [Ibid]. Actions should not be overshadowed in complex security or political environments or measured solely against security concerns. Further, children previously associated with the armed forces or armed groups should be regarded "primarily as victims" [Ibid.]. This will help counter their portrayal as perpetrators of alleged crimes and avoid further stigmatization. This principle will help facilitate alternatives to their prosecution and detention, especially in the context of violent extremism. Additionally, a "child's right to life, survival, and development" should be accorded paramount importance and not be limited to their physical well-being [Ibid]. This needs to be accompanied by an overall development of their spiritual, moral, and social prosperity, where education plays a decisive role.

Failing to do so could potentially have long-term impacts on social cohesion and economic development, with them growing up to contribute to the reversal or stalling of future peace processes. Given that their only exposure to reality has been violence and gruesome bloodshed, reintegrating former child soldiers who were affiliated with militant groups back into civilian life may initially be an arduous task. As they are rebuilding their lives, leaving behind the chronic cycle of barbarity, their past traumatic events, and frequent stigmatization for their former roles causes a carryover effect in their civilian lives and may be a major hindrance to their effective reintegration. Programs not adapted to the context of the local community and made palatable to the children's needs lead to their further exclusion and isolation from mainstream society. Further, it is essential to adopt a gender-sensitive lens on the agenda, as women and girls have vulnerabilities unique to their gender and status in society and suffer specific consequences from rape and sexual violence, making them reluctant to join such reintegration programs.

Unlearning and Relearning: The Role of Peace Education

Prior to engaging in the rehabilitation and reintegration process, understanding the impetus for youth to join armed groups is a necessary precursor for deliberating well-informed means of preventing their future engagement. An auxiliary plan of action needs to be considered in discussions surrounding this issue to counter the culture of violence and masculinity that has been ingrained into the societal fabric by romanticizing the gory details of destruction and glorifying the virtues of men who, defying morality, 'fought for the cause'. Targeting the hidden intricacies that fuel and sustain perpetual wartime societies requires studying the enthusiastic behaviors towards war and the normalization of violence resulting from experiences of nationalistic bias and expulsion from the mainstream narrative. This is where peace education comes in. 'Teaching for peace' rather than 'teaching about peace' has the potential to foster a climate conducive to positively addressing years of neglect and actual and perceived injustices for a pragmatic shift towards rekindled hope and understanding.

Regardless of the agreements concocted in the aftermath of peace talks and ceasefires, initiating specific programs aimed at establishing new foundations of life and normalcy and curbing the psychosocial impacts is nowhere near the agendas of the groups involved. While devising a blueprint to counter issues of insurgency and small arms proliferation is in the works, efforts to heighten awareness about child recruitment and deter influential factors are equally essential. This can be achieved as a two-way mechanism: by involving civil society organizations and community groups to monitor and report recent developments, and by the government devising strategies for action plans that are accessible to the remotest corners and uniquely catered to the immediate and long-term needs of the people. Lessons learned from successful grassroots innovations, such as those in Uganda, can be replicated by accommodating local incentives and conditions for strategic interaction among the warring groups [Bhattacharya 2011].

To prevent cloning the essentialist approach of adopting a homogenized lens to understand the 'difficult histories' of Northeastern conflict, it needs to be ensured that a Western-centric model of peace education is not copied and pasted to this region. As underlined in Freire's Pedagogy of the Oppressed, communicating in a language where people feel heard and seen is the only way for them to move out of the cultural schizophrenia of "being present and yet not visible, being visible and yet not present" [Freire 2005]. By imparting the critical tools to reflect, understand, and process what it means to be at the periphery, peace education has the potential to equip people with constructive ways to express their "tensions, contradictions, fears, doubts, hopes, and "deferred" dreams" [Ibid].

This is where the unlearning happens, for both the victims and the policymakers. To move beyond the image of the Northeast as a Shangri-La of escape, using historically accurate euphemisms and warranting agency over the language and tone of the subject allows citizens to circumvent policy blind spots and representation of its histories in "academic selective selection" of bodies of knowledge [Freire 2005]. Engaging in critical discourses will not only enable them to deconstruct the colonial and hegemonic paradigms but also underscore the fact that peace cannot be taught without actually addressing the factors anchored in the competing histories and ideologies that generated it in the first place [Ibid]. In this context, Freire's pedagogical orientation of dialogical teaching seems fitting, which is to create a dialogical platform for learning and knowing about lived experiences and a group therapy space for stating grievances without overindulging in exoticizing these experiences [Ibid]. Being able to transform their lived experiences into knowledge and utilize it to unveil and make sense of new information about the world will enable students to make peace with their past. Having a curriculum compatible with addressing cognitive biases and contradictions in knowledge and epistemology delivers a language of clarity to deconstruct ideologies of oppression.

The issue of child soldiers in the context of Northeast India is a fairly hidden subject given the lack of record-keeping on their precise roles and numbers in addition to the normalization of their labor as unacknowledged members [Bhattacharya 2011]. While it could have been the mainstay of insurgent groups for decades and a successful endeavor in hiding from the purview of national and international attention, away from media scrutiny, the issue has been brought to the limelight in the past decade with renewed energy on the part of researchers, journalists, and other intellectuals who have taken a greater interest in uncovering the truth. As long as the multifarious issues of the region persist, rabidly luring spaces will continue to create opportunities for children as a way for them to meet their basic survival and individualistic needs. Beyond a pacifistic phenomenon, the pedagogical intervention in the Northeast, at the state level in school curricular and informal discourses, should entail a continuous process of intervention to imbibe human-centric values and re-center the moral tug of war between the psychological and social modalities of the post-conflict generation. Only then can we expect a peaceful transition of the region and its people, catapulting it to the more vexed matters of the 21st century.

References

Asian Human Rights Commission. (n.d.). INDIA: Child soldiers being used as expendable pawns in armed conflicts. Asian Human Rights Commission. Retrieved May 3, 2023, from http://www.humanrights.asia/news/alrc-news/human-rights-council/hrc6/al-024-2007/

Asian Center For Human Rights. (2013, May 8). India's child soldiers: Government defends officially designated terror groups' record on the recruitment of child soldiers before the UN Committee on the Rights of the Child - India. Relief Web. Retrieved July 11, 2023, from https://reliefweb.int/report/india/india%E2%80%99s-child-soldiers-government-defends-officiall y-designated-terror-groups%E2%80%99-record

Banerjee, R. (2015, December 13). Kids who bit the bullet. The Week. https://www.theweek.in/theweek/cover/northeasts-child-soldiers.html

Baruah, Sanjib. (2020). In the Name of the Nation: India and Its Northeast. N.p.: Stanford University Press.

Beber, B., & Blattman, C. (2013). The logic of child soldiering and coercion. International Organization, 67(1), 65–104. https://doi.org/10.1017/s0020818312000409 Bhattacharyya, R. (2011, August 15). The Child Guerrillas of the Northeast - II. Indian Defense Review. Retrieved July 11, 2023, from http://www.indiandefencereview.com/news/the-child-guerrillas-of-the-northeast-ii/

Bhattacharyya, R. (2011, August 15). The Child Guerrillas of the Northeast - I. Indian Defense Review.

http://www.indiandefencereview.com/news/the-child-guerrillas-of-the-northeast-i/

Child Soldiers International. (2001). Child Soldiers Global Report 2001 - India. Refworld. Retrieved July 11, 2023, from https://www.refworld.org/docid/498805f12d.html

Choudhury, R. (2015, September 10). Resurgent NSCN-K on a mission to recruit 'child soldiers'. Deccan Herald. https://www.deccanherald.com/content/500109/resurgent-nscn-k-mission-recruit.html

Freire, Paulo. (2005) Pedagogy of the Oppressed. New York: Continuum International Publishing.

Ghosh, G. (2018). Deciphering Legal Safeguards for Child Soldiers in Northeast India Vis-a-Vis International Standards. Child Rights Law & Policy Review, 1(1), 19-31.

Karmakar, S. (2014, December 3). Kids face the brunt in Assam, Manipur. Telegraph India. https://www.telegraphindia.com/india/kids-face-the-brunt-in-assam-manipur/cid/283871

Mukhim, P. (2016, July 3). Child soldiers of Northeast: Straddling between boundaries. The Northeast Today. https://thenortheasttoday.com/oped/child-soldiers-of-northeast-straddling-between-boundaries/ci d2546648.htm

Nepram, Binalakshmi. (2002). South Asia's Fractured Frontier Armed Conflict, Narcotics & Small Arms Proliferation in India's Northeast. N.p.: Mittal Publications

Office of the Special Representative of the Secretary-General for Children in Armed Conflict. (2018, January 21). REINTEGRATION of Former Child Soldiers.

Peoples, S. (2013). Embodying the military: Uniforms. Critical Studies in Men's Fashion, 1(1), 7–21. https://doi.org/10.1386/csmf.1.1.7_1

Ramanis Blog. (2014, December 10). Child Soldiers Of India – Ramanisblog. https://ramanisblog.in/2014/12/10/child-soldiers-of-india/

Riyani, M., Wasino, Suyahmo, Brata, N., Shintasiwi F., (2021). Making Peace with the Past: Peace Education in Post-Conflict Aceh Societies through the Application of Cognitive Behavioral Therapy. Journal of Social Studies Education Research, 330-376

ROUL, A. (2014, November 3). Catching Them Young: Child Soldiers Of India's Myriad Mutinies. Society for the Study of Peace and Conflict. https://www.sspconline.org/opinion-analysis/catching-them-young-child-soldiers-indias-myriadmutinies-mon-11032014-1200

Sen, A. (2014, March 24). There Are at Least 500 Child Soldiers Fighting in Northeast India, and the World Hasn't Noticed. TIME. https://time.com/33008/child-soldiers-recruited-into-northeast-india-insurgencies/

Sen, A. (2015, April 29). Aim and Shoot: Child Soldiers of Northeast India. Royal Society for Asian Affairs. https://youtu.be/KqoErUYNU3g

Shah, M. (2022, March 7). AFSPA, Unemployment and Trafficking In Manipur: Children Of Northeast Lured By Militancy. Outlook India. https://www.outlookindia.com/national/afspa-unemployment-and-trafficking-in-manipur-childre n-of-northeast-lured-by-militancy-news-185579

Siddiqui, A. B., & Siddiqui, N. (2015, April). Child Soldier In India. International Journal of Advanced Research in Management and Social Sciences, 4.

The Northeast Today. (2016, August 22). Is Assam ready to tackle 'child soldiers' of ULFA? The Northeast Today. https://thenortheasttoday.com/states/assam/is-assam-ready-to-tackle-child-soldiers-of-ulfa/cid255 2512.htm

Tombing, T. (2018). Legal Pluralism and the Notion of Rights of Child Among the Tribal Communities of the Northeast India: A Critical Analysis. Child Rights Law & Policy Review, 1(1), 71-79.

Vinet, F. (2023, February 1). Child Recruitment and Use – Office of the Special Representative of the Secretary-General for Children and Armed Conflict. Children and Armed Conflict. Retrieved July 11, 2023, from https://childrenandarmedconflict.un.org/six-grave-violations/child-soldiers/

THE DEMAND FOR JUSTICE: REDISCOVERING INTERDEPENDENCE IN THE CONCEPT OF JUSTICE

DOCTOR SAPHIMOSHA W. BLAH

Unsurprisingly, the present century is referred to as an age of extremes—a century of illusions and disillusionments. The world is currently facing unprecedented uncertainty, which has given rise to various conflicts and crises. Conflict has always been a prominent aspect of the human experience throughout the ages. These conflicts act as barriers and create differences among people. Researchers have considered conflicts at different levels of analysis, ranging from interpersonal conflicts to those involving many people, where differences can be on the basis of nationality, race, gender, and language, to mention a few. Intrapersonal conflicts involve only the individual's personal beliefs, being true to one's convictions, and maintaining integrity. In other words, conflict can exist globally between nations, locally among various cultural groups, in the relationship between two people, and within an individual itself. Conflicts of any sort must be addressed for progress to occur. Until and unless an individual or community feels safe, the role of justice will always be questioned, and conflict is bound to follow. Hence, efforts have been made to resolve these conflicts, which is necessary for creating prospects for developing global culture and sustainable peace. One pertinent way of achieving this transformation of conflict in the individual is education.

When we turn our attention to India, we find terms like 'conflict,' 'insurgency,' and 'militancy' are so closely associated with the Northeastern region of India. The Northeast region is comprised of eight states: Assam, Arunachal Pradesh, Manipur, Meghalaya, Mizoram, Nagaland, Sikkim, and Tripura. The total area covered by the states is over 255,088 sq. km. The Northeast region's unique aspect is that it is home to more than 160 Scheduled Tribes belonging to five major ethnic groups and many other minor tribes, as well as a large and diverse non-tribal population. By 'scheduled tribes, ' we only refer to the tribes listed in the Sixth Schedule of the Indian Constitution. Thus, the region is characterized by extraordinary ethnic, cultural religious, and linguistic diversity, and almost 400 languages and dialects are spoken here.[1] Conflicts in the Northeast region, like in many other regions of the world, have indeed been a source of great suffering and have had far-reaching consequences, especially for innocent people. These conflicts often arise from various factors, including historical grievances, economic disparities, political marginalization, land disputes, and cultural differences. While the specific nature and causes of these conflicts can vary, the focus has often been centered on the role of how the government or government authorities promote or fail to establish policies to support the rights of the tribal people. In such a situation, the various ethnic groups have asserted their unique identities based on cultural, linguistic, and religious factors. Some have demanded greater autonomy or even separate states within or outside the Indian Union or SC/ST statuses. These demands have sometimes led to the emergence of insurgency groups that engage in armed conflicts with the Indian state. As a result, the region has experienced confrontations that have escalated into conflicts and violence. Eventually, this has created significant challenges for the Indian government and the affected communities. Take, for instance, the case of Dimasa versus Karbis in Assam, the Garo-Rabha conflict in the recent past in Meghalaya, Mizo versus Hmars and Reangs in Mizoram, and Naga versus Kukis in Nagaland.[2] The latest and most recent is the ethnic violence in Manipur, which erupted on May 3, 2023, between the Meitei community and the Kuki tribal community from the surrounding hills. So deeply rooted is the concept of conflict in the Northeast region that we have a generation of children associating the Independence Day and Republic Day celebrations with the 'bandhs' called by the various militant outfits. This characteristic in the Northeast has been aptly put forward by Choudhury when she writes that there is a growing trend in North-East India of idealizing 'little nations' against the larger idea of a 'nation' for the simple reason of preserving one's unique identity. This will only cause a drift and divide the various communities in the North-East.[3]

---

[1] Nityananda Kalita, "Resolving Ethnic Conflict in Northeast India," *Proceedings of the Indian History Congress*, Vol. 72, PART-I (2011):1354, accessed 30 Mar 2020, https://www.jstor.org/stable/44145746.

[2] Indrani Choudhury, "Negotiating Nations Within a Nation: Reading Rabindranath Tagore and the Ethics of Nationalism," *The Heritage: Multi-lingual Research Journal on Indology* Vol. IV, Issue-2 (2013): 9

[3] Ibid., 10

In all the unrest that the people of the region experienced, one thing that was very prominent in almost all the various agitations held at different places was that people questioned the role of justice. They would call out and carry slogans in various agitations that read, "We demand justice!". 'Rather than the possibility of peace, one believes that it is the continued memory of injustice and lack of official accountability that will define the strategies adopted by political actors in the region.'[4] Thus, the inability of the government or government authorities to be inclusive of human, social, and sustainable development is resulting in an increased concern about the role of justice in society.

The concept of justice has continuously been a major concern of social theorists and political philosophers from antiquity to the present. Thus, it is not surprising that theorists and activists involved in analyzing and critiquing the concept of justice have developed various ideas and proposed several socio-political practices to promote social justice. However, despite the seeming differences that can be found in the concept of justice, as reflected in the various theories of justice, some fundamental principles hold them together. However, before we look into these common fundamental principles, let us first examine the meaning of the concept of justice.

What is justice? This is an age-old question that has been asked for centuries. The fact that this question is still being asked even today shows that we still need clarification about the meaning of justice. According to some writers, justice has always been regarded as a political virtue.

As a virtue, it is understood that justice is concerned with individuals living in a society. The concern is, however, a restricted kind of concern. Justice looks toward the individual with a dispassionate gaze. It sees the individual without the various aspirations, idiosyncrasies, and weaknesses associated with the individual. The individual is viewed in relation to other individuals in society. In this way, we can say that justice is a neutral virtue. However, the universal attributes possessed by the members of society are of core importance to justice because they form the basis of rational judgment. It should also be noted that although justice is concerned with the individuals in a society, it is only concerned with the individual's past and present. Justice is not concerned with the individual's

---

[4] Sanjay Barbaro, "Rethinking India's Counter-Insurgency Campaign in North-East," *Economic and Political Weekly*, Sep. 2-8, 2006, Vol. 41, No. 35 (Sep. 2-8, 2006), 3805, Accessed 06 May 2023, https://www.jstor.org/stable/4418651.

future because the future is open.[5] Thus, justice implies that the individual should be treated in a non-arbitrary manner, where there is consistency, and where each person is to be treated as a unique rational agent.

So far, we have been looking at a very individualistic perspective of justice, that is, justice strictly from the point of view of the individual itself. However, it only seems logical that if we are to have a comprehensive understanding of justice, it has to be understood from an all-inclusive point of view. In this way, the concept of social justice comes into view. Social justice is concerned not only with the individual alone but with the whole society. Social justice includes not only the interactions among the different individuals but also the relationships of the individuals to their surroundings. Given the current global situation, the task of social justice is indeed challenging and complex. Another essential aspect that we should keep in mind is the fact that everything in this world changes constantly. Similarly, justice, which exists in the individual's thoughts and deeds, also changes with time. Perhaps this is the reason why the question of justice is always relevant.

We live in a globalized world where different cultures intersect and mingle. In such a multicultural and globalized world, the individual must be overtly or covertly engaging in processes that affect our social world, and these interactions will ultimately affect our understanding of justice. Cultural differences are expressed through language, religion, cuisine, family structure, lifestyles, and attire. These cultural differences can constrain effective communication, eventually leading to international misunderstandings and violence.

Coming up with an understanding of justice that includes the various views of the different social groups will not be easy. Nonetheless, there are fundamental principles that hold them together. The fact that the concept of justice has always enticed human minds cannot be denied. Therefore, apart from the seeming differences, there ought to be some similarities or common footholds somewhere. In order to determine this common foothold, this paper intends to look into the concept of justice as put forward by John Rawls, which has been called the most influential theory of twentieth-century political philosophy, and the view of justice as expressed in the worldview of the Khasi tribal culture, an indigenous

---

[5] J.R. Lucas, "Justice," Philosophy, Jul., 1972, Vol. 47, No. 181 (Jul., 1972): 229, accessed 22 Aug 2020, http://www.jstor.com/stable/3750151.

group of people from the Northeast region where conflict is widely experienced.

In his article, *Justice as Fairness: Political, not Metaphysical,* John Rawls states that the classical theories on justice tend to be very teleological because they stress one rational conception of the good. These classical theories were put forward by Plato and Aristotle, and the Christian tradition was characterized by Augustine and Aquinas. According to Rawls, they have no practical answers that are appropriate for a political conception of justice for a democratic society.[6] Thus, Rawls put forward his understanding of the concept of justice as a political concept in a democratic society.

According to Rawls, the conflicting disagreement in the present scenario prevents a person from realizing the values of liberty and equality in the basic structure of society. *Justice as Fairness* tries to solve these problems by proposing two principles of justice to serve as guidelines and to enable citizens to view themselves as free and equal persons. The two principles of justice are:

1. Each person has an equal right to a fully adequate scheme of basic rights and liberties, compatible with a similar scheme for all.
2. Social and economic inequalities are to satisfy two conditions: first, they must be attached to offices and positions open to all under conditions of fair equality of opportunity, and second, they must be to the most significant benefit of the least advantaged members of society.[7]

The aim of justice as fairness is very practical, for it represents itself as something that can serve as the basis of an informed and willing political agreement between citizens who are viewed as free and equal persons. To reiterate, Rawls discusses some basic ideas that make up justice as fairness. The idea of a society as a system of fair social cooperation between free and equal persons is considered to be an essential idea. The idea of social cooperation plays an integral part in Rawls's theory. To emphasize this point, Rawls put forward the following three elements:

---

[6] John Rawls, "Justice as Fairness: Political not Metaphysical," *Philosophy & Public Affairs*, Vol. 14, No. 3 (Summer, 1985): 248 – 249
[7] Ibid., 227.

1. Cooperation is distinct from merely socially coordinated activity, for example, from activity coordinated by orders issued by some central authority. Cooperation is guided by publicly recognized rules and procedures that those cooperating accept and regard as properly regulating their conduct.
2. Cooperation involves the idea of fair terms of cooperation; these are terms that each participant may reasonably accept, provided that everyone else likewise accepts them. Fair terms of cooperation specify an idea of reciprocity or mutuality: all who are engaged in cooperation and who do their part as the rules and procedures require are to benefit in some appropriate way as assessed by a suitable benchmark of comparison. A conception of political justice characterizes the fair terms of social cooperation. Since the primary subject of justice is the basic structure of society, this is accomplished in justice as fairness by formulating principles that specify basic rights and duties within the prominent institutions of society and by regulating the institutions of background justice over time so that the benefits produced by everyone's efforts are fairly acquired and divided from one generation to the next.
3. Social cooperation requires an idea of each participant's rational advantage or good. This idea of good specifies what those engaged in cooperation, whether individuals, families, associations, or even nation-states, are trying to achieve when the scheme is viewed from their own standpoint.[8]

From the idea of society as a fair system of cooperation, Rawls talked about his conception of humans, an idea that he assumed would support his view of society. According to him, a person is understood as a full participant in a fair system of social cooperation. Such a person is attributed with two moral powers, namely, a capacity for a sense of justice and a capacity for a conception of the good. A sense of justice is the capacity to understand, apply, and act on the basis of the public conception of justice, which characterizes the fair terms of social cooperation. The capacity for a conception of the good is the capacity to form, revise, and rationally pursue a conception of one's rational advantage or good. In the case of social cooperation, this good is understood as a concept of what is valuable in human life.

---

[8] Ibid., 232

Moreover, this concept of good comes with specific attachments and loyalties, which give rise to affection and devotion. Eventually, the individuals and associations considered the objects of these sentiments and part of the conception of the good would flourish. In such a conception, Rawls also includes a view of our relation to the world's religious, philosophical, or moral. In this way, the conception of persons is also assumed to be one of the basic ideas for justice as fairness. Thus, the strength of a concept like justice as fairness lies in social unity, which is understood in terms of society as a system of cooperation between free and equal people. Secondly, in the concept of a person who, according to Rawls, is a citizen who is a fully cooperating member of society over a complete life.[9]

The Khasis, an indigenous group of people found in the Northeastern part of India, like other indigenous communities, have a very close relationship with nature. So close is the relationship that the culture has an ongoing dialogue with nature that influences the Khasis' thoughts and actions. This learning from nature or close proximity to nature shapes the individual's character and sense of moral virtue. It is here that a worldview that is based on the old-fashioned way of life is found. That is a worldview where we are sensitive to the flow of nature through us and its direct implications for our ways of life.[10] This close communion with nature enables a Khasi to understand the surrounding natural world.

The Khasis tradition is an oral tradition. The Roman script used today was introduced to the Khasis by Rev. Thomas Jones, a Christian missionary from Wales, only in 1841. Though there are no written records and its past is undocumented, the oral narratives have documented the Khasi traditional wisdom and knowledge in nature all over the Khasi Hills.

Every aspect of nature is equally valuable to a Khasi. Humans do not occupy any special position in Khasi belief but are considered part and parcel of one creation. The fact that animals and birds are part of the human community has been reflected in most of the Khasis' folklore. Thus, when it comes to the question of justice, a Khasi is always of the opinion that a human cannot decide on the justice of another human or, for that matter, on the justice of the animals and plants, that is, the entire

---

[9] Ibid., 233 – 234.

[10] Holmes Rolston III, "Can and Ought We to Follow Nature?," in *Environmental Ethics: An Introduction with Readings,* Comp. John Benson (New York: Routledge, 2000), 238.

natural surroundings. Eventually, therefore, any plea for justice must be made to a higher authority, that is, *Ka Hok.*

Ka Hok, for a Khasi, is an eternal truth with no beginning or end. In fact, *Ka Hok* is considered to be a dispenser of justice. According to the Khasis, *Ka Hok* encompasses the whole existence, and it is connected to humans through *Ka Kren,* or the spoken word. *Ka Kren* is speech or communication in the collective conscience among the Khasis. It is a language understood by all co-existents that is not necessarily verbal or vocal. It is through *Ka Kren* that the individual relates itself to its surrounding world, that is, outside the individual. In this way, the individual, through communication, will connect or link itself to *U Blei* (God) and the other co-existents in the world. Consequently, through communication, the individual will establish *Jutang,* or covenant with *U Blei* and the other co-existents in the world. *Jutang,* for the Khasis, is sacred, *'lah ïatang,'* because it is bound to the foundation of *Ka Hok,* and therefore, it is considered a sanctified conviction or commitment established between two parties. For the Khasis, the sanctity of the *jutang* is established on *Ka Kren,* which is grounded on the all-encompassing *Ka Hok.* For a Khasi, humans live amidst various *jutang.* Like any other covenant, *jutang* also has witnesses. The nature, or *Mariang* is considered the witness or witnesses of the various *jutang* made. As mentioned above, nature has always been considered a living document for the Khasis. Since *jutang* is established on the basis of *ka Hok,* the Khasi forefathers warn their fellow beings to take *jutang* seriously. Once a *jutang* is made, breaking it without any fatal consequences is very difficult.

According to a Khasi, justice will come into play whenever there is a breach in the *jutang.* Justice will be served at any time and any place; there is no need for the victim to appeal for justice to other humans. The party that disrespects the *jutang* will be punished by being struck to death by lightning or killed by a tiger and other wild animals at any unexpected time or place. For instance, whenever there is a land dispute about the boundary, the victim will plead to the divinity as the judge and call upon the witness or witnesses of the *jutang,* which is nature, to restore the balance and settle the dispute. The verdict in such an appeal will come from nature, the fair witness to the whole ordeal. This is the law of the Khasis. *Ka Hok,* which encompasses nature, is the living law and the judge that will decide the fate of all people, animals, demigods, and evil in this world.[11]

A closer analysis of all the theories mentioned above reveals an element of interdependence that lingers in the background of these theories on justice. A theory of justice will directly or indirectly touch upon the element of *interdependence*.

In John Rawls's *Justice as Fairness,* this element of interdependence can be seen in his idea of social cooperation. According to Rawls, social cooperation is a concept that cannot be understood narrowly but rather as a conception of what is valuable in human life.[12]

Unlike the Western worldview that separates nature from humans, the Khasi worldview rejects such dualism and stresses that there is no separation between humans and other beings on Earth. In fact, the world is being viewed as the body of God. According to the Khasi worldview, the importance of interdependence has been expressed in the *jutang,* which are sacred and are not to be taken for granted. Whenever these *jutang* are disrespected, the Justice delivered is the verdict of the universe as a whole.

Now the question we are faced with is: how do we make a section of people who are made to think that they are backward, underdeveloped, and different realize that the value of their traditional practices that they have inherited from their ancestors can be compared with the theory given by someone from the so-called developed world? For instance, how do we make an indigenous person, like a Khasi, see that the core of its notion of justice is more or less similar to Rawls's Theory of Justice? That is, both theories stressed the importance of interdependence. It sure is very overwhelming and intimidating for an indigenous person to even think that the idea of justice is of some importance. This sense of inadequacy and, hence, a feeling of being intimidated or different from the 'other' is very noticeable when we look at the situation in the Northeast region of India. The region where conflicts are generally based on identity. This awareness of the 'other,' often associated with the 'fear of the other,' can be considered one of the leading causes of conflict. In such a conflicting

---

[11] Fabian Lyngdoh, *Ka Thymmei Pyrkhat U Khasi* (Shillong: Don Bosco Press, 2018): 198.
[12] John Rawls, "Justice as Fairness: Political not Metaphysical," *Philosophy & Public Affairs*, Vol. 14, No. 3 (Summer, 1985): 233.

situation, it is a human tendency only to pay heed to the differences and to ignore or be blinded to all the points of similarity or interdependence that exist among the different groups. In such a situation, the only apparent solution to mend the drift and bring unity among the different groups is to change the mindset or viewpoint of the people. Education as a pedagogical tool can significantly assist in bringing about this desired change. Education can act as a catalyst for bringing people together and making them see that they are all human beings first, with few differences between them. It can also make them realize that they have many things in common with each other. Education can be an eye-opener to the various groups in the Northeast region and worldwide. There is no need to resort to conflict or violence while seeking justice, as the truth of justice ultimately lies in interdependence. Although this may sound easy, it sure is a herculean task for education.

In this context, one is reminded of Rabindranath Tagore's innovative and pioneering ideas on education. It is crucial to delve into his broader philosophy of life, which is heavily influenced by the teachings of the Upanishads. Tagore viewed the entire universe as a manifestation of a single, all-encompassing force that exists throughout time and space. Consequently, any sense of difference or separation between individuals is an illusion born out of ignorance, which often manifests itself in conflicts.[13]

Tagore's concept of true wisdom revolves around recognizing the interconnectedness of all things, seeing the one within the many, and vice versa. Those who attain this heightened state of consciousness liberate themselves from suffering and pain. Eventually, they view every other person as a reflection of themselves, making it impossible to harbor ill feelings toward others. Here, love is pivotal in achieving this state, serving as the only force capable of uniting people worldwide.[14] Love is also the fundamental driving force behind creation and the ongoing continuity of life. This perspective explains why Tagore observed the principle of unity within diversity at work in all aspects of existence. He firmly believed that there is a divine essence within every living being, motivating him to respect and love all of God's creation. This belief underpins his naturalism, humanism, and internationalism.

---

[13] Salamatullah, "Tagore as educationist," *Indian Literature*, Oct. 1960/Sept.1961, Vol. 4, No. 1/2, Tagore Number (Oct. 1960/Sept.1961), 133 – 134, accessed 07 Sep 2023, https://www.jstor.org/stable/24157437.
[14] Ibid., 134.

However, having mentioned that Tagore's thinking was deeply rooted in ancient Indian culture, it does not mean that he was utterly oblivious to the currents of the modern world. Tagore's outlook was genuinely international, even when many leaders of the Indian national movement sometimes indulged in chauvinistic fervor. He recognized the limitations of narrow nationalism and urged his fellow citizens to transcend it. He stated, "The most important lesson today is how to free ourselves from arrogant nationalism. The history of tomorrow will begin with a chapter on internationalism, and we will be ill-prepared for the future if we hold onto any customs, habits, or modes of thought that contradict universalism." In a world rife with discord, he offered the profound principles of Shantam, Shivam, and Advaitam—Peace, Purity, and Oneness.[15]

Tagore unequivocally criticized the narrow interpretation of nationalism that often fused ethnic identity with national identity, resulting in a loyalty to an abstract ideal that prioritized the prejudices of specific dominant communities over the unity of humanity.[16] In the novel *Home and the World,* Tagore narrates his view on nationalism through his three characters: Nikhilesh, the wealthy zamindar Bimila, who is Nikhilesh's wife, and Sandip, an extreme nationalist leader in India's Swadeshi Movement. Nikhilesh is a man who is very deeply rooted in his traditional culture and yet, at the same time, very international in his outlook. He is the kind of person who is firm and would never bend his sense of justice and righteousness, even for the love of his country. This outlook is reflected when Tagore writes, "Our country quakes under every gaze, be it God's or the constable's. Now, in the name of freedom, if you bring back terror with a new name to it, if you want to plant your victory flag through oppression, then the ones who love the country would never bow down to that rule of terror…The limit of that terror determines how free the people of that land are. If it is used solely to curb violence against the others then it's obviously there to protect every individual from the cruelty of another individual. But if the reign of terror determines what one should wear, where he should buy his goods, what he should eat, and with whom he should have his meal, then it denies the basics of individual freedom. And

---

[15] Banshi Dhar, "The Humanism of Rabindranath Tagore," *Indian Literature* January-June 1973, Vol. 16, No. 1/2 (January-June 1973): 150-151, accessed 07 Sep 2023, https://www.jstor.org/stable/24157437
[16] Indrani Choudhury, "Negotiating Nations Within a Nation: Reading Rabindranath Tagore and the Ethics of Nationalism," *The Heritage: Multi-lingual Research Journal on Indology* Vol. IV, Issue-2 (2013): 10

it is tantamount to denying man his human rights."[17] In contrast, Sandip is a radical nationalist who is driven by fanatical nationalism and jingoistic devotion to his nation and is found to be a person who is unable to be a true man of his home, country, or to the world. "We will not gift desi clothes to the man who wants to buy foreign clothes. He is the one to be punished, not us. If they went to court, we would set their crops on fire; the gentle approach wouldn't work. Hey, Amulya, don't look so shocked. I don't get kicks out of setting the farmer's crops on fire. But this is war......"[18] Similarly, if education is to bring about any changes in the mindset of the people towards conflict, it is the mindset of Nikhilesh that one needs to imbibe. The outlook that Tagore portrays through his character Nikhilesh transcends the boundaries of the different states and even international boundaries. The love for humanity at large should be the pedagogical aim of education.

In conclusion, the current state of affairs is marked by degradation, not only in the Northeast region of India but as a global phenomenon. Over centuries, modern humanity has exploited the planet for progress, success, and economic development, resulting in an inner and spiritual depletion. Conflict and confusion pervade every aspect of society, from politics and social dynamics to individual experiences. Long-standing principles, objectives, and institutions are now being questioned. Mutual distrust, jealousy, fear, and suspicion drive the world, accompanied by rising poverty, violence, and intolerance. This contemporary society lacks a sense of basic consensus. In such a fragmented world where everyone is questioning justice, the path to resolution lies in reconnecting with ancient wisdom, emphasizing the insignificance of our magnified differences. Therefore, the need of the hour is to recognize that the feeling of oneness is the core that can hold everything together.

The concept of interdependence is at the heart of justice. Justice, as demanded in conflicts and protests, underscores cooperation and interdependence. Much like Rabindranath Tagore, we should prioritize our shared humanity. Tagore believed that humans are fundamentally moral beings, capable of treating others as moral agents with the capacity to make decisions. This ability enables us to form bonds and relationships with fellow human beings. Realizing our interdependence can help us address numerous global challenges. Change is constant, and our

---

[17] Rabindranath Tagore, *Nationalism & Home and the World* (India: Penguin Books, 2021), 231-232.
[18] Ibid., 214

understanding of justice evolves with time. However, a closer look indicates that, although prima facie, we may seem different from each other, we are all linked by the thread of interdependence. This realization can occur when we broaden our perspectives and look beyond the confines of narrow divisions. That is when we widen our mindsets and look beyond the 'narrow domestic walls.' To end in the words of Tagore,

> "Where the mind is without fear and the head is held high;
> Where the world has not been broken up into fragments by narrow domestic walls;
> Where words come out from the depth of truth;
> Where tireless striving stretches its arms toward perfection;
> Into that heaven of freedom, my father, let my country
> awake".[19]

Bibliography

1. Barbaro, Sanjay. "Rethinking India's Counter-Insurgency Campaign in North-East." *Economic and Political Weekly*, Sep. 2-8, 2006, Vol. 41, No. 35 (Sep. 2-8, 2006), 3805-3812. Accessed 06 May 2023, https://www.jstor.org/stable/4418651.

2. Choudhury, Indrani. "Negotiating Nations Within a Nation: Reading Rabindranath Tagore and the Ethics of Nationalism." *The Heritage: Multi-lingual Research Journal on Indology* Vol. IV, Issue-2 (2013): 7-15.

3. Dhar, Banshi. "The Humanism of Rabindranath Tagore." *Indian Literature* January-June 1973, Vol. 16, No. 1/2 (January-June 1973): 147–152. Accessed 07 Sep 2023, https://www.jstor.org/stable/24157437.

4. Kalita, Nityananda. "Resolving Ethnic Conflict in Northeast India." *Proceedings of the Indian History Congress*, Vol. 72, PART-II (2011): 1354–1367. Accessed 30 Mar 2020, https://www.jstor.org/stable/44145746.

5. Lucas, J.R. "Justice." Philosophy, Jul., 1972, Vol. 47, No. 181 (Jul., 1972): 229-248. Accessed 22 Aug 2020, http://www.jstor.com/stable/3750151.

6. Lyngdoh, Fabian. *Ka Thymmei Pyrkhat U Khasi.* Shillong: Don Bosco Press, 2018.

7. Rawls, John. "Justice as Fairness: Political not Metaphysical." *Philosophy & Public Affairs*, Vol. 14, No. 3 (Summer, 1985): 223 – 251.

---

[19] https://www.spiritualbee.com/media/gitanjali-by-tagore.pdf Gitanjali poem no. 35

8. Rolston III, Holmes. "Can and Ought We to Follow Nature?." In *Environmental Ethics: An Introduction with Readings,* Comp. John Benson, 237–242. New York: Routledge, 2000.
9. Salamatullah. "Tagore as Educationist." *Indian Literature*, Oct. 1960/Sept.1961, Vol. 4, No. 1/2, Tagore Number (Oct. 1960/Sept.1961), 133 – 139. Accessed 07 Sep 2023, https://www.jstor.org/stable/24157437.
10. Tagore, Rabindranath. *Nationalism & Home and the World.* India: Penguin Books, 2021.
11. https://www.spiritualbee.com/media/gitanjali-by-tagore.pdf Gitanjali.

Education:
Society's Cornerstone Institution for Improving the Quality of Life

ASSISTANT PROFESSOR MANEK NARZARY
AND DOCTOR LEON MILLER

Education is a liberating social activity that aims to develop or bring out the best qualities of the individual and is a means of developing the best quality of life for society (Dewey 2004, 106).

Introduction

In many ways, establishing the best type of learning experience for a classroom and the best type of atmosphere throughout a school is similar to what it takes to build a thriving community—it is all about the nature or quality of relationships. Without the right approach to relationships, we will be no more successful in the practice of pedagogy than we will be in the endeavor to build a thriving community. In the classroom, the school, and the community, building quality relationships is a matter of interacting in such a way that there is equal respect, mutual benefit, and mutual growth. In such relationships, each participant achieves what is in his or her best interest by relating to others in a way that creates benefits that are shared by each participant. In social terms, this means an approach to social relations where the personal development of each individual contributes to an improved quality of life for the entire society of which each is a part. In other words, the nature of the relationship contributes to the personal development of the members of society, which increases the quality of life within that social system. In short, education is a cornerstone institution for improving the quality of life for individuals and society as a whole. In order for the practice of pedagogy to be successful in this role, it must simultaneously be a method of teaching, an approach to personal growth and development, include a strategy for social development, be based on a viable social and socio-political philosophy, and, as well, be based on a communication theory effective for promoting and disseminating constitutive socio-political values and principles. Constitutive socio-political values and principles are the collective values of a community that constitute a type of normative power (i.e., having the power to enact the values and principles as social practice).

These desirable social outcomes can be achieved by viewing pedagogy as activities and processes that promote individual growth and development, social learning, and social development. This means an approach to pedagogy that promotes the holistic development of the individual members of society as the basis of social development. In other words, pedagogy plays a key role in empowering individuals and social groups to live in accordance with what they value most and to achieve what they aspire to do and/or be (Sen 1999, 74 & 87). Therefore, it is necessarily an integrative social mechanism with a special emphasis on modeling patterns of relating and communicating that are positive, creative, and respectful (based on etiquette, decorum, and wisdom as the mediums of interaction). When put into practice, it is effective because it establishes a model of inculcating civility by means of its relational dynamics and processes. In addition, there is an emphasis on the importance of Constructivist-type communication and collaboration among participants, thus interactions that involve a critical analysis and response to "real-world situations" (Bansal 2018, 680).

In order for the relational dynamics to be effective, participants must learn to accept and respect each other's differences. In doing so, participants will not merely interact with each other with tolerance but with a sense of mutual respect. In fact, the need for developing the virtuous character of individuals as the basis for increasing civic virtue is sparked by a decline in appreciation for tolerance. Such a decline is resulting in a rise in intolerance, incivility, and violence. Therefore, it is important to understand the relationship between the fundamental principles of human growth and development, pedagogy, and improved civic relations as a step towards reducing interethnic, class, intercultural, racial, and ideological conflicts.

Pedagogy, human growth and development, and social development are intricately linked in that they all have the aim of increasing the extent to which individuals experience the full development of their capabilities, holistic well-being, and happier, more successful lives. In addition, they aim to increase the extent to which individuals learn to live together in society in a way that maximizes the benefits and enjoyment they experience in their relationships with each other and the environment. This includes the members of society cooperatively engaging in civic activities in order to make desirable things happen for themselves rather than having the feeling that undesired things are happening to them over which they have no control (i.e., the members of society engage in co-creating desirable social outcomes) (Giddens, 1994, 15). There is also an emphasis on principles and values that, when put into practice, result in the optimal level of performance of both individuals and society by establishing the basis for "the learning society" (Dewey 2008, 320–322; Yang & Yorozu 2015, 10). In this respect, the philosophical framework, values, principles, and practices of this approach to pedagogy, personal development, and social development are relevant to educators as well as social theorists (i.e., teachers, psychologists, social psychologists, and public administrators). In both theory and practice, teaching individuals the connection between their own self-cultivation and their role in progressive social development is an important component of education, particularly in areas where individuals and social groups are subject to various types of discrimination, where there is tension between different ethnic and cultural groups, and, as well, in areas that are affected by or prone to conflict.

The goal of an integrative approach to personal growth and social development is to diminish, or even eradicate, a variety of problems that cause social fragmentation, conflict, inequality, prejudice, intolerance, discrimination, environmental destruction, injustice, violations of human rights, and other social problems. Therefore, the approach contributes to equal rights, justice, an improved quality of the environment, creating a world of peace, and other positive features (Bar-Tal 2005, 28). Linking education with human and social development contributes to reducing social conflict and promoting peacebuilding by generating a greater degree of social harmony, solidarity, cohesion, social order, and social justice. This is achieved by perpetuating certain principles, norms, and practices that have constitutive power—thus, an approach that is value-laden. The question is: what value is to be realized and how (Reardon 1988, 23)?

The value to be realized can primarily be described as improvements in how the members of society relate to each other, how they relate to their public authorities and public institutions, and increased evidence of social interactions that adhere to the principles of Cosmopolitanism (i.e., respect for the rights and dignity of every human being). Therefore, the integrative approach emphasizes the importance of developing the capabilities of individuals with the aim of training them to choose a life that enables them to realize what is of intrinsic value and, as well, enables them to contribute to creating the types of public value that enhance their collective social life. Therefore, the principles explain the most powerful and effective means of achieving positive social transformation and sustainable peace. Change means accepting new ideas that lead to progressive social development. In addition, in terms of what values are to be realized, fundamental pedagogical principles emphasize that "True education must be in touch with every aspect of people's lives: e.g., intellectual, eco-aesthetic, economic, social, and spiritual; and our educational institutions should be in the very heart of our society, connected with it by the living bonds of varied cooperation. True education is to realize at every step how our training and knowledge have an organic connection with our surroundings" (Tagore 1921, 2). In other words, the principles and values emphasize that human and social development does not occur by merely dispensing information. Personal growth and social development involve the school as a cornerstone institution of society, demonstrating a type of power of influence that extends from its core to the community and from the community to the greater society.

This chapter proposes that education and learning are social goods thus involve not only the interests of the students, the teachers, and the school but of the community and entire society. This chapter explains the fundamental concepts, principles, and values of the integrative approach. This chapter also explains the role of pedagogy in putting such principles and values into place as social practice. To realize these principles as social practice, society entrusts its teachers and the schools with the mission to develop the full capabilities of each student, to train them in the principles of mutuality, equal respect, tolerance, and social inclusion, and, in doing so, to ensure that, in return, the society enjoys a stable, prosperous, and peaceful future. The chapter points out that, given the complexities of society (especially when the level of ethic, cultural, and language differences is added), it is the nature of the relationship between individuals and the overall society that determines the quality of social life. In this respect, the chapter emphasizes why a Constructivist approach to teaching, interacting, and communicating promotes relational and interactive dynamics that result in complementary, mutually beneficial, and mutually enhancing agent-social structure interactions (Giddens 1984, xx-xxi & 14–16).

The following section of the chapter explains the principles underlying the integrative approach to pedagogy and the role of those principles in promoting human and social development. The section emphasizes that the effectiveness of this approach lies in the fact that it is simultaneously a method of teaching, an approach to personal growth and development, a strategy for social development, is based on a state-of-the-art perspective on social theory, and, as well, is based on a communication theory effective for promoting and disseminating constitutive socio-political values and principles. In this respect, this approach simultaneously impacts learning at the micro level (when teaching in formal, non-formal, and alternative settings) and at the societal level (when applied as a means of promoting social learning and engaging in networks of social discourse). Therefore, when applied as an approach to human and social development, the principles establish an ideal framework for a learning society. Ultimately, the section explains principles prescribing how the enhanced quality of life of the individual participants becomes evident in the quality of life of the social contexts where the model is applied.

The concluding section of the chapter explains the factors involved in putting the model into practice. This section provides an analysis of the types of interactions taking place between individuals, network facilitators, and the social sphere that create an improved quality of life. To illustrate how the model works, the concluding section explains the nature of casual powers that contribute to facilitating agent-structure complementarity. This power emerges from initiating particular processes that shape the nature of the relationship between the structure and its individual members (i.e., its agents). This establishes the basis for explaining why the relational approach to human and social development represents a coherent strategy for integrating individual and social causal mechanisms in a way that establishes complementary agent-structure dynamics. Most importantly, the concluding section explains how the application of the factors contributes to establishing a learning society and why agent-social structure interactions generate an increase in public value. Therefore, by marrying Constructivism with an integrative approach to human and social development, we end up with a model of how to co-create social reality. In other words, by integrating the concepts and principles underlying the Constructivist approach to pedagogy with those of the integrative approach, it is possible to determine the factors for co-creating an increase in social benefits that are mutually beneficial and satisfactory for the participating stakeholders.

The Conceptual Framework for a Pedagogical Approach to Improving the Quality of Personal and Social Life

"I would confine the term education exclusively to wisdom, justice, virtue, and righteousness. Education is the highest blessing bestowed on humanity, and it is the best of them on whom it is most fully bestowed. Schooling inspires the recipient with a passionate and ardent desire to become a perfect citizen" (Plato 1934, 21).

Education is one of the cornerstone institutions of society. As a cornerstone institution, it plays a major role in human, social, and sustainable development. A fundamental way of defining education is the activities and processes connected with personal growth and development. However, education can also be defined as a social institution that primarily focuses on developing the capabilities of the learners. In other words, education engages individuals in processes and activities that promote their personal growth and development (or that promote their self-cultivation), which involves far more than merely disseminating relevant knowledge. In fact, the etymology of the term education can be traced back to the root meaning of training individuals in how to enjoy a better personal and social life and how to have a better relationship with the natural order. If social pedagogy is added to the description of education, then the scope is expanded to include care for the growth and development of individuals throughout their entire lifespan. Therefore, this clearly does not only mean caring for students during the time teachers are in a relationship with them in the classroom. If education contributes to individuals having a happier, healthier, more successful, and more meaningful life (throughout their lifespan), then the responsibility educators have to learners extends beyond the classroom. That is to say that the success of this endeavor depends on the social dynamics that play a role in the well-being and success of the individual members of society. Consequently, educating also includes the responsibility of addressing the social dynamics that impact the lives of students.

Thus, the scope of educational activities necessarily includes the relationship between the school and society (i.e., in that society plays a key role in the continued growth and development of its individual members). This makes education a multidisciplinary activity that includes the personal growth and well-being of individuals, training in citizenship, and, as well, promoting the type of ongoing human and social development that can only occur in connection with establishing *a learning society*. The learning society, an educational philosophy advocated by UNESCO, goes beyond formal learning by including social pedagogy and lifelong learning as the keys to social development. The learning society is a broader concept that harnesses the elements of systems that facilitate the lifelong learning capacity of individuals. The ideal of a learning society is "Meant to be more than organizing principles of education; rather, it depicts a worldview of a democratic society in which all citizens have equal learning opportunities that enable them to unleash their full potential and participate in building the societies in which they live" (Elfert 2015, 92–93).

Conceptualizations of the relationship between the learner and society are based on fundamental principles of the science and philosophy of human and social development. From the perspective of the fundamental principles, the education of individuals and social groups involves instructing them on how to interact, relate, communicate, and engage in transactions that maximize the benefits they co-create and enjoy in their relationship with each other. Therefore, when we view teaching from the perspective of fundamental principles, it necessarily involves more than just institutional learning. In fact, an explanation of the foundational principles and The Philosophy of Education can be summed up by emphasizing the connection between the word college and the word collegiality. The etymology of both the words college and collegiality can be traced back to the same root meaning pertaining to the nature of a collegium (i.e., members of a particular school of thought, members of a school of philosophy, those who loved and pursued wisdom, and members of the earliest forms of a college who viewed themselves as equal in status or as colleagues). Both the concepts of college and collegiality refer to a community where interactions are based on a core unifying value or principle. In terms of how social behavior is structured in such communities, it means adherence to the ethos, principles, and standards of relationships that govern behavior among people of equal power. In other words, a participatory approach to power and governance.

But collegiality was also a principle emphasized at the earliest centers of learning. Therefore, both words can be traced back to an association of (or society formed by) members of a community who are respected for their insight, vision and foresight, wisdom and knowledge, and their ability at transformational leadership. Such associations were famous for teaching principles that optimized the impact that an integration of the various fields of knowledge had on human, social, and sustainable development. They were famous for teaching socio-political principles that prescribed how to elevate the human experience. They also prescribed how adherence to particular principles, ethics, and values contributes to increasing public value. Value is *the end result* of what social action is meant to achieve, and values reflect the knowledge humanity has gained regarding what how to realize what has value. Wisdom and knowledge are the basis for ensuring that society employs the best instrumental means for achieving its desired future goals.

If social life (e.g., whether tribal, village, or in complex societies) is essential for the growth and development of individuals and the flourishing of a social group, then developing collegiality (i.e., learning to socialize) is essential for the development of society. Learning to socialize means training that develops the virtuous character of individuals, which contributes to civic virtue. In terms of the ideals of pedagogy, this means a relational approach to teaching that not only contributes to developing the capabilities of the learner but also brings out the best in the learners (in terms of developing excellence in character). The learners, in turn, realize how to interact in ways that promote collegiality (within the community, the state, and the world) (Confucius 1869, 298–305).

In this respect, the relational approach to pedagogy plays a role in influencing the collegial-type relationships that shape the nature of society. It is in this way that "Education plays a role in encouraging and assuring robust democratic citizenship, deliberative spaces, participatory processes, collaborative practices, relationships of care, and shared futures" (UNESCO 2021, 40). This means that, on the basis of the relational aspect of pedagogy, there is mutual growth and development of both the teacher and the students (i.e., human development), which spills over into society (i.e., social development). Education is ideally a form of interaction where there is mutual respect, growth, and development for both the instructor and the learner. This means there is a transformational aspect involved in that the relational style inspires higher levels of motivation, performance, and integrity (Burns 1978, 4 & 18-21). Transformation occurs for both the teacher and the learner when the interaction dynamics of the relationship are mutually stimulating and elevating. Such transformational-type relationships ultimately become moral in that they raise the level of human conduct and the ethical aspirations of the teacher and the learners.

In other words, the values and communication style personified by the educator and taught to the participants in the learning experience (e.g., students, the future leaders of the civil body, and future public authorities) will enrich their lives in such a way that those values will become the shared values reflected in various aspects of social processes and activities. At this point, it should be stressed that personal and social morality are very much connected with understanding the relationship between the individual and the nature of society. Of course, this can only mean that there is an essential interdependence and interrelatedness between the individual and society, and as long as basic human rights are protected and relations are based on the basic principles of the "golden rule", the moral or ethical aspect of social existence is realized. The process of learning that serves to develop this way of thinking is designed to inspire a higher level of awareness, which also sparks the personal freedom necessary for creating "the good life". This is the type of knowledge that truly empowers and liberates individuals and social groups. The ideal is to awaken something within the inner nature of the learner (i.e., authenticity, sincerity, and self-actualization) (Tagore 1922, 187–188; Tagore 1917, 155–159). Therefore, the teacher draws from the depths of his or her own being to awaken something deep within the inner nature of the student. What is awakened can be referred to as a source of power that has a personal and socially liberating impact.

In this respect, those concerned with the role that education plays in elevating the human experience must address "The question of what should be the ideal of education" (Tagore 2007, 515). The ideal is that teachers must clearly explain the connection between the student's usual pursuit of instrumental means for achieving their endeavors and the role that higher-order intrinsic values play in realizing what is in their best interest. This includes explaining the role that intrinsic values play in achieving the highest good and establishing a just society. According to the foundational principles of educational philosophy, education involves not only disseminating knowledge but also relating to learners in a way that awakens something in the deeper levels of their inner selves. It also involves training individuals in how to relate to or communicate with others in a way that awakens something in the deeper levels of their being. In that respect, education not only involves preparing individuals for a life of success and happiness and how to be good citizens, but also matters of the highest good. This calls for an approach to pedagogy where the teacher acts as a "wise friend, guide, and helper" (Sri Aurobindo 2003, 390).

Therefore, to achieve this, the teacher must be a model of authenticity, sincerity, and self-actualization (Quintilian 1959, 511–513). Parents entrust their children to the school with the expectation that the teacher will take a benevolent "Attitude toward pupils and think in terms of being the representative of those who have committed their children to the school. Therefore, the teacher should be free from vice and refuse to tolerate it in others. Above all, the teacher must be a good model of the ideals and principles that he or she teaches" (Quintilian 1980, 213). The teacher plays the role of a person with excellent character. But it is better if it is not merely a role, but the teacher's character truly reflects what is good and honorable. It is in this respect that the teacher models the ideals of social relations: e.g., the teacher provides fair and equal treatment to everyone, never shows favoritism, and rewards strictly on the basis of merit. Because both authenticity and sincerity are involved, education is a moral process or moral relationship (both for the teacher and the student). As an activity with moral implications, it involves the relationship or duty that both the teacher and the student have to themselves, to others, to society, and to promoting a harmonious relationship with the environment, or, in other words, with the forces shaping the natural order (Trilling 1972, 5-6 & 9-11).

Relationships based on benevolence increase the possibility that good will be reflected in the interactions in the school and are expanded to include the other personal and social networks of the students and teachers. Consequently, the learning environment acts as a basic social value sphere (i.e., a basic social unit or function) that represents an intermediary value that operates on the basis of ideal-type relationships between the individual and the micro-level community and between the community and the greater society. It exists not merely for itself but for the one and the other and to help them fulfill each other (Sri Aurobindo 1997, 69; Confucius 1896, 311-312). It is in this way that the relational approach to education, the school, and the community form a pedagogical triangle, which establishes the basis of the learning society. This makes the relational approach to pedagogy (i.e., pedagogies of solidarity) "Vital for reparative justice and solidarity, which has recently become an important pedagogical aim in both formal and less formal learning. Pedagogies of solidarity help to transcend oppressive regimes by building consciousness of the need for collective awareness and action" (UNESCO 2021, 55). In this respect, the integrative approach to pedagogy enhances the psychological and social well-being of the individual members of society and, in addition, establishes more positive and beneficial interactions between the members of society and their public officials. This awakens an intention to cooperate in determining and undertaking the right type of social action for achieving the goals that the organized social body aspires to. However, more importantly, with the emphasis on training in human and/or natural rights, there is also a focus on the mutual realization of these rights (Confucius 1869, 152 & 226).

The fact that the institution of education impacts the total scope of social activities and processes means that there are many theories, sciences, and philosophies that address the different ends that the system of education must realize. "But when any of these comes under some single faculty, then in all cases, the end of the master science is more worthy of choice than the ends of the subordinate sciences. This means that we are inquiring about the most authoritative science, the highest master science. And this is obviously" socio-political science (Aristotle 2004, 4). It might be surprising for many readers that one of the world's most famous social psychological, ethical, and political economic philosophers would equate education with socio-political science. Therefore, the question is: why is education given socio-political significance?

Education is given socio-political significance because, from the perspective of classical pedagogical philosophy (in the Far East, South Asia, and the West), education involves praxis philosophy (i.e., an authentic and dialectical activity involving reflection and action). The ideal construction of education is one that is ethical and utopian, one that can make the public sphere more harmonious and produce a just social structure in which humanity is protected and the human condition improved. Therefore, from the perspective of classical pedagogical philosophy, education has socio-political significance because teachers ensure that students learn "The most authoritative science, the master science. Its end will include the ends of the others and will therefore be human good. The master science employs the other sciences and also lays down laws about what we should do and refrain from doing. Since knowledge seeks some good", the master science teaches students about the highest good (Aristotle 2004, 4 & 5).

Also, education is related to the master science because "Education is that terrain where power and politics are given a fundamental expression, since it is where meaning, desire, language, and values engage and respond to the deeper beliefs about the very nature of what it means to be human, to dream, and to name and struggle for a particular future and way of life" (Freire 1985, xiii). Consequently, when undertaking our professional educational mission in accordance with the fundamental principles of educational philosophy, we should actually teach students about what the master science prescribes as the means of achieving the highest good. Pedagogy has socio-political aspects because personal growth and social development involve a broad range of knowledge that includes the social sciences, critical pedagogy, ethics, socio-political philosophy, socio-political theory, and, as well, good governance. Teachers must instill socio-political literacy by enabling their students to reflect on, understand, and act on "The recognition of the world, not as a given world, but as a world dynamically 'in the making'" (Freire 1985, 106).

A Pedagogical Approach to Cognitive Development, Moral Development, and Social Development

Teachers display "Perfect virtue when by first taking the time to establish others, which is the means of establishing themselves. When they first help others to become prominent, they become prominent—this may be called the art of virtue or the master science" (Confucius 1869, 152).

"What can we do today so that tomorrow we can do what we are not able to do today" (Paulo Freire 2014, 115)?

This chapter addresses the role of pedagogy in shaping the socio-political reality of society. The chapter argues that pedagogy, as a cornerstone institution of society, is a key factor in shaping the nature of social life. The relationship between the teacher and the learner, the personal growth and development that individuals experience as a result of that relationship, the knowledge the learners gain about themselves and their world, and the relationship between the school and the community shape the quality of our future social life. In this respect, education and educators are the architects of social reality. That is to say that there is a visionary aspect to quality education. In addition to providing information, teachers also motivate and inspire students to transform their knowledge into innovative and socially entrepreneurial solutions to our current challenges.

This final section of the chapter explains how pedagogy can be simultaneously a method of teaching, an approach to personal growth and development, a strategy for social development, a viable social and socio-political philosophy, and, as well, a communication strategy effective for promoting and disseminating constitutive socio-political values and principles. The concluding section explains a strategy for teaching what encompasses both human and social development. Thus, the final section of the chapter explains how this can be achieved by structuring the learning experience so that it is simultaneously training in personal growth development (Confucius and Plato); an activity where the growth of the learner is based on knowledge/wisdom, experience, and reflection (Dewey, Tagore, and Sri Aurobindo); and structuring the learning experience in a way that demonstrates how pedagogy can be a powerful mechanism for development communication, communication for social transformation, and emancipation (Dewey and Freire).

Classical educators and philosophers viewed pedagogy as having a liberating impact. For classical educators and philosophers, the liberating impact is the result of teaching learners how they can experience a higher level of awareness (Plato 2003, 215-223). Therefore, it is essential that education involves a process of self-cultivation, which leads to individuals being able to simultaneously act with greater self-determination while at the same time acting in ways that earn them greater respect and admiration in society. Enlightened individuals follow the rules of propriety because they realize that by doing so, they increase the likelihood of being able to experience the value outcomes they ultimately desire (Confucius 1869, 190–193). Achieving a higher level of awareness enables individuals to discern how to act in ways that are in their best interests and experience their highest good. In fact, Mahatma Gandhi thought of liberation in similar terms. Gandhi asserted that freedom is achieved when individual consciousness is rooted in what is truly of enduring value rather than what has instrumental value. In Gandhi's own words, "The way to achieve freedom or liberation is to do pure and good deeds, to live truth", and to achieve freedom by means of restoring peace with others and harmony with nature (Gandhi 2005, 37).

Contemporary proponents of pedagogy, who prescribe education as a means of personal and social development, use the term *consciousness-raising* to describe its liberating impact. That is to say that critical pedagogy theorists stress that the young learners we work with in our classes and many members of the communities where we carry out informal, nonformal, and alternative education programs realize that they have not reached their full potential and do not feel that they are yet able to completely live in accordance with what they value most. Therefore, they are conscious of the need to learn more about how to develop their full capabilities and live fully in accordance with their ultimate values. Individuals and social groups therefore view the education process as a means by which they can become more fully human. Consciousness raising involves enabling individuals and social groups to conceive of and perceive possibilities (i.e., practical solutions) that can be achieved to improve the quality of their lives (Freire 2005, 113–114).

Why is it that consciousness-raising sparks the freedom to live a life of one's own choosing and making (i.e., shaped by self-determination) despite the social and economic constraints of society? The answer is that self-awareness increases the courage to be one's own person, to creatively express one's unique individuality, to draw from (or be rooted in) one's own value stance and convictions, and to express oneself authentically. Education does indeed train individuals to successfully satisfy their basic survival needs in ways that are prescribed by society, thus enabling them to have a good lifestyle in society. However, it is equally important to teach individuals that they potentially have available a mediating power (what Mahatam Gandhi referred to as knowledge of our authentic selves) that acts as a creative force that provides the ability to satisfy natural drives in ways that not only help individuals to be successful in social and economic terms but, as well, to express themselves in their own unique way and to realize what has ultimate intrinsic value for them, thus in ways that are more personally meaningful, rewarding, and fulfilling for them. In other words, by teaching individuals how to achieve a higher level of self-development (i.e., a higher level of consciousness), we are also teaching them a primary means of achieving independence and how to align their actions with their deepest convictions and values. Thus, they are empowered to experience what they value most as the outcome of their actions.

In contemporary terms, this is referred to as a value-centered approach to leadership, success, and happiness. This means an approach to pedagogy that is inclusive of teaching leadership, values clarification, and how to maintain a focus on intrinsic values. To accomplish this, the teacher must train students to be intrinsically motivated or self-motivated rather than extrinsically motivated. Of course, leadership also involves training in persuasion (i.e., a form of motivation), how to be convincing and influential, and how to empower others. This is why rhetoric (i.e., the art of public speaking) was such an important part of classical education, especially in regard to leadership training. In short, it is important that education focuses on how to awaken within the students a vision of a better future and how to make the best use of available resources to accomplish it. The learning experience should be structured in a way that helps the learner understand transformational leadership (i.e., how they can develop the ability to transform a current situation into a better or more preferred one). The teacher does this by awakening the students to a higher level of consciousness, which enables them to perceive, conceive, and experience reality in a better or more enlightened way. Therefore, the teacher must appeal to and cultivate something in the deepest nature of the student (the term to describe the deepest nature in ancient philosophy is the psyche), and the teacher must train the student to both trust in and have an intuitive attunement with their own inner nature.

It is in this respect that the teacher reflects sage-like wisdom, and the knowledge passed on to the students is of a sage-like nature. It is only in this way that the teacher can motivate the students to holistically develop their full potential and to have great achievements in life. Therefore, leadership training is not only an important aspect of the course content but an approach to the relational style of the teacher, e.g., the lesson brings out the best in the students and gives the students a sense of how to relate to others in a way that brings out their best (Confucius 1869, 196). Teachers become transformational leaders when they structure the learning experience so that it includes a transformation of the attitudes, beliefs, and behaviors of the learners. This means that there should be transformational dynamics that shape the student's growth, development, and heighten their level of awareness. In other words, students learn leadership skills that empower them to become influential, transformational leaders. Transformational leaders inspire others "To act for certain goals that represent the values and the motivations—the wants and needs, the aspirations and expectations—of both leaders and followers. Thus, transformational leadership occurs when one or more persons engage with others in such a way that leaders and followers raise one another to higher levels of motivation and morality" (Burns 1978, 19 & 20).

Both classical and contemporary social theorists view aesthetics as a means of raising the level of awareness and consciousness of learners and of the members of a social community. In short, lessons in aesthetics aim at teaching individuals how to turn their lives into a beautiful experience (i.e., into a work of art) (Foucault 1984, 350). Aesthetics is a means of connecting the learner to the highest level of awareness and, if employed effectively, serves to establish peace, harmony, and solidarity in society. Plato, in the section of his political philosophy (i.e., The Republic) that uses the cave as a metaphor to explain a lack of higher awareness, points out that it can be equated to being in the dark and only experiencing a shadowy glimpse of reality. Aesthetics is regarded as providing a creative and illuminating experience, which results in elevating, ennobling, and enriching the human experience. In this respect, aesthetics empowers individuals to find creative means to overcome the struggles and challenges they face in the endeavor to increase what is good and pleasurable in their individual and social experiences. Aesthetics enhances the quality of life by providing works of art that uplift the spirit and beautify the human experience.

Classical social theorists and socio-political philosophers viewed lessons in aesthetics as a means of teaching the art of living, living beautifully, and the aesthetics of self-making. This includes the art of having experiences that are more satisfying and fulfilling, as well as acting in ways that contribute to beautifying the life of the community one is a part of. Teaching aesthetics involves training individuals in how to connect with what is most real and meaningful in their innermost being and express that in ways that elevate social life. Aesthetics spark a feeling of experiencing a fuller sense of oneself in the world and a stronger sense of having a harmonious connection with existence. "Thus, it is not limited to what is beautiful in nature and art but embraces the whole realm of morality and manners" (Gadamer 2006, 34). That is the reason why Confucius proposed aesthetics as a means of elevating individuals to higher levels of success and achievement. "An aesthetic aptitude is awakened by poetry [or the Songs], established by ritual, and perfected in music" (a translation of Confucius 1869, 164). Confucius' teachings about aesthetics, personal growth and development, and social development are referred to by the principle "Wen" (which is translated as "The Arts of Peace").

Aesthetics enables individuals to connect with their deepest longings and provides the creative freedom to express them in ways that contribute to the beauty, ecological, and cultural aesthetic enrichment of society. Therefore, by training individuals and social groups in aesthetics, the teacher enables them to focus on realizing, appreciating, and creating more of what beautifies, enriches, and elevates the human experience. By teaching aesthetics, we awaken our students to the interrelatedness of things. We help them to become aware of the fact that "Reality is not based on the substance of things but on the principle of relationships" (Tagore 134). We help our students learn that reality (i.e., reliable knowledge) is the unfolding of the truth of existence in the deeper consciousness of the creative individual. Therefore, the ability to turn one's life into a beautiful experience—what is referred to as the aesthetic epiphany or an aesthetic awakening—is achieved by training individuals and social groups in the importance of aesthetics (Miller 2011, 1-2).

Liberationist Pablo Freire stressed that aesthetics is an important part of teaching individuals how to transform undesirable conditions into outcomes that are more rewarding and fulfilling. Therefore, he argued, the lack of creativity causes individuals to lack confidence, to become misguided, and to fail to develop or experience their full humanity. "Creativity stimulates action, thereby responding to the need that individuals must be authentic and engaged in creative transformation. Hence, it is prophetic (and, as such, hopeful). It affirms individuals as beings who transcend themselves, who move forward, and look ahead" (Freire 2014, 84). Education must be a means of connecting individuals with the source of their inner-most creative potential so that they can clearly understand who they are and so that they are empowered to use their potential creative ingenuity to more wisely build the future.

From the classical perspective, pedagogy aims to train individuals to either make a valued contribution to their societies or to become future teachers who would train others to contribute to elevating the quality of life in society. Toward that end, the focus is on character development, virtue ethics, developing sage-like wisdom, and developing foresight or vision. In some respects, this involves holistically developing the full potential of the student. If explained from a contemporary perspective, pedagogy involves engaging students in three stages of personal growth and development: (1) training students in how to meet their basic needs by making a valued contribution to society; (2) providing lessons that spark emotional, character, and moral development, which enables students to grow beyond dependency and a lack of self-determination toward independence and interdependence; and (3) providing the type of training, guidance, and influence that motivate students to experience both peak experiences and optimal performance. In short, pedagogy empowers students so that they are able to successfully experience all three levels of the classical and contemporary hierarchy of values, which means achieving their highest good. The teacher devises a lesson plan that has a transformational effect. In the words of the founder of the contemporary hierarchy of value theory, Abraham Maslow, the teacher structures the learning experience so that students learn to live meaningful and fulfilling lives, they become the best that they are capable of being, they experience self-actualization in terms of fully becoming their authentic selves, and they develop or are developing to the full stature of which they are capable (Maslow 1970, 150).

The foundational principles for The Philosophy of Education for the social sciences and political philosophy stress that one of the important aims of pedagogy is to train the future leaders of society, train future teachers who will provide instruction on leadership, or train individuals who will be among the most respected in society because of their exemplary character and wisdom. In other words, the foundational principles stress that achieving "the good life" and accomplishing the ideal goals that social activity aims to achieve require that teachers train their students in the art of leadership. Leaders "Care for all the things [concerning the various aspects of social life] and weave them all together most correctly" (Plato 1984, III.60). This means that the character of the teacher should be inspirational or motivational. For the classroom to have such an impact, the teacher must motivate and/or inspire by example, meaning that the character of the teacher and his or her teaching style must be transformational. Therefore, teachers are themselves models of exemplary leadership, which enables them to motivate or inspire participation in a larger vision, a greater goal, or a higher ideal.

Structuring Lessons so that they Encompass Knowledge/Wisdom, Experience, and Reflection

Students (both those in secondary schools and those studying in higher-level educational institutions) are oriented toward one of three levels of growth and development: dependence, independence, and interdependence. "We each begin life as infants, totally dependent on others. Then, over the years, as we continue to grow, we become more and more independent, until eventually we can take care of ourselves, becoming inner-directed and self-reliant. As we continue to grow, we become increasingly aware that all of nature is interdependent and that there is an ecological system that governs nature, including society" (Covey 1990, 49). Individuals who are dependent continue to rely on being sheltered by others; they rely on others for direction, and they feel that they cannot get what they want in life without the support of others. Therefore, dependency implies a need for growth toward becoming one's own person (i.e., it implies a need for becoming mature). In this respect, education is the process of guiding growth so that it produces a person with qualities that contribute to independence.

Independent people have acquired enough of the fundamentals of learning to give them confidence in their ability to decide for themselves and to effectively manage their life affairs. They are, in fact, experimental in that they are deeply immersed in intelligently applying their knowledge of how to care for themselves. Therefore, successfully managing independence requires knowledge of the best instrumental means of attaining the end value one ultimately desires, which means learning that this almost always requires cooperation with others. The knowledge and actions of the independent individual may be sufficient to initiate a course of action, "But the outcome depends upon the interaction of his or her response with energies supplied by other agencies" (Dewey 2004, 143). So gradually, as individuals continue to grow and develop, and as they continue to experience and reflect, they learn that the ultimate fact of existence in the natural and social worlds is interdependence.

Interdependence is the paradigm of being essentially interconnected with others in society and with nature. However, in practical terms, it involves having matured to the point of having learned how to act in ways that are mutually beneficial and mutually satisfactory and that generate these positive outcomes on a sustainable basis. Therefore, one of the most important aspects of pedagogy is teaching students interdependence. This requires structuring lessons so that they encompass knowledge, wisdom, experience, and reflection. In doing so, the learning experience includes an aspect of personal growth and development that empowers, in that it teaches students to understand the nature of the interdependence between themselves and their natural and social environments. Therefore, when classes are structured to include knowledge, experience, and reflection, students learn the connection between interdependence and cooperative, collaborative, communicative social activity (Miller 2022, 159 & 159–197).

Knowledge is not static or passive in that it merely affords students prolonged periods of blissful reverie that they can enjoy as a result of having reached a certain level of consciousness. Knowledge is active in that it teaches students how to apply it toward a better quality of life for themselves, their families, and their communities. That is to say that learning is relevant when it enhances the student's life experience. The object of inquiry and reflection is that they become "A factor in the completion of a course of events in which the student is engaged and by whose outcome the student is affected" (Dewey 2004, 146). The information the student learns becomes knowledge when the student understands how it can be applied to experience to create an outcome that the student desires. Thus, the information the student is acquiring in the classroom is useful when it can be applied as knowledge of how to create a desired experience and an outcome that the student prefers. When reflection reveals that the change from a less desirable experience to a more desirable one is made possible by what is taught, then the lessons are filled with meaning and significance.

Therefore, this section of the conclusion focuses on how to transform the theoretical principles and values, which are explained above, into a practical course of action that is beneficial for students, their families, and their communities by means of a learning process that encompasses knowledge, experience, and reflection. In other words, this section explains an approach to learning that enables individuals to not only envision possibilities that do not now exist but, as well, ways in which they can engage in practical experiential and communication activities that increase the possibility of bringing them to fruition, even with very limited resources. In this respect, this section focuses on learning, relational, and communication strategies that not only contribute to personal growth and development but also generate positive social outcomes (Kohlberg 1981, 26–27 & 54–59). In addition, as part of a pedagogical process, it includes a means of evaluating the impact that learning, relational, and communication strategies have on individuals, social communication processes, and social life.

We imagine the school years as a period of time that students spend in the "ivory tower", focused on their personal growth and development, and sheltered from the pressures of life, which the years of schooling will, supposedly, teach them how to manage effectively. However, it is increasingly clear that in the second decade of the 21st century, that is not necessarily the case. Students today are experiencing an inordinate amount of personal and social pressure. For example, The New York Times reports that gun fatalities are the leading cause of death for children and youth (ages 1–17). The article goes on to report that the child gun fatality rate has doubled since 2013. And a number of these fatalities are increasingly occurring in schools at a staggeringly high rate. The National Institute of Health adds to this report by pointing out that the extent of such violence is often associated with significant mental health issues, including anxiety, traumatic stress, and depression, which are affecting the mental health and cognitive development of our youth.

Both UNESCO and UNICEF stress that the youth of today are experiencing challenges that make it difficult for them to achieve happiness, peace of mind, and true fulfillment. The difficulties they face are challenges to their principles, character, and integrity; challenges to balancing what is best for themselves personally with what is best for their communities; and, as well, even challenges to their health and psychological well-being. Our students are hearing it reported by several media outlets on an almost daily basis that humanity has put itself on a course that is not sustainable. And they are increasingly realizing the consequences of this unsustainable path in their own personal lives. Consequently, according to the CNBC news channel, youth suicide rates rose by 62% between 2007 and 2021. UNICEF reports that suicide is the second leading cause of death among young people in Europe today. There has been more than a 32% increase in youth suicides in India in recent years, and the suicide rate among 5 to 14-year-olds in China has quadrupled in the last decade.

Certainly, the intent here is not to paint a gloomy picture of the state of today's youth. But a point should be made that teachers are remiss if they only focus, for example, on math, science, and commerce but fail to address what really has meaning in the lives of students today. In fact, because these are such troublesome times for youth, many secondary school districts and higher educational programs around the world have asked their school administrators and teachers to find ways to include character training, values clarification, moral development, lessons in integrative and holistic well-being, and paths toward individual and environmental well-being into their school's curriculum and classroom lessons.

It is certainly true that it is easier to steer the class content toward personal growth and development in courses like psychology, educational psychology, value clarification, and ethics. However, it is equally true that motivation and focusing on bringing out the best in the students are even important in classes like physics and biology. In addition, the significance of issues like climate change, sustainability, and increased health threats makes topics like the interconnected web of existence, relationality, integrality, and holistic well-being extremely important, even when teaching classes like governance and public administration. Finally, even for studies of business and commerce, topics like the co-creation of value, creating shared value, and the co-creation of social reality have become extremely popular in organizational, management, and social economic courses. And the shift to the sustainability paradigm opens the way to teach students about topics like Systems Theory (i.e., the reliance of the economy on its greater ecosystem and the fact of nature-human interdependence).

One of the most important and basic aspects of teaching is motivation. In terms of classroom teaching, to motivate students means to captivate their attention, which involves strategies for keeping them interested in the subject matter throughout the lesson. The key to motivation is to connect the subject matter of the class to something that is very important or meaningful in the life experience of the student. Students at the upper secondary level take a number of classes every day; most of them are required. Therefore, the student is not necessarily highly motivated in the subject matter of each of those classes. Certainly, a primary task and challenge of teaching is arousing the interest of the student. During the early years of higher education students are beginning to think about a major, which is usually a career choice as well. This means that students are more likely to be motivated by courses related to their profession. But there are still others that are required; thus, motivation continues to be a factor. At both levels, in many respects, the motivation of the student depends on the relational and communication style of the teacher.

In fact, when students are asked to reflect on the teachers that impressed them the most or that they admire the most, they usually remember teachers because of their personalities. Students even report that they were able to perform better in courses they did not find particularly interesting when the teacher had the type of character or personality that motivated the interest of the students. As with many other areas where relationship building and communication skills are important, individuals who are best at relating and communicating do not merely focus on the topic being discussed. They regard the topic as an opportunity for and as the medium for relating. In other words, those teachers understand that, for example, they have one hour with a group of students. Both the teacher and the students want that one hour to be as enjoyable, meaningful, and informative as possible. Therefore, what comes across to the students is not only the informative aspect, but the teacher uses relational and communicative strategies for raising the level of enjoyment and meaning the students experience during that hour.

The activities and dynamics of the classroom and the school that elevate the life experience of students and bring out their best can be divided into two types: (1) those taking place within the classroom and (2) experiences students have with teachers and the school during extracurricular activities. As mentioned above, the ability of the activities and dynamics of the classroom to motivate and inspire students depends on the character of the teacher and the extent to which the teacher balances concern for the subject matter with concern for the growth and development of each and every student. Students are impressed, motivated, and even inspired when teachers demonstrate dedication. Dedication, primarily in the sense that Quintilian advocated in his pedagogical philosophy means foremost that the teacher must demonstrate having achieved some degree of self-cultivation and the teacher's knowledge of the subject matter should reflect insight and wisdom. And, as was advocated by both Quintilian and Confucius, although the teacher is an authoritarian figure, he or she also demonstrates having a sincere interest in the student (an interest that is similar to the concern of a parent). Therefore, there is a dynamic of benevolence that is sensed by the students, although balanced with guidance and discipline. Students are motivated when the teacher acts in accordance with the principles of virtue ethics as prescribed by Aristotle. Teachers who are best at motivating students seem to love (or even be excited about) their subject matter. Thus, they are able to reveal facets of the subject in a way that arouses interest—by pointing out aspects that are unique, interesting, meaningful, and important to the life experience of the students. But equally important teachers that impress students the most seem to love their interactions with the students. The positive energy they generate seems to be contagious in that it establishes the dynamics of the classroom atmosphere.

Then where does the process of knowledge, experience, and reflection fit into classroom motivational strategies? The knowledge, experience, and reflection learning process are the basis for transforming the students outlook from that of "I want" or "I hope" to that of "I will". But just as the teacher is a positive influence on the students, the student should begin to understand the connection between his or her self-cultivation and having a positive impact on others and on society. The reputation of the school is significantly influenced by the success of its students. Therefore, it is helps teachers to motivate students by making sure they understand that their success is important to them because it means success for the school. Students are motivated and act more proactively when teachers make it clear that the lessons in the classroom and the school itself provide resources to help them accomplish what they aspire to do and/or be. But for this to work, the teacher must explain the basics of inner direction, self-motivation, and critical thinking.

Therefore, the best teachers and those most familiar with and confident with their subject matter can contract with each student by training them in the basic aspects of the art of living, self-direction, and self-motivation.

This involves asking students to reflect on what they need most from what the class has to offer (and, as well, what the school has to offer), how they want to demonstrate having mastered their learning experience in the class, and in what ways the learning experience can be applied to their practical affairs. In effect, the teacher is asking the student to describe how the learning experience can provide them with practical benefits and be both meaningful and fulfilling. Of course, this ideally includes asking the student to reflect on and explain how the knowledge gained from the class and the insight gained from their reflections and their experiences in the class can be applied toward making the world a better place.

During the early years of university training, most students have not yet mastered the principles connected with raising the level of their consciousness and the principles that empower them so that they experience a greater sense of self-determination. Thus, there is a need to deepen their understanding of the principles connected with the art of living and the art of self-making. In fact, even when students have reached the master's level, they usually just try to do their best in their studies, hope to land a good and rather high-paying job after school, and, as a result, enjoy the life of a professional, which can offer a rather good lifestyle. This means that even if students are focused on preparing for a future job and their hoped-for good salary, teachers must not forget that it is equally important that students understand the significance of and experience some degree of self-discovery (i.e., the students need to learn the significance of reaching the highest level of the value hierarchy described in Humanistic Psychology, or what virtue ethicists refer to as achieving their highest good and what is in their best interest).

However, if the teacher is to fulfill the responsibility of bringing out the best in the student and indeed elevate the life experience of the student, then the teacher must help the student learn the significance of a value-centered approach to life, which includes having convictions, being a person of integrity, and being true to oneself. A strategy for doing this is to ask the students to reflect on the meaning of what the Cheshire cat said to Alice (in Lewis Caroll's novel "Alice in Wonderland"). To paraphrase, in order to make it more meaningful for the students in your class, the idea is, "You can't get what you want if you don't know what you want." Or perhaps it is a bit more explicit when stated as "you can't get what you want until you know what you want". Wishing and hoping are not enough; students really need to reflect on the connection between the values that motivate their behaviors and what they experience as a result.

It is when students begin to understand the connection between values and the fact that their values shape their life experience and the nature of social life that they increase their chances of achieving what they aspire to, despite the obstacles, traps, and distractions in social reality.

Those activities and dynamics taking place during the school's extracurricular activities are also of two types: those that play a role in the character development of the student and those where the focus is on training students in creative and constructive ways to address important issues in life. Sports, for example, is a good means of training students in self-cultivation in that it provides a holistic approach to developing their potential, character development, and learning to cooperate with others to achieve a collective aim. Sports training also teaches youth how to balance concern for themselves with concern for others, and that the success they are hoping for depends on cooperating with others. Lessons in sportsmanship train talented individuals in team leadership, the coaching style of leadership, and belief in the ability to accomplish a goal despite all obstacles. And of course, sports psychology teaches individuals how to motivate other teammates. But in addition to sports, debate club is an activity students can engage in to address vital social issues. The school newspaper (or journalism) is also a way students can learn to address issues that are important to the lives of the students, to the school, and to the community. A school drama club is a good way of using theater to address and/or reveal important issues about the nature of being, tragedy, and facing and overcoming life's most difficult challenges. In most cases, lessons in the classroom contribute to the student's intellectual development. However, teachers should also be mindful of engaging students in ways that help them develop their creative potential. Actually, creative activities help students get in touch with the deeper level of their being and express their unique individuality in creative ways.

Finally, getting students to explore alternative media (e.g., social media) by encouraging or even, in some cases, assigning them to actually participate in a significant social network that operates for the purpose of community development is a good way of engaging students in meaningful extracurricular activities. The aim is to engage students in dynamic interactive activities, processes, and networks that create value for themselves and others. This process is structured to first have students reflect on the conditions in society that are most likely to be an obstacle for them, engage in dialogue to generate knowledge of the best way to deal with the challenges, and finally plan a course of action that they believe is practical and beneficial. In this way, the process nourishes the student's personal, cognitive, and moral growth and development (Kohlberg 1981, 54 & 57). It is in this way that teachers are combining the moral development of students with teaching them that to protect their own best interests, they must be concerned with promoting and protecting the best interests of others. The idea is that students will find such activities satisfying, meaningful, and fulfilling when they perceive them as having a positive impact on their own lives and the lives of others that they care about (Brodie et al. 2019, 173–188). Thus, in this way, teachers train students to understand the connection between their intellectual development and their moral development (between personal virtue and civic virtue). But in the long run, this involves addressing real-world concerns and issues that could affect the life of the student and the student's ability to achieve what he or she aspires to.

Pedagogy, Public Discourse, and Social Transformation

"Universities will be judged, and learn to judge themselves, by the variety and vitality of their interactions with society. Those interactions are what we term 'engagement'. Twenty-first century academic life must champion engagement with the wider society and its concerns" (Smerek et al., 2001, i).

At the earliest stages of human existence, when people lived in small tribes and were closely bound together by kinship ties, and later, when they lived in communal villages with looser and more extended ties, collective agreement was easily achieved by means of public deliberation, which also established the norms that everyone conformed to. In that respect, public discourse and determining the collective will can be regarded as means by which a social group is bound together in cohesion, solidarity, and harmony. When society became more complex (following the emergence of city-states, kingdoms, and empires), collective agreements were established by individuals deliberating within social networks. However, it should be kept in mind that those deliberations, and thus the decisions they made, primarily represented the voice and influence of the elite, who deliberated within networks of power. Those networks of power could include the ruling authorities, intellectual elites (i.e., scholar officials and those who had powerful and very influential rhetorical skills), and those who displayed sage-like wisdom that could influence the powerful elite. In the Far East, scholar officials were ministers of the court; in the West, those with powerful and influential rhetorical skills were referred to as Sophists, and in both the West and the Far East, those displaying sage-like wisdom were founders of philosophical schools and visionaries. This continued right up to the founding of the nation-state. Nation-states represented a shift toward establishing governments that were "of the people, for the people, and by the people". But for a society and its government to actually enact the will of the people, certain principles have to be adhered to. Political philosophers and theorists refer to public discourse as one of the most important or essential principles. Public discourse is a form of deliberation in which collective agreement on decisions is reached.

The point is that throughout the history of human existence, the fundamental principle of social formation has been and continues to be that personal well-being is enhanced by safeguarding collective well-being. However, getting the individuals of a complex society, made up of millions of people, to interact in ways that shape a collective will and, thus, in ways that enact the will of the people, proves to be an overwhelming task. The fact is that in large, complex, and diverse societies, multiple publics exist, and these publics typically have different interests, competing claims, and different understandings of how to communicate in ways that form a collective agreement. However, even though there is a tendency for individuals to be consumed with their own self-interests—thus, to focus on their individual concerns, their personal challenges, and their endeavor to establish their desired lifestyle—the fact remains that because of our interdependence, what is in our best interests is directly correlated to the good of all (i.e., the good of all means making things better for everyone). A collective public agreement that establishes practices, processes, and patterns of social activity that will establish the good of all can only happen when individuals participate in some form of public discourse.

Of course, public deliberation is an approach to decision-making that calls into consideration not only the value that the members of society are hoping to achieve but also the means of achieving that value. Public discourse is the means of determining a collective agreement on what constitutes the best, most legitimate, and just means of achieving social goals. Therefore, to the extent to which self-interest thwarts participating in relational and communicative activities for co-creating the good of all, individuals not only suffer personal and social loss, but they hinder the prospect of establishing a society that is *of the people, for the people, and by the people*. In fact, even if communicative action takes place within a microsocial network, it can produce a discourse that is admired, accepted, and endorsed by the larger public. So, such a discourse is worth the undertaking.

But the question might be, how does that involve classroom teaching, the patterns and dynamics of relations in the classroom, and thus, communications in the classroom? Or, if asked in the form of the question that Socrates put to Protagoras in the dialogues of Plato, in what ways will the student become a better person by attending your class, how is civic virtue improved because of your class, and/or in what ways will the world become better as a result of your class (Plato 2002, 11–18)? The answer is that it is easy to see the connection between pedagogy, becoming a better person, social development, and a better world if one thinks in terms of the famous "ripple effect" put forward by Professor Edward Lorenz (the winner of Japan's highest and most prestigious award for lifetime achievements in the arts and sciences). The "ripple effect" proposes that one small change in the conditions of one state of being can create a ripple effect that results in consequences that impact a larger system. Thus, when students engage in practicing the prescribed approach to relationality and communication within their own social network, a ripple effect can be generated. This section focuses on pedagogy as a powerful form of communicative action, although it occurs within a particular public network. The public is defined in the sense stressed by Dewey. "The public consists of all those who are affected by the transaction" and who agree that the issues addressed demand an appropriate response (Dewey 2016, 69).

This section of the chapter focuses on pedagogy as a powerful form of communicative action that occurs within a particular network of social relations and establishes a form of social discourse. This section explains the significance of deliberations in the classroom, between the teacher and the students, within the school, and between the school and society. Therefore, it provides examples of how pedagogy can be an effective form of social discourse. The focus is on the connection between pedagogy, public discourse, and social learning. This calls for an approach to pedagogical communication that teaches students the significance and potential power of their agency and the role they play in the co-constitution of social reality. That is to say that the pedagogical communication theory explains the nature of the agency of each individual and the impact that agency has on the social system. This section re-emphasizes the importance of learners becoming aware of the powerful communication forces in society that can shape their perceptions, how they feel about themselves, and their learning and growth. Some of which have a subtle subliminal effect that has become internalized (Mezirow 1981, 12). Thus, it explains the impact that pedagogical communications have on establishing a "learning society". This includes explaining the impact that the classroom and school have on creating public value.

What better place is there than the classroom to teach students how to engage in co-creating a better future? A good starting point is a classroom discourse on Nobel Prize Winner Amartya Sen's concept of *Development as Freedom*. This is likely to arouse the interest of the student for two reasons. First, because the better future it advocates involves empowering them to live in accordance with what they value most, achieve what they aspire most to do and/or be, and thus experience a better future. Secondly, because the discussion involves a critical analysis of the inadequacies of the prior paradigm, which emphasized what has value for exchange and an increasing a country's GDP. However, material things only represent an instrumental means or a steppingstone to a better life, but the material emphasis downplays what has ultimate value for the individual (i.e., intrinsic values, which for many cultures also refer to higher-order human values). This means that if the classroom discourse is not progressive, it will merely train students to seek their future happiness and success by acquiescing to the very social forces that limit the possibility of their acting in accordance with their intrinsic values, finding meaningfulness, and experiencing fulfillment (Sleeter 1991, 61–65). In addition, the prior development paradigm has placed humanity on a path that is not sustainable. Thus, it is likely that students will understand the connection between their own personal well-being, that of their community, and planning for a sustainable future.

Taking such an approach accomplishes two things that are beneficial to the student and the school. First, it establishes an alignment between what is vitally important to the individual student, to the school, to the locality of both the students and the school, what is a major concern of society, and what is a vital concern of the global community. In fact, the United Nations has proposed that integrating Amartya Sen's approach to empowering the individual (i.e., his approach to human development and his Capability Theory) with a sustainability approach to development is a preferred approach to planning the future. Secondly, this approach to empowerment not only gives voice to the individual student, but it also plays a role in improving the image and reputation of the school. In fact, where tertiary schools are concerned, it contributes to improving their international ranking. That is to say that the ranking of a college or university is improved when the school, its students, and its teachers are involved in discourse addressing vital concerns and when that discourse takes place in international networks of collaboration and exchange. In other words, for the reputation, image, and ranking of the school to improve, teachers and the school must engage their students in a critical analysis of issues that are most important for their lives, society, and the global community.

In addition, the process should include interpretation, criticism, and evaluation, which results in students constructing a new narrative that expresses what they believe promotes human, social, and sustainable development. In this respect, the discourse between the teacher and the students forms a narrative that depicts experience in the real world and has meaning for them. "Pedagogy refers to the process by which teachers and students negotiate and produce meaning. This, in turn, takes into consideration how teachers and students are positioned within discursive practices and power/knowledge relations. Pedagogy, then, refers to how we represent ourselves, others, and the communities in which we live" (McLaren 1995, 34). Shaping such narratives forms the basis of self-empowerment and social transformation and contributes to teachers and the school truly having a liberating and empowering impact on the lives of their students. Pablo Freire, who impressed educators worldwide with his ideas about the role of pedagogy in personal and social transformation, stressed that the most important characteristic of such a discourse is its power to transform (Freire 2014, 73). He referred to the process as establishing a narrative to counter that of the prior paradigm. The transformational power of narrative lies in the fact that it can spark a shift from one overarching framework or set of beliefs to another, often resulting in a shift in mindset and a transformation in how people perceive, think, and act. The central point is that narrative has the power to "Operate as an instrument in the construction of reality—in fact, constitute it" (Bruner 5-6 & 13).

"Without a narrative, life has no meaning. Without meaning, learning has no purpose" (Postman 1996, 7). Therefore, without developing a relevant narrative, teaching begins to lose its meaning and purpose. Of course, the most powerful narratives are those that raise the student's awareness, affirm their sense of personal identity, give them an understanding of their power of agency (i.e., make them feel empowered), and make them feel better integrated within their natural and social environments. Therefore, teachers should themselves understand and make use of the constitutive power of a certain type of rhetoric that they have the potential to exercise. It is only by doing so that teachers help students understand the potential power they have to co-create social reality. When teachers engage in Constructivist-type communicative interactions with students and participate with their students in various types of academic and social discourses and networks, they train them in what it means to co-create social reality. Students should be taught the significance of engaging in Constructivist-type social action because it provides a model of co-creating mutually beneficial and satisfactory outcomes for all social stakeholders, thus reducing social conflict and promoting peaceful coexistence.

Secondary, college, and university students typically view their time in school as steps in a process that leads them to where they want to get in the future, i.e., school is a means to an end in that it is the process that enables them to reach their future goal. That is to say that they expect that what is presented to them by their teachers is information that will help them experience what they are hoping for in the future. Thus, they view their experience at school as having instrumental value. This means that students do not usually feel that school is providing them insight into what has ultimate and intrinsic value, e.g., self-making, self-creation, and the power individuals have to create their own personal and social space. At the same time, there are issues that are pressing into the personal lives of the students that are not addressed. Students are experiencing peer pressure, the temptation of drug and alcohol abuse, the threat of new and extremely dangerous viruses, economic pressures, and instances of violence that seem to break out unpredictably at any time and place. But this means two things: first, the schools fail to address things that are vital in the student's current everyday life situation, and second, the students are hoping to, in the future, fit into a world that is not of their making (they just have to accept it as it is). This perspective on the educational process prevails unless the teacher and the school (e.g., its vision statement and its mission) speak deeply to the student and inspire them, and thus, the values and principles of the school influence the student's values and convictions.

Students are in a transitionary stage when they are comparing their established assumptions about meaning and the actions that are appropriate for achieving their aspirations with the constituted forms of meaning-making prescribed in their learning experiences. Deliberations in the classroom are important at this stage in that students are anxious to know if their established frameworks are effective for achieving their desired success and realizing lasting happiness. Therefore, the discourse between the student and the teacher, within itself, has constitutive power in that it prescribes the best course of action for achieving a desired outcome. In that respect, the teacher's knowledge, insight, and wisdom shape the student's understanding of what is meaningful, influence the way the student perceives vital issues, and ideally serve to raise the level of the student's awareness. So, in terms of the classroom, the teacher engages the students in a type of communicative action that establishes a micro-network of relations that plays a major role in meaning-making. However, teachers are at their best when the micro network of relations becomes an open discourse platform. In this way, students learn by experience and reflection the significance of deliberative engagement and collectively determining the best course of action. That is to say that students learn from their practice in the classroom and from reflections on the experience the significance and power of public discourse.

The ability of the school to establish a discourse that makes some type of meaningful reflects its image and reputation while making a meaningful impression on society begins with its motto. The school's motto is a statement of how it views itself in terms of its vision and mission. What a school has to offer to a prospective student and to the community should be evident in the school's mission statement. (i.e., vision statement or motto). Schools, like other private organizations and public institutions, have a vision, mission, or goal that they profess to achieve, which ideally motivates the teachers, inspires the students, and establishes the basis of the school's image and reputation. Therefore, the vision statement should not be just words that look good on paper. It should send a message to its students and the community that reflects its image and its mission. Therefore, the mission statement should really represent a message that has meaning for the students, the school, and the community.

It also portrays what the students should expect in terms of the dynamics they experience in the various school activities. Teachers and the school should establish the type of dynamics that enable students to feel that they have joined a vibrant community (a living tradition) where they experience the first stages of happiness and success, themselves as equals in power, creative ability, and relational and communicative skills to those of students at any other school. A good example is the film Dangerous Minds, starring Michelle Pfeiffer. The film portrays a school in an underprivileged neighborhood that has a reputation and image that establishes the impression it makes on society. The film portrays students from underprivileged backgrounds whose social and economic condition results in underperformance and the feeling of an inability to have any meaningful impact on the forces that perpetuate their social and economic condition. Michelle Pfeiffer introduces a way of relating and communicating that motivates students to unexpected levels of higher quality performance. The film indicates that pedagogy can be a form of public discourse, which becomes even more essential in contexts where students are subject to "oppression, domination, discrimination, racism, conflict, and other forms of cultural struggles due to differences in ethnicity, class, religion, sexual orientation, and other identity markers" (Frey and Palmer 2017, 362). Students from upper-class families have a greater degree of self-confidence; they can attend the best schools; they feel assured of getting the best jobs when they complete their education; and they believe they will be influential in society. But students from the disadvantaged segment of society can't afford the best schools (average yearly tuition for top universities worldwide is around 23,500 dollars, not counting dormitory fees, food, travel, and books). In addition, students from underprivileged backgrounds do not feel certain that they can achieve what they most aspire to after schooling, and they do not envision having a real influence in society. Therefore, it is even more important that their classroom and school experience teach them the power of agency and the ability to use their relational and communication abilities to neutralize power differences.

In fact, a dialogue with society is essential aspect of the role that the educational system is assigned by society. Society is dependent on its educational system for its growth and development. The growth and development of society are based on the extent to which the educational system generates what social theorists refer to as a learning society. Social growth and development are manifestations of what society has learned about what produces flourishing and how to avoid what causes stagnation, disorder, and social conflict. A failure in this respect increasingly encroaches on the sanctity of the educational institution itself. For example, what message is society sending to schools if they are increasingly subject to violent attacks? Several news media report that there were almost as many school shootings as there were days in 2023, which some analysts are describing as reaching a point of almost one school shooting every day. And this number does not include the other types of violent attacks occurring worldwide that schools are increasingly subject to (from the lowest level of education to the highest). These violent attacks have resulted in mass injuries, and many have even resulted in fatalities. The problem has reached such a level that several fashion outlets are advertising that it is best for parents to protect their children by investing in bullet-proof vests and helmets, which are now easily available on Amazon.

People do not become a community merely by living in proximity to each other. "Not only is social life identical with communication, but all communication (and hence all genuine social life) is educative" (Dewey 2004, 6). Thus, the role of the school consists primarily of enriching social life through communication. Since education was established as a cornerstone institution of society, there have been three creative dimensions of social life that society relies on from its schools: (1) generating knowledge that is believed to contribute to human, social, and sustainable development; (2) explicating knowledge of the relational and communicative practices that spark human, social, and sustainable development; and (3) an analysis of the practical networks that disseminate such knowledge. Consequently, the ideal of a society in which the good of all is realized is achieved when schools, by means of practice, example, and knowledge dissemination, promote engagement in inclusive social networks. Indeed, "Few social institutions are better situated to stimulate significant community improvement than schools (i.e., especially colleges and universities). These institutions are physically rooted in their communities" (Smerek et al., 2001, 7).

The ability of pedagogy (i.e., teacher-student relations, their communicative activities, and the school itself) to have an impact on society is only fixed by the quality and scope of the relational and communication interactions in which they participate. Contemporary communication theory describes each point of contact during a social interaction as an engagement in a social network. Each point of engagement is a node, and the number of nodes in the network determines the extent of its influence. Nodes are "The direct and indirect points at which the actors and actions within the network are connected, which potentially extend almost without limit (Miller 2022, 84). Therefore, communicative action greatly extends the reach of the teachers, the students, and the school, as well as their potential for creating a ripple effect. Nodes represent an extension of the influence of the individuals who participate, so that it prompts others, even at a distance, to reflect on their experience when deciding their own course of action. Therefore, as a student, even communicating within a micro-level social network has the potential for almost unlimited reach. It is in this respect that even a micro-level social discourse (enhanced by connecting to a network of nodes) can contribute to breaking down barriers of class, ethnicity, gender, race, and nationality (Dewey 2004, 93). Such an approach to relationality and communication liberates the powers and capabilities of students, which would otherwise be suppressed. It overrides exclusion and opens the way for the inclusiveness that the individual student communicating in a micro-level social network helped to establish.

Students, even from otherwise disadvantaged sections of society, are taught in this way to realize the nature of the power that they have to achieve what they aspire to most. Teachers and schools that engage in such relational and communication practices awaken their students to the role that agency plays in structure-agent relations. The social system (i.e., the social environment), in a sense, is thought of as "the structure", and students, along with the other members of society, are its agents. And "Education is defined as consisting in the acquisition of those habits that affect the adjustment of an individual and the individual's environment" (Dewey 2004, 50). Therefore, it should be kept in mind that interdependence is a fundamental fact of human society. Interdependence means that mutuality is a fundamental feature of a good society. Mutuality implies a balance of power (what liberalism refers to as equal rights). "Power is an integral element of all human relationships. However, it must be borne in mind that the balance of power, like human relationships in general, is at least bipolar and usually multipolar. And balances of power are always present wherever there is functional interdependence between people" (Elias 1978, 74). This means that the relational and communicative lessons taught in the classroom and by the school are a form of empowerment. Thus, students are learning not only about the power of their personal agency but that power in today's world is increasingly regarded as relational. This means that power lies in the hands of individuals who are effective at managing relationships and communicating. Teachers and schools that help their students understand the nature of power in today's interdependent society increase the students' power of self-determination. and self-motivation. This, in turn, increases their feelings of volition, connectedness, and belonging (Ryan and Deci, 2020, 1–5). And activities that satisfy the student's personal and social needs increase the student's engagement in such activities, the meaningfulness they find in them, and the fulfillment they experience.

References

Aristotle. (2004) *Nicomachean Ethics*. (Crisp, Roger. Trans.) Cambridge, UK: Cambridge University Press.

Bansal, Sonam. (2018). A constructivist perspective towards collaborative learning. *International Journal of Research in Social Science. Vol. 8.*

Bar-Tal, Daniel. The Elusive Nature of Peace Education. *Peace Education: The Concept, Principles, and Practices Around the World.* (Salomon, Gavriel. & Nevo, Baruch. Edits.). Mahwah, New Jersey: Lawrence Erlbaum Associates.

Brodie, R., Fehrer, J., Jaakkola, E. and Conduit, J. (2019) Actor engagement in networks: defining the conceptual domain. *Journal of Service Research*. Vol. 22 No. 2, 173-188.

Bruner, Jerome. (1991) The Narrative Construction of Reality. Critical Inquiry. Volume 18, Number 1, 1-21.

Burns, MacGregor. (1978) *Leadership*. New York: Harper & Row Publishers.

Confucius. (1869) *The Life and Teachings of Confucius*. (Legge, James. Edits.). London: N. *Trübner & Co.*

Covey, Steven. (1990) *The Seven Lessons of Highly Effective People*. New York: Fireside Publications.

Dewey, John. (2004) *Democracy and Education*. New Delhi: Aakar Books.

Dewey, John. (2008) *The Later Works, 1935-1953*. (Boydston, Jo Ann. Edit.). Carbondale, Illinois: Southern Illinois University.

Dewey, John. (2016) *The Public and Its Problems*. Athens, Ohio: Ohio University Press.

Dewey, John. (1932) The School and Society. Chicago: The University of Chicago Press.

Elfert, Maren. (2015) UNESCO, the Faure Report, the Delors Report, and the Political Utopia of Lifelong Learning. *European Journal of Education*. 50(1), 88–100.

Elias, N. (1978) *What is sociology?* New York: Columbia University Press.

Etzioni, Amitai. (2002) The Good Society. *Seattle Journal for Social Justice*. Volume 1, Issue 1, 83-96.

Freire, Paulo. (2014) *Pedagogies of Hope*. London: Bloomsbury Academic.

Freire, Paulo. (2014) *Pedagogy of the Oppressed*. New York: Continuum International Publishing Group.

Freire, Paulo. (1985). *The politics of education: culture, power, and liberation*. New York: Bergin & Garvey.

Frey, Lawrence. & Palmer, David. (2017) Communication activism pedagogy and research: communication education scholarship to promote social justice. *Communication Education, 66(3),* 362–367.

Foucault, Michel. (2002) *Archaeology of Knowledge.* Oxon, UK: Routledge Classics.

Gadamer, Hans-Georg. (2006) Truth and Method. (Weinsheimer, Joel & Marshall, Donald). London: Continuum Publishing Group.

Gandhi, Mahatma. (2005). *Hindu Dharma.* Delhi: Vision Books, LTD.

Giddens, Anthony (1994) *Beyond Left and Right: The Future of Radical Politics.* Cambridge: Polity Press.

Giddens, Anthony (1984) *The Constitution of Society.* Cambridge: Polity Press.

Kohlberg, Lawrence. (1981) Essays on Moral Development (vol.1) - The Philosophy of Moral Development. Harper & Row.

March, J. G., & Olsen, J. P. (1995) *Democratic governance.* New York: Free Press.

Maslow, Abraham. (1970) *Motivation and Personality, 2nd ed.* New York: Harper and Row.

McLaren, Peter. (1995) *Critical Pedagogy and Predatory Culture: Oppositional Politics in a Postmodern Era.* London: Routledge.

Miller, Leon. (2018) Social Networking Strategy for Creating Public Value in Eastern India. *Journal of Ethnic and Cultural Studies.* Vol. 5, No. 1, 85-93.

Miller, Leon. (2011) The Aesthetic Epiphany. *Consciousness Connection.*

Mezirow, J. (1981 A Critical Theory of Adult Learning and Education. *Adult Education, 32(1),* 3–24.

Pew Research Foundation. (1923) Gun deaths among U.S. children and teens rose 50% in two years. Washington, D.C.: Pew Research Foundation Publications.

Plato. (2003) *Plato's Republic.* Cambridge, UK: Cambridge University Press.

Plato. (1984) *Plato's Theaetetus, Sophist, and Statesman.* Chicago: The University of Chicago Press.

Plato. (2002) *Protagoras.* Oxon, UK: Oxford University Press.

Plato. (1934) *The Laws of Plato.* (Tayler. A. Trans.). London: J. M. Dent & Sons, LTD.

Postman, Neil. (1996) *The End of Education: Redefining the Value of School.* New York: Vintage Books.

Quintilian. (1959) *Institutio Oratoria.* (Volume III). (Butler, H. Trans.) London: Published by William Heinemann.

Quintilian. (1980) *Institutio Oratoria.* (Books I-III). Cambridge, Massachusetts: Harvard University Press.

Reardon, Betty. (1988) Comprehensive Peace Education: Educating for Global Responsibility. New York: Teacher's College Press at Columbia University.

Ryan, Richard. and Deci, Edward. (2020) Intrinsic and extrinsic motivation from a self-determination theory perspective: definitions, theory, practices, and future directions. *Contemporary Educational Psychology.* Vol. 61, 1-11.

Sen, Amartya. (1999) *Development as Freedom.* New York: Alfred Knopf.

Sleeter, Christine. (1991) *Empowerment through Multicultural Education.* Albany, New York: The State University of New York.

Smerek Ryan. Pasque, Penny. Mallory, Bruce. & Holland, Barbara. (2005) Partnerships for Engagement Futures. *Higher Education Collaboratives for Community Engagement and Improvement.* (Pasque, Penny. Smerek, Ryan. Dwyer, Brighid, Bowman, Nick, & Mallory, Bruce. Edits.). Ann Arbor, Michigan. National Forum on Higher Education for the Public Good.

Sri Aurobindo, Ghosh (2003) Cultural Writings. *The Complete Works of Sri Aurobindo, Volume One.* Pondicherry, India: Sri Aurobindo Ashram Press.

Tagore, Rabindranath. (1922) *Creative Unity.* Lonon: Macmillan and Company.

Tagore, Rabindranath. (2007) *Essays.* New Delhi: Atlantic Publishers.

Tagore, Rabindranath. (1917) *Personality.* New York: Macmillan and Company.

Tagore, Rabindranath. (1921) *The Center of Indian Culture.* Madras: Society for The Promotion of National Education.

The Communication for Social Change Consortium. (2002) *An Integrated Model for Measuring the Process and Its Outcomes.* New York: The Rockefeller Foundation and Johns Hopkins University Center for Communication Program.

The National Institute of Child Health. (2022) *Preventing Gun Violence, the Leading Cause of Childhood Death.* Rockville, Maryland: The National Institute of Child Health Information Resource Center.

UNESCO. (2021) *Reimagining Our Futures Together: A New Social Contract for* Education (Volume 2, Part 2). Paris: The United Nations Educational, Scientific and Cultural Organization.

Vygotsky, Lev. (1978) *Mind and Society: the Development of Higher Psychological Processes.* Cambridge, Massachusetts: Harvard University Press.

Yang, Jin. and Yorozu, Rika. (2015) *Building a learning society in Japan, the Republic of Korea and Singapore*. Hamburg: UNESCO.
Xin, Cindy. & Feenberg, Andrew. (2006) Pedagogy in Cyberspace. *Journal of Distance Education*. Volume 21, Number 2, 1-25.

Pedagogy and Social Development (with an Emphasis on the Role of Indigenous Knowledge in Social Development)

Indigenous Knowledge and Social Development in Northeast India

Doctor Amita Gupta

Introduction

The rich cultural ecology of Northeast India provides a canvas where traditions, rooted in the indigenous communities' collective memory, continue to flourish while adapting to the prevailing winds of globalization and modernization. This chapter, "Indigenous Knowledge and Social Development in Northeast India," endeavors to present a lucid exploration into the intricate dynamics of knowledge preservation, cultural identity affirmation, and socio-political transformation within this uniquely diverse context.

The term 'indigenous knowledge' takes on a multidimensional meaning in this setting, one that is meticulously dissected in the insightful work by Singh and Misra (2016). They expound on the themes of knowledge, not as an isolated entity but as a holistic construct that is intrinsically linked with people's daily lives, customs, and societal structures. In this context, social development becomes a manifestation of the innate expression of the local populace's lived experiences, a theme eloquently expounded upon by scholars like Sharma and Haque (2018).

An enriching layer to this discussion is introduced through the pioneering research by Bhattacharjee and Devi (2019), elucidating the resilient dynamism inherent within these tribes. They not only have safeguarded their ancestral wisdom but have also manifested an adaptive spirit, assimilating and refining external influences to foster a harmonious coexistence of tradition and modernity.

As we delve deeper, the role of education, especially its non-formal and informal variants, becomes profoundly salient. The educational paradigms here are as diverse and multifaceted as the tribes themselves. Roy's (2020) comprehensive analysis presents education as a vehicle that transports ancestral wisdom, ethical values, and societal norms across generations. It is an enlightening window through which the tribes view and interact with the world, maintaining a delicate balance between preservation and evolution.

Integrating a broader perspective, Das (2017) brings to the fore the significant interplay between the political and cultural realms. The tribes, through the prism of their unique cultural identity, engage in a dialogical process with the broader political entities. This dynamic interaction is instrumental in carving out spaces where traditional wisdom and practices not only survive but also thrive amidst the complexities of the modern world.

This chapter aspires to offer an immersive journey through the breathtaking landscapes of Northeast India, where every hill, river, and forest is steeped in the stories and wisdom of the indigenous tribes. We aim to weave together the vibrant threads of cultural richness, social development, and political engagement to present a tapestry that is as illuminating as it is enchanting. Through their silent yet eloquent narratives, the indigenous communities invite us to a world where the past and present converge and tradition and innovation dance to the timeless tunes of resilience, adaptability, and identity.

Historical Context

The historical panorama of Northeast India, rooted in a robust ecological, cultural, and communal framework, lends itself to a nuanced exploration of the indigenous educational traditions. It's a context where learning and wisdom are not confined to institutionalized structures but are breathed into life through the rich tapestry of community interactions, storytelling, and rituals. From Aristotle's (2004) ethics and human development perspective, the learning ethos here is akin to a living entity, a dynamic process intimately woven into the individual, societal, and environmental wellness fabric.

In revisiting the genesis of indigenous pedagogical traditions, Barua (2012) underscores that the richness of these practices is encapsulated in the diversity of ethnicities, languages, and cultural practices in the region. The traditional societies of Northeast India are repositories of a communal and collective approach to learning, rooted in oral traditions and experiential learning, echoing Geertz's (1973) observations.

During the colonial period, the education system in this region underwent transformative changes. Nath (2015) provides an in-depth analysis of this transformation, highlighting the complexities arising from the intersection of indigenous pedagogical practices with the formalized educational structures introduced by the colonial powers. Nussbaum's (2000) discourse on the nuanced dance between cultural traditions and developmental aspirations provides a lens through which this transformative period can be understood.

In the post-independence period, the tribal communities found themselves navigating the complex terrains of cultural preservation, national integration, and political recognition. Sharma and Sharma (2017) highlight the role of education as a platform for articulating identity, cultural preservation, and rights. This discourse resonates with Sen's (1999) notion of development as freedom.

The contemporary context of the indigenous communities is aptly described by Misra (2019), who underscores the pivotal role of education as a medium of empowerment, resistance, and identity formation amidst the wave of globalization. Freire's (2005) work on education as a practice of freedom finds resonance in the contemporary adaptations and evolutions of indigenous pedagogical practices.

Thus, this rich historical context unfurls an evolving narrative, meticulously woven through the threads of time, echoing the voices of the indigenous communities, their silent triumphs, enduring resilience, and dynamic transformations. It transcends beyond a mere historical recounting, morphing into a vibrant, living entity that breathes life into the ongoing dialogue between the ancient and the modern, the traditional and the contemporary, and the local and the global.

1. Case Studies of Northeast India Tribes

1.1 The Naga Tribes: Identity, Conflict, and Reconciliation

Spread across Nagaland, the Naga tribes comprise several ethnic groups, each possessing distinct languages and traditions. Their age-old customs showcase a profound respect for nature, reflecting Aristotle's assertion of the intertwined relationship between personal development and the politics of communal living (Aristotle, 2004). The Nagas' festivals, such as *Hornbill*, emphasize their rich cultural heritage and the role of traditional knowledge in shaping their social constructs and relationships with neighboring tribes and the state (Figure 1).

Figure 1: Cultural Time Capsule: Naga Tribesmen of the 1890s" Bourne and Shepherd's striking studio portrait of Naga tribesmen in the 1890s. This image showcases five Naga men adorned with their distinctive boar tusk headgear, offering a glimpse into the rich cultural heritage of Nagaland, a northeastern state in India. (*After The British Library Board*).

This intricate mosaic of cultural diversity among the Naga tribes also presents challenges in the form of ethnic and territorial conflicts. Their unique identity, though a source of pride, has often become a center of contestation both internally and with the Indian state (Yhome, 2019). The tribes' assertion of autonomy and distinct identity has led to a prolonged conflict that has shaped their social, political, and economic landscapes (Haksar, 2018).

Despite the longstanding conflicts, the Naga tribes' inherent affinity for nature and their community-centric way of life continue to thrive. Their rich biodiversity is celebrated through traditional practices and festivals, blending art, music, dance, and nature worship, illustrating a harmonious coexistence of varied customs and beliefs (Singh, 2014). The *Hornbill* festival is the epitome of this cultural richness, offering insights into the tribes' resilient spirit and persistent efforts towards unity amidst diversity.

Efforts towards reconciliation and peacebuilding, facilitated by both governmental and non-governmental interventions, have gained prominence. The ongoing peace talks and engagements aim at resolving conflicts and recognizing the distinct Naga identity while ensuring integration within the Indian Union, echoing an intricate dance of autonomy, identity, and nation-building (Goswami, 2017).

1.2 The Khasis of Meghalaya: Balancing Modernity and Tradition

In the hills of Meghalaya, the Khasis stand out for their matrilineal system, where lineage and inheritance are traced through the female line. This social structure, unique in the broader Indian context, underscores Nussbaum's (2000) emphasis on the role of women in development. Integrated into their societal structure is their relationship with the environment, manifested in sacred groves preserved for generations, exemplifying their intrinsic understanding of sustainable living. (Figure 2)

Figure 2: Discovering the Rich Tapestry of Khasi Women: Unveiling Meghalaya's Unique Cultural Heritage" *(After Mala Chandrashekhar)*

Figure 3: "Innocence in Black and White: Khasi Children, 1944" An endearing capture of Khasi children from 1944, preserved in the Salesians of Don Bosco, Guwahati, India collection. This evocative photograph immortalizes the vibrant spirit and youthful exuberance of the Khasi children in a bygone era. *(After Salesians of Don Bosco, Guwahati, India collection)*

The Khasis' matrilineal system promotes gender equity and empowers women to be pivotal figures in societal development and decision-making (Kharkongor & Mishra, 2016). This inherent gender balance within Khasi society offers a unique perspective in the discourse of women's roles in societal development, aligning with Nussbaum's emphasis on women's centrality in societal progress (Nussbaum, 2000).

Sacred forests, a significant aspect of Khasi ecology and spirituality, are biodiversity-rich areas preserved due to their cultural and spiritual significance (Sarma et al., 2020). These groves are microcosms of the tribe's environmental ethics, showcasing their commitment to ecological preservation and sustainable living. Their traditional ecological knowledge, rooted in centuries-old practices, contributes to the conservation of biological diversity and the environment.

The Khasis' adaptation to modernity while retaining their cultural and traditional essence is a delicate balancing act. In the face of globalization, the community has shown resilience in maintaining its distinct identity and traditions (Kharshiing, 2019). (Figure 3) The integration of modern education, technology, and societal norms with their rich cultural heritage demonstrates the dynamism of Khasi society.

1.3   The Mizo Tribes: Harmony in Hills

In the lush landscapes of Mizoram, the Mizo people offer insights into a society where communal living is the norm and the entire community participates in significant events, be they agricultural tasks or cultural festivities. Their Tlawmngaihna principle, stressing the importance of selfless service, aligns closely with Cicero's natural law teachings (Cicero, 2004).

Tlawmngaihna, an unwritten social law, govern Mizo society, emphasizing self-sacrifice and welfare for others (Lalremruata, 2017). This philosophy underpins their societal structure, influencing their political organization, social interactions, and even economic activities. The Mizo's agricultural practices, particularly the Jhum cultivation, are deeply rooted in community participation (Laldinpuii, 2018).

Cultural festivities, an intrinsic part of the Mizo tribes, not only embody their rich traditions but also strengthen communal bonds. (Figure 4) The Chapchar Kut festival, for instance, highligshts the robust social fabric of

Mizo society, featuring traditional dances, music, and crafts, all of which echo the Tlawmngaihna principle (Lalthangliana, 2011).

Figure 4: Cultural Elegance: A Glimpse into the Rich Heritage of the Mizo Tribe in Mizoram. *(After Saumya Bansal)*

In their journey to maintain the essence of their culture while navigating the terrains of modernity, the Mizo tribes have demonstrated adaptability. They have managed to intertwine traditional values and modern elements, resulting in a dynamic yet harmonious society that continues to thrive in the picturesque hills of Mizoram (Laldinpuii, 2018).

1.4   The Bodos of Assam: Autonomy and Cultural Preservation

The Bodos, one of the ancient tribes of Assam, are renowned for their Bathouism religion and the vibrant Bwisagu festival (Brahma, 2015). Their intricate weaving patterns, traditional dances, and folklore serve not only as cultural expressions but also as pedagogical tools reflecting their socio-political realities (Geertz, 1973). The Bodos' meticulous preservation of these cultural aspects underscores the deep ties between their identity, traditions, and the land they inhabit (Brahma, 2019).

Bathouism, central to their identity, is rooted in the worship of Bathoubwrai (Lord of the Earth), where five elements—air, fire, water, earth, and ether—are revered. The Bwisagu festival, marking the Bodo New Year, is characterized by colorful attire, traditional music, and dances that encapsulate the community's history, myths, and aspirations (Basumatary, 2013).

Over the decades, the Bodos' quest for autonomy and cultural preservation has been marked by both conflict and negotiation with the state and other ethnic groups (Nath, 2017). The Bodoland Territorial Region (BTR) is a testament to their ongoing struggle and accomplishments in securing a political space for the autonomous flourishing of their cultural and social practices (Misra, 2000).

Educational institutions and cultural organizations among the Bodos play a pivotal role in sustaining their rich cultural legacy. The intricate weaving patterns of the Bodos narrate their history, struggles, and victories, with women notably the custodians of this artistic tradition (Boro, 2019).

Figure 5: Bodos of Assam: Nurturing Autonomy and Safeguarding their Cultural Heritage. *(After Shaan Academy)*

As the Bodos navigate the complexities of autonomy, cultural preservation, and broader socio-political integration, their indigenous knowledge systems, vibrant culture, and traditional practices stand as pillars of their identity and resilience (Nath, 2020). Every dance, song, and woven pattern is a chapter in the Bodos' ongoing narrative, echoing the rhythms of their past, present, and anticipated future.

1.5 Sikkim's Ethnic Diversity: From Lepchas to Bhutias

Sikkim, with its diverse tribal groups like Lepchas and Bhutias, represents a confluence of various cultural streams. The narratives of these tribes offer insights into their worldviews and their responses to external influences and modernity. Tran's work (2012) illuminates the historical interactions of these tribes within the political realms, with a specific focus on tax, land, and clan politics, revealing the complexities these tribes navigate in maintaining their cultural identities.

The Lepchas, regarded as the original inhabitants of Sikkim, have distinct language, customs, and traditions. Their connection to the natural environment is integral to their culture, as manifested in their agricultural practices and rituals (Shneiderman & Turin, 2006). The preservation of this rich heritage faces challenges and transformations induced by modernization and external cultural influences.

Figure 6: Sikkim's Vibrant Ethnic Tapestry: Discovering the Lepcha Culture. *(After bltribeofsikkim Blogspot)*

Bhutias, on the other hand, brought with them influences from Tibet, contributing to the intricate tapestry of Sikkim's cultural landscape (Arora, 2008). (Figure 7) Their religious practices, social organizations, and art forms enrich Sikkim's cultural diversity and have adapted over the years to accommodate and resist various forms of change, showcasing their resilience.

Figure 7: Sikkim's Ethnic Mosaic: Exploring the Bhutias' Rich Heritage. (After bpibs.ebsb)

Efforts to document and preserve the languages and traditions of the Lepchas and Bhutias underscore the importance of cultural preservation amidst rapid globalization (Plaisier, 2007). Initiatives to revitalize indigenous languages and traditions are central to maintaining the identity and heritage of these tribes in the contemporary context.

1.6 Arunachal's Tribes: A Mosaic of Cultures

Home to numerous tribes like the Monpas, Adis, and Apatanis, Arunachal Pradesh is a melting pot of cultures. These tribes, each with distinct customs, languages, and rituals, highlight the importance of indigenous knowledge systems. From the Dree festival of the Apatanis to the Losar celebrations of the Monpas, these customs signify the tribes' intrinsic pedagogical values, reflecting the core ideas presented by Freire (2005) in his exploration of oppressed pedagogies.

The Apatanis, particularly noted for their sustainable agricultural practices and unique methods of paddy cum fish culture, are indicative of their intricate connection with the environment and their adeptness in resource management (Mibang & Chaudhuri, 2004). The Dree Festival, a significant agricultural event, is not just a cultural celebration but a nuanced educational process through which the Apatanis pass down generational wisdom related to agriculture and environmental preservation. (Figure 7)

Figure 7: Exploring Arunachal's Cultural Tapestry: The Apatanis *(After Vajiram and Ravi)*

The Monpas, inhabiting the icy terrains of the Tawang district, are distinct for their Tibetan Buddhist practices. The Losar festival exemplifies their cultural richness, blending religious rituals with social gatherings, an indicator of their holistic approach to community living and education (Sarkar & Roy, 2006). They portray a vibrant culture where religious teachings are integral to their educational and social upbringing. (Figure 8)

Figure 8: Journey Through Arunachal's Cultural Kaleidoscope: The Apatanis. *(After Orang Srang)*

Adis, another prominent tribe, have a strong oral tradition, and their folklore, myths, and stories encapsulate their history, values, and norms, forming an integral part of their educational system (Pandey, 2009). They exhibit a dynamic interaction between their cultural heritage and educational processes, showcasing a lived experience of Freire's concept of pedagogy. (Figure 9)

Figure 9: Preserving Traditions: An Elderly Adi Woman Leading a Folk Song in Gete Village, Yingkiong District, Arunachal Pradesh. *(After RIWATCH)*

1.7 Tripura's Tribes: Reconciling Modernity and Tradition

The tribes of Tripura, such as the Tripuris, Reangs, and Jamatias, showcase a dynamic balance between modernity and ancient traditions. Their age-old customs are interwoven with contemporary practices, illuminating Giddens' (1994) articulation of radical politics and the co-creation of societal outcomes. The amalgamation of the past and present within these tribal societies is not merely a passive occurrence but an active process, imbued with reflections, dialogues, and interactions that are as complex as they are enriching.

The Tripuris are particularly noted for their indigenous architectural styles and handicrafts (De & Tripuri, 2015). Their traditional bamboo and cane works bear testament to intricate craftsmanship that has managed to survive and adapt amidst the encroaching waves of modernity. Such adaptability illustrates Giddens' concept of modernity's influences in reshaping traditions.

The Reangs, one of the largest tribes in Tripura, maintain distinct cultural practices, including traditional dance and music, despite the profound impacts of modern influences (Das & Kharbani, 2020). Their Hojagiri dance, a reflection of their cultural essence, is an expressive narrative of their ancestral roots and contemporary journey, depicting a community in constant conversation with its past and future. (Figure 10)

Figure 10: Unveiling Tripura's Cultural Richness: The Reang Tribe. *(After tripura.gov)*

Jamatia tribes are known for their community-centric living and the Huk or Hukumani institution, a traditional system of self-governance that has evolved over the years (Roy, 2019). (Figure 11) This system exemplifies a dynamic equilibrium where ancient traditions are not fossilized constructs but living entities, continually molded and remodelled by contemporary realities.

Figure 11: Exploring the Cultural Tapestry of Tripura: The Jamatia Tribe (*After tripura.gov*)

In these tribal societies, an interplay of identity, culture, and modernity is observable, echoing Giddens' sentiments on the dialectical relationship between tradition and modern influences. The tribal communities of Tripura stand as exemplars of societies that are neither entirely swayed by the tides of modernity nor rigidly anchored in the past but are in a perpetual dance of cultural negotiation and adaptation.

2   Integration and Synthesis: A Collective Narrative

The Northeast is a rich mosaic of diverse tribes, each with its own distinct narrative yet collectively contributing to a vibrant socio-political tapestry. The Chakma et al. study (2016) illuminates this diversity, highlighting the collective contribution of these distinct tribes to social development. Each tribe, though rooted in its unique indigenous wisdom, is an active participant in the broader socio-political narrative, embodying Sen's (1999) reflections on development as freedom. Expanding on the diverse tribal communities, one sees a dynamic interface where traditional knowledge and contemporary global influences meet. Each tribe, from the Bodos of Assam and the Khasis of Meghalaya to the numerous tribes of Arunachal Pradesh, exhibits a unique adaptation strategy to modern challenges while preserving their cultural heritage (Nath, 2018). The tribal education systems, especially, are exemplary of Freire's (2005) Pedagogy of the Oppressed. These systems integrate indigenous knowledge and wisdom, making education a tool of empowerment and social transformation, not just literacy (Dutta, 2017). This emphasizes a collective evolution where each tribe, while maintaining its uniqueness, contributes to a shared narrative of development and empowerment.

Furthermore, the socio-political engagements of these tribes are not isolated but rather intersecting and interdependent. They represent diverse yet interconnected narratives of struggles, resilience, and adaptations (Misra, 2019). These tribes are not just passive recipients of developmental policies but active contributors to the discourse of social, political, and economic development. As such, the Northeast becomes a vibrant space where indigenous knowledge and modernity are not antithetical but are in a dialogic relationship. This synthesis underscores Sen's (1999) argument that development is deeply embedded in the freedom of the people to carve their destinies, rooted in their cultural, social, and political contexts.

The case studies of tribes from Northeast India, such as those of the Magars and Bodos, reveal an intricate narrative of resilience and adaptation. Each tribe embodies a rich indigenous wisdom that is dynamic and continually evolving in response to contemporary challenges and opportunities. They stand as a testament to the enduring and lively interplay between traditional wisdom and contemporary socio-political realities.

In the wake of globalization and rapid modernization, tribes like the Adis, Apatanis, and Khasis have showcased remarkable adaptability, harmonizing their age-old traditions with new-age demands (Goswami, 2014). Their indigenous knowledge systems, replete with unique traditions and customs, are not relegated to the annals of history but are actively informing and being informed by modern developmental narratives.

Freire's (2005) Pedagogy of the Oppressed finds resonance in the educational narratives of these tribes, particularly in the realm of experiential and context-specific learning (Devi, 2019). Their educational practices, rooted in indigenous knowledge, affirm that learning is an active, participative process where learners are not mere recipients but active participants in the creation of knowledge.

The stories of these tribes are emblematic of a broader, more profound interplay between indigenous wisdom and contemporary socio-political dynamics. For instance, the Naga tribes, in their quest for identity assertion and autonomy, reflect the intricacies of navigating political landscapes, underscoring Sen's (1999) concept of development as freedom (Jacobsen, 2014).

In this multifaceted dialogue, there is a dance between preservation and transformation, echoing the profound reflections of thinkers like Geertz (1973) on the interpretation of cultures and Nussbaum (2000) on human development and capabilities. These insights shed light on the indomitable spirit of the tribes, their unyielding commitment to cultural heritage, and dynamic socio-political engagement (Singh & Misra, 2016).

In essence, the vibrant narratives of Northeast India's tribes encapsulate a dynamic interplay of education, indigenous knowledge, and socio-political engagement. They present a rich resource for reflection and engagement for scholars, policymakers, and global citizens, contributing insights to broader discourses on cultural preservation, societal development, and the transformative power of education.

3 Indigenous Pedagogical Practices

3.1 Storytelling: A Dynamic Learning Experience

Storytelling, a cornerstone of indigenous education in Northeast India, is not merely a form of entertainment but a vibrant pedagogical tool. According to Das (2017), storytelling serves as a platform where historical, ethical, and cultural knowledge is imparted. This practice is rich in moral narratives, aligning with Aristotle's notions of moral development (Aristotle, 2004), and serves as a dynamic conduit for transferring communal wisdom, fostering identity, and instilling societal norms.

3.2 Experiential Learning: Nature as the Classroom

The indigenous tribes, notably the Naga and Mizo, embrace a form of holistic experiential learning rooted in environmental interaction (Barua, 2018). They embody Freire's concept of learning from the environment and real-life experiences (Freire, 2005). It is a symbiotic relationship where nature is not just the backdrop but an active participant in the learning process, fostering an intrinsic understanding of ecology and biodiversity.

3.3 Rituals and Ceremonies: Living Lessons

Rituals and ceremonies are pedagogical in essence, embodying complex societal, ethical, and spiritual lessons. Sharma (2015) illuminates how these intricate rituals, akin to Geertz's semiotic systems (Geertz, 1973), are multifaceted, integrating aspects of history, spirituality, and community ethics. They are a living curriculum, imbuing each participant with ancestral wisdom and communal ethos.

3.4 Mentorship and Apprenticeship:
The Intergenerational Transmission of Skills

Building on Giddens' structure and agency theory (Giddens, 1994), the mentorship and apprenticeship systems among these tribes offer a balance of structured learning and individual agency. According to Deka (2020), elders impart not just technical skills but the wisdom and ethical considerations underpinning each craft, establishing a holistic learning environment.

3.5 Community Participation: A Collective Endeavour

Indigenous education is communal, where every member has an educational role, echoing Nussbaum's capabilities approach (Nussbaum, 2000). Bhattacharjee (2019) highlights that this participatory model fosters a sense of belonging, responsibility, and mutual respect, emphasizing that learning is not an isolated but a shared journey.

3.6 Indigenous Knowledge and Governance: Leadership Rooted in Tradition

Drawing insights from Thapa (2002), governance in these societies is a rich blend of ancestral wisdom and adaptive innovations. It underscores the vibrant role of indigenous knowledge in shaping responsive, participatory, and ethical governance models that are rooted in tradition yet attuned to contemporary challenges.

3.7 Environmental Ethics: The Harmony of Existence

Echoing Cicero's insights (Cicero, 2004), environmental ethics among the tribes is a lived experience. According to Verma (2016), nature is revered and integral to their worldview. Every element of nature is embedded with lessons of respect, sustainability, and interconnectedness, fostering an ethic of coexistence.

3.8 The Synthesis of Pedagogical Practices: A Journey of Wisdom

Northeast India's indigenous educational paradigms weave a rich tapestry of wisdom that is dynamic, evolving, and integrative. Sen's development as freedom (Sen, 1999) finds its embodiment in these practices that are not just about knowledge acquisition but holistic development. According to Mishra (2021), these pedagogical practices offer a harmonious blend of the ancient and contemporary, fostering an education that is deeply rooted yet expansively connected.

4. Socio-Political Implications of Indigenous Knowledge and Social Development in Northeast India

Understanding the socio-political fabric of Northeast India requires a nuanced exploration of indigenous knowledge and its pervasive influence in shaping community relations, governance, and societal norms. This knowledge, rich in historical context and ecological wisdom, underscores a paradigm of social development intrinsically linked with environmental sustainability and cultural preservation.

The role of indigenous knowledge in nurturing cultural integrity and individual identity cannot be overstated. Banerjee (2017) illustrates how local myths, rituals, and traditions, embedded within this knowledge, contribute to a collective identity that is integral to fostering social cohesion and political stability. Aristotle's theories on moral and ethical upbringing find a resonant echo in these processes, wherein community values and norms are ingrained from childhood (Aristotle, 2004).

Building on Freire's pedagogical theories (Freire, 2005), Roy (2019) explores how incorporating indigenous knowledge into mainstream education amplifies political participation and empowerment. Indigenous communities, armed with a critical consciousness, navigate and influence political landscapes, asserting their rights and contributing to democratic processes.

The contributions of indigenous knowledge to environmental stewardship are pivotal. Singh (2021) highlights the alignment with Sen's development model (Sen, 1999), where enhanced capabilities and freedom emerge from an intimate, respectful relationship with the environment, fostering policies and practices that are sustainable and equitable.

In a landscape often marred by ethnic and political tensions, indigenous knowledge serves as a catalyst for peace. Gurung (2009) highlighted the role of cultural identity in conflict resolution, where indigenous norms and practices facilitate dialogue and consensus, nurturing social harmony and political stability.

Bharali (2020) discusses the transformative potential of integrating indigenous perspectives in policy and governance, resonating with Giddens' advocacy for inclusive political dialogues (Giddens, 1994). Such integration fosters policies that are responsive, equitable, and rooted in the complex realities of diverse communities.

The intricate dance between land and identity is captured in Tran's analysis (2012), where indigenous knowledge underscores claims to land rights and autonomy. This knowledge, encapsulating historical, cultural, and ecological narratives, becomes a powerful voice in legal and political arenas, asserting the indigenous communities' intrinsic ties to their ancestral lands.

With the richness of indigenous knowledge on medicinal and healing practices, community health finds a strong anchor. Nussbaum's capabilities approach (Nussbaum, 2000) is enriched by Sharma's findings (2018), which spotlight the role of indigenous knowledge in enhancing health outcomes and overall community wellbeing.

Thapa's insights (2002) into social stratifications are complemented by Dutta's research (2021), which emphasizes the role of indigenous knowledge in ecological conservation. These practices unify diverse social strata, fostering collective actions that are anchored in the respect and preservation of biodiversity.

In the quest to unravel the intricate dynamics of social development in Northeast India, indigenous knowledge emerges not just as a repository of historical and cultural wisdom but as a living, evolving entity that shapes and is shaped by the socio-political landscape. Each strand of this knowledge, as Geertz posited, is a symbol and narrative woven into the intricate fabric of society (Geertz, 1973).

The resultant tapestry is one of resilience, diversity, and adaptability. It's a landscape where politics, culture, and ecology converge, each a reflection and embodiment of the other. In this convergence, as elucidated by Goswami (2020), lies the transformative potential for a social development paradigm that is as robust as it is nuanced—a narrative where the echoes of the ancestors resound in contemporary policy, governance, and societal norms.

5. Contemporary Challenges and Opportunities

The fluid relationship between contemporary challenges and opportunities is pivotal in understanding the evolution of indigenous knowledge and social development in Northeast India. These dichotomies, although complex, harbor the potential for the regeneration and sustainability of indigenous communities amidst evolving global paradigms.

The pervasive waves of globalization and a unified modern culture pose a threat to the richness of indigenous cultures. Smith (2013) highlights the erosion of indigenous languages and traditions as a crisis of cultural identity, corroborating Geertz's findings that underscore the fragility of cultural systems amidst rapid modernization (Geertz, 1973).

With expanding urbanization and industrialization, the ancestral lands of indigenous communities face unprecedented threats. Sharma (2015) delves into the struggles against land dispossession, corroborating Tran's explorations of the encroachment and exploitation of indigenous territories (Tran, 2012).

Sarma (2018) elucidates the political sidelining of indigenous communities, echoing Gurung's insights on the exclusionary practices embedded within political structures that often undermine indigenous voices (Gurung, 2009).

The integration of indigenous knowledge into mainstream education remains a formidable challenge. Kikon (2020) echoes Freire's perspective, calling for a pedagogical shift to encompass and valorize the profound wisdom encapsulated in indigenous narratives (Freire, 2005).

A renaissance of indigenous cultures is emerging. Singh (2019) documents global endeavors to resurrect indigenous languages and traditions, affirming Nussbaum's proposition of cultural preservation as a central tenet of human development (Nussbaum, 2000).

Das (2021) highlights innovative initiatives integrating indigenous wisdom in addressing contemporary ecological and societal challenges, reinforcing Chakma et al.'s advocacy for indigenous knowledge as a cornerstone for rural development (Chakma et al., 2016).

In the digital era, technology emerges as a conduit for the globalization of indigenous narratives. Hazarika (2017) examines how digital platforms are archiving and disseminating indigenous knowledge, resonating with Giddens' assertion of technology as a transformative agent in society (Giddens, 1994).

Baruah (2020) analyzes the UNDRIP's impact on amplifying the voices of indigenous communities, marking a pivotal moment in the global recognition and protection of indigenous rights and knowledge.

In the midst of these challenges and opportunities, the synergistic alignment between traditional indigenous wisdom and modern innovation emerges as a catalyst for social transformation. Education, as Freire professed, transcends conventional norms, metamorphosing into an instrument of empowerment and identity reaffirmation (Freire, 2005).

Sen's conceptualization of development as freedom finds embodiment in the amalgamation of traditional wisdom and modern innovation (Sen, 1999). Pathak (2022) elucidates how this amalgamation fosters an ecosystem where indigenous knowledge evolves, adapting and contributing to contemporary socio-economic and political discourses.

The trajectory of indigenous knowledge and social development in Northeast India is sculpted in the crucible of challenges and opportunities. It's a narrative of resilience, adaptability, and the incessant quest for identity affirmation amidst the cascading waves of globalization. The harmonization of indigenous wisdom with modern innovation crafts a pathway teeming with possibilities—a future where cultural preservation and social development coalesce, birthing a society that is as diverse as it is unified.

6. Indigenous Knowledge and Human Rights

Indigenous knowledge and human rights in Northeast India, navigating through the intricate corridors of cultural identity, social justice, and education. Indigenous communities, adorned with an abundant heritage of distinct knowledge and traditions, often find themselves on the peripheries of the overarching socio-political narrative (Geertz, 1973). As Kymlicka (2002) attests, the validation and celebration of cultural identities are fundamental to human dignity and rights. In line with Freire's analysis (2005), educational and societal structures have at times morphed into conduits of oppression. The echoing sentiments of marginalization and cultural erosion resonate deeply, as exemplified by the extensive documentation of identity suppression by Smith (2012).

Yet, amidst this, a progressive shift burgeons, underscored by the global awakening to the symbiosis between human rights and indigenous knowledge. Sen's discourse on the interweaving threads of development, freedom, and rights places indigenous knowledge as a pivotal aspect of cultural and social affluence (Sen, 1999). On the global forefront, milestones like UNDRIP stand as testaments to indigenous rights recognition. Yet, within the specific contours of Northeast India, a nuanced adaptation of these standards is pivotal, as explored by Xaxa (2005), ensuring that policies intertwine international norms with local contexts.

Nussbaum's advocacy for an inclusive, culturally attuned education (2000) finds its echo here, where pedagogical innovations stand as bridges connecting human rights and indigenous knowledge. Aristotle (2004) and Cicero (2004) accentuate the ethical pillars of this journey, engraving the moral edicts of respect and preservation of diverse knowledge forms into societal norms.

Delving into the intricate social fabric of regions like Sikkim, Thapa's revelations (2002) offer windows into the complex dance of ethnicity and politics. The indigenous knowledge narratives, as amplified by Chakma et al. (2016), form the substratum of economic and societal advancements. In the realm of such complexities, the dialogue between traditional wisdom and modern legal frameworks become, instrumental. The work of Bose (2018) illuminates these interactions, proposing an integrated approach to human rights that is both global in its outreach and local in its sensitivities.

The empowerment of indigenous communities transcends mere inclusivity, morphing into a vibrant assertion of identity and rights. As echoed by Roy (2020), pedagogy becomes not just an educational endeavor but a profound celebration of diversity and human rights, interweaving indigenous knowledge into mainstream. narratives. The delineation of indigenous knowledge within the vast expanse of human rights unveils a dynamic, multifaceted landscape. It's a realm where education, culture, and rights coalesce, weaving a narrative that's as diverse as the myriad tribes of Northeast India. Each strand of knowledge and tradition, intricately woven, underscores a tale of resilience, identity, and the ceaseless quest for recognition and respect in the contemporary world.

7. Policy Recommendations

A multipronged policy approach is crucial to enhancing the integration of indigenous knowledge (IK) and fostering social development in Northeast India. This section outlines policy recommendations leveraging the insights from key philosophical, sociological, and developmental thinkers. Freire's (2005) insights indicate a culturally responsive pedagogical approach is paramount. Integrate IK into the educational curriculum, ensuring that indigenous perspectives are included and valued, fostering an environment where learning is dialogical and participative. As Geertz (1973) highlighted the intricate richness of cultural systems, policies should prioritize preserving and promoting indigenous languages, arts, crafts, and traditions. Implement programs that document, preserve, and promote the diverse cultural expressions of the indigenous communities.

Drawing from Tran (2012), ensure that indigenous communities have legal rights to their lands and natural resources. Policies should protect these rights, ensuring that any developmental activities are sustainable and equitable. Inspired by Sen (1999) and Nussbaum (2000), developmental policies should be inclusive, ensuring that the indigenous communities are active participants in the decision-making processes affecting them. Apply a capability approach to development, focusing on enhancing the freedoms and capabilities of the indigenous people. Gurung (2009) and Thapa (2002) provide insights into the intricate dynamics of ethnic and cultural identity in the political process. Policies should ensure fair political representation and participation of indigenous communities in local, regional, and national governance structures. Drawing from Chakma et al. (2016), implement policies that focus on the economic empowerment of indigenous communities. Promote indigenous entrepreneurship, provide access to credit facilities, and enhance market access for indigenous products.

From the perspective of the socio-political principles of Aristotle (2004) and Cicero (2004), policies should be grounded in ethical and moral considerations. Respect for the indigenous communities' dignity, rights, and cultural heritage should be at the core of every policy initiative.

This includes promoting interdisciplinary research and collaboration to explore, document, and integrate IK. Ensure that research is participative, with indigenous communities being active contributors and beneficiaries. Leverage technology to document, preserve, and promote IK. Implement initiatives that bridge the gap between traditional knowledge and modern innovation, ensuring that IK contributes to contemporary solutions for social, environmental, and economic challenges.

Collaborate internationally to share best practices, learnings, and innovations in integrating and promoting IK. Ensure that policies align with international standards on the rights and well-being of indigenous peoples. The intersection of indigenous knowledge, social development, and human rights in Northeast India presents a unique landscape rich with opportunities yet fraught with challenges. Policies grounded in respect for cultural diversity, human dignity, and social justice, as advocated by global thinkers like Freire (2005) and Sen (1999), can usher in an era where indigenous knowledge is not a sidelined relic but a dynamic, valued, and integral component of the nation's socio-political and developmental tapestry.

Conclusion

The exploration of Indigenous Knowledge (IK) and its significant influence on social development in Northeast India, as presented in this chapter, is akin to unearthing a treasure trove of intricate cultural narratives, resilient social structures, and insightful educational systems that have stood the test of time. The intrinsic interrelationship between IK, social structures, and the natural environment, as articulated by scholars like Baruah (2015), epitomizes the holistic nature of indigenous ways of life.

Communities in Northeast India, as outlined throughout this chapter, are not passive repositories of traditional knowledge but active agents of cultural preservation, social transformation, and economic innovation. In the face of globalizing pressures, these communities have demonstrated formidable resilience and adaptability, as noted by Hazarika (2019), maintaining the vibrancy and vitality of their traditions while forging pathways to contemporary relevance.

The integration of IK into contemporary social and economic development initiatives isn't an option but an imperative. Bera (2020) elaborates on the multifaceted advantages offered by the alignment of indigenous knowledge and modern development practices, emphasizing the creation of sustainable, equitable, and contextually relevant development outcomes. The practices, rituals, and wisdom ingrained in these communities serve as pragmatic solutions to contemporary challenges and an insightful blueprint for future societal advancements.

The overarching narrative emerging from this chapter underscores the pivotal role of dialogue, collaboration, and integration. No longer can IK be sidelined or marginalized. The insights from scholars like Das (2017) make it explicitly evident that the incorporation of IK within national and international development discourses will usher in an era of enhanced inclusivity, sustainability, and cultural respect.

These indigenous communities, embedded in diverse and rich cultural ecosystems, hold the keys to a harmonious coexistence of humanity with nature. In their traditions, there is a profound wisdom, an unspoken connection to the earth, and a deeply rooted sense of community that transcends the individual to embrace the collective. Singh (2019) elucidates how indigenous customs and traditions offer invaluable insights into sustainable environmental management, biodiversity conservation, and climate adaptation.

This chapter does not merely aim to document or archive the richness of IK but to advocate for its integration, adaptation, and respect in the broader spectrum of social development. In the intricate dance between tradition and modernity, therein lies a narrative of hope, resilience, and transformation. The indigenous communities of Northeast India, with their intricate mix of cultures, languages, and traditions, embody a lived experience of sustainable development that is as profound as it is intricate. The chapter leaves us with a clarion call to not only respect and preserve but also learn, adapt, and integrate indigenous wisdom in the quest for a more inclusive, sustainable, and equitable global society.

References

Arora, V. (2008). The Forest of Symbols Embodied in the Tholung Sacred Landscape of North Sikkim, India. Conservation and Society, 6(2), 132-153.

Aristotle. (2004). *Nicomachean Ethics*. Cambridge, UK: Cambridge University Press.

Banerjee, S. (2017). *Indigenous Narratives and Cultural Preservation in Northeast India.* Cultural Studies Journal, 21(1), 45-60.

Bharali, A. (2020). *Indigenous Knowledge in Policy Formulation: Northeast India Context.* Journal of Public Policy Research, 7(3), 215-230.

Bareh, H. (2001). *Encyclopaedia of North-East India: Meghalaya.* Mittal Publications.

Baruah, B. (2015). *Indigenous Knowledge Practices among Communities of Northeast India: An Anthropological Perspective.* Ethno Research, 1(1), 45-52.

Barua, P. (2018). *Experiential Learning Among the Mizo and Naga Tribes: An Ethnographic Insight.* Journal of Educational Ethnography, 6(2), 45-59.

Basumatary, R. (2013). *The Cultural Politics of Festival: A Study of Bwisagu of the Bodos.* Cultural Studies, 12(45), 340-355.

Bera, A. (2020). *Aligning Indigenous Knowledge with Modern Development: Opportunities and Challenges in Northeast India. International Journal of Social Development*, 6(1), 120-135.

Bhattacharjee, D. (2019). *Community Participation and Indigenous Education.* Indian Journal of Educational Research, 8, 56-68.

Bhattacharjee, J., & Devi, A. (2019). *Cultural Preservation Amidst Modernity: The Resilient Tribes of Northeast India.* Cultural Studies, 33(6), 1002-1020.

Boro, M. (2019). *Embroidery of the Bodos: Tradition and Change.* Indian Journal of Traditional Knowledge, 18(4), 700-705.

Bose, S. (2018). *Human Rights and Indigenous Realities: Challenges and Opportunities in Northeast India.* International Journal of Human Rights, 22(5), 702-719.

Brahma, K. (2015). *The Bodos: Children of Bhullumbutter.* Pratibimba.

Brahma, K. (2019). *Bodo Women and the Weaving Tradition.* Textile Society of India, 70(3), 260-267.

Chakma, B., Nongbri, T., Basumatary, C., Marak, Q., & Singha, K. (2016). Economy and Social Development of Rural Sikkim. Journal Space and Culture, India, 4(2), 5-17. https://doi.org/10.20896/saci.v4i2.198.

Chakma, B., Reang, D., & Tripura, A. (2016). *Tribal Development in Tripura: A Study of Social and Economic Indicators.* Social Change, 46(3), 474–483.

Cicero. (2004). *On Moral Ends (Woolf, Raphael. Trans.).* Cambridge: Cambridge University Press.

Cicero, M.T. (2004). *On Duties* (M.T. Griffin & E.M. Atkins, Eds.). Cambridge University Press.

Das, B. K., & Kharbani, W. (2020). *Reang Tribe in Tripura: A Sociological Study on their Customs and Traditions.* International Journal of Advanced Education and Research, 5(1), 35-37.

Das, P. (2017). *Oral Tradition and Moral Lessons: Storytelling Among the Tribes of Northeast India.* Journal of Indigenous Studies, 4(1), 12-26.

Das, S. (2017). *Indigenous Knowledge in Sustainable Development: A Case Study from Northeast India.* Journal of Rural and Community Development, 12(3), 135-148.

Das, R. (2017). *Political Engagement and Cultural Resilience: The Indigenous Tribes of Northeast India in the Modern State. Politics, Groups, and Identities,* 5(3), 456-472.

De, B. K., & Tripuri, B. (2015). *Socio-Cultural Life of Tripuri Tribe.* Journal of Culture, Society and Development, 10, 45-51.

Deka, M. (2020). *Mentorship and Skill Transmission Among the Indigenous Artisans.* Journal of Indigenous Arts, 3(1), 78-92.

Devi, O. (2019). *Indigenous Knowledge and Sustainable Development in Northeast India.* Journal of Global Resources, 5(01), 48-55.

Dutta, P. (2017). *Integration of Indigenous Knowledge in Addressing Climate Change.* Indian Journal of Traditional Knowledge, 16(1), 115-120.

Dutta, P. (2021). *Ecological Conservation through Indigenous Knowledge in Assam.* Journal of Biodiversity, 32(1), 11-27.

Freire, P. (2005). *Pedagogy of the Oppressed.* New York: Continuum International Publishing.

Geertz, C. (1973). *The Interpretation of Cultures.* New York: Basic Books.

Giddens, A. (1994). *Beyond Left and Right: The Future of Radical Politics.* Cambridge: Polity Press.

Giddens, A. (1994). *Living in a Post-Traditional Society. In Reflexive Modernization: Politics, Tradition, and Aesthetics in the Modern Social Order.* Stanford University Press.

Goswami, N. (2017). *The Politics of Autonomy: Indian Experiences.* SAGE Publications India.

Goswami, U. (2014). *The Magic of Diversity: An Ethnographic Account of Northeast India.* Cultural Studies Journal, 8(2), 123-137.

Goswami, R. (2020). *Indigenous Knowledge and Socio-Political Development: A Northeast Perspective.* Journal of Northeastern Studies, 15(4), 49-66.

Gurung, S. (2009). Ethnic cultural identity and the political process: A study of relationship between ethnic politics and political institution and organization of Sikkim. (Doctoral Thesis, Shod Ganga). Retrieved from http://hdl.handle.net/10603/137600.

Haksar, N. (2018). *The Naga Chronicles: The Naga War & the Peace Process 1951–2018.* Zubaan Publishers Pvt. Ltd.

Hazarika, M. (2019). *Resilience and Adaptation: Indigenous Responses to Natural Disasters in Northeast India.* Journal of Indigenous Studies, 4(2), 23-38.

Jacobsen, M. (2014). *Ethnic Identity, Autonomy, and Development: The Case of the Nagas of Northeast India.* Journal of Developing Societies, 30(3), 327–347.

Kharwanlang, L. (2019). *Community Conservation and Livelihoods at the Sacred Groves of Meghalaya, India.* International Journal of Ecology & Development, 34(1), 1-14.

Kharkongor, R., & Mishra, B. K. (2016). *Economic Empowerment of Women and Matriliny: A Study among the Khasi of Meghalaya.* International Journal of Advanced Research and Development, 1(10), 47-50.

Kharshiing, E. V. (2019). *Transformation and Adaptation: An Anthropological Study on the Encounter of the Khasis with Christianity.* International Journal of Research in Humanities, Arts, and Literature, 7(7), 49-58.

Kymlicka, W. (2002). *Multicultural Citizenship and Indigenous Rights.* Oxford Journal of Legal Studies, 22(3), 487-514.

Lalremruata, V. (2017). *The Mizo Uprising: Assam Assembly Debates on the Mizo Movement, 1966-1971*. Abhijeet Publications.

Laldinpuii, J. (2018). *Jhum Cultivation and Its Impact on the Environment and Rural Economy: A Case Study of the Mizo Hills*. International Journal of Advanced Research, 6(12), 862-871.

Lalthangliana, B. (2011). *History and Culture of the Mizos*. Mizoram Publication Board.

Lamare, S. (2017). *Traditional Institutions, Governance and Development in Meghalaya, India*. International Journal of Humanities and Social Sciences, 10(2), 44-56.

Mibang, T., & Chaudhuri, S. K. (2004). *Ethno-Medico-Botany of Arunachal Pradesh*. Bishen Singh Mahendra Pal Singh.

Mishra, P. (2021). *Indigenous Pedagogical Practices: Blending Tradition and Modernity*. Journal of Tribal Studies, 15(1), 1-17.

Misra, U. (2000). *The Periphery Strikes Back: Challenges to the Nation-State in Assam and Nagaland*. IIAS.

Misra, P. K. (2019). *Tribes of Northeast India: Bio-Cultural Perspectives*. Bio-Cultural Diversity, Ecotourism, and Conservation, 8, 157-174.

Nath, D. (2018). *Ethnic Identities and Social Conflict: The North-East Experience*. Indian Anthropologist, 48(1), 47-61.

Nath, D. (2017). *Insurgency and Identity: Reimagining State and Society in Assam*. Springer.

Nath, D. (2020). *Politics of Identity and the Bodo Movement in Assam*. Routledge.

Nussbaum, M. (2000). *Women and Human Development: The Capabilities Approach*. Cambridge University Press.

Pandey, B. B. (2009). *Oral Tradition, Rituals and Folklore: A Reflection on the Adis*. Journal of the Indian Anthropological Society, 44(2), 207-214.

Plaisier, H. (2007). *A Grammar of Lepcha. (Doctoral dissertation)*. Leiden University, Netherlands. Retrieved from https://hdl.handle.net/1887/11996

Roy, A. (2020). *Education, Identity, and Indigenous Rights: Navigating the Challenges in Northeast India*. Comparative Education Review, 64(1), 45-63.

Roy, A. (2019). *Indigenous Knowledge and Political Participation in Northeast India*. Journal of Asian Politics, 18(2), 124-142.

Roy, D. (2020). *Education and Cultural Preservation: The Tribal Paradigms of Northeast India*. International Journal of Educational Development, 75, 102218.

Roy, B. (2019). *The Jamatia Hoda: An Indigenous Knowledge of Self-Governance.* International Journal of Humanities and Social Science Invention, 8(9), 56-60.

Sarkar, A., & Roy, R. D. (2006). *The Monpas of Tawang: A Profile.* Himalayan Journal of Social Sciences, 1(1), 123–131.

Sarma, R. R., Hajong, S. R., & Shukla, A. C. (2020). *Sacred groves of Meghalaya, India – are they the last bastions of rich biodiversity?* Current Science, 118(8), 1275–1282. DOI: 10.18520/cs/v118/i8/1275-1282.

Sen, A. (1999). *Development as Freedom.* New York: Alfred Knopf.

Singh, R. (2019). *Indigenous Customs and Environmental Sustainability: Insights from Northeast Indian Communities.* Ecology and Society, 24(2), 1-16.

Singh, S. (2014). *Conflict and Reconciliation: The Politics of Ethnicity in Assam.* Routledge.

Singh, P. (2021). *Ecological Wisdom and Sustainable Development in Tribal Societies.* Environmental Anthropology, 27(1), 33-48.

Singh, A. & Misra, P. K. (2016). *Social Change Among the Tribes of Northeast India.* Social Change, 46(3), 430–444.

Singh, K., & Misra, A. (2016). *Indigenous Knowledge and Sustainable Development in Northeast India.* Journal of Development Policy and Practice, 1(2), 234-248.

Sharma, A. (2015). *Rituals as Pedagogical Tools in Northeast Indian Tribes.* Asian Ethnology, 74(1), 135-152.

Sharma, S., & Haque, I. (2018). *Traditional Wisdom and Modern Development: A Case Study of Tribes of Northeast India.* Social Change, 48(4), 590-607.

Shneiderman, S., & Turin, M. (2006). *Seeking the Tribe: Ethno-politics in Darjeeling and Sikkim.* HIMALAYA, the Journal of the Association for Nepal and Himalayan Studies, 26(1), 17–28.

Smith, L.T. (2012). *Decolonizing Methodologies: Research and Indigenous Peoples.* Zed Books Ltd.

Thapa, S. (2002). Ethnicity class and politics in Sikkim Centre for Himalayan Studies (Doctoral thesis, University of North Bengal) Retrieved from http://hdl.handle.net/10603/149379.

Tiwtawati, H. (2018). *Traditional Forest Management Practices of the Khasi Tribes in Meghalaya,* Northeast India. IOSR Journal of Humanities and Social Science, 23(1), 20-26.

Tran, H. (2012). Chogyal's Sikkim: Tax, Land & Clan Politics. (Doctoral Thesis, SIT). Retrieved from https://digitalcollections.sit.edu/isp_collection/1446.

Tran, L. (2012). *Governance on the Ground: Innovations and Discontinuities in Cities of the Developing World.* Woodrow Wilson Center Press; Johns Hopkins University Press.

Verma, S. (2016). *Indigenous Environmental Ethics and Sustainable Development: A Study on Northeast Indian Tribes.* Journal of Human Ecology, 21(2), 123-130.

Xaxa, V. (2005). *Transformation of Tribes in India: Terms of Discourse.* Economic and Political Weekly, 40(24), 2418-2422.

War, B. D. (2013). *The Matrilineal System of the Khasi-Jaintia of Meghalaya.* International Journal of Social Science & Interdisciplinary Research, 2(10), 118-127.

Yhome, K. (2019). *Conflict Management in Northeast Asia: A Comparative Study of India's Look East Policy and Japan's Eurasia Diplomacy.* International Journal of Business and Globalisation, 22(4), 487–502.

VIETNAMESE INDIGENOUS KNOWLEDGE AND SOCIAL DEVELOPMENT

ASSOC. PROF. HO NGOC SON AND DOCTOR HA MINH TUAN

Introduction

The important role of indigenous knowledge (IK) in achieving the Sustainable Development Goals (SDGs) and addressing the most pressing global problems is reflected in its inclusion in many global environmental governance forums. The World Heritage Convention of the United Nations Educational, Scientific, and Cultural Organization (UNESCO), the Convention on Biological Diversity (CBD), and the Food and Agriculture Organization (FAO) all explicitly acknowledge the contributions of IK to sustainable development. In addition, the importance of mainstreaming indigenous knowledge systems for the realization of human rights, sustainable development, poverty eradication, and disaster reduction has been recognized in a series of international instruments such as the United Nations (UN) Declaration on the Rights of Indigenous Peoples, the Ahmadabad Framework on Environmental Education, the UN Declaration on Human Rights, the UN Covenant on Civil and Political Human Rights, and the UN Covenant on Economic, Social, and Cultural Rights (Masoga and Shokane, 2019).

Indigenous knowledge is sometimes referred to as local knowledge, traditional knowledge, or local ecological knowledge. It serves as the foundation of many environmental solutions for problems related to agriculture, the health care sector, food preparation, natural resource management, and education (Ty and Cuc, 1998). IK has been the foundation of indigenous peoples' identities, cultural heritage, civilizations, livelihoods, and coping strategies for several centuries. Therefore, indigenous knowledge can offer valuable responses to climate change, food insecurity, reducing inequalities, and other challenges that we are trying to resolve through the Sustainable Development Goals. IK remains a valued asset in many societies around the world, and Vietnam in particular. Its role in establishing the individual and community's identity within history cannot be disputed (Pascalia et al., 2022). IK is a crucial building block of local social capital, which is essential for sustainability because it facilitates cooperation and reciprocity among community members (Vu, 2010).

Vietnam is a multi-ethnic country with 54 ethnic groups, of which 53 are ethnic minority groups. The government of Vietnam does not apply the term "Indigenous Peoples" to any of these minority ethnic groups. The term "ethnic minorities" is used instead. The term "ethnic minorities" is often used interchangeably with "Indigenous Peoples" by international agencies working in Vietnam. There is no specific law on ethnic minorities, but an agency at the ministerial level, the Committee on Ethnic Minority Affairs, is in charge of the affairs of ethnic minorities. Ethnic minorities in Vietnam account for about 14.1 million people, or around 14.7% of the country's total population of about 96 million (2022). Poverty is still high among ethnic minorities. In 2022, the multidimensional poverty rate registered for ethnic minorities was 23.7%, while the national poverty rate was 4.3% (Statistical Yearbook, 2022). All ethnic minorities have Vietnamese citizenship, and the Vietnam Constitution guarantees that all people have the same rights. Ethnic minority groups have their own culture and different traditions. Ethnic minority groups, especially those with small populations, mostly live in mountainous and highland areas with very limited access to infrastructure, health care, and education (World Bank, 2009; Phung & Do, 2014).

Indigenous knowledge systems in Vietnam are rich and greatly varied in every aspect of development, including nature conservation, health protection, farming systems, and plant and animal varieties. This reflects the vast differences in physical conditions and the different needs of different local people. Such knowledge and diversity have been developed and practiced over many centuries of local experience (Ty and Cuc, 1998; Tran et al., 2007). In Vietnam, indigenous knowledge is relevant to all fields of the life of local peoples, especially those living in rural areas, relating, in particular, to local livelihoods through such practices as crop cultivation, food preparation, rearing of animals, seed storage, traditional medicine, hunting, and natural resources management (Giang, 2010).

Social development is a broad concept, and it may include efforts to reduce poverty and inequality, improve access to education and healthcare, and promote civic engagement and community participation. In this chapter, the role of Vietnamese indigenous knowledge in social development through improving natural resource management, enhancing community resilience to climate change, agricultural production, use of medicinal plants, economic and livelihood opportunities, local institutions and spiritual life, social management, and education are discussed.

Indigenous Knowledge for Improved Natural Resource Management

There are many examples where indigenous knowledge has contributed to effective natural resource management in Vietnam. For example, the use of indigenous knowledge has been effective in maintaining vegetation, creating new landscapes and increasing soil fertility, limiting weeds, increasing water permeability and water retention, reducing erosion and surface leaching, limiting floods in the rainy season and maintaining water for the dry season, limiting forest fires, contributing to a sustainable ecological environment, and limiting pests and diseases in plants (Pham et al., 2019). A study found that indigenous knowledge plays an important role in forest, water, and land management. Ethnic minorities such as the Hmong, Thai, Dao, Van Kieu, Ja Rai, E De, and Ba Na peoples living in various provinces throughout Vietnam often have sacred forests that are used for devotions, much like the Kinh majority use temples and clan altars. The Thai people have "ghost forests", the Hmong and the Tay people have "forbidden forests", and they are like the "rừng cãi or arguing forests" of the La Chí people: they are usually watersheds or primal forests. There is a custom law that says people are not allowed to disturb the forests; they have to respect and protect them in order to bring majesty to the forests (Le, 2017). Specific customary laws govern forest areas for water, where water spirits are worshipped. Different customary laws govern different forest areas for the production of forest products, such as medicinal plants, firewood, and materials for handicraft. This type of community forest management plays a strong role in the cultural practices, as well as the livelihoods, of many ethnic minorities in Vietnam.

Mountain communities in Vietnam often have their own way of classifying forests, treating each type of forest separately. For example, the S'tieng, Ma, and M'nong ethnic groups in Central Highland have the same way of classifying forests, which are divided into old forests, young forests, ghost forests, and watershed forests. Meanwhile, the Choro people in Ba Ria Vung Tau divide forests into four types: old forests, medium old forests, bamboo forests, and bud forests. It is for the benefit of the community that they are all conscious of protecting the forest. Anyone who violates will be prosecuted based on customary law. Ethnic minority communities have a very high awareness of forest protection. They are attached to the forest land; they are "forest eaters", but they do not destroy the forest when exploiting it. They only exploit certain types of forests and have specific regulations so as not to destroy the forests. In particular, ethnic minorities in the Southeast of Vietnam often associate forests with "sacred" elements to protect forests. For them, forests are a source of food, construction materials, and medicinal plants, and forests are also a shield to support community life. Since ancient times, the Ede people have had a very correct concept: As long as there are trees in the forest, there will still be a water wharf; if the water wharf is still there, the village will still be there. Therefore, all people in the village must keep the forest trees so that their water will always flow, bringing a source of life to the people in the village (Tran and Nguyen, 2016). When people have "faith" and "fear" of gods, this is the best way to protect the forest. The study also found that indigenous knowledge of Khmer people in Southern Vietnam has played an important role in making land use decisions, which can support solving land-use conflicts to achieve the most sustainable management of land resources. The Khmer attach great importance to land. The Khmer consider land a place to live, a means of production, a homeland, and have sacred feelings for the land (Pham et al., 2017).

Similarly, indigenous knowledge of water resources management may be seen throughout the country, but especially in lowland areas or upland water catchment areas. This knowledge is based around spiritual forces and the customary laws of small communities; they combine with the management of other resources such as land and forest. Vietnamese people believe that water is given and managed by the Water Spirit, while other beings, such as the Rain Deity and Forest Spirits, also influence water resources. Therefore, people must maintain their relationship with water resources by respecting the gods and spirits and obeying the laws handed down by such creator-beings in order to have enough water and avoid disasters such as flooding and droughts that occur due to the anger of these forces. For example, Dao people engage with water spirits and forest spirits through their ceremonies. They believe that there is a close relationship between water and the forest. Any activities that violate forest and water sources will impact the spirit world and will be penalized. Dao people have laws to protect watershed areas, distribute water to households and rice fields, and prohibit any wastewater discharging activities to other families, and these laws are reinforced through ceremonies (Nguyen and Ross, 2017).

Indigenous Knowledge of Medicinal
Plant use for Health Care

Each ethnic group living in Vietnam has accumulated its own system of knowledge and experience in using plants to prevent and treat diseases. For a long time, ethnic minorities in Vietnam have had a tradition of healing with medicinal plants (Huong and Thanh, 2016). The number of medicinal plants in Vietnam can reach 6,000 species (Loi, 2005). In Vietnam, there are 3948 medicinal plants identified by the indigenous knowledge of 54 ethnic groups (Hop et al., 2020). Most of the upland households can use tens to hundreds of medicinal plants that are available in the communities to heal normal diseases such as headaches, diarrhea, and fever. There are often some herbalists in every community in the upland. They are the persons who hold knowledge and experience in finding and using medicinal plants for healing in the communities (Phuc, 2019). Ethnic minorities in Vietnam have rich experience in using medicinal plants because their lives have been based on forest resources. For example, a study found that the Cho Ro community at Dong Nai Cultural Nature Reserve could use 76 species belonging to 52 families of 3 phyla for health care and disease treatment (Kieu et al., 2020). Similarly, Co Tu people in Quang Nam province often use medicinal plants in traditional medicine practices (59 species), particularly in treatments of arthritis and diseases of the digestive system (Dang et al., 2022).

A study found that the Van Kieu and Pa Ko ethnic groups in Quang Tri province have 56 known poisonous plant species in their surrounding environments. Their knowledge is valuable for their daily lives and provides fundamental information for further phytochemical and biological investigation to ascertain the toxic compounds of poisonous plants that may be used for the treatment of appropriate diseases (Chi et al., 2023). Thus, medicinal plants, which are used by local people to treat diseases, are significant materials that can help scientists further research those plants whose medicinal properties may be useful in the development of new drugs and provide a basis for the conservation and sustainable development of this knowledge (Kieu et al., 2020). The medicinal plants not only protect public health but also contribute to hunger eradication and poverty reduction in the uplands. Medicinal plants have been regarded as special goods in the uplands of Vietnam. Several communities in the uplands are involved in collecting, processing, and selling medicinal plants (Tran et al., 2007).

Indigenous Knowledge Enhances Community Resilience to Climate Change

Indigenous knowledge is an essential asset for communities to adapt to climate change by knowing the land, using local natural resources, sharing capital, and taking a community approach to local issues. In the NMR of Vietnam, to cope with cold spells, the Hmong people often make earthen walls for buffalo stalls. They also feed buffalo with rice straw or prepare rice or corn porridge for animals with cardamon and salt to 'keep their bellies warm' in the cold winter. The Hmong communities in Bac Kan province have different indigenous strategies, including those focused on the management of resources related to water, land, crops, and livestock. For example, in agricultural production, Hmong communities were found to use local drought-resistant crops and switch from rice to other cash crops when necessary. Hmong people also grow heirloom crops such as Hmong peas, Hmong maize, or soybeans on upland farms, as these crops do not require much water. Yao people still use any local crop varieties and traditional farming practices to adapt to climate change (Son et al., 2019; 2021).

IK is also considered one of the most effective strategies in response to climate change issues among the Xo Dang ethnic minority groups in Tra Doc commune, Bac Tra My district, and Quang Nam province in Central Vietnam (Chuong et al., 2020). A study on IK and flood adaptation in Hue found a strong relationship between local knowledge and flooding adaptation (Tran and Ubukata, 2020). A study in An Giang province found that many IKs and practices remain valuable in predicting and adapting to floods. However, this knowledge has not been specifically recorded and stored appropriately for transmission to the latter and is widely shared in the community (Phu et al., 2019). Indigenous knowledge also contributes as an important early warning system to understand the resource distribution, ecosystem, and impacts of climate change and sea level rise and potentially provide a needed edge to a more effective management of production in the context of changes (Pham et al., 2017; Son et al., 2019).

IK provides more solutions and options for climate change adaptation. Indigenous crops and/or livestock are more resilient to extreme weather events, bearing fewer diseases than new varieties; intensive farming and rearing requirements are not high; thus, they are optimal for community residents, including the poor. IK helps people live with self-sufficiency and self-determination. It makes them feel less dependent on external factors; hence, they can reduce their vulnerability to climate change impacts. Farmers are likely familiar with indigenous techniques; they can understand, adapt, and maintain such techniques better than the newly introduced ones from outside, and as a result, the experience and voice of the community can be properly promoted. Local residents have more community-based choices to adapt to climate change impacts rather than relying on external factors, e.g., new varieties (Son et al., 2019; Son et al., 2021). Therefore, policymakers should pay more attention to indigenous knowledge to combat climate change in future national policies and projects.

Indigenous Knowledge Creates more Livelihood Opportunities

Indigenous knowledge could contribute to income generation and livelihood opportunities for local people in many different ways. There have been some typical achievements in combining indigenous knowledge with modern science and technology to create sustainable livelihoods for ethnic minority communities, especially in the fields of exploitation and sustainable development of forest resources, ensuring food security for people in the face of drought, floods, and extreme weather conditions caused by climate change. For example, many youths and women in Vietnam are doing good business growing and selling indigenous crops, animals, and non-timber forest products, which are in high demand by people in the city centers. Both medicinal plants and non-medicinal plants are known as the main economic supply of rural areas, especially with ethnic minorities in the mountainous countryside of Vietnam. The cultivation, collection, and sale of medicinal plants and non-medicinal plants, which are non-timber forest products, contributes to the livelihood improvement of many people, especially poor households (Dang and Tran, 2006). The knowledge of traditional plant use is still essential to the families living in the forest areas (Cuong et al., 2021).

Indigenous knowledge in the form of cultural heritage is increasingly used by local communities to do business about cultural tourism. Tay and Nung people in Cao Bang province of North Vietnam have created unique traditional cultural heritages containing many historical and cultural values in all areas of social life, such as food production, food, livestock, food storage and processing, collection, use of medicinal plants, and treatment methods; transmitting knowledge through generations in education; protecting, managing, and reasonably exploiting natural resources;

community management organizations; social values; and traditional laws in villages. Cultural identity is also expressed vividly through the cultural forms, costumes, festivals, folk games, crafts, cuisine, customs, and practices of residential communities. It is the uniqueness and diversity of culture that creates the attraction for tourists to explore, experience, and learn about the traditional culture of ethnic minorities in Cao Bang as well as in many other places in Vietnam. Community and cultural tourism in some villages and hamlets where many ethnic minorities live initially has brought positive results, contributing to poverty reduction and creating additional sources of income for the communities.

Indigenous Knowledge in Agricultural Production

Indigenous knowledge plays a key role in farming and agricultural production, especially among ethnic minority people in Vietnam. It could support the design of sustainable agricultural systems, increasing the likelihood that rural populations will accept, develop, and maintain innovations and interventions. For example, terraced rice in many provinces of Vietnam is an indigenous water management approach in the upland region. The rice terraces are a great system of irrigation and water management that are rooted in the depths of the H'Mong culture. The terraced rice fields have been created by people living in mountainous and hilly terrain, where there is a shortage of flat land for rice cultivation. They are also representative of a living culture's harmonious interaction with nature. The indigenous culture has transformed the mountain's harsh natural conditions (Son and Tuan, 2022). In Vietnam's northern region, especially the Dong Van and Meo Vac Districts of Ha Giang Province, the topography is made up of karst limestone mountains and deeply cut valleys and gorges. The H'Mong people cultivate maize by means of "rocky pocket agriculture". The pockets are found on the mountainsides, from the valleys to the higher reaches. Maize is grown in these pockets as long as there is enough soil to support it. The pockets act as catchments for both soil and water and provide some protection for the plants from the wind and other elements. Maize is a traditional type that villagers have planted for many generations, and it has a number of advantages. It requires very little fertilizer. It also has thick and tough cornhusks that cover the cob until the seeds are dry, effectively protecting it from the rain, insects, and birds in the fields. In the rocky pockets, the local people often use their indigenous knowledge through intercropping and crop rotation methods between maize, beans, peas, and other vegetables (Tran et al., 2007).

For the ethnic Khmer in the mountainous area in An Giang province, the IK of peanut cultivation has been developed over time and focused on dealing with the sandy soil and the water shortage. They have applied cow dung and the broadcasting method to increase yield and save labor. The farmers effectively apply the broadcasting method and are knowledgeable about the benefits and harms of using cow dung and applying the broadcasting method to peanut crops over the years. This sowing method is still of useful value in the community. In addition, farmers understand how to blend indigenous and scientific knowledge, such as crop rotation, crop calendar, varieties, and chemical fertilizer application, for increasing yield and improving adaptive capacity to climate change (Bui et al., 2023). Ethnic minorities in Bu Dang (Binh Phuoc), such as M'nong, Ma, and S'tieng, often choose red or yellow soil for farming. Because these two types of soil have high moisture and retain moisture well, they are good for plants and drought-resistant. Local people do not choose white soil for farming as it has poor fertility. The Cho ro people in Dong Nai, Ba Ria, and Vung Tau, through their experience, also choose red soil with high fertility to exploit cultivation. The M'nong people in Bu Gia Map also prioritize red soil for exploitation (Le et al., 2020). It can be said that the indigenous knowledge of local people has played an important role in agricultural production.

Indigenous Knowledge, Local Institutions, and Spiritual life

Traditional institutions in Vietnam play important roles in ethnic minority communities. They could promote the dissemination of ideas, the linkages and cooperation, the voice and accountability, the participation and empowerment, the conservation and development of traditional characteristics and culture, and community-based social security. In areas where traditions and customs are still strong, village heads receive support from notables for village operation and management. Village heads often ask notables for their advice and experiences in handling community issues. Village institutions in some ethnic minority communities in Vietnam have well-conserved traditional faith and spiritual practices. These play an important part in the activities of ethnic minority communities. For example, for the Van Kieu people in Quang Tri province, village notables organize God worship ceremonies every year at the holly forest area with contributions from village households. In addition, there are many other spiritual events organized within families and households, such as new year rituals such as rice seedling, rice blossom, year-end, and household peace worship under the coordination of family heads (Oxfam and ActionAid International Vietnam, 2013).

The new rice celebration is a long-standing custom of ethnic groups living in the Central Highlands, usually held in November every year to pray for good rain, good winds, good harvests, and family prosperity. The new rice ceremony is also a traditional cultural feature with profound humanity that Thai people value and preserve from generation to generation. This is an opportunity for family members and neighbors to reunite, have fun, share business, build a family, and tighten community solidarity. The water wharf worship ceremony is a traditional ritual with a unique cultural feature that is rich in humanity and has profound educational significance for the young generation about the morality "When drinking water, remember the source" of the H're ethnic people. The water wharf worship ceremony is an opportunity for people to express their gratitude to the water source for helping them get through a good season of plowing and sowing.

For ethnic minorities residing in Vietnam's mountainous area, the meaning of forest does not simply refer to materials, environment, and resources but also to the spiritual culture. The spiritual forest has been located in the consciousness and life of the ethnic minority for a long time. Religious beliefs formed spiritual forests in Vietnam, and this helped preserve truly primeval forests. Moreover, spiritual forests have played an important role in the material, spiritual, and social lives of ethnic minorities. The roles of the spiritual forests in social life can be seen in the activities of maintaining and creating the social space where people practice and hand down customs, indigenous knowledge, taboos associated with forest trees, wild animals, and rituals with offerings for the god of the forest (Le, 2017). For example, worshiping the forest god is an important traditional ritual in the spiritual life of the Pu Peo people. In the religious life of the Pu Peo people in Ha Giang province, the custom of worshiping the forest god has existed for a long time. The worshiping ceremony creates a close relationship in the community and village, raises awareness about preserving the forbidden forest, and contributes to protecting the increasingly depleted forest resources and domestic water sources for the people. The areas where the Pu Peo people live all have a separate forbidden forest, where the god of the forest resides, preserved and protected by the people by customary laws. For the Pu Peo people, the forest god has a particularly important position, has the most influence, and is prayed for in most worship rituals. The ceremony to worship the forest god is held periodically every year on the sixth day of the sixth lunar month. Pu Peo people believe that this is a time when heaven and earth are sacred, all things are peaceful, and it is also a time to wait for the results.

Indigenous Knowledge, Customary Law, and Social Management

Indigenous knowledge can be seen in the form of customary law. Customary law is a compilation of community knowledge into regulations that are mandatory for all members of the ethnic community. Customary law has strong local elements associated with a specific community. Vietnam's customary laws have existed and been applied in various forms and to various extents, having contributed to the management of villages and hamlets in particular and the management of traditional countryside in general. They still exert positive impacts on rural development at present (Ngo et al., 2016). In rural areas where people of various ethnic groups live, the customary laws have positively contributed to the preservation and management of natural resources, particularly forests, cultivated land, and water sources, to the determination of relations of ownership over the natural resources, that is, public ownership by the village or hamlet communities and the rights to use them by individuals of such communities within the framework of the state's current land law, as well as to the consolidation of social relations and the building of a healthy cultural life at the grassroots.

Most ethnic minorities in Vietnam do not have writing, so all knowledge accumulated in life is passed down orally from generation to generation. In most ethnic minorities, that knowledge is expressed in customary law. As a product of the community, the customary laws of ethnic groups aim to create friendly relationships between people and between people and nature. A study found that the customary laws of ethnic minorities in the Southeast cover most aspects of ethnic life, including regulations on community organization and management (Le, 2019). Thus, in any ethnic group, customary laws bear the imprint of ethnic culture and serve as a principle in social management and administration.

Conclusions and Recommendations

Today, indigenous people or ethnic minority communities in Vietnam and elsewhere are facing unprecedented challenges because of globalization, urbanization, and tourism expansion. However, indigenous knowledge can be the key to reconciling the needs of development, cultural preservation, and ecological conservation. The indigenous knowledge of farmers is considered an important source of information about the local farming systems, experiences, institutions, and culture. This knowledge system plays a significant role in designing formal and efficient extension services. Indigenous populations have managed to survive for centuries, adapting in many different ways to adverse climate conditions and managing to create sustainable livelihood systems. Diverse forms of knowledge, deeply rooted in their relationships with the environment as well as in cultural cohesion, have allowed many of these communities to maintain a sustainable use and management of natural resources, to protect their environment, and to enhance their resilience. Their ability to observe, adapt, and mitigate has helped many indigenous communities face new and complex circumstances that have often severely impacted their way of life and their territories. Indigenous knowledge and climate-resilient agricultural practices and technologies, which are cost-effective, lead to food security at the household level as they can easily be carried out by resource-poor or small farmers.

In Vietnam, IK contributes to the sustainability and productivity of many systems, including forest management, farming practices, land management, biodiversity conservation, fisheries monitoring, and climatic adaptations. Indigenous knowledge also contributes to enriching the culture, improving economic development, and ensuring the social stability of ethnic groups. Indigenous plant varieties and animal breeds are associated with the traditional cultures, voices, and agency of ethnic minorities in Vietnam. Ethnic minority people not only use indigenous knowledge for maintaining their economic and cultural livelihoods but also as a cornerstone for natural resource management and biodiversity conservation. Indigenous knowledge is a critical factor for sustainable development. Empowerment of local communities is a prerequisite for the integration of indigenous knowledge in the development process. The integration of appropriate indigenous knowledge systems into development programs has already contributed to efficiency, effectiveness, and sustainable development impact. Indigenous knowledge needs to be constantly used, challenged, and further adapted to evolving local contexts. While the government of Vietnam emphasizes preserving indigenous and ethnic cultures and customs, making use of indigenous knowledge is not highlighted.

IK needs to be addressed and integrated into educational programs. Indigenous knowledge can act as a powerful tool in a learning environment to teach students. When IK is integrated into classroom settings or learning environments, students better connect to the material taught and can become a major knowledge source for their community's sustainable development. Applying ethnic indigenous knowledge to teaching folklore, a cultural element of the ethnic group, is a new approach that is very suitable for the current Vietnamese educational environment and views. It is the use of contexts, documents, sources of traditional cultural values, and vivid real-life contacts in the locality to create classroom situations, extra-curricular activities, projects, and student research. Through these activities, learners have the opportunity to reinforce classroom lessons, learn more practical lessons, apply learned knowledge to solve local real-life problems, and practice skills of analysis and synthesis (Pham et al., 2022). However, learning environments need to be adapted to help students build on their indigenous communities' knowledge and recognize students' culture and value systems. Educators can further this type of education by combining appropriate pedagogical techniques (WB, 2005).

The new sustainable development agenda encompasses many issues that are directly affecting indigenous peoples' lives. Education, poverty, access to justice, and climate change are only a few of the challenges that indigenous people have been and are currently facing. Their knowledge and know-how, deeply rooted in the relationship of indigenous peoples with nature and community, have proven to be efficient in responding to some of these challenges. Knowledge loss has already been responsible for increasing vulnerability and risk for indigenous populations. It is, therefore, important that the national and international community start recognizing indigenous peoples and their knowledge as valuable allies in the fight against climate change and sustainable development challenges and in maintaining global biodiversity. Joint efforts are urgently required to develop and implement suitable initiatives to empower indigenous peoples to uphold and realize their rights and be involved in the decision-making process, becoming in this way active agents of change (Sultana et al., 2018).

References

Bach, T. S., Lebel, L. and Nguyen, T.T., 2009, Indigenous knowledge and decision making in Vietnam: Living with floods in An Giang Province,

Mekong Delta, Vietnam Pages 445-458, in *Indigenous Knowledge and Disaster Risk Reduction: From Practice to Policy* by Rajib Shaw, Anshu Sharma, Yukiko Takeuchi (editors), Nova Science Publishers, Inc. 490 pages

Benyei, P., Calvet-Mir, L., Reyes- García, V., & Villamayor-Tomas, S., 2022. Indigenous and Local Knowledge's Role in Social Movement's Struggles Against Threats to Community-Based Natural Resource Management Systems: Insights from a Qualitative Meta-analysis. *International Journal of the Commons*, 16(1), pp. 263–277.

Bui, T.M.P, Nguyen, V. H., Le, T. P., Nguyen, T. N. T., Nguyen, H. C., 2023. Indigenous Knowledge of Peanut Cultivation of the Ethnic Khmer Resident in the Mountainous Area in An Giang Province, Vietnam, *International Journal on Advanced Science Engineering Information Technology*, 3(1): 250-259.

Cuong, H.N., L Averyanov, A Egorov, Doi, T. B. and Quyet, T. P., 2021.Traditional knowledge on non-medicinal plants used by the tribal people in Nam Dong Commune, Quan Hoa district, Thanh Hoa provice, nothern Vietnam, IOP Conf. Series: Earth and Environmental Science 876 (2021) 012053.

Chuong V. H., Quy, N. P. L., Mai, T. H. N., Phuong, T. T., Tan, Q. N., Tung, G. P., Linh, H. K. N., Loan, T. D. N., Ha, N. T., 2020. Indigenous knowledge in relation to climate change: adaptation practices used by the Xo Dang people of central Vietnam, Heliyon, 6 (12).

Chi, M. N., My, T., Huong, G.V., Van, T. B., Van, A. N. T., & Khac, B. N. (2023). Indigenous knowledge of poisonous plants from Van Kieu and Pa Ko ethnic groups in Quang Tri province, Vietnam. *Academia Journal of Biology*, 45(2), 89–103.

da Silva, C., Pereira, F. & Amorim, J.A., 2023. The integration of indigenous knowledge in school: a systematic review, *Compare: A Journal of Comparative and International Education*.

Dang, N.H., Vu, D. D., Le, X. D., Pham, M.P., 2022. Indigenous knowledge of the

Co Tu group for medicinal plants used in the Tay Giang district (Axan and Tr'Hy commune), Quang Nam province, Vietnam, *Journal of Forestry Science and Technology* No.12: 122-128.

Dang, V. Q. and Tran, N. A., 2006. Commercial collection of NTFPs and households living in or near the forests: Case study in Que, Con Cuong and Ma, Tuong Duong, Nghe An, Vietnam, *Ecological Economics*, 60 (1): 65-74.

Hop, N.V., Xiong, C.C, Yun X.L, Ha, N.T, Hanh, N.T., 2020. Diversity and indigenous knowledge of using medicinal plants of the Dao people in Ta Dung National Park, Vietnam, *Journal of Medicinal Plants Studies*, 8(1):45-49.

Kieu, M.H., Nguyen, V. H., and Doan, A. V., 2020, Indigenous knowledge on using medicinal plant of Cho Ro ethnic group in Vietnam: A case study at Dong Nai culture nature reserve, *Journal of Medicinal Plants Studies*, 8(6): 123-130.

Le, N. V., 2019. "Indigenous knowledge of ethnic minorities - viewed from development resources (The case of the Southeast region)". Proceedings of the 4th International Scientific Conference on Vietnamese Studies: Issues in Vietnamese language teaching and Vietnamese research in today's world. Ho Chi Minh City National University Publishing House, pp. 1183-1197.

Le, A.T., 2017. The role of spiritual forests in life of ethnic minorities in the Vietnam's central mountainous area, *Religious Studies*, 11 (3&4): 60-75

Le.T.N.P., 2019. Indigenous knowledge of using herbal and animal products as medicinal treatments among ethnic minorities in Lac Duong district, Lam Dong province, Journal of Ho Chi Minh Open University, 14(1), 45-58.

Le T. T. H. and Nguyen, T. T., 2016. Research knowledge and usage experience Medicinal plants of ethnic minorities in Thai Nguyen province for conservation and sustainable development, Journal of Science and Technology, Hanoi National University, 32 (1): 55-64.

Loi, D.T.2005. Vietnamese medicinal plants and medicine. Medical Publishing House, Hanoi.

Masoga, M.A. and Shokane, A.L., 2019, Viewpoint: Indigenous knowledge systems and environmental social work education: Towards environmental sustainability, *Southern African Journal of Environmental Education*, 35: 1-11.

Mbah, M.F. and Johnson, A.T., 2021. Special Issue Introduction: Exploring the Role of Indigenous Knowledge in Postsecondary Policies and Practices Toward Sustainable Development, *Journal of Comparative & International Higher Education, 13 (3): 7-19.*

Ngo, V. L., Huynh, N. T. and Ngo, T.P. L., 2016. Minority ethnic groups' indigenous knowledge in sustainable development: A case study from the Southeast region (in Vietnamese), 393 pages, National Political Publisher, Hanoi.

Nguyen, T.H. and Ross, A. 2017. Barriers and opportunities for the involvement of indigenous knowledge in water resources management in the Gam River Basin in north-east Vietnam, *Water Alternatives* 10(1): 134-159.

Nguyen, C.M., Tran, M. L., Vu, H. G., Bui, V. T., Nguyen, T. V. A., Ninh, K. B., 2023. Indigenous knowledge of poisonous plants from Van Kieu and Pa Ko ethnic groups in Quang Tri province, Vietnam. *Academia Journal of Biology*, 45(2): 89–103.

Oxfam and Action Aid International Vietnam, 2013. Roles of village institutions in poverty reduction in some typical ethnic minority communities of Vietnam: Case studies in Dien Bien, Quang Tri, Dak Lak and Tra Vinh provinces, Research report.

Pascalia, J.S., Akoth, S.O. and Dzinekou, J.Y., 2022. The role of Indigenous knowledge: practices and values in promoting socio-economic well-being and equity among Endorois community of Kenya, *AlterNative 18(1):* 37–45.

Pham, T.V., Hieu, T. N., Tuan, H. V., Pham, D. T. V., Quang, T. L., 2017. Integrating indigenous knowledge for participatory land use planning (PLUP) in Tra Hat hamlet, a climate-smart village in the Mekong River Delta, Vietnam, *Vietnam Journal of Science, Technology and Engineering*, 59(3): 32-38.

Pham, T.K., Paingha, A.S and Dorgu, T.E., 2022. Learning individual knowledge of the Southern Khmers in Vietnam and applying to teaching of folk literature, *Himalayan Journal of Humanities and Culture Studies*, 3 (3): 1-6.

Pham, X.P. and Ngo, T.B.C., 2020. The Role of Indigenous Knowledge and Livelihood to Adapt to Floods in Sustainable Development in Mekong Delta, Vietnam (A Case Study in An Giang Province). *Acta Scientific Agriculture* 4 (10): 10-15.

Pham, P. X., & De, N. N., 2016. The Situation and Solutions for Using Indigenous Knowledge of Local People in Adaptation to Floods in an Giang Province, Vietnam. *Asia-Pacific Journal of Rural Development*, *26*(2), 72-96.

Pham, T.T., Pham, V. D., Le, T. B., Giang, K. B., 2019. Promotion of local knowledge for forest protection in the Central Highlands Region of Vietnam, *International Journal of Advanced Research and Publications*, 3(10): 39-41.

Pérez-Caselles, C., Brugarolas, M. & Laura Martínez-Carrasco, L. (2020), "Traditional varieties for local markets: A sustainable proposal for agricultural SMEs", *Sustainability* Vol. *12* No.11, pp.4517.

Sergon, P. J., Akoth, S. O., & Dzinekou, J. Y., 2022. The role of Indigenous knowledge: practices and values in promoting socio-economic well-being and equity among Endorois community of

Kenya. *AlterNative: An International Journal of Indigenous Peoples*, *18*(1), 37–45.

Son, H.N., and Tuan, B.T., 2022. Mu Cang Chai Rice Terraces and its water management, The cultural heritages of water in Eastern and South-Eastern Asia, *ICOMOS Thematic Study*, page 151-155.

Son, H.N., Kingsbury, A. and Ha, T. H, 2021. "Indigenous Knowledge and the Enhancement of Community Resilience to Climate Change in the Northern Mountainous Region of Vietnam", *Agroecology and Sustainable Food Systems*, 45(4): 499-522.

Son, H.N. and Kingsbury, A., 2020. Community adaptation and climate change in the Northern Mountainous Region of Vietnam: A case study of ethnic minority people in Bac Kan Province, *Asian Geographers*, 37(1): 33-51.

Son, H.N., Kingsbury, A. and Dong, L. C., 2019. Indigenous knowledge and climate change adaptation of ethnic minorities in the mountainous regions of Vietnam: a case study of Dao people in Bac Kan province, *Agricultural Systems*, 176 (2019) 102683

Sultana, R., Muhammad, N. and Zakaria A.K.M., 2018. "Role of indigenous knowledge in sustainable development", *International Journal of Development Research*, 8 (02): 18902-18906.

Tran, C.T., Le, X. Q. and Vu, V. H., 2007. The Role of Indigenous Knowledge in Sustainable Development: A Case Study of The Vietnam Mountain Regions, Tribes and Tribals, Special Volume No. 1: 215-224 eds. Emmanuel K. Boon and Luc Hens, Editors, *Indigenous Knowledge Systems and Sustainable Development: Relevance for Africa*

Tran, H. B. C. and Ubukata, F., 2020. Understanding local and scientific knowledge about flooding adaptations in low-lying areas of Central Vietnam, *Journal of Vietnamese Environment*, 12(2):123-131.

Tran, C. K. and Nguyen N. S., 2016. Indigenous knowledge in conservation of genetic resources and roles of the community, Forum on building a partnership forum on biodiversity conservation and sustainable use of ecosystem services, Dated 20/5/2016 Hanoi (in Vietnamese).

Ty, H. X. & Cuc, L. T., 1998. Indigenous knowledge of upland people in agriculture and natural resource management. Agriculture Publishing House.

Vu V. C. and Tran, T., 2017. The role of indigenous knowledge in adapting to climate change, Journal of Climate Change Science Issue No. 2, 6/2017, pages 25-30 (in Vietnamese).

Vu, T. G., 2010. Preserving indigenous knowledge of ethnic minorities in Vietnam, Journal of Ethnicity, 111: 28-39 (in Vietnamese).

World Bank, 2005. Education: Building on Indigenous Knowledge, IK notes, No.87.

CONCLUSION

KNOWLEDGE, POWER, AND THE PROGRESSION OF CIVILIZATION

DOCTOR LEON MILLER

What the laws of existence have ordained is called The Way; living in accordance with The Way is called The Path of Duty; the regulation of this path is called Pedagogy (Confucius 1869, 283).

"Early in the fourth millennium B.C., there occurred a phenomenon of lasting importance for the history of humanity: the appearance in quick succession of a group of culture foci that gave rise to self-contained and characteristic civilizations" (Oppenheim 2009, 31). Civilization emerged in astonishingly parallel fashion in various places in the world ushering in a decisive change that established a deep hold on human consciousness, spirit, and socio-political activity world-wide. Generally, civilization refers to more complex, structured, and organized systems of political economy that both expanded and advanced the village stage of social life. Civilization is described as a large-scale and long-term pattern of social-historical reality, encompassing a plurality of coexisting and successive social formations. In other words, a civilization is a large-scale social-historical system or long-term pattern that is able to influence its region with its culture, ideology, and traditions. The important aspects of what characterizes a civilization are a clearly established institutional framework for social life that extends over a rather large geographical region; the ability to exercise social, cultural, and political power over a prolonged period of history; and a civilization encompasses a plurality of coexisting socio-cultural groups whose development follows a prescribed pattern established by a highly developed and well-organized socio-political, socio-cultural, or ideological system.

Civilization represents a way of organizing individuals and social groups into a complex socio-political structure based on power, status, and *psychologization*. Psychologization is defined as "Complex webs of interdependence that spread over greater distances. Less abstractly, more people are forced more often to pay more attention to more people, in more varying circumstances" (Elias 1998, 18). Therefore, civilization necessarily demands a more inclusive sense of social relations and social order, a more inclusive sense of social identity, and a more inclusive sense of community or society. In addition, fundamental to a civilization is a school of thought that wide segments of the people of the region accept as reliable knowledge regarding what is best for shaping society, the nature of social relations, social justice, and having a beneficial relationship with the forces shaping the nature of existence. Knowledge is the understanding that individuals, a social group, or a society have that provides the ability to address and resolve the challenges they face. Such knowledge is believed to be reliable, not only because it is based on viable principles that explain how individuals can have the most beneficial relationships with others and with the environment but also because it is based on insight into what has ultimate meaning. The establishment and dissemination of such knowledge played a role in the development and expansion of civilization and was even the reason a civilization could have an impact that is trans-civilizational. That is to say that there was a civilizing force at work that represented a type of power, distinct from political and military power, that established the basis of what is regarded as classical wisdom.

Civilization provided its members with a particular socio-cultural worldview: e.g., a particular set of norms, ethics, and values; a particular approach to how to obtain what is needed from the environment to satisfy material needs; a particular view on the nature of existence; and religion. Such knowledge was regarded as indisputable and was established either because of the power of rhetoric or because it was believed to be irrefutable truth. This enabled structuring society in such a way that flux, uncertainty, and unpredictability could be managed in ways that produce predictable outcomes. In addition, such knowledge included insight into how to manage various environmental forces that could otherwise threaten society. Such knowledge included insight into how to avoid the types of conflict that can arise when one social political system believes that another competing ideological system is threatening its own perceived categorization of existence (Mannheim, 1954, 50–58). Even though such wisdom is clearly a social construct, it is believed to be based on the true nature of existence, thus has a unifying impact. Therefore, a civilization is described and characterized in terms of the knowledge, ideas, and socio-political philosophy by which they are recognized (i.e., their way of living together, culture, and worldview). Such knowledge also prescribes the basis of individual integrity, how to shape social relations, how to sustain the socio-economic flourishing of society, how to structure political authority, and the operations and processes of good governance. Because it touches on every aspect of social life, it provides insight into life's most worthwhile and valuable pursuit and what advances civilization in spite of obstacles.

The intellectual elite and sages who proclaimed such wisdom envisioned civilization as a means of establishing a socio-political system that would elevate humanity. Such a vision underlies much of the social, ethical, and political philosophy of the major centers of civilization. Most analysts agree that in its earliest uses, civilization was almost wholly moral and prescriptive, with the elevation of the whole of humanity as a primary aim of social, political, and economic development. Therefore, most analysts agree that in its earliest uses, the term civilization—its worldview and social and political philosophy—was a prescription for human and social development as well as achieving sustainable peace. For example, the established schools of thought prescribed a means of developing the virtuous characters of the individual members of society in order for them to experience the highest good, live "the good life" (i.e., live well), and experience civic virtue. Being trained in "Goodness was thought to inspire the recipient with a passionate and ardent desire to become a perfect citizen, knowing both how to wield and how to submit to righteous rule" (Plato 1934, 21). In other words, those transmitting such knowledge aim to instill in citizens the type of beliefs and values that would ensure a harmonious and well-ordered society.

Civilization emerged as a result of "Deep-seated intellectual shifts that occurred in different forms but with striking, if relative, simultaneity in" the major centers of civilization (Wittrock 2012, 108). That is to say that a civilization is shaped by particular ideals that were promulgated by schools of philosophy, social theorists, and/or religion. The political significance of this intellectual ferment was twofold. First, it created something like an ideology, that is, a received set of ideas for the proper ordering of socio-political systems by which later generations could judge the performance of their political leaders. The main purpose of ideology in social life is that it establishes a "Theory of the social life that helps to constitute and reconstitute the reification of social relations. The reification of social relations, or the discursive naturalization of the historically contingent circumstances and products of human action, is one of the main dimensions of ideology in social life" (Giddens 1984, 25–26). Second, "The mobility of intellectuals encouraged the growth of something that looked increasingly like a national culture" (Fukuyama 2011, 115). In other words, the security of society and its members was increasingly believed to be based on reliable knowledge, e.g., discerning the nature of existence (or even better, knowledge of how the forces of existence could work in favor of society and its members), how to have a beneficial relationship and exchange with the forces in the environment, and how to effectively manage forces that could otherwise be threatening.

Knowledge mechanisms are the means of transforming the conditions imposed by reality into outcomes that are favorable for society and its members. The growth and spread of such knowledge sparked the emergence of something that looked increasingly like a regional unifying force and acted as a means of expanding the influence of a civilization. The new possibilities envisioned by the great teachers and philosophers (i.e., lovers of wisdom), schools of thought, and religious leaders gave rise to formative practices that outlasted and had influence beyond the societies in which they first appeared. In this respect, a civilization is characterized by the knowledge that shaped its culture, and culture in turn, like the major schools of thought, influences all activities, organizations, and institutions of society. Therefore, there was a close connection between the advancement or expansion of a civilization and its "belief system". A belief system is a set of principles or an ideological perspective that helps individuals understand the very nature of existence and serves as a guide for their everyday activities. This has led many scholars of history to stress that civilization is shaped by a type of knowledge that has ideological power, and such knowledge is, as well, the basis of political, economic, and religious power. Ideological power, as used to shape civilization, took the form of a *Weltanschauung* (i.e., a worldview built upon what is believed to be the most reliable knowledge regarding the forces shaping the natural order and the nature of existence).

The emergence of civilization was a tumultuous undertaking marked by villages being absorbed by kingdoms, followed by kingdoms being absorbed by empires, and empires constantly engaged in attempts at conquering and invasion. Because of the conflict-prone nature of interactions between socio-political systems, there was a need to establish a unifying principle that would generate a sense of interdependence that would unite the various social, ethnic, and economic interests that intersect at the boundaries of different social units. The leaders of the schools of thought, religions, and schools of philosophy recognized how essential the unifying force is to society's attempt to provide its members with knowledge that would safeguard them from the threats otherwise imposed by various forces (e.g., internal forces, threats in the environment, and the threats posed by adversarial fringe groups). Therefore, the literati prescribed strategies for effectively managing the threatening challenges imposed by various internal and external forces. This included how to manage the struggle to maintain socio-economic stability, security threats, the challenge of managing larger, more diverse social systems, and the problem of interethnic rivalry. Such knowledge and the benefits it affords in terms of generating resources for the flourishing of civilization attracted fringe groups into alliances, which extended the scope of civic administration. However, to serve this purpose (or to act as a unifying force), knowledge had to have a syncretistic effect. In other words, it had to be a mechanism by which ideology could be embraced and internalized by fringe groups.

Therefore, providing reliable knowledge regarding how to overcome the obstacles to establishing a thriving socio-political and economic system and how to avoid socio-political disorder and disaster was essential for providing "the good life". In many cases, this took the form of schools of thought that focused on prescribing higher-order human values; an ethical philosophy for the cultivation of individuals; how to develop the full capabilities of the members of society; how each member of society could experience holistic well-being; and, as well, an ethical philosophy that established the basis of political theory. Such "Knowledge transcended religious, geographic, and political boundaries" and established the foundation of the impact of a civilization on a geographical region (Tampio 2013, 823). Therefore, understanding the nature of the various forms of ideological power sheds light on "Why a few ideological movements conquer their region and even much of the world" (Mann 1986, 22). In other words, understanding the nature of such power sheds light on why schools of thought, philosophy, or religion serve as an essential force for progressing civilization and if there are things to learn from the process that can advance humanity to an even higher level of existence.

This chapter analyzes the relationship between knowledge generation and dissemination (e.g., schools of thought, ideology, the world's most cherished wisdom traditions, culture and cultural worldviews, and socio-political philosophy) and the progression of civilization. Therefore, the chapter analyzes the impact that the emergence of a "New type of intellectual elite had on transforming the shape of human societies and history in what seems to be an irreversible manner" (Eisenstadt 1982, 294 & 295). The chapter examines how knowledge systems function as a mechanism for improving human existence; in fact, knowledge can even elevate the human experience. The chapter explains why those individuals who were gifted with such knowledge had persuasive influence over others. Therefore, *Knowledge, Power, and the Progression of Civilization* is an interdisciplinary examination of the socio-political dynamics of the role that knowledge plays in establishing the good life. Thus, the chapter analyzes the connection between schools of thought and social life, social formation, politics, collective action, and as a means of expanding the influence of a civilization.

In addition, this chapter also points out that knowledge was employed by sage-like visionaries as a mechanism for promoting goodness, avoiding what would cause harm, and guiding individual and social behaviors toward what would improve the quality of social life. That is to say that in the major centers of civilization, human and social development were prescribed as a means of avoiding corruption, fragmentation, and deprivation. Above all, the chapter explains dialectics as an approach to generating and disseminating knowledge that improves personal and social life and, as well, improves the activities and processes of governance. Therefore, this chapter explains various perspectives on the concept of dialectics and also explains the role of the dialectic concept in establishing a type of ideological force that has a civilizational impact.

The following section (section 2), Knowledge, Power, and the Progression of Civilization, explains the role that a civilization's most cherished wisdom tradition played in the "Ethical orientation that shaped the criteria of evaluation and justification of activities and institutional formations— criteria that then served as the regulation of the flow and distribution of resources and media of exchange in a society" (Eisenstadt 2012, 290). In addition, this section explains the role that scholars played in reconciling the dichotomy between agency as a powerful force for organizing society on the basis of the ideals provided by the most respected wisdom traditions (i.e., Idealism) and the notion that agency is best utilized to amass power over the proverbial other, who is regarded as a threat that either has to be controlled or eliminated (i.e., Realism, which often means a split between knowledge and ethics).

This is followed by section three entitled Knowledge and the Power to Overcome the Forces that Threaten Civilization, which explains the nature of the ideas, ideals, schools of thought, philosophies, and religions that played a key role in establishing large-scale and long-term patterns of social-historical reality in China, ancient Mesopotamia, and the West. This section points out the important aspects of what characterized the foundation of each of these major zones of civilization that had a deep and lasting influence on history. In particular, there is emphasis on the nature of the type of knowledge that shaped each civilization, gave the civilization a trans-regional impact, and continues to impress people today from other regions of the world. This includes explaining the particular perspective on dialectics employed in each of these civilizational zones, how dialectics relate to their conception of reliable knowledge, and its role in human and social development.

The fourth section, *The Expansion of Civilization and the Civilizational State*, uses India as an example of a civilization whose perennial wisdom, schools of thought, philosophy, and worldview influenced other parts of South Asia, much of the Far East, and parts of Southeast Asia. In fact, the civilizational-type knowledge coming out of India ultimately impressed the rest of the world. That is, in addition to its impact on Asia-Pacific, the world was influenced by such Indian traditions as yoga and meditation; its ayurveda tradition; its perspective on self-actualization, non-violence, and environmentalism; and the religious traditions it introduced to the world— Hinduism, Buddhism, Jain, and Sikhism. Therefore, this section of the chapter emphasizes the type of knowledge that not only shaped impressions of India's legitimacy and power but also established its civilizational impact. For example, in the last century, India's civilizational impact on the world was felt by offering a "middle way" (i.e., a Buddhist term meaning steering clear of extremes) by proposing its peaceful co-existence vision of non-alignment. In that respect, it is important to take a closer look at the significance of the Indian traditional commitment to tolerance. Tolerance is a particularly important principle in contexts that are ethnically, religiously, and linguistically diverse. Therefore, India is chosen as a point of entry for explaining the significance that symbolic, ideational, normative, and soft power play in today's globalized world.

The concluding section, Global Dialectics, explains the nature of the type of knowledge that drives the expansion of civilization to the global level of social existence and increases global interdependence. The conclusion summarizes the role that knowledge plays in promoting a progressive global value transformation. A value transformation refers to a change from an existing state to one that is more desirable, and the more desirable state reflects the type of value transformation that is more conducive to the present stage of global social existence (Boulding 1978, 225). However, the conclusion emphasizes that, given the present state of global existence, the knowledge generated and disseminated must be of a particular type. That is, it must provide reliable knowledge regarding how to co-create peaceful coexistence, sustainable human and social development, an improved quality of life, and the elevation of the human experience. The concluding section of the chapter explains the contemporary significance of the type of knowledge that will enable social agents (interacting at the various levels of social interactions) to relate in such a way that they manage the challenges humanity faces by co-creating outcomes that are mutually beneficial and satisfying.

Knowledge, Power, and the Progression of Civilization

The emergence and progression of civilization involved the endeavor to realize the level of growth and development that the sage-like visionaries of the major centers of civilization believed humanity is capable of. But the question is: what type of potential is there, and what is the best method for achieving it? The major schools of thought in the major centers of civilization articulated a vision of awakening a higher level of consciousness, the possibility of establishing a complementary connection between what is in the best interest of the individual and the common good, achieving the good life and social flourishing, good governance, and having the most beneficial relationship with the natural order. The scholars who played the role of sage-like visionaries articulated a progressive vision of what promotes "Human flourishing and hence inevitably also the structure of society" and how to gain the most benefit from the environment, upon which this flourishing is achieved (Taylor 2012, 35). In this respect, they prescribed a means by which society could experience long-term well-being. Therefore, the schools of thought played a highly significant role in socio-political life because they explained the meaning of life and how to realize the goal that organized social activity aims to achieve. Such knowledge was believed to provide a buffer against the intrusion of misfortune, disorder, and chaos. Therefore, knowledge, wisdom, and humanity's rational ability were regarded as the highest blessing bestowed on humanity, and those who developed this gift to the highest level were regarded as either amongst the most respected members of society or a sage-like member of society (Plato 1934, 21).

Their insight impressed the public because it was imparted with exceptionally appealing rhetorical powers. However, the most outstanding intellectuals were never merely sharing information. Knowledge was associated with power in that it shaped the cultural worldview, understanding of self and self-other relations, understanding of the nature of reality, and, as well, the political, social, economic, and religious nature of society. Therefore, the wisdom and knowledge espoused by the intellectual elite of society permeated all social activities and ends, which included medicine, the economic, ethical, philosophical, artistic, scientific, technological, political, and religious. For much of the classical world, this involved explaining how to eliminate the dichotomy between that which would promote the elevation of humanity and the oppressive forces that would deprive humanity of enjoying higher levels of growth and development. Therefore, pedagogy became linked with ethics (i.e., principles prescribed by the most respected philosophies and the types of values that have constitutive meaning). Constitutive, in this sense, refers to a normative mechanism that has the power to bring about the type of social activity that is aligned with prescribed ethics, principles, and values. This ultimately resulted in knowledge production and dissemination becoming associated with socio-political power. Therefore, schools of thought and ideology have been of particular interest to those interested in acquiring and employing power.

Consequently, "Scholars and literati were enshrined as the highest human type, higher than even the warrior" or the ruler (Fukuyama 2011, 115–116). In the major centers of civilization, this evolved into the idea that educators, those with wisdom, and the lovers of wisdom who devote their lives to the pursuit of knowledge were some of the most influential members of society. For example, in South Asia, it resulted in the idea that sages, educators, those with wisdom, and those who devote their lives to the pursuit of higher-order human values have a status that is even higher than that of rulers. The point is that as civilization progressed, the ruling authorities realized that to use their power in the most effective and progressive way, those in positions of authority and/or leadership must learn from the most established and respected scholars (i.e., from their socio-political philosophy, their ethics, and their theory of justice). "Thus, there emerged the conception of the accountability of rulers and of the community. Concomitant with the emergence of conceptions of accountability, there began to develop autonomous spheres of law and conceptions of rights" (Eisenstadt 1982, 303). Therefore, the ruling authorities were increasingly subject to and constrained by scholars and the knowledge that they taught regarding how to shape socio-political affairs. The point is that as civilization advanced, kings were not omnipotent but were constrained by ethics and principles based on viable political philosophies.

Thus, the progression of civilization was accompanied by a tension (perhaps even, at some points, a dichotomy) between society ruled by the absolute authority of the sovereign and government systems that were inclusive of governance processes and activities shaped by the influence of scholar-officials and administrative officials. Administrative officials were government officials who acted as ministers responsible for certain aspects of public affairs. They introduced governance strategies for organizing society in a way that is in accordance with social and political ideals. And their ideals were explained in a way that is compatible with the knowledge proclamations of social psychology, ethics, physics, biology, and socio-political philosophy, thus in terms that were regarded as reliable knowledge. That is to say that they explained how a virtuous individual character and the moral/normative structure of society can override the threats imposed by the unpredictable, perplexing, and contingent nature of reality. The scholar-officials provided insight into how to institutionalize a strategy for structuring society so that it could encompass a wide diversity of classes that vary in terms of status and geographically and incorporate them into social cohesion. They did this by establishing an agreement to engage in social activity based on a shared goal and common values. The scholar-officials articulated a means of establishing cultural crystallization based on integrating a traditional sense of an unqualified good with rational conceptualizations that increased epistemological reliability and had more universal appeal. The unqualified good became the goal that organized social action aimed to achieve.

The intellectual elite of the time "Developed a strong tendency to constitute distinct collectivities and institutional arenas as the most appropriate carriers of a particular vision—creating new 'civilizational' collectivities, which were often—though not always — [ideological] in nature but, in any case, distinct from the existing 'primordial', 'ethnic', local, political, or religious collectivities" (Eisenstadt 2012, 280). How to describe the change or transformation of the basic traditional, cultural conceptions of social relations, the nature of existence, and the goals that organized social activity aims to achieve? The process involved transforming the clan and village-based notion of social order into a socio-political and economic order that would promote the cosmopolitan ideal of the human family. "Within these discourses, the tension between new cultural concepts and mundane reality was centralized and promulgated" (Eisenstadt 2011, 205). The most important of these tensions concerned, first, the great range of possible cosmopolitan liberal visions and the ways of their implementation; second, the distinction between practical reality and the cosmopolitan ideal. Thus, they explained transcendental ideals in a way that also addressed worldly concerns like natural laws and rights, social justice, defending the masses, and being very critical of oppression.

The knowledge disseminated by the literati provided insight into the nature of reality and legitimate human and social purposes and explained them in terms that transformed what heretofore were localized mythological explanations. They employed forms of rhetoric and logic that awakened new levels of consciousness and rationality. Therefore, their epistemological claims came to be regarded as a more valid and reliable approach to knowledge. An essential aspect of this endeavor was the attempt to construct an expanded sense of consciousness, which would align socio-political activities with higher ethical principles and values. In addition, they prescribed a means by which a type of enlightenment could be experienced by engaging in self-cultivation, developing a virtuous character (i.e., inner moral perfection), and realizing the complementary connection between the biological principles of nature—that are ordained by the forces of creation—and humanity's biological nature (i.e., the natural impulse to seek the freedom to develop one's full potential and to experience holistic well-being) (Huxley, 1947, 8–11). In many ways, although what each of the most respected schools of thought portrayed was distinct, they also expressed—either one of or all three—closely related and integrated strands of social development thought: the transcendental ideal; the social psychological; and the ethical, rational, or philosophical. In other words, the sages and intellectuals prescribed a means of experiencing goodness in both personal and social terms—a good that is not limited to a particular clan, tribe, or village (Taylor 2007, 152-153).

Pedagogy (i.e., schools of thought) is regarded as the institution that generates and disseminates the knowledge, ideas, ideology, philosophy, or doctrines that shape the nature of a civilization. The wisdom (beliefs, knowledge, and worldview) of a civilization takes the form of religion, art, philosophy, ethics, and/or science. Therefore, the knowledge generated by the pedagogical system of a civilization shapes the capabilities of all those who manage society's organizations and institutions. In this respect, knowledge production and dissemination are associated with power. Consequently, pedagogy eventually became recognized as a socially sanctioned institution that provides the most valid prescriptions regarding personal growth and development, social development, political economy, and how to enjoy sustainable growth. Pedagogy, as a socially sanctioned institution, represents what can be described as the genetic cause of a civilization. That is to say that "Education can be seen as transmitting the concentrated epitome of a culture, and as such, it is inseparable from the form of that culture" (Sullivan 2012, 411). Pedagogy and its equivalents—schools of thought and ideology—serve the purpose of stabilizing, extending, and perpetuating a socio-cultural reality. Therefore, there is a widely shared belief that there is a complementary connection between what education means for the individual, what it means for society, and what it means for a nation, which, in other words, means that education is essential for human and social development and for the progression of civilization. Therefore, it is possible to talk about schools of thought, philosophy, or cultural worldviews that play a role in the development and progression of certain civilizations, and some that even had an impact that is trans-civilizational. When a civilization has this type of impact, it represents a progressive movement toward the fulfillment of a trans-millennial vision.

The transmitters of a perspective on knowledge or wisdom that earns the highest respect propose taking a critical, reflective, and questioning stance toward the status quo, and they offer a vision of the ideal-type possibilities that lie ahead. That is to say that such knowledge provides humanity with a comparative criterion for evaluating the current state of affairs. The body of knowledge they establish represents a collective value orientation and an axiological identity. A collective value orientation and axiological identity are shared values, convictions, ideologies, and senses of moral obligation. The shared ideas, moral obligation, and value orientation influence society's understanding of values that will enable it to flourish and enjoy sustainable growth. In fact, pedagogy, as an academic discipline, has the power to override the fragmentation that usually occurs with one system of belief attempting to claim greater validity and authority over its rivals. Because of the impact that the scholar elite had on society, many historians viewed the established schools of thought as responsible for the moral education of the people (or, in particular, those who would themselves become the leaders, educators, and intellectual elite of society). It is in this respect that the intellectual elite play a significant role in the ability of a society to produce forms of cultural capital that not only sustain, perpetuate, and legitimate it but also impress those from other cultures, thus spreading the influence of the culture.

Knowledge and the Power to Overcome the Forces that Threaten Civilization

The wisdom traditions that had the greatest impact on China arose at a time when there was an urgent need to save the region from disorder, violence, and chaos (i.e., the upheaval of the Warring States period of ancient China). The scholarly sages that emerged at this time were well aware of the need to formulate a school of thought powerful enough to diminish the destructive forces of Realism. In undertaking this challenge, they devised schools of thought aimed at resolving the dichotomy between pristine traditional values and political power struggles for dominance over rivals. In doing so, they expressed a vision of a new order based on ideals and perennial wisdom, and some even included social activism in their teachings (i.e., a strong sense of the type of civil organizing needed for the progression of civilization).

The Hundred Schools of Thought that arose at this time established the wisdom traditions that shaped China's civilizational impact (e.g., Confucianism, Daoism, Mohism, Legalism, the School of Names, the Yin-Yang School, Agriculturalists, Diplomats, Eclectic School, and Storytellers, just to name a few of the most recognized schools). These schools of thought, philosophers, and sages endeavored to construct an ideological means of overcoming the great disorder, confusion, and deplorable conditions that had overcome the region. The most prominent schools of thought, scholar officials, and sage-like philosophers of this period developed an ideological stance that, altogether, transformed what had up to that point been a region composed of distinct ways of life, traditions, subsistence regimes, and social groups ruled by chieftains. They attempted to transform a strong sense of filial bond with members of one's clan (and the group's strong identity with or attachment to its environmental space) into an approach to social organizing effective for managing the emergence of complex societies, technological advancement, and regional political authority. This meant an ideological stance that sparked a sense of a regional culture that would increasingly have a civilizational impact on the region. This resulted in harmonizing systems of etiquette, normative expectations, and social customs over broader spatial realms. Such an ideology proved to contribute to unifying this fractious landscape and establishing the foundation of Chinese civilization.

The literati transformed these principles, which were foundational to the culture and heritage, into a theory of how individuals could develop sage-like wisdom and intuitive insight and how they could enjoy holistic well-being and social harmony. In doing so, they incorporated thoughts about nature, freedom, effortless action, going with the flow, social etiquette, health preservation, outdoor life, and explanations about astronomy, art, and aesthetics. Such knowledge is rooted in the ancient understanding of the concepts 無為 (Wu Wei, or effortless action), 休 (Xiū, or to rest your mind and body), and hsien (i.e., the role of heritage and ancestry in social life). The ancient wisdom traditions of China proposed that a lack of knowledge regarding the significance of such principles will have a negative impact on posterity. In sum, they proposed what could be referred to as a Systems Theory type explanation of the complementary and interdependent relationship between micro and macro phenomena, or, in other words, a complementary relationship between individuals, social activity, ancestral heritage, and the forces shaping the natural order.

The intellectual elite prescribed an approach to social relations that tempered the rule of authority and force with the ideal of society structured on the basis of moral codes, with scholar-officials playing an important role in governance. They explained the "Mandate of Heaven" as a superordinate political and moral force that, if abided by, would enact a power that had the effect of universalizing but not mandating uniformity, thus integrating elements of diversity into social harmony. Therefore, the "Mandate of Heaven" became a proclamation declaring that the primary aim of political rulers was properly undertaking their moral or ethical responsibility (Confucius 2007, 8). They proposed that the social order, harmony, solidarity, and sustainable peace that the state desired could not be achieved without the self-cultivation of the individual members of society, which included the self-cultivation of public authorities.

This means that, taken all together, the intellectual elite were teaching what is translated into English as virtue, goodness, what is worthy of praise and celebration, and, in addition, harmony with Tao: i.e., the sense of being fortunate as a result of feeling that things are unfolding in a good way and the way one hopes. The sage-like visionaries proclaimed that freedom, filial piety, and social harmony are all interconnected principles derived from the culture's heritage. In addition, they prescribed a means of reconciling the dichotomy between a rational, humanistic, proto-scientific, and ethical socio-political philosophy and an earlier philosophy of nature that proclaimed spontaneity, realization of pristine authenticity, and "Free and Easy Wondering" – all of which were based on insight into socio-cultural heritage and the popularization of folk wisdom (Needham 1956, 33–35). Therefore, the intellectual elite of China attempted to reconcile the difference between social hierarchy and class and the egalitarianism of the rural villagers (i.e., they proposed mutuality and meritocracy balanced with respect for seniority, with respect for seniority being regarded as tantamount to respect for authority). They proclaimed nobility as a matter of character and self-cultivation, not as a matter of birth or status (Yu-Lan 1948, 214). This gave birth to principles emphasizing a path to authenticity and self-cultivation, detailed moral or ethical knowledge, and an explanation of the connection between personal virtue and civic virtue. They envisioned that virtuous character traits would shape the nature of social relations and dynamics, would manifest as personal and social good fortune, and would diminish social and political unrest (Needham 1956, 9).

In ancient China, contemplation was believed to spark an integrative perspective on existence that harmonizes that which otherwise would seem oppositional. Although individuals perceive the various entities in existence as discrete, they can also experience a sense of harmony by prioritizing awareness that the distinct components are all essentially interconnected within the seamless web of existence. The whole, which harmonizes what otherwise would seem to be distinct or could even seem oppositional, is called "The Tao". In terms of ancient Chinese wisdom, phenomena exist as the means by which individuals gain experience, reflect on what on the surface is experienced as dialectic opposition, sense an impulse that motivates individuals to be well-integrated within the fabric of existence, and, as a result, intuitively gain insight into a harmony that transcends duality. In other words, the wisdom elite of the Far East attempted to raise the consciousness level of individuals by arousing awareness of the fact that although we tend to view things in the natural world as particulars—as either-or, e.g., winter-summer, night-day, male-female, good or bad, etc.—natural phenomena actually exist in a complementary relationship (Lao Tzu 2008, 10). They used ancient traditions, their understanding of the phenomena of the natural order, and filial piety as a means of motivating individuals and social groups to achieve social order, harmony, and cohesion.

The aim was the elevation of humanity, raising the consciousness of individuals, and elevating the quality of social life by means of the ancient Chinese notion of dialectics. Dialectics was an ancient Chinese philosophical tradition that prescribed a means of resolving the dichotomy between transcendental idealism and practical, mundane reality. "It is the recourse to this dialectic between the absolute and the phenomenal that makes it possible to arrive at higher awareness. Truth—which is perfect sincerity (ch'eng)—goes beyond distinction and opposition between basic nature and passions. Here we have the basic dialectical approach of the ch'an school transposed into the vocabulary of the Classics and of the Mencius" (Gernet 1999, 219 & 294). The dialectic approach to the elevation of consciousness established an ideological mechanism that was an effective social psychology based on the wisdom of respected sages who prescribed a means of increasing good fortune and reducing misfortune (Xunzi 2014, 153 & 323). In this respect, ideology, tradition, cultural heritage, and socio-political philosophy played a role in the civilizational impact of China. In sum, they revived the ancient Chinese system of dialectics in a way that resulted in transforming primitive communism into a vision of social harmony that is in line with the notion of "great harmony" (i.e., ta-t'ung, which was proposed by the school of Kung-yang and later to be popularized right up to today). The starting point was stressing knowledge of the aim or goal of social life. With such knowledge, individuals could be empowered to experience the highest good, and, when employed as an approach to social relations, the principles would elevate the quality of social life.

Ancient Mesopotamia gave rise to four religious traditions that played a major role in shaping the development of the region, and all four have subsequently spread to other parts of the world: Zoroastrianism, Judaism, Christianity, and Islam, with the latter three each having a number of sub-sects. Their wisdom, philosophical insight, transcendental ideals, and prophetic proclamations played a significant role in the socio-cultural dynamics of the region, the region's notion of the source of the power for establishing a socio-political system that has a civilizational impact, and consequently the basis for how the region gained the reputation as the Cradle of Civilization. Knowledge was thought of as essential wisdom that should be transmitted from generation to generation, philosophical and ethical ideals, and revelatory insight (i.e., prophecy). In ancient

Mesopotamia, wisdom was regarded as one of the most respected and highly regarded virtues, and those possessing it were thought to have insight into the very nature of the forces shaping existence. The earliest forms of knowledge in the region included protoscience, but with a slant towards understanding the relationship between the human experience and the forces shaping the natural order. The tremendous respect for wisdom was reinforced by acknowledging the validity of the oracle-like proclamation that those who abide by it will experience good fortune and those who go stray will experience misfortune.

Wisdom was associated with the type of knowledge possessed by a certain class of intellectual elite: e.g., a small number of individuals from the leisure class, scribes, priests, artists, leaders (meaning those with knowledge of how to effectively manage public affairs), and those who were experts in divination. It is also certain that the type of knowledge we are talking about developed "In close connection with the introduction of writing. Writing in all other centers of civilization came demonstrably later" (Speiser 1940, 706). Therefore, educational training during the earliest stages of civilization in ancient Mesopotamia included training scribes. The main theme addressed by the texts was how to protect and perpetuate human existence by effectively managing some of the challenges that perplex the human experience. This means that they were concerned with how to resolve the dichotomy between the socio-cultural activities and socio-political forces that adhere to the principles of transcendental Idealism (as the basis of personal and social development) and the opposing forces. Therefore, the basic concern that the prophetic visionaries addressed was a question raised by people of many other cultures: how can the oppositional forces of existence be overcome so that humans can experience peace, security, well-being, and prosperity? In the wisdom traditions of Mesopotamia, the answer is by faithfully abiding by the principles prescribed by transcendental Idealism.

Hence, the earliest scripts known to humanity prescribed principles for how to achieve personal well-being, socio-cultural harmony, and, as well, socio-political order. The wisdom literature proclaimed that by adhering to the prescribed principles, individuals and public officials will make wise decisions that will contribute to personal good fortune and societal flourishing. Therefore, the texts also established the cornerstone of the infrastructure of power. The texts were evidence of the fact that "The basic feature of society was attested overwhelmingly in cuneiform law, perhaps the most characteristic and abundant expression of ancient Mesopotamian civilization. The law applied to ruler and subject alike" (Speiser 1940, 707). Thus, the knowledge proclaimed by sage-like visionaries was meant to promote an allegiance to the principle prescribing good faith and eliminate hindrances to good faith. In other words, they taught their adherents that there is a strong connection between what is demanded by the transcendental moral order, what promotes civic virtue, and the ability to establish sage-like political leadership.

A good place to start to analyze the type of knowledge that laid the foundation for the civilizational impact of ancient Mesopotamia is with a myth that reflects the composite character of the region. The myth involves a depiction of cosmology, with aspects that relate to all four monotheistic traditions. In Mesopotamian creation myths, there is first a separation of darkness and light, with each becoming a metaphor that has meanings that have moral significance. This is followed by a dichotomy between the heavens and earth (i.e., earth is regarded as a lower realm that becomes the center of conflict between the forces adhering to transcendental Idealism and its opposing forces). The aspects of this ancient Mesopotamian cosmology that explain the creation of the earth begin with a primordial force first forming a primordial sea, and ultimately there is a separation of the primordial water elements and the establishment of the earth. Therefore, the story reflects a stage in the earliest Mesopotamian wisdom traditions when those who developed proto-scientific knowledge began to understand the relationship between the forces of nature and what was beneficial for establishing civilization. This included an understanding of the relationship between individual and social well-being plus personal and societal good fortune (Lambert 1996, 1–15).

The main characters in one of the earliest creation myths are Tiamat (a primordial goddess who personifies archaic primordial stasis) and Marduk (one of the progenies of Tiamat who emerges as the most outstanding of a youthful pantheon of gods that intends to overthrow the older established order). Thus, the story involves a conflict within the core of the cosmic pantheon. In ancient Mesopotamian mythology, Tiamat was the personification of the primordial sea and the established primordial order. Marduk disrupts the perpetual primal statis by participating in a revolutionary attempt to overthrow the established primal order. Marduk ultimately kills Tiamat, cuts her into parts, and uses her body parts to form creation. The myth explains how a younger generation of gods overthrows the older generation and gradually becomes conceptually transformed from representing the forces of existence (or of nature) into an ideological force that both personifies and rationalizes the transcendental ideal. The transformed ideology explains the socio-cultural and socio-political benefits of wisdom (i.e., the highest virtue) and how the transformed ideological perspective on personal, social, and political affairs is aligned with the transformed understanding of the forces shaping the nature of existence.

An important point to note is that, at the outset of this myth, both the older generation of gods and goddesses and their progeny primarily represent natural forces. Consequently, Marduk, who was initially a lower god in the pantheon of ancient Mesopotamian deities, becomes the most elevated god and, as well, comes to stand for wisdom, moral authority, and the fundamental ethical principles of political philosophy that, if adhered to, would establish ideal human and social conditions. The transformation occurs when Marduk (i.e., a champion of the youthful gods) overthrows archaic natural patterns to establish a new order. This conceptualization of the forces of existence provides an ideological boost to the historians and empire-builders of the time. Marduk was referred to as apkal ilī ('the sage of the gods'). For indeed, establishing a city-state in the desert required altering nature in ways that allowed for building a complex society. Therefore, "The supreme lord of heaven and earth, who fixes the destiny of the land, had committed to Marduk the rule of all humanity, making his name supreme, making it preeminent in the regions of the world, and establishing therein an enduring kingdom, firm in its foundation like heaven and earth" (Hammurabi 2004, 29). From the perspective of this myth, it is also easy to understand why the original nature-based understanding of paradise is transformed from "the garden" into a civilizational-based concept—the kingdom to come with its capital being a city.

The story is, indeed, a cosmology with the major events initially happening on a cosmic scale, but one could also conclude that this is where the belief systems of Zoroastrianism, Judaism, Christianity, and Islam all share the view of a cosmic conflict that afflicts the human realm. Therefore, from this perspective, the nature of the conflict becomes evident as civilization emerges and progresses. The ultimate aim of human existence is to play a role in the resolution of this conflict. In addition, there are two factors related to this initial Mesopotamian perspective on what shapes the human experience that played a major role in the development of civilization not only in the Near East but in other civilizational zones and continue to have an impact on the human experience. This has to do with a problem of psychological and social nature, which is particularly highlighted in Judaism, Christianity, and Islam. They all stress the fact that there is a deeply rooted conflict within the nature of existence that shapes the nature of civilization.

On the one hand, this myth depicts an initial state of archaic stasis, which is disrupted by a younger generation of gods who demand space for their boisterous expressions. The younger generation overthrows the undifferentiated stage of existence, which results in establishing a dialectical dualism that humanity experiences as an aspect of existence that manifests as a struggle between good and evil. However, on the other hand, the wisdom literature also implies that this creates a problem that strikes at the very core or foundational unit of society. This warning has aspects that are repeatedly emphasized in Judaism, Christianity, and Islam. That is to say that in Judaism, Christianity, and Islam, the crisis in the foundational unit of society ultimately occurs between the two children of the Father of the Faithful (Abraham). The two brothers Ishmael (whose descendants establish the Islamic faith) and Isaac (whose descendants establish the Jewish faith) represent a theme that plays a central role in the shaping of the dynamics of the Middle East and the development of civilization and has significance regarding the continued advance of civilization. In other words, the changes depicted by the creation myth "Corresponded to broad changes in real social life. Thus, they had a high truth content" (Mann 1986, 157).

It should be kept in mind that the sage-like visionaries of ancient Mesopotamia were documenting what they understood to be the socio-political dynamics resulting from the transition from the egalitarian agricultural village stage of socio-cultural existence to city-states and ultimately to kingdoms and empires. Of course, their transcendental ideals were based on their understanding of the close bonds, initial family ties, and kinship-based relations of social periods closer to nature (e.g., the transition from Enlil, the god who represents a natural vital life force, to the god Marduk, who represents wisdom, the power of rationality, a civilizing force, and the patron god of an empire). This transition gradually gave way to increased social stratification: "A federated empire of elites, an emerging ruling class, and the literate elite. In this respect, Mesopotamian religion and culture did more than merely reflect a real social situation" (Mann 1986, 160). However, and this is the central point—the significance of the ancient Mesopotamian worldview is that it also reveals the necessity of (and a historical struggle) to ultimately resolve the tension between personal behavior, social activity that adheres to ideal transcendental principles, and the types of behaviors and activities that reflect the conviction that one's personal and social benefits increase by maintaining a power advantage and control over the underprivileged. That is to say that ancient Mesopotamian wisdom literature portrays the nature of human existence as involving a dialectic process that will inevitably generate eschatological dualism.

The prophetic visionaries proclaimed that humanity struggles with dialectical dualism because it is manifest in the human experience as a conflict between the transcendental moral order and mundane social reality. Therefore, dialectical dualism is a deep-rooted psychic force that plays an important role in how we view each other, plan social and economic relations, plan international relations, and plan our common future. According to the ancient Mesopotamian visionaries, resolving the dichotomy would usher in an era of peace, harmony, and prosperity. In other words, the prophetic visionaries promise that resolving the dichotomy will create a golden age-type era that can come about as a result of conforming human consciousness, character, and behavior, as well as social activity, to the transcendental ideal. Thus, they propose adherence to transcendental Idealism as a means of overcoming the problems of dualism and human fragmentation. In other words, they prescribed a means of achieving social harmony, order, cohesion, and solidarity in social life. Knowledge of social etiquette and propriety was regarded as the means of freedom in that it liberated individuals from biological determination while prescribing a means by which they could maintain their pristine authenticity.

Consequently, the most respected form of knowledge was associated with a particular type of wisdom that explicated the supremacy of a type of power necessary for realizing humanity's ideal personal, social, and political aims. It is important to understand the nature of this knowledge (especially in terms of how it shaped the development of civilization in the Near East and impacted other parts of the world). In addition, it is important to understand how the institutionalization of such knowledge established a close connection between the priesthood and the socio-political elite of the Near East and subsequently continues to play a similar role. The ancient Mesopotamian wisdom tradition makes for a useful comparison of the role of knowledge in achieving social aims, the significance of dialectics in shaping civilizational knowledge and ideology, and the prospect of eschatological dialectics resolving humanity's most perplexing problems. That is to say that all four monotheistic traditions promote the possibility of eschatological dialectics as a means of transcending what plagues the human experience.

The formulation of a Western perspective on what contributes to human and social development, the challenges humanity is confronted with, and humanity's relationship with the forces shaping the natural order passed through four foundational stages that shaped its development: the eras of ancient Greece, pre-Socratic Greece, classical Greece, and the Greco-Roman periods. It should first be noted that several of the fundamental ways that existence was viewed in ancient Greece are similar to those of ancient Mesopotamia. First, as was true in the ancient Mesopotamian creation myth, the Greek gods were born of the Great Mother Goddess. In other words, the matriarchal goddess, whose functions resemble those of the corresponding figures in the ancient Near Eastern pantheons, appeared as the Great Mother (i.e., Rhea) (Voegelin 2000, 124). In addition, (again, as is similar to the Mesopotamian myth), there is conflict within the family of the gods, which results in the triumph of the younger progeny over the older generation (i.e., ultimately the triumph of Zeus). A version of the rise of the Olympian gods that is somewhat popular is the myth of the conflict between Zeus and Metis. Metis was an *Okeanide,* or one of the goddess-nymphs, who presided over the sources of the earth's fresh-waters. Although Zeus, as the story goes, was indeed intimate with her, he was also threatened by her (or afraid that she would be the source of his downfall), so he ultimately annihilates her (Hesiod 1988, 29).

There is, as well, the story of Perseus, a younger male demigod who represents the newly emerging eras of Greek naturalism, rationalism, and humanism. Perseus overthrows the older "hag" Medusa (who represents an older generation of demigods, an antiquated worldview, and pre-rational and pre-humanistic Greek pagan beliefs). "Perseus beheads the Gorgon Medusa, much as Marduk, the Babylonian hero, kills the she-monster Tiamat, Goddess of the Sea" (Graves 1955, 17). Finally, there is the fact that the ancient Greek description of the human condition also depicts a dialectic tension within the cosmic forces that impacts the human experience. However, in describing the nature of existence this way, ancient Greek literature is also portrays the human condition as influenced by dialectical dualism, which subsequent Western intellectual elites attempted to address and resolve. In the earliest worldview of ancient Greece, the forces impacting the human condition were thought of as natural and/or cosmic forces, natural and cosmic forces that gradually became anthropomorphized, or as cosmic beings that controlled natural forces. Again, as was true with the cosmic pantheon in ancient Mesopotamia, this dialectic tension that strikes at the very core of the family of the Greek pantheon ultimately impacts the human experience.

In addition, there is conflict that results from the human-like passions that the gods themselves experience (i.e., desire, jealousy, resentment, and favoritism) that impact the human experience. On the one hand, there is favoring and disfavoring of individuals by the gods, which can cause one person to experience good fortune and the other to be unfortunate. For example, the members of the heavenly pantheon live on Mount Olympus (within the human realm but on a higher plane), and on occasion they interact with humans. Therefore, the Olympian gods, although more powerful, can seriously impact the human experience, and most importantly, in terms of impacting the human experience, some even mate and have children with mortals. Some members of the Olympian pantheon are known to be resentful of the fact that their spouses mated with mortals and consequently had children among the human race. Some of these members of the Olympian pantheon take their resentment out on the human offspring by causing them calamities and suffering.

The ancient Greek worldview (particularly as described by the epic poet Homer) was full of legendary characters and ancient Greek mythology blended with history. On the one hand, the early epic hymns that established the pan-Greek cultural identity addressed the problems that occur when passions (i.e., the irrational impulsive aspect of human nature) are not tempered by higher-level ethical values and principles. The ancient Greek literature that laid the rudimentary foundation of Western Civilization stressed that a failure to develop a virtuous character diminishes the prospect of personal and social well-being while increasing the likelihood of disorder (Voegelin 1957, 151 & 158). However, on the other hand, the early Greek literature reflects a criticism of bad leadership and a preference for those who possess the chieftain-like or socio-political leadership qualities of valor, wisdom, a clearly noble character, those who have logical and persuasive rhetorical skills, those who gained their status by merit, and those who are favored by the forces shaping the natural order (i.e., they are blessed with good fortune) (Hesiod 1988, 43–45).

Therefore, they taught that there is a close relationship between power and integrity. However, integrity was described in both personal and socio-political terms. In other words, rhetoric, logic, and personal virtue were core subjects taught to those learning *paideia*. That is to say, the ancient Greek literature, which laid the foundation for a growing sense of Greek culture and identity, was highly critical of the limited *paideia* of an aristocratic ruler compared to the superior *paideia* of the true leader. Paideia refers to educational training that focuses on developing a virtuous character, a broad and enlightened outlook, a balanced and well-integrated personality, and training in how to become a model of a good citizen. What stands out as both highly unique and highly significant about ancient Greece is its tendency to establish a growing cultural unity that was balanced by, while at the same time, respecting or maintaining a preference for heterogeneity. This means there was indeed an increasing sense of Greek identity while maintaining the autonomy of each subregion. Thus, cultural unity did not evolve into political unity.

In the second phase of the Greek tradition, the intellectual elite were recognized as pre-Socratic philosophers. They pondered the nature of noumena, i.e., the fundamental component or "first cause" that they believed must constitute an intelligible world. They were opposed to the gods being anthropomorphized, although they did acknowledge an animating force in nature that is tantamount to a vital life force. In addition, as was true with the astrology of ancient Mesopotamia, India, and China, they accepted the likelihood that the forces that make up the universe have a bearing on earthly existence. They explained the vital life force and cosmic dynamics in terms of an archetypal ideal that is a creative or constitutive force—the *seminal logoi.* Seminal logoi can be understood as natural laws or the natural organizing principles inherent in existence that make humanity political by nature. The ancient notion of seminal logoi was regarded as having paradigmatic value. The *seminal logoi* were believed to have an effect on the psyche and the emotions, and being educated in the *seminal logoi* was effective for taking away the causes of human suffering. Thus, education came to be thought of as training individuals in what establishes personal and social well-being despite the contingencies in life.

That is to say that pedagogy, in the pre-Socratic context, involved training in the connection between the effect of *seminal logoi* on personal and social experience and the motivational power that drives the human tendency to develop culture, transform culture into the polis, and establish a civilization (i.e., a civilizing force). Therefore, the second stage of the ancient Greek heritage involved a type of educational training that rationalized what, heretofore, were ancient myths describing the nature of existence. They were transformed into conceptualizations of and principles explaining the nature of the underlying forces of existence. In other words, these early Greek intellectuals were teaching what many contemporary specialists in ancient Greek educational philosophy refer to as natural philosophy. Although education also involved teaching logic and rhetorical skills, it appealed to something at a deeper level of consciousness. In this respect, it trained individuals in how to relate to or communicate with others in a way that awakens something at the deeper level of their consciousness (Gorgias 1982, 24–27).

In this respect, gaining wisdom was believed to be reflected in cultivating the self to the point of displaying the best personal qualities and social virtues. Two of the primary skills that education was to impart were critical thinking (i.e., deep self-reflection) and how to arrive at reliable knowledge (i.e., progressing towards the type of knowledge that will enable a person to understand and experience his or her highest good, or, in other words, to understand and experience life's most worthwhile, important, and valuable pursuit). Both of which should increase the power to do good and influence others in a way that enables them to experience their highest good. Education was a social process that involved self-cultivation and resulted in nobility of character. The development of nobility of character was preferred over having oligarchical-type authoritative power given by birth but having no training in character development (Isocrate 1945, 7 & 17-27).

The third phase of the Greek contribution to the Western intellectual heritage begins with transforming concerns about the First Principles and an inquiry into the most fundamental features of the natural world into a philosophical inquiry into ethics, social formation, and socio-political philosophy (Irwin 1978, 258). This included an emphasis on the significance of self-knowledge, realizing the highest good, achieving lasting happiness and good fortune, and the importance of the sage-king. In this respect, the foundational principles that shaped Western Civilization's understanding of how best to effectively manage the human dilemma and how to promote human and social development during the third phase were initially based on Idealism (Plato 1888, 77 & 167–169). It was in this third phase that Western Civilization firmly established principles for how individuals could experience goodness, rational self-sufficiency, and what in life has intrinsic value. In short, this meant knowledge of how to experience goodness and how to enjoy the feeling of true inner contentment. Training in how to achieve this level of personal growth and development included prescribing how to realize life's most worthwhile pursuit (i.e., the benefits of devoting one's life to *Sophia*—or devoting one's life to the love of wisdom) and the benefit of developing wise evaluative judgement and prudence. Wise evaluative judgement or prudence was proposed as a means of increasing the ability "To do the actions that tend towards the aim individuals have set before themselves and to achieve it" (Aristotle 2004, 116). It was during this third phase that education came to mean cultivating individuals to understand and personify what had come to be thought of as the best in Greek philosophical wisdom, culture, and heritage.

Educational training focused on developing magnanimity, what nourishes the soul, or what connects individuals to their innermost being, and how to avoid that which would result in misfortune, disgrace, and dishonor. Therefore, training focused on learning *logoi politik*: e.g., moral rectitude or virtue, management of a polis, civil leadership, good governance, and socio-political authority. The intellectual elite who taught logoi politik conceptualized the state in a radically new way that came to be Western Civilization's fundamental perspective on socio-political order. They described the polis as a citizen-state. "This close identification of the polis with its citizens presupposed a high degree of solidarity, and this could take root only in a general civic interest that transcended all particular interests. The state was grounded in its citizens, not in an autonomous state apparatus. The citizens constituted the state" (Meier 1990, 21 & 144). In other words, the early Greek intellectuals envisioned governance in the early Greek municipalities and early city-states as occurring in the form of public assemblies rather than in the form of authoritative government. This meant that in the earliest forms of ancient Greek social formation, wealthy nobles and civil leaders planned social activities by using rhetorical powers to persuade in a public assembly, which was made up of those who had the status of citizen.

Knowledge was not regarded as absolute but as an understanding acquired through dialectic engagement with others. That is to say that it was regarded as a matter of inquiry and the outcome of a willingness to come to an agreement, collaborate, share ideas, argue, and persuade. They proposed that reliable knowledge results from being critical of errors in beliefs and progressing towards reliability by means of good reasoning. However, the critical stance also encouraged self-criticism, or, in other words, self-reflection. In addition, reliable knowledge was thought to play a role in human and social development and true freedom, which result from dialectically synthesizing all the opinions of the invested parties, special interest groups, and the political authorities to produce the common good and the necessary conditions for free citizens. Therefore, both education and wisdom were thought of as a type of consciousness-raising that involved dialectics and deliberation (Aristotle 2004, 107–108). This makes dialectics an important aspect of what contributes to the rise of Western Civilization.

The pedagogues who taught these ideas deliberated with an elevating, unifying, and authoritative voice. It was a type of authority that is comparable to that of a ruler or religious leader. Consequently, the pedagogues exercised a type of power that shaped the socio-cultural and socio-political dynamics of society. They prioritized displaying the art of rhetoric, superior logic and reasoning to win arguments, dialectically aiming for reliable knowledge above asserting one's opinion(s), and promoting personal and civic virtue above gratifying the powerful in an attempt to win favor. Fringe social groups were attracted to their influence because it seemed to enrich not only their lives and social conditions but, as well, their innermost being in ways that are comparable to how exercise strengthens the body (Isocrates 1928, 11). However, where exercise is beneficial for the body, the wisdom articulated by the pedagogues seemed to produce a type of personal growth and development that is beneficial to one's whole being and life experience.

Self-knowledge was involved because the outcome of training in self-cultivation and developing rhetorical skills is becoming aware of the nature of something at a deeper level of one's being, which sparks reverence and a love for justice (Plato 2005, 141-142 & 305-311). Self-knowledge was also prescribed as the key to understanding the connection between *seminal logoi* and logoi politik. In other words, understanding the connection between one's innermost being and the principles of natural law. Self-knowledge is the basis for becoming a well-integrated person who communicates with and relates to others in a way that establishes a well-integrated society. It was thought of as a type of enlightenment that results from connecting with the deep logos, which is awakened by self-cultivation (i.e., educational training), deep self-reflection, and contemplation.

Self-realization came to be regarded as the basis of not only good citizenship but, as well, practical freedom or political freedom in that it results in establishing a complementary connection between the authentic self and natural laws. In other words, the classical Greek intellectuals had great regard for the admonition to "know thyself" because it was tantamount to a type of happiness that can be equated with being blessed, being fortunate, experiencing good fortune, enjoying true happiness, and true contentment. "If happiness is activity in accordance with the highest virtue, then this will be the virtue of the best element. This best element naturally rules and guides us and has insight into matters noble and divine, and its activity, in accordance with its own proper virtue, will be complete happiness. This activity is that of contemplation, for this is the highest activity" (Aristotle 2004, 194). For, indeed, the classical Greek philosophers were among "The first to propose the connection between the substance of things hoped for and the evidence of things not seen, i.e., the connection between the potential inherent in one's *psyche* and realizing one's ultimate hopes" (Miller 2019, 62).

The Greek classical philosophers were well aware of the ancient Greek notion of dialectical dualism as a fundamental aspect of the nature of existence, evident in the nature of the gods, and impacting the human experience in terms of the problem of evil. The classical Greek philosophers addressed the issue from the perspectives of socio-political philosophy (i.e., as in Plato's theory on how to organize our relationships with each other, how to organize society, and our relationship with the natural order) and, as well, ethical philosophy (i.e., as in Aristotle's claim that it is possible to subject evil to the sphere of the moral order) (Aristotle 1995, 745-746). This set the stage for the fourth phase of what established the foundation of the civilizational impact of Western Civilization. The fourth phase combined Plato's and Aristotle's approaches to dealing with the challenge of dialectic dualism, emphasizing the role that natural law plays in philosophical claims about how life ought to be lived, how we should relate to each other and with nature, and how political activity ought to be conducted. It was during this fourth phase (the Greco-Roman period) that early Roman philosophers drew from and refined natural law, which continued to be a cornerstone of Western political theory and philosophy.

The Greco-Roman understanding of the nature of existence, their understanding of the challenges humanity faces given the nature of reality, and the best type of socio-political arrangement for promoting human and social development reflected a perspective on the issue of dialectic dualism that was evident throughout the development of Greek thought. Therefore, the Roman political philosophers provided training in "Those primary things that are in accordance with nature, what is well suited to human nature, things that are attractive within themselves, and capable of arousing our desire (what the Greeks call hormê). In other words, what moves us in this way is the natural object of our desire from the moment we are born" (Cicero 2004, 123 & 124). Hence, they taught how adherence to natural law can enable individuals to enjoy goodness and avoid evil. Natural law philosophy is based on the premise that humans are naturally inclined toward that which they perceive to be or experience as good and that which is contrary to good—evil—is regarded as harmful to individuals and society (Cicero 2004, 38-43 & 83-86). Natural law proposes that individuals have a naturally motivated positive feeling toward what they perceive as beneficial, and they naturally regard what seems harmful as bad. "It must be the case, then, that every right act of avoidance or pursuit is aimed" at experiencing what is regarded, felt, or conceived to be good and avoiding evil (Cicero 2004, 124).

The Greco-Roman pedagogues accepted that fortuity is a part of the nature of reality. Therefore, they realized that it was important to address it as an aspect of educational training. They stressed that there clearly is a reliable providential force that shapes nature into underlying reliable patterns of consistency, which, however, does allow for spontaneity. Humanity experiences such unpredictability as the forces of destiny, fate, or chance. Such forces have the causal power of change, which can mean growth or decline or a reversal of fortune. However, the Greco-Roman pedagogues stressed that contingency (which, although it does not act in accordance with predictable patterns), is also an act of nature and, in that respect, does not offset the reliability of the providential force. Therefore, the intellectual elite proclaimed that the outcome of the conditions imposed by the impact of contingency is neither determined by fate nor by chance. For they declared, in accordance with ancient Greek philosophy, that a person's character determines his or her destiny (Seneca 2007, 4-5; also see Heraclitus 2001, 128). They stressed the fact that although we cannot control the conditions that reality confronts us with, we can control our response, our attitude toward them, and the meaning we assign to them. This means that there cannot be a predetermined outcome, for chance will be impacted by our evaluative judgement, our moral convictions, and by being committed to acts that are in accordance with what will enable experiencing intrinsic value ends (Seneca 2007, 3–17).

That is to say that the pedagogues of the Greco-Roman era taught their students the art of self-making (i.e., self-creation, self-determination, and self-sufficiency). Knowledge was intended to contribute to the development of a good person, a good citizen, and a person with the ability to be a good civil leader. The development of the inner person with the aim of amalgamating the individual's natural qualities (Quintilian 1996, 349). What they taught were prescriptions for how human and social development could be achieved by adhering to the principles and ideals of socio-political philosophy (e.g., honor and integrity; having a strong sense of justice; refinement of character; excellence in demeanor, speech, discourse, and behavior; and displaying a lofty and courageous spirit). They believed that one of the most unfortunate things that could happen to Roman society is that public authority would fall into the hands of those without these qualities (Dionysius of Halicarnassus 1940, 221-227). Therefore, the most well-known Greco-Roman philosophers, statemen, and pedagogues took a firm stance in support of the Roman Senate in opposition to imperial Rome. Above all, they admonished that "There is nothing in all the tasks of life that is more important than sagacity, and without it, all formal instruction is given in vain" (Quintilian 1921, 521).

The Civilization State and the Expansion of a Civilization

India's Foreign Minister, Subrahmanyam Jaishankar, asserted that India must be recognized is a civilizational state. A civilizational state is defined as a geographical region with national boundaries that are established by means of an operative socio-political system. Civilizational states are enduring, large-scale, socio-cultural formations that have a high degree of social and cultural development and are characterized by trans-ethnic affinities. They have a well-established underlying cultural heritage that guides and shapes their identity and traditions. The underlying heritage is established on the basis of a worldview that has an impact on art, literature, religion, philosophy, and scholarly traditions. In addition, a civilizational state has historical continuity and a cultural unity that transcends ethnic, linguistic, and religious differences. On the one hand, what Jaishankar stresses is that India embodies territories that were historically disunited and are now undergirded by cultural linkages, principles, and values that stretch back to the Vedic period of social existence. This means that India, as a civilizational state, compresses the tangled Indic web of Indo-Aryan, indigenous, colonial, and post-colonial Anglophone influences into the narrative framework for identity consolidation. But, on the other hand, as devised within the context of India's domestic socio-political practices and activities, the concept of the civilizational state suggests that the Indian subcontinent, one of the most ethnically diverse regions in the world, is a living testimony of the enormous challenge involved in integrating an intermixture of ethnic, religious, linguistic, and cultural traditions. Therefore, on the basis of the terms proposed by Jaishankar, understanding the rise of a civilizational state requires gaining insight into the power and consolidating force of the foundational principles, ideals, values, and ideational framework that underlie a cross-culturally acceptable sense of civilizational unity.

This section of the chapter analyzes the ideological schools of thought, perennial wisdom, and philosophy that shaped India's socio-cultural values, principles, and ideals and subsequently played a role in India having a civilizational impact. To understand how a culture is able to have a civilizational impact, it is important to analyze the integrative principles, ideals, and values that establish a consolidated sense of socio-cultural unity throughout a region. In the case of India, this involves addressing three key points that play a role in India's impact as a civilization: (1) its knowledge, wisdom, religious, and philosophical traditions; (2) the emphasis in India's most cherished wisdom traditions on the importance of reconciling Idealism and Realism; and (3) the need to reconcile the dichotomy between Swaraj in terms of the self-rule of the Indian state and Swaraj in terms of the self-determination of every Indian citizen, e.g., every tribal-villager, member of its various religious communities, and every member of its indigenous cultures.

India's wisdom tradition is grounded on a deep analysis of "The utility, the effect, and the result of knowledge" (Vivekananda 2011, 280). In the Indian cultural worldview and philosophical tradition, the pursuit of knowledge (Jnana), wisdom (Pragyaa), and truth (Satya) have always been regarded as the most important life pursuits. In one of India's sacred texts, Lord Krishna describes knowledge as a means of purifying and liberating the self (Bhagavad Gita 2007, 120–121). Therefore, knowledge, wisdom, and truth are important to self-cultivation, social development, and freedom. The pursuit of knowledge enables each and every Indian citizen to achieve Stithprajna (i.e., a person who has achieved total self-mastery and thus has become a true Satyagrahi). Perhaps the best term for describing the role that knowledge plays in personal and social development is Dharma. Dharma is a concept of great complexity and paramount importance in Indian thought. The concept includes ideas about self, society, the natural order, ethics, the responsibility individuals have to themselves and to each other, the meaning and ultimate aim of life, and the laws of existence. Dharma, in this respect, emphasizes the totality of how individuals engage the outside world (natural and social). However, the concept also stresses that the nature of the interaction between individuals and the outside world is determined by the level of the individual's physical, psychological, and consciousness development.

Conceptualizations of Dharma include ontological explanations regarding humanity, the natural order, and the nature of existence. That is to say, Dharma shapes the experience of individuals in that it acts as an inherent motivational force within individuals that shapes how they act in relation to the natural and social environments (but based on their inclinations and level of consciousness). In other words, Indian philosophy describes human activity as motivated by either the senses (e.g., impulse, biological determinism, or passion), cognitive abilities (e.g., acts that are the outcome of a deliberative process of self and/or collective reflection), or higher consciousness. According to the Dharma Sastra, knowledge is pursued as a means of developing one's physical and cognitive abilities in ways that "Help the consciousness in its upward ascent and at the same time promote the general welfare" (Motwani 1958, 54). Therefore, knowledge sparks insight into how individuals can develop a holistically well-integrated character, enjoy the benefit of all three aspects of their potential, and act in ways that are socially acceptable and admired.

Because Indian philosophy is concerned with knowledge regarding the relationship between the inner life (*atmavidya*) and the forces shaping the natural order, the Indian philosophical tradition is inclined toward Idealism. But first, let us say what is meant by ideal. The ideal is to cultivate one's character, which will consequently manifest as social conduct and interactions based on equal respect and true mutual empathy. Consequently, the ideal is that "Political, social, and economic life will all be forms of an arrangement by which people collectively can [realize, experience, and enjoy higher-order human values]. Those who distrust this ideal hinder a collective advance towards the power, peace, unity, and harmony of the divine nature of humanity" (Aurobindo 2011, 63). The ideal is each and every citizen working together for the sake of the cultural, social, economic, and sustainable development of India. "From the highest intellectual to the simple unread and untaught villager, India's normative ethics are still a living force in the lives of the Indian people. The ideals play a role in building up a unity of outlook among the people, which was to survive and overshadow all diversity" (Nehru 1994, 99–100). India continues to cherish ideals that are based on its heritage; thus, those values and principles have a continuous and pervasive influence on the minds of all its citizens.

The wisdom, ethics, and principles of India's heritage are rooted in the rural society of the Vedic period, which itself developed from knowledge disseminated by semi-nomadic intellectuals known as the Parivrajakas and Samghas. Their aim included the moral cultivation of the individual, developing civic virtue, establishing social unity and harmony, and elevating humanity. These saintly-type intellectuals when gathered together, formed a community, which established what was referred to as a vidyasthdna (place of learning). They proclaimed Vedantic insight into humanity's essential interdependence and the interconnectedness of every aspect of reality. In other words, though differences and great diversity appear in the human condition, the higher-order knowledge that results from self-cultivation enables appreciating and respecting the unity within the diversity (e.g., the ancient Indian concept of Vasudhaiva Kutumbakam, translated as the family of humanity).

The significance of knowledge, *wisdom*, and truth propagated by the schools of thought in India's culture was made evident in establishing one of the world's earliest institutions of higher learning. In fact, historians credit India with opening the world's first residential university (Nalanda University). Nalanda University was famous for teaching principles that optimize the impact that the integration of the various fields of knowledge has on human, social, and sustainable development. It was also famous for teaching socio-political principles that prescribe how to enrich the quality of life, how individuals can realize and achieve their highest good, how to plan a future that balances prosperity with holistic well-being, and how to live in accordance with higher-order human values. Higher-order values are those that increase the happiness and well-being of the members of society (in addition to increasing prosperity and public value). Value is the end result of what social action is meant to achieve, and values reflect the knowledge humanity has gained regarding what has value. Wisdom and knowledge are the basis for ensuring that society employs the best instrumental means for experiencing its cherished ideals. Thus, India's foundational perspective on the role of knowledge in shaping the social, political, and economic reality of society played a key role in India establishing itself as a unified cultural zone. Consequently, the principles, values, and worldview that informed this perspective not only shaped the civilizational development of the South Asian region but went on to influence that of Southeast Asia and the Far East and subsequently impressed the rest of the world.

However, many readers might find it interesting that the Indian wisdom tradition, although rooted in higher-order human values and transcendental Idealism, also addresses the socio-political challenges society faces because of Realism. In other words, there is within India's heritage a deep insight that was applied to addressing and resolving the dichotomy between Idealism and Realism. India's wisdom tradition achieves this through its use of dialectics. Dialectics is an approach to reconciling what appears to be opposites and differences. India's knowledge tradition is based on the premise that wisdom is gained through an openness to various perspectives. Therefore, dialectics incline wisdom-seekers to be open-minded. One of the most recognized forms of Indian dialectics is the term Neti-Neti, which is also employed as a means of invoking the realization of the highest form of knowledge. Neti-Neti can be translated as neither this nor that. Of course, on the one hand, Neti-Neti represents a type of Idealism (i.e., all differences are synthesized into a harmonious unity). In this respect, the term specifies a means of shifting the emphasis that is typically based on differentiation into a higher level of consciousness that enables one to be aware of harmonious unity. Therefore, on the other hand, in social and political terms, Neti-Neti, as a form of Indian dialectics, also implies neither this nor that in response to the usual tendency to differentiate (i.e., the usual tendency to be either for or against). In other words, in social and political terms, "not this" (one side of a particular stance) and not that (a contrasting stance) also reflect that what is seemingly oppositional should be blended into a synthesis that reflects a higher ideal. The synthesis reflects a preferred perspective that is in line with the aim of social and political activity that is prescribed in India's heritage. Adhering to these principles results in social order, cohesion, solidarity, and harmony.

It is in this respect that ideally the Indian tradition employs dialectics as an ideological device for blending its diversity, plurality, and complexity into an inclusive and composite culture. Dialectics, as a key aspect of Indian philosophy, reflects its endeavor to embrace pluralism. Pluralism can be defined as the peaceful coexistence of different types of people who have different beliefs and opinions; therefore, it is a system that allows for a diversity of views rather than endorsing a single viewpoint. Embracing pluralism is the basis for establishing social justice and overriding the "it must be this and cannot be that" type of divisiveness that can stem from debates on class, caste, ethnicity, religion, and gender. The commitment to pluralism "Can be traced back even to the *Upaniṣads*—the dialectical treatises that were composed in about the eighth century BCE and which are often taken to be the foundations of Hindu philosophy" (Sen 2005, 7). The general moral and political principle can be summed up as "For he who does reverence to his own sect while disparaging the sects of others wholly from attachment to his own sect, in reality inflicts, by such conduct, the severest injury on his own sect" (Sen 2005, 18).

Therefore, the Indian heritage, especially as portrayed in the Practical Idealism of Mahatma Gandhi, demonstrated the effectiveness of a dialectical means of transcending what is otherwise a dichotomy between Idealism and Realism (Radhakrishnan 1967, 4). It is the effectiveness of a dialectic means of transcending what is otherwise a dichotomy that enables individuals to take the necessary steps to becoming a Satyagraha or Satyagrahi (i.e., adapting ahimsa as a creed). By practicing Practical Idealism, it is possible for India to once again demonstrate the type of leadership that established its legitimacy and power in the years shortly after independence (Nehru 1970, 306-398). The power and legitimacy that India established shortly after independence can be summed up with the concept of Panchsheel, i.e., non-interference, self-determination, a powerful force for peaceful coexistence, a synthesizing power, and a normative power.

The disruptive problems resulting from the conflict between Idealism and Realism are a central theme in India's sacred texts. From the Ramayana, we learn that the vision of achieving Ram Rajya (righteous rule) and the unfolding of a societal-wide Satyug (a blissful era of truth) can be disrupted by outside malevolent forces. From the Mahabharata, we learn that Realism does not establish a win-win outcome; it even does not ensure a win-lose outcome, and quite realistically, it can result in a lose-lose outcome. Yet both the Ramayana and the Mahabharata are concerned about Dharma, or social order. Thus, both are continuations of ideas deeply rooted in India's heritage regarding how to respond to or manage the challenge of divisive forces, and they both highlight the distinction between Idealism and Realism. Therefore, the two epics can be said to complement each other. The Ramayana can be described as an epic tale of the struggles with and ultimate triumph over divisive forces (i.e., the ultimate triumph of good over evil). The Mahabharata (especially the Bhagavad-Gita) can be described as addressing a similar theme. However, in the Ramayana, the divisive force comes from outside the community, but in the Mahabharata, the crisis does not arise from outside but from divisive forces within (even between relatives).

The dichotomy between Idealism and Pragmatic Realism can also be explained in terms of the difference between India's pre-independence Idealism and the factors that led India to "Cross the Rubicon". *Crossing the Rubican* occurs when it appears that society is faced with imposing forces that can only be dealt with by means of power in the form of force. That is to say that the principles of Dharma and Karma yoga acknowledge that there are forces in reality that are best dealt with by the Kshatriyas (i.e., warriors and those with the ability and responsibility to protect society). However, the problem with Realism is that it places great emphasis on the necessity of amassing material power. Those who espouse Realism believe that the use of force is necessary; thus, they emphasize the necessity of prioritizing economic and military power (Mohan 2003, xix-xxii & 268–269). Therefore, following independence, the Realist – who were heavily influenced by international experts who introduced a top-down plan for economic development, concentrated on centralized economic planning, heavy industries, establishing India's military advantage over perceived threats, and other trappings of the International Modernization Development Theory. Hence, a solution to India's challenges cannot be achieved without understanding the factors that compel it to adopt Realism.

Indian ideals, however, express a commitment to establishing independence, legitimacy, and power by means of a "middle way". The middle way portrays India's image as a Vishwaguru (i.e., taking the moral higher ground, promoting peaceful coexistence, non-violence, non-alignment, and integrating democracy with what is often called social democracy, which indeed reflects the principles that won its independence). The "middle way" is based on the pre-independence ideal of the sovereignty of the people, the cultivation of their inner being, and prioritizing socio-cultural development. The idealists prioritize pure moral authority and assert that such ideals will increase civic virtue and result in realizing Ram Rajya and a societal-wide Satyug. Idealists propose that there is a connection between Swaraj and life's most important and worthwhile pursuits (i.e., knowledge – Jnana, wisdom – Pragyaa, and truth – Satya). That is to say that the pre-independence reformers took Swaraj to mean self-determination, which, indeed, is one way it could be translated. Swaraj certainly meant the freedom of India from British rule, but as well, it referred to individual freedom (self-determination) and Gram Swaraj (the freedom of the village—i.e., decentralized, human-centric, and participative governance). In other words, a democracy that is truly "of the people, by the people, and for the people". However, the primary way in which Swaraj was used during the independence movement highlighted the self-rule of India. Consequently, the freedom of individuals and villages was overshadowed by the focus on the political aspect of Swaraj.

Ultimately, according to the Bengali reformers, there is a practical aspect to Swaraj and one that is based on higher-order human values. However, both the practical and the aspects based on higher-order human values can be integrated by means of a certain type of knowledge. The Dharma Shastra emphasizes that social forces, processes, and values promote the welfare of the people. The emphasis is placed on the role of civil and religious leaders, with the state and government following their lead. It should also be noted that a diverse society faces a major problem when religion and politics become co-mingled. However, India's wisdom traditions draw a clear differentiation between religion and politics (political authority was secularized, and the sacred, in its many facets, was a separate and distinct institution from politics). Accordingly, obtaining Swaraj requires keeping in mind the Dharmic injunction. The Dharmic injunction means that which is indicated by the injunctions of the Veda. According to the injunctions of the Veda, the welfare of all the people of India is a social process that prioritizes self-development as the basis for social development. That is to say, true Swaraj involves bringing the personal, social, and political aspects into harmony. "The emancipation of our physical nature is in attaining holistic well-being, of our social being in attaining goodness, and of our [authentic] self in attaining love. Those who are wise harmonize their wish for self-gratification with their wish for the social good, and only thus can they realize authentic being" (Tagore 1915, 47 & 48).

For Gandhi, the true nature of Swaraj is rooted in India's wisdom heritage, i.e., the authenticity of being and the self-determination of every Indian citizen, which is achieved by fully developing the capabilities of each (Gandhi 2009, 39). In Gandhi's own words, "Swaraj has to be experienced by each one for himself or herself" (Gandhi 2009, 73). Thus, Swaraj has to do with eliminating the conditions that trap individuals and social groups in illusion, suffering, disharmony, injustice, and oppression. "Hind Swaraj is the rule of all the people; it is the rule of justice. It can never be the rule of the majority community, i.e., the Hindus" (Gandhi 1995, 113). Therefore, if India does indeed establish cultural unity across a large geographic region as a civilizational state, then the power of India's unifying ideals, values, and principles must override the differences and act as a force that reconciles the dichotomy between India's social ideals and its social reality. In this way, India continues to act as a civilizational state that establishes cultural linkages that act as a superordinate mechanism for transcending the vast differences in India's society. In the context of India, this involves resolving the dichotomy between cultural ideals, principles, and values (that are based on one of the oldest and most respected wisdom traditions in the world) and India being prone to domestic and foreign practices and policies based on Realism. The discrepancy results from prioritizing instrumental means over intrinsic value ends, such as, for example, failing to balance the material development and prosperity of India with improving the quality of life. The inability to override the dichotomy "Leads to disastrous politics, which puts groups that need to unite in order to be effective against each other. Instead of finding ways to live with these differences and to (if fleetingly) coalesce, fratricidal critique becomes politically suicidal" (Krishna 1993, 391 & 400).

One of the best examples of the ideal principles that India espouses for shaping its social reality is the preamble of its constitution. These principles guarantee justice to all the people of India (in social, economic, and political terms), liberty, equality (i.e., in status and opportunity as well as equality before the law), and mutuality (i.e., fraternity, social harmony, and solidarity). The people of India placed their hopes in these constitutional ideals and principles. They dreamed that such cultural values would shape India's post-independence growth and development. However, there were various factors that thwarted India's aim to shape society on the basis of its values and ideals, e.g., first, India, out of necessity, is prompted to pursue the power and advantages that are provided by adopting Practical Realism and second, the prior development paradigm that dominated from shortly after independence until just recently reinforced the shift to Economic Realism in that it emphasized economic growth (which is easily converted into military power and the competitive advantage of individual economic agents). Therefore, Realists prioritize establishing a comparative advantage by means of competition (in contrast to the more cooperative emphasis espoused by, for example, social democracy). In particular, the prior emphasis on increasing GDP was not matched with human development, social development, or improving the quality of life. Third, the government has its own convictions and agenda; therefore, it uses its power and resources to promote its aims and ideal convictions, which diminishes its ability to operate as a representative of the people and be devoted to enacting the will of the people.

The emphasis on GDP resulted in post-independence India adopting a top-down approach to planning political economy, which was also reflected in its approach to governance, public administration, and political authority. The inability to match its social performance with its cherished cultural values results in mounting social problems and conflicts throughout various segments of society. India's social problems and social conflicts can be defined as activities that are contrary to what contributes to realizing the social goals it aims to achieve. Social conflicts can also be described as behaviors out of harmony with other members of society. Social conflict occurs when the endeavors of one social group to achieve its aims cause another social group to feel that its identity, preferred way of life, or even its very existence is threatened. In particular, discontent with the quality of life will be felt most strongly with tribal groups, the populations of particular regions (especially those most remote), and with particular ethnic and religious groups. One way of describing the problem is that without matching India's rather good performance on GDP with human, social, and sustainable development, large numbers of people will be discontent with their quality of life. India ranks with the world's top performers in GDP—that is to say, India ranks with the top performers in the world in terms of GDP but with the countries ranked significantly lower in quality of life.

Rather than knowledge being used for the benefit of each and every citizen, India prioritizes economic growth, which means that the contemporary sense of knowledge only reflects one aspect of the value perspective that inspired the freedom movement. Therefore, many tribal cultures continue to experience a struggle to realize self-determination and liberation from the various forms of deprivation they face. Such conditions leave many of the most marginalized people still crying, "Swaraj is my birth right, and I shall have it"! That is to say that there remains a struggle to resolve the lack of balance between Swaraj in political and economic terms (i.e., India's commitment to moving up even higher in the GDP ranking) and Swaraj in terms of human and social development. This means balancing economic value theory with social value theory (with economic growth merely being a means for elevating the quality of life for all Indian citizens, not the ultimate end value). Therefore, there are really two distinct issues here that must be faced and resolved. First, it is a fundamental mistake to give economic wealth to the status of an end. "Economic prosperity is no more than one of the means to enrich the lives of people. Secondly, even as a means, merely enhancing average economic opulence can be quite inefficient in the pursuit of the really valuable ends" (Sen, 1989, 42). Balancing economic development with human, social, and sustainable development ensures that planning does not continue to suffer from costly confusions of ends and means. We need to reconsider the value ends that Swaraj is meant to achieve and assess policy, governance practices and activities, and development planning on the basis of those ideals. In this respect, long-cherished cultural values, principles, and ideals will be enacted as both the process and the goal. In other words, they become the instrumental means for achieving those long-cherished intrinsic values.

The solution lies in integrating a framework for human, social, and sustainable development with India's high economic performance. It could be argued that the *Development as Freedom* and Capability Theory introduced by Nobel Prize Winner Amartya Sen is a viable means of achieving self-determination and Swaraj for achieving India's pre-independence ideal of promoting human and social development and thus reducing social conflict. Sen's model, when put into practice, is a state-of-the-art strategy for increasing public value, aligning the aims of government with the will of the people, conflict reduction, and peacebuilding. In addition, the viability of such a model was made evident by the United Nations adopting it to form its Human Development Agenda (UN 2010, 2 & 12-16). Consequently, as a result of the UN adopting Sen's model, it has now become an important aspect of the UN's Development and Sustainability Goals.

Sen's perspective on Swaraj was nurtured by his experience with India's pre-independence cultural reform movement (i.e., the Bengal Cultural Renaissance, centered in Calcutta, which was then regarded as the cultural capital of India). For example, the fact that at Sen's birth his father asked Rabindranath Tagore to name him and that during his formative years he attended Tagore's school clearly suggests that Sen was heavily influenced by India's philosophic, cultural, and religious traditions. Therefore, Sen thought of Swaraj (*Development as Freedom*) as the development of the capabilities of individuals and empowering them to live in accordance with what they have reason to value. In other words, he thought of freedom as resulting from clarifying one's personal core values, living in accordance with those values, and realizing the significance of India's cultural values. He described self-determination in terms of his Capability Theory, i.e., enabling individuals to shape their own destiny and achieve the things they aspire to do and/or be (Sen 1999, 53–65 & 85–86).

Therefore, establishing a balance between improving its GDP ranking (i.e., experts believe that India is posed to move up even higher in GDP ranking in the near future) and matching its GDP ranking with that of human and social development would certainly fulfill India's aim of becoming the best functioning democracy in the world. Knowledge of how to balance the plans introduced by international experts for continued economic development with its own internal need to focus on human and social development is tantamount to applying the knowledge of its inherent wisdom traditions to its "Approach to power and the effort to temper Idealism with a strong dose of Realism" (Mohan 2003, xv). India's earliest strategies for achieving its social, political, and economic goals involved generating knowledge of how to achieve the highest good possible by means of organized social activity. This includes insight into "the art of living", how to maximize the enjoyment and benefit the members of society experience in their relationships with each other and with the environment, and how to have a harmonious relationship with the forces shaping the natural order. That is to say that India's principles of human and social development are based on how individuals and social groups can experience the highest good achievable by human social action. The principles are an explanation of the connection between the holistic well-being of each individual member of society and that of society as a whole, as well as an explanation of how to adhere to Dharma.

India's traditionally established insight into dialectic transformative political power (at the local, regional, national, and international levels) can override some problematic aspects of both classical Idealism and Realism (Radhakrishnan 1967, 3–4). In fact, given the conditions of reality, it is not possible to truly achieve Swaraj without resolving this dichotomy. All in all, India still maintains a vision of achieving social harmony, solidarity, cohesion, and social order based on its inherent sense of goodness. India's notion of the responsibility of each citizen displaying that goodness is portrayed as the symbol of Ashoka's Wheel of Law in the national flag. The symbol represents the Dharma concept (i.e., a personal virtuous character and a collective morality that would override the disruptive forces that incline society toward disorder). Swaraj would be a widely acclaimed example of a model of human, social, and sustainable development that would contribute to improving human existence globally. Thus, we would certainly establish India as Vishwaguru (i.e., a civilizational impact based on knowledge of how to elevate the human experience). Therefore, what is preferred by both the overall public and public authorities are social relations, social activity, and governance processes that effectively enact the principles that bind India as a civilizational state. This is preferred because those principles minimize social divisiveness and evil.

Conclusion: Dialectical Constructivism

This chapter provides an overview of the role that the most cherished wisdom traditions of the major centers of civilization played in human and social development. This includes explaining "The ideals which were formed on the basis of them within the social and intellectual context which generated them, and in which they have subsequently been invoked and specially privileged" (Yun Lee 1998, 8). In addition the chapter explains the principles of socio-political philosophy, ethics, and religion produced by the intellectual elite and sage-like visionaries of the major centers of civilization. The principles prescribed a means by which humanity could enjoy flourishing, sustainable socio-economic development, and security, as well as be well-integrated within the fabric of existence. In other words, they introduced a system of thought that reconciled the earlier sense of clan bonding and harmony with nature with the increasing complexity of society and the demand to harness the power of nature for the sake of the advancement of civilization. Thus, such knowledge provided a transformative force that undergirded the transformation from city-states to regional powers, and the knowledge contributed to the regional powers ability to have a civilizational impact. The type of knowledge they introduced had an integrative or unifying effect, which played a role in binding people together into cooperation and cohesion despite the many differences in the make-up of their social groups. Such a force was needed to provide the ideological, ethical, and religious foundations of civilization.

The chapter emphasizes a particular type of knowledge that made the members of society more conscious of respecting differences despite an increase in social complexity and diversity. Such insight included both knowledge based on observation of phenomena as well as insight into higher-order human values, which provided an effective force for overriding the tendency for political and economic rivalry to prevail (Mirsepassi 2011, 130). That is to say that the intellectual elite mediated and reconciled the dichotomy between universalistic ideals and a tendency for society to operate on the basis of social, political, and economic power and status (Shils 1972, 7). Or, to put it another way, they mediated and reconciled the dichotomy between the masses who struggle for justice (i.e., a fairer and more egalitarian distribution of social resources) and the elite, who tend to use their power to protect the status quo.

The intellectual elite and sage-like visionaries spoke of the family of humanity as related on the basis of an interdependent bond that contemporary social scientists refer to as organic solidarity. The shift involved transforming the naturally formed bond that individuals have with a tribal-village community (and its natural surroundings) to that of a cosmopolitan individual in relationship with an envisioned cosmic order and essentially interconnected by the ties inherent in humanity's social make-up that make humanity political by nature. "The outcome was the growth of ideologies that were at the same time innovative and germinal to the social and religious philosophy and ethical thought of subsequent periods" (Thapar 1975, 119 & 122). One of the most important aspects of this, that is relevant for the current stage of the progression of civilization, was transforming the belief that there is inevitable conflict between social groups competing for resources into the belief that civilization provides a means of integrating resources for the benefit of the various social, ethnic, and religious groups it encompasses (e.g., for the benefit of all the village, clan, and tribal groups encompassed within civilization). The intellectual elite proclaimed that humanity's social and political nature inclines it to shape societies in a way that will maximize goodness (personally and socially). Therefore, the intellectual elite developed and disseminated a socio-political philosophy that prescribed "Knowledge of the good, the concern of the most authoritative science, the highest master science" (Aristotle 2004, 4).

This concluding section summarizes the role that knowledge played in the progression of civilization and, as well, summarizes why such knowledge allowed humanity to better understand how to effectively manage the challenges it faces and to structure socio-political activities in such a way to not only realize the goal social action aims to achieve but, as well, contribute to continued human and social development. In other words, the concluding section emphasizes that the epistemological reliability of the knowledge that shaped civilization (rooted in the foundational principles for ethics, personal and social development, and a well-functioning and just socio-political system) continues to be relevant to contemporary plans for the sustainable future of civilization. In particular, the study reveals that sustainable human and social development is promoted by a type of knowledge that is not limited to development solely from an economic viewpoint but rather informs the economic and political forces of society. That is to say that knowledge has always determined the course of both social and economic development. Throughout the history of civilization, political authorities regarded the welfare of the state as primarily based on acquiring knowledge of how to increase the social and economic welfare of society and develop the technologies necessary to ward off threats (Beckley 2010, 46).

A study of the power of knowledge in shaping the progression and nature of civilization indicates the validity of the aphorism "knowledge is power". (Yun Lee 1988, 9). "Humanity, which certainly cannot survive without nourishment and protection, cannot survive without knowledge. In fact, such knowledge must be handed down from generation to generation in order for the culture to survive. Like the means of satisfying other needs, satisfying the requirement for knowledge can serve as a basis for power" (Elias 1987, 230). From the earliest stage of human culture, when knowledge was evident in the shaman, to its manifestation in the intellectual elite at the initial stages of civilization, right up to our present stage of global social existence, pedagogues and sage-like visionaries have always been and continue to be associated with a highly valued and essential form of power. However, there is, as well, an aspect of such power that acts as a force that motivates people to cooperate to form a collective will, which enhances the ability to establish the type of ideological power that advances civilization (Mann 1986, 6 & 199-225). Knowledge, in this sense, prescribes a way to overcome social dislocation, alienation, and disorder. Thus, knowledge is tantamount to insight into what provides individuals, social groups, cultures, and entire societies with the most beneficial outcomes from their efforts to effectively deal with the forces they are confronted with. Therefore, knowledge is equated with "Power [because it] corresponds to the ability not just to act but to act in accord" (Arendt 1970, 44). Such insight is regarded as both reliable knowledge and a source of legitimate power. Power is the ability of individuals and social groups to pursue and attain their goals by implementing effective means of managing challenges in a way that contributes to continuous growth and development.

Knowledge generation is conceived of as building increasingly complex and integrated networks of dialectical Constructivist-type engagements that take place between individuals and between individuals and their environment. "The construction of a new level of integration is necessarily difficult, fragile, and fraught with contradictions" (Eisenstadt 1982, 309). However, success in generating such knowledge means that a socio-political regime can expand its influence, power, and legitimacy by exercising ideological power over socio-political systems and practices that are less effective for creating such integration (Baltrusch et al. 2011, 1). Thus, dialectics continues to play a role in transcending differences and increasing reliable knowledge, promoting open-minded inquiry, and eclectic agreement. Dialectical Constructivism is rooted in the premise that growth and development are concrete processes that result from Constructivist-type dialogic engagement in the construction of knowledge. The process leads to implementing cooperative and collaborative strategies for managing challenges in a way that is mutually beneficial and satisfactory. Therefore, dialectics point the minds of people to The Way and "To compel the people to do right and to prevent them from following wrong. Hence the dialectic contributes to the great refinement of human activity" (Yu-Lan 1952, 311).

In other words, by integrating the various ways in which the major centers of civilization view Dialectic Constructivism, it can be conceived of as the knowledge generated in reaction to the forces shaping the current reality they are confronted with. Such knowledge can direct the course of further human and social development. From this perspective, the source of the knowledge needed for continuous human and social development is co-created in Constructivist-type interactions between individuals and between individuals and the environment, which result in a new synthesizing of the prior contradictions that inhibited human and social development. The prior inhibitions are shaped into a more desirable future course of action. In other words, knowledge generation and dissemination involve co-creating a reciprocal relationship between the social agents interacting at the multi-levels of social interaction (e.g., in the micro-social context, in regional and national engagements, and in the interactions occurring in the global arena). In this respect, the development of knowledge needed for sustainable human and social development is no exception to the general rule; it, too, is "Subject to the fundamental law of development, which knows no exceptions and appears in the general course of psychological development as the outcome of the same dialectical process" (Vygotsky 1978, 46). The principle is fundamental to the educational philosophies that explain the basis of personal growth and development. However, as the article emphasizes, by adding dialectics, the processes and outcomes of strategies for human and social development have increased in socio-political significance and play a greater role in elevating the human experience (Giroux 2004, 36–39).

In fact, the effectiveness of the Dialectical Constructivist approach to human and social development is attested to by the role it played in the rise of each of the civilizations highlighted in this article. In this respect, the contemporary notion of the co-creation of social reality can be regarded as a dialectical Constructivist perspective on social relations at each of the levels of social engagement and the relationship between a society and its environment. Such relationships cannot involve differences in perspectives, values, and interests without disrupting the interdependent relationship that is a fundamental aspect of the nature of social existence. There can be no doubt whatsoever that human growth and development are dependent upon developing such dialectical relationships with others and with the environment. "But always and everywhere, adaptation is only accomplished when it results in a stable system, that is to say, when there is equilibrium between accommodation and assimilation. In short, the knowledge needed for human growth and development, like every other kind, consists of putting an assimilatory mechanism and a complementary accommodation into progressive equilibrium" (Piaget 1952, 7).

The driving force of civilization has certainly been its commitment to such ideational principles and values. There has never been and will never be a time when society does not have to clearly distinguish between what elevates the human experience and what threatens to harm the human experience. Continued human and social development is based on affirming such principles and values. The nature of the knowledge and power that shaped the progression of civilization has been evident in its response to two ideological forces impacting human and social development. These two forces can be described as those that promote what is "for the people, by the people, and of the people" (i.e., Liberal Idealism) and those that represent holding power and advantage over other social agents (i.e., political and economic Realism). Without reconciling the dichotomy between the way these two ideological forces impact the human experience and global social existence, the most likely outcome is that we are heading for more than an inevitable and unavoidable "Clash of Civilizations", which could even lead to the destruction of civilization. Therefore, resolving this manifestation of dialectic dualism is essential to future human and social growth, regardless of which civilization you are a part of. In other words, the nature of the knowledge that shaped civilization reveals a constant attempt to address the issue of dialectic dualism that disrupts the lives of individuals and society and therefore must ultimately be resolved.

In our contemporary world, dialectics can also be thought of as a collaborative Constructivist-type dialogue to contribute to the endeavor of individual social agents to meet their needs and satisfy their interests and the need to be sensitive to and respectful of our increasing interdependence and interconnectedness. As was true regarding the significance that the term dialectics has for each of the centers of civilization referred to in this article, the conclusion emphasizes that dialectics is an approach to determining how to understand and manage the challenges to the human experience. Dialectics is effective because it is simultaneously a way of conceptualizing the nature of reality (an ontology) and an approach to deriving more reliable knowledge about how to deal with the nature of reality (an epistemology).

When viewing the possibility of a sustainable progression of civilization from the perspective of the concept Dialectical Constructivism, greater consideration must be given to the fact of the integrative power of a co-creation of social reality approach to establishing a multi-civilizational field. In terms of both the ancient, classical, and contemporary notions of personal growth and development (as well as social development) such an integrative network would enable humanity to better manage its current environmental, climate, and health challenges. Therefore, knowledge, construed on the basis of Dialectical Constructivism, could resolve the inevitable contradictions that can occur during the course of deciding what is best for shaping the future.

A study of the role of knowledge in shaping civilization reveals the nature of the mechanisms that enabled humanity to establish institutionalized systems of cooperation despite cultural, ethnic, and value differences. Today, more than ever, there is a need for "Creating a forum—outside of the partisan schools—in which the perspective of and interest in the whole is safeguarded" (Mannheim 1954, 144). In other words, the analysis provides insight into how to build a global social order on the basis of an ideological vision that is rooted in the foundational ethics, values, and principles that established each civilization. In both the history of knowledge and of social existence, there is historical continuity with cumulative effects that have reached the global scale. Because intellectuals reflect a social position that transcends class, they develop a "Broader point of view and an ability to view social issues from the perspective of the whole of the social and political structure, which provides for a wider possibility of choice" (Mannheim 1954, 143).

This chapter has emphasized a non-exclusionary-based vision of an expanded community that reflects human solidarity (i.e., the Cosmopolitan view of Tianxia – All Under Heaven). In addition, the chapter provides a vision of an integrative strategy for moving beyond the Idealism-Realism divide that has challenged harmonious human existence throughout the history of civilization. The new knowledge that will shape the continued progression of civilization is, as knowledge generation has always been, constructed as a synthesis that resolves the inevitable contradictions arising during the course of such interactions. In fact, in line with the theory of knowledge proposed in this article, the future of development lies in integrating the co-creation of the knowledge needed for sustainable human and social development with a perspective on futurology determined by the dialectic dialogue. Consequently, educators worldwide will "Recast concrete, local, and particular understandings into abstract, global, and universal knowledge. Thus, the entities, capacities, and relationships comprising the basis of reality can be understood in a global vocabulary. There will be a growing interpenetration of the global and the universal with the local and the particular" (Meyer and Frank 2007, 28).

References

Arendt, Hannah. (1970) *On Violence*. New York: Harcourt, Brace & World, Inc.

Aristotle. (2004) *Nicomachean Ethics*. (Crisp, Roger. Trans.) Cambridge, UK: Cambridge University Press.

Aristotle. (1995) *The Complete Works of Aristotle*. (Barnes, Jonathan, Trans.). Princeton, New Jersey: Princeton University Press.

Aurobindo, Ghosh. (2011) The Renaissance in India. *Indian Philosophy in English*. (Bhusan, Nalini. & Garfield, Jay. Edits.). New York: Oxford University Press.

Bhagavad Gita (2007) (Easwaran, Eknath. Trans.). Tomales, CA: Nilgiri Press.

Baltrusch, Ernst. Bonatz, Dominik. Cancik-Kirschbaum, Eva. & Klinger, Jörg. (2011) Politcal Governance and Governed Space. *Journal for Ancient Studies*. Special Volume 1, 1-12.

Beckley, Michael. (2010) Economic Development and Military Effectiveness. *The Journal of Strategic Studies*. Volume 33, Number 1, 43–79.

Boulding, Kenneth. (1978) *Ecodynamics: A New Theory of Society Evolution*. Beverly Hills, CA: Sage Publications.

Cicero. (2004) *On Moral Ends*. (Annas, Julia. Edit. & Woolf, Raphael. Trans.). Cambridge, UK: Cambridge University Press.

Confucius. (2007) *The Analects of Confucius*. (Watson, Burton. Trans.). New York: Columbia University Press.

Confucius. (1869) *The Life and Teachings of Confucius*. (Legge, James. Edits.). London: N. Trübner & Co.

Dionysius of Halicarnassus. (1940) *The Roman Antiquities of Dionysius of Halicarnassus*. (Cary, Earnest. Trans.). Cambridge, Massachusetts: Harvard University Press.

Eisenstadt, Shmuel. (1982) The axial age: the emergence of transcendental visions and the rise of clerics. *European Journal of Sociology*. Volume 23, Issue 02, 294-314.

Eisenstadt (2011) The Axial conundrum. *Análise Social*. Volume 199, 201-217.

Eisenstadt, Shmuel. (2012) The Axial Conundrum between Transcendental Visions and Vicissitudes of their Institutionalizations: Constructive and Destructive Possibilities. *The Axial Age and Its Consequences*. (Bellah, Robert. & Joas, Hans. Edits.). Cambridge, Massachusetts: Harvard University Press.

Elias, Norbert. (1998) *Civilization, Power, and Knowledge*. Chicago: The University of Chicago Press.

Elias, Norbert. (1987) The Retreat of Sociologists into the Present. *Theory, Culture, and Society*. Volume 4, Issue 2-3, 223-247.

Fukuyama, Francis. (2011) *The Origins of Political Order*. New York: Farrar, Straus, and Giroux.

Gandhi, Mahatma. (2009) *Hind Swaraj*. Cambridge, UK: Cambridge University Press.

Gandhi, Mahatma. (1995) *The Wit and Wisdom of Mahatma Gandhi*. New Delhi: The New Book Society of India.

Gernet, Jacques. (1999) *A History of Chinese Civilization*. New York: Cambridge University Press.

Giddens, Anthony. (1984) *The Constitution of Society*. Oxford, UK: Polity Press.

Giroux, Henry. (2004) Critical Pedagogy: *Revitalizing and Democratizing Teacher Education*. *Education Quarterly*. Vol. 31, No. 1, 31-47.

Gorgias. (1982) *Encomium of Helen*. (MacDowell, D. Trans.) London: Bristol Classical Press.

Graves, Robert. (1955) *The Greek Myths*, Volume 1. Baltimore, Maryland: Penguin Books.

Hammurabi. (2004) *Hammurabi's Laws*. London: T&T Clark International Publishers.

Heraclitus. (2001) *Fragments: The Collected Wisdom of Heraclitus*. New York: Penguin Publishing.

Hesiod. (1988) *Theogony and Works and Days*. Oxford, UK: Oxford University Press.

Huxley, Aldous. (1947). *The Perennial Philosophy*. London: Chatto and Windus.

Irwin, Terence. (1978) First Principles in Aristotle's Ethics. *Midwest Studies in Philosophy*. Volume 3, Issue 1, 252-272.

Isocrate. (1945) *Evagoras*. (Hook, Larue. Trans.). Cambridge, Massachusetts: Harvard University Press.

Isocrates. (1928) To Demonicus. *Isocrates*. (Norlin, George. Trans.). London: William Heinemann, LTD.

Krishna, Sankaran. (1993) The Importance of Being Ironic. *Alternatives: Global, Local, Political*. Volume 18, Number 3, 385-417.

Lambert, W.G. (1996) *Babylonian Wisdom Literature*. Winona Lake: Eisenbrauns.

Lao Tzu. (2008) *The Tao Te Ching*. (Legge, James. Trans.). The Floating Press.

Mann, Michael. (1986) *The Sources of Power: A history of power from the beginning to A.D. 1760*. Cambridge, UK: Cambridge University Press.

Mannheim, Karl. (1954) *Ideology and Utopia: An Introduction to the Sociology of Knowledge*. New York: Harcourt, Brace & Co., Inc.

Meier, Christian. (1990) *The Greek Discovery of Politics*. Cambridge, Mass.: Harvard University Press.

Meyer, John. & Frank, David. (2007) Worldwide Expansion and Change in the University. *Universities between Global Trends and National Traditions*. (Krücken, Georg. Kosmützky, Anna. & Torka, Marc. Edits.). Bielefeld, Germany: transcript Verlag.

Miller, Leon. (2019) Self-knowledge: Based on Knowledge of the First Cause of Creation (Aristotle's Conception of the Soul). *Tattva-Journal of Philosophy*. Volume 11, Number 1, 53-70.

Mirsepassi, Ali. (2011) *Political Islam, Iran, and the Enlightenment: Philosophies of Hope and Despair*. Cambridge: Cambridge University Press.

Mohan, Raja. (2003) *Crossing the Rubicon: the shaping of India's new foreign policy*. New Delhi: Viking.

Motwani, Kewal. (1958) *Manu Dharma Sastra*. Madras: Ganesh and Company.

National Educational Policy 2020. Ministry of Human Resource Development. The Government of India.

Needham, Joseph. (1956) *Science and Civilization in China: Volume 2*. Cambridge, UK: Cambridge University Press.

Nehru, Jawaharlal. (1970) *Jawaharlal Nehru's Speeches*. New Delhi: Government of India.

Nehru, Jawaharlal. (1994) *The Discovery of India*. New Delhi: Oxford University Press.

Oppenheim, Leo. (2009) *Ancient Mesopotamia*. Chicago: University of Chicago Press.

Piaget, J. (1952) *The Origins of Intelligence in Children*. New York: International Universities Press.

Plato. (2005) *Euthyphro, Apology, Crito, Phaedo, and Phaedo*. Cambridge Massachusetts: Harvard University Press.

Plato. (1934) *The Laws of Plato*. London, Dent & Sons ltd.

Plato. (2003) *The Republic*. (Ferrari, G. Edit. & Griffith, Tom. Trans.). Cambridge, UK: Cambridge University Press.

Plato. (1888) *The Timaeus of Plato*. (Archer-Hind. Edit. & Trans.). London: MacMillan and Company.

Quintilian. (1996) *Institutio Oratoria*, Books I-III. (Butler, Harold. Trans.). Cambridge, Massachusetts: Harvard University Press.

Quintilian. (1921) *Institutio Oratoria*, Books IV-VI. (Butler, Harold. Trans.). London: William Heinemann.

Radhakrishnan, Sarvepalli. (1967) *The Mind of Mahatma Gandhi*. (Prabhu, R. K. & Rao, U. R. Edits.). Ahmedabad: Navajivan Publishing House.

Sen, Amartya. (1989) Development as Capabilities Expansion. *Journal of Development Planning*. Number 19, 41-58.

Sen, Amartya. (1999) *Development as Freedom*. New York: Alfred Knopf.

Sen, Amartya. (2005) *The Argumentative Indian*. New York: Farrar, Straus, and Giroux.

Seneca. (2007) On Providence. *Seneca: Dialogues and Essays*. (Davie, Tobias. Trans.). Oxford, UK: Oxford University Press, 3-17.

Shils E. (1972) The intellectuals and the powers: some perspectives for comparative analysis. In The Intellectuals and the Powers and Other Essays, pp. 3–22. Chicago, IL: Univ. Chicago Press.

Speiser, Ephraim. (1940) Ancient Mesopotamia and the Beginnings of Science. *The Scientific Monthly*. Volume 55, Number 2, 159-165.

Sullivan, Willian. (2012) The Axial Invention of Education and Today's Global Knowledge Culture. *The Axial Age and Its Consequences*. (Bellah, Robert. & Joas, Hans. Edits.). Cambridge, Massachusetts: Harvard University Press.

Tagore, Rabindranath (1915) *Sadhana*. New York: MacMillan.

Tampio, Nicholas. (2013) Promoting Critical Islam: Controversy, Civil Society, Revolution. *Politics and Religion*. Volume 6, Issue 4, 823–843.

Taylor, Charles. (2007) *A Secular Age*. London: The Belknap Press of Harvard University Press.

Taylor, Charles. (2012) What Was the Axial Revolution? *The Axial Age and Its Consequences*. (Bellah, Robert. & Joas, Hans. Edits.). Cambridge, Massachusetts: Harvard University Press.

Thapar, Romila. (1975) Ethics, Religion and Social Protest in India. *Daedalus*. Volume 104, Issue 2, 119-132.

UN. (2010) *Human Development Report*. New York: Published for the United Nations Development Program.

Vivekananda. (2011) Jnana Yoga. *Indian Philosophy in English*. (Bhusan, Nalini. & Garfield, Jay. Edits.). New York: Oxford University Press.

Voegelin, Eric. (2000) *The Collected Works of Eric Voegelin*. Columbia, Missouri: University of Missouri Press.

Vygotsky, Lev. (1978) *Mind and Society: the Development of Higher Psychological Processes*. Cambridge, Massachusetts: Harvard University Press.

Wittrock, Björn. (2012) The Axial Age in Global History. *The Axial Age and Its Consequences*. (Bellah, Robert. & Joas, Hans. Edits.). Cambridge, Massachusetts: Harvard University Press.

Yu-Lan, Fung. (1952) *A History of Chinese Philosophy*. Princeton, New Jersey: Princeton University Press.

Yun Lee, Too. (1998) *Pedagogy and Power*. New York. Cambridge University Press.